Susan Chitty, Antonia White's eldest daughter, was born in London and educated at Godolphin School, Salisbury, and at Somerville College, Oxford, where she read Modern History. She won the *Vogue* talent contest in 1952 and then worked on *Vogue* in London. She has written works of fiction, travel, fashion and biography, as well as articles and reviews. Her biographies include *Gwen John, The Woman who wrote Black Beauty* (Anna Sewell) and *The Beast and the Monk* (Charles Kingsley). She has also written a personal memoir of Antonia White, *Now to My Mother*. Her most recent book was a biography of Edward Lear, *That Singular Person called Lear*. Susan Chitty lived in Africa for two years, and for three years in the United States, at the universities of Illinois and Boston. She and her family live in Sussex.

Virago also publishes the first volume of Antonia White's *Diaries* 1926–1957.

Antonia White

DIARIES

1958–1979

EDITED BY SUSAN CHITTY

Published by VIRAGO PRESS Limited 1993
20–23 Mandela Street, Camden Town, London NW1 0HQ

First published in Great Britain by
Constable and Company Limited 1992
Copyright © Susan Chitty 1992
This edition offset from Constable 1992 edition
The right of Susan Chitty to be identified as the author of this
work has been asserted by her in accordance with the Copyright,
Designs and Patents Act 1988

*A CIP Catalogue record for this book is available from
the British Library*

Printed in Great Britain by Cox & Wyman Ltd, Reading, Berks

Contents

Contents

Illustrations

Author's note

The diaries have been reproduced, as to spelling and style, as Antonia wrote them except in a few cases where, for the sake of the sense, I have corrected errors of punctuation. On page 321 there is a list of biographical sketches giving some details of the main characters referred to in the diaries. A † following a name indicates that a biographical sketch is supplied.

S.E.C.
1992

Introduction

THE Introduction to Volume I, which related the main facts of Antonia White's life, is reprinted below, so that readers of this second volume can learn, or remind themselves of, the story so far. This volume begins in 1958, not long after Antonia's reconciliation with her daughter Susan Chitty, and shortly before her move to Courtfield Gardens which was to be her last home.

It might be supposed that the last twenty years of Antonia's life would be less interesting than the earlier ones. The great love affairs were over and no more novels were to appear. Yet there is not a dull page in the later diaries. Antonia writes of a succession of people she met through translating from the French, from Jacques Maritain to a maddening lady who 'couldn't write French, let alone English'. She writes also of eccentrics met by chance, from a tame burglar to a gay lodger who excelled in Spanish cooking but wouldn't pay the rent. And there was the extraordinary episode as writer-in-residence at St Mary's College, Indiana.

But above all Antonia remained chiefly concerned with inward problems: her inability to write, her guilt about her father, now thirty years dead, and her religious doubts. In pursuit of answers she travels back into the past many times.

There were two great moments of success in this period, but both were followed, like *Frost in May*, by disasters. The publication of the widely acclaimed series of letters, *The Hound and the Falcon* (1965), led to the third of her nervous breakdowns. The highly successful re-issue of all her novels by Virago (1979) was followed a year later by her death. Yet as long as she could hold a pen, and long after her writing had ceased to be legible, Antonia continued to keep her diary and so record, as truthfully as she could, the process of her dissolution.

Antonia White was born a year before the beginning of the twentieth century, of which she was so much a part. She was the only child of

Cecil Botting and his wife Christine White. Her mother always called her Tony, although her real name was Eirene, spelled in the Greek manner. Her father came of a long line of Sussex yeomen but had risen to become head of the classics department of St Paul's School, London, and was co-author of the famous Hillard and Botting Latin and Greek text books. Antonia's early years were spent at 22 Perham Road, West Kensington, where she largely occupied herself by inventing adventures for her rocking horse, Sceptre and her toy poodle, Mr Dash. She was to relive those first four years with increasing affection for the rest of her life and, even when she was in revolt against most of the things her father held dear, she never moved far from West Kensington.

The Sussex background, however, was very much part of her childhood and of her life. Her summer holidays were spent at Binesfield, the cottage standing back from Bines Green where Cecil Botting's maiden aunts, Clara and Agnes Jeffery, lived. Bines Common is between the villages of Ashurst and Partridge Green, near Horsham and the South Downs. Old Stepney, the gardener, used to wheel a handcart four miles to Steyning, at the foot of the Downs, once a week on market day.

When Antonia was nine her father, who had become a convert to Catholicism, sent her as a boarder to the Convent of the Sacred Heart at Roehampton, a southern suburb of London, near Richmond Park and only a bus ride from West Kensington. She worked hard there and won many prizes for work and morals, but disaster struck when she was fifteen. A book she was writing for her father was discovered in somebody else's desk. It was to have been the story of some people with 'unspeakable vices' ('unspeakable' because Antonia did not know what they were) who were ultimately converted. Unfortunately Reverend Mother read it before the young author had had time to write the end. Antonia had always understood that she was expelled from the convent, but she discovered years later that her father had withdrawn her.

She was now sent to St Paul's Girls' School, Kensington. At St Paul's the frivolous side of her nature came to the fore and, from having wanted only to please her father, she now seemed to wish only to annoy him. She failed to work hard enough for the Cambridge Higher Local Examination to win a scholarship, and so to go on to

Cambridge in his footsteps. Instead she experimented with clothes and make-up, and, finding by chance that she had a knack for writing advertising copy, she was soon earning £250 a year from Dearborn's Beauty Preparations advertising a product called Mercolized Wax.

Antonia left St Paul's at the age of seventeen, as she had been offered a job by the Lattey family as their governess. During the next three years she supported herself with odd teaching jobs and worked in government offices. Then she did something that must have been still more of a shock to her father: she took a year's course at what is now the Royal Academy of Dramatic Art, and went on to tour the provinces as the *ingénue* in a farce called *The Private Secretary*. She never pretended to be a good actress but she had a fluffy blonde charm which saw her through. Even in youth she was attractive rather than beautiful and her looks changed according to her mood.

In 1921, Antonia made a disastrous and incomprehensible marriage to Reggie Green-Wilkinson, a gangling young man of good family whose passions were for driving fast cars and hanging about the theatre. He also drank too much. The only interest the young couple shared was playing toy soldiers in their toy house at 38 Glebe Place, Chelsea.

After three years the marriage was annulled, legally and by the Catholic Church, and Antonia returned to her parents' home. By now she had fallen in love with a handsome officer in the King's Own Scottish Borderers. He was called Robert Legg and he was lucky to have survived the trenches. The two appear to have established telepathic powers of communication when apart. Three weeks later Antonia was certified insane – terrified, she later insisted, by his amorous advances – and spent a year in Bethlem Royal Hospital, often under restraint.

Soon after her sudden and unexpected recovery she returned to her parents' home and spent a night with Jim Dougal, a seedy journalist. He was her first lover, in the physical sense. She conceived a child and underwent an abortion.

The memory of her madness and the fear that it might return did not leave Antonia for the rest of her life. It may explain her second marriage which was not to Robert, who had married somebody else while she was in Bethlem, but to Eric Earnshaw Smith, a Cambridge-educated civil servant whom she had venerated as little less than a seer since she was a drama student at the age of twenty-one. Despite later entanglements, Antonia's veneration for Eric, her closest friend, lasted until his death. Together they moved to 55 Paulton's Square, Chelsea. By now she had a well-paid job as head woman copywriter at W.S. Crawford's advertising agency. It was Eric who persuaded her to abandon her Catholic faith.

During her second marriage, Antonia began to take lovers to compensate for the affairs her husband was having with young soldiers. Her admirers were mostly men whom she met on holiday, and included Yvon from Martinique and Edo from Austria, but one, Bertrand Russell, was far from unknown and not particularly young. Encouraged by Eric, she had introduced herself to Russell after one of his lectures.

In 1928 a tall, handsome young man with a slightly melancholy charm, Rudolph Glossop, known as Silas, crashed into this uneasy household. He was brought there one day by a friend, Frank Freeman, because his motorbike had broken down outside. Silas is my father. He was not the kind of person Antonia was likely to meet at the Chelsea parties she frequented. Although he was well read in French and English literature, he was by profession a mining engineer, often obliged to work abroad. He was undoubtedly attracted to Antonia by her literary powers as well as her charm and became her lover.

Antonia had by now taken on a part-time job, as assistant to Desmond McCarthy, editor of *Life and Letters*, in addition to her work at Crawford's. It was in this review that her first short story appeared. 'The House of Clouds' was based on her experiences in the asylum. She signed it with the pseudonym 'Antonia White', taken from her childhood name, Tony.

In August 1929 I was born and, three months later, Cecil Botting died. Cecil was fifty-nine and had enjoyed only three years of his early retirement, living at Binesfield. To add to the complications of this period of her life, Antonia now fell in love with Tom Hopkinson, a junior copywriter at Crawford's. Tom was one of the four sons of a north country parson. He was recently down from Oxford and was considered a promising novelist.

Antonia was divorced from Eric in the autumn of 1929. She had the greatest difficulty in deciding whether to marry Silas Glossop or

Tom Hopkinson, and kept them both in suspense until Silas took a mining post in Canada and went there to await her decision. In 1930 she married Tom and in 1931 my half-sister Lyndall was born. Antonia and Tom moved to 18 Cecil Court in Hollywood Road, Fulham, engaged a nurse for us children and for a few years established a nearly normal home.

Frost in May, Antonia's first and most successful novel, based on her experiences at the convent and published in 1933, was written with Tom's encouragement. He insisted on having a new chapter read aloud to him every weekend. The book was the first and last to be published by a new firm, Desmond Harmsworth (Harmsworth had just set himself up with the money he'd won in a sweepstake) and its dust jacket was designed by Antonia's old friend the painter Joan Souter Robertson. Like her subsequent novels, it was largely autobiographical.

Antonia's celebrity brought her many new friends including the amazing trio of American women, Djuna Barnes, author of *Nightwood*, Emily Coleman, author of *The Shutter of Snow*, and Peggy Guggenheim, the art collector. With them she spent a holiday at Hayford Hall, in Devon (better known as Hangover Hall). Success, however, did not have a good effect on her marriage. Although Tom's short stories were admired, and he was later to achieve fame as the wartime editor of *Picture Post*, none of his novels received the attention accorded to *Frost in May*. It was a cruel turn of fate for Antonia that, just at this moment of recognition, 'The Beast', as she described her madness, returned. This time it came in the form of neurosis rather than insanity and she underwent a Freudian analysis. The same year (1935) she left Tom and moved into a room at 105 Oakley Street, Chelsea, and began a period of almost hectic promiscuity. She had close relationships with the group of young poets of which Dylan Thomas was a member: David Gascoyne, George Barker and Norman Cameron, with the West Indian sculptor Ronald Moody and others in the art and theatre worlds.

In 1938 she divorced Tom Hopkinson and began freelance fashion writing for the *Sunday Pictorial* (Cecil King, its owner, was a friend). For once she had no financial problems and she moved into a handsome two-storey flat in Cornwall Gardens, South Kensington, with my sister and myself, and continued her affair with Ian

Henderson, son of her friend Wyn. But with the War her jobs folded, Ian enlisted and the Cornwall Gardens flat was bombed.

Perhaps it was not surprising that Antonia should have chosen this moment to return to the Catholic Church, after a twenty-year absence. She considered that the moment was chosen for her by God when she entered the Carmelite Church in Kensington just before Christmas, 1940 and found herself pushed 'quite against my will' toward a confessional. Father Hugh, the Irish priest who heard her confession, helped her back to belief. Now she began to explore her religion intellectually with a thoroughness she had never known in her youth. She wrote newspaper articles and gave lectures about it and contributed pieces, one on her beloved St Thomas Aquinas, to French and English religious periodicals. She also wrote a series of letters to Peter Thorp, a stranger who had written to her. He had once been a Jesuit. These were published many years later under the title *The Hound and the Falcon*.

During the War Antonia had been obliged to return to fulltime office work. She had a period with the BBC Overseas Department, then moved to SOE (Special Operations Executive). Once the War was over she determined to devote herself to writing novels. She by now had a flat in Kensington at 13 Ashburn Gardens.

It was not until 1950, sixteen years after *Frost in May*, that she produced her second novel, *The Lost Traveller*. It carried Nanda, the child heroine of the first novel, now renamed Clara, through her late adolescence. In a period of rare fertility, Antonia produced two more novels in the next four years, *The Sugar House* (1952) and *Beyond the Glass* (1954). The first was based on Antonia's experiences in the theatre and her marriage to Reggie Green-Wilkinson (renamed Archie Hughes-Follett). The second was about her madness. During the 'forties (more or less) Antonia wrote half a dozen short poems at intervals. They were only squeezed out of her under pressure of strong emotion: thus 'Epitaph' was for a beautiful friend who died a brutal death, and 'The Double Man' was about Ian Henderson. By far the longest, 'Sed Tantum Dic Verbo' concerned the eating of Christ's body.

Now that Antonia no longer received a salary, much of her time had to be devoted to writing for money. She wrote novel reviews for Janet Adam Smith, the literary editor of the *New Statesman*, but relied for serious income on translations. With her first, Maupassant's *A*

Woman's Life, she won the Denyse Clairouin prize in 1949. There were thirty-four titles to follow, many of them the novels of Colette, the last translation appearing in 1967.

At this time Antonia also wrote some pieces for such magazines as *Punch* and *Lilliput* (a pocket-sized humorous magazine edited by Tom Hopkinson). Her sense of humour unfortunately could not encompass her relations with Lyndall and myself. I had gone up to Oxford in 1947 and in 1948 Lyndall began a year's stage production course at the Old Vic Theatre School. Antonia's response to any success we had was one of extreme jealousy leading to hostility. I had a severe nervous breakdown on coming down from Oxford and was still recovering from it when she turned me out of her flat on a trivial pretext. I married Thomas Chitty (Hinde) and did not communicate with her for five years. In 1952 I won the Vogue Talent Contest and was rewarded with a job on the magazine which I held until our first child was born. Lyndall moved permanently to Italy. Antonia was not an easy woman to be involved with emotionally. She had at least two intense relationships with women (Benedicta de Bezer, a religious friend, and Dorothy Kingsmill, her friend and analyst)· during the post-war period and both ended explosively.

My mother and I were reconciled in 1957, when she met her first grandchildren, Andrew and Cordelia. Lyndall always kept in touch. Antonia later declared that the last twenty-five years of her life were the happiest. Alone in her fourth-floor flat at 42 Courtfield Gardens, to which she moved in 1961 and where her work room looked over the trees and the church in the square, she spent most of the day working at her father's desk surrounded by her books. In the late afternoon she occasionally had a friend in for a glass of sherry (whisky for a priest). Her conversation was anecdotal and often very funny, and she abandoned herself to it with obvious pleasure. She would end a particularly naughty story with a special laugh I can still hear. When I was little more than a child she had kept me up much too late with those stories. I never complained.

As her infirmities increased, the ninety-seven stairs up to the flat became a problem, but she would not move to the ground-floor flat that Lyndall offered. During this period she was threatened with a third nervous breakdown and had weekly consultations with a Dr Ployé.

Luckily, of her surviving friends some were young and strong. A great companion of her last two years was the publisher, Carmen Callil of Virago Press. Besides bringing Antonia's novels back into print, she even did her shopping on the way to work. Antonia was now earning enough to spend her last years without the financial worries, many of them of her own making, that had dogged her all her life. She had usually been in debt to Harrods, Selfridges, or Peter Jones. She was a shameless recipient of handouts, often from people who could ill afford to give ('I know she is hard up,' she said of her friend, Phyllis Jones, 'but it is in her nature to give and I cannot prevent her'). Lyndall provided her with a small income throughout her last years.

Sadly, Antonia did not live to see the *Frost in May* serialization on BBC Television in 1981. She died on 10 April 1980.

Antonia White left behind diaries that spanned more than half a century and filled forty notebooks and ring files. It amounted to a million words, of which I have selected a quarter, and have divided this into two volumes of which this is the second. The first volume of the diary (1926) tells of an aeroplane trip to Paris. The last (1979) records the journey towards her own death. Had it not been for an unfortunate bottle of Pommard 1937, consumed with Benedicta de Bezer, the diary would have gone back to 1921. On that occasion two 'enormous old journals' were burnt and the Office of the Dead was said over them.

Besides the ordinary diaries there are three which differ from the rest. One is 'the Analysis Diary', started in 1935, in which Antonia attempted to record her three-year psychoanalysis with Dr Dennis Carroll. The second is the 'Basil Nicholson Diary' of 1937. On the cover of this separate notebook Antonia wrote 'B.N.' Its more sexual passages were in French. The third is the 'Benedicta Diary', a tiny notebook in which she recorded the events of her tempestuous affair with Benedicta in 1947. In fact none of these (with the exception of the first few pages of the Benedicta Diary and the French passages of the Nicholson Diary) differs greatly in style from the normal diaries, and they have been incorporated chronologically with the rest.

It has been suggested that Antonia's diaries were in fact not diaries but writer's notebooks. She herself referred to them by both names.

Certainly they were not diaries in the conventional sense. Sometimes she did not make an entry for many months or even a year. Sometimes, when she was in love or wrestling with a personal or theological problem, she would fill twenty pages at a sitting. External events, even important ones, were by no means always recorded, indeed sometimes they were not recorded *because* they were important. Of her first meeting with her grandchildren she wrote, 'It means too much. I don't need to record it.'

So the diaries, in her small neat hand, were largely an internal affair, 'telling myself about myself', as Julien Green said of his journals. In them, Antonia wrestled with her psychological problems and particularly with the guilt she felt about her father. Many of her dreams were about her father. Dreams form so much a part of the diary that at first it is often hard to tell a dream entry from a real one. During her three periods of psychoanalysis (with Dr Carroll, Dorothy Kingsmill and Dr Ployé) the dreams become exceptionally vivid. Most vivid of all was a dream (recorded elsewhere) in which she was ritually raped by her father and actually felt him penetrate her. It is hard not to suspect that Cecil may have, even if only to a small degree, sexually abused Antonia as a child. Father and daughter had the ground floor of 22 Perham Road to themselves, with a lavatory used only by them (as Antonia always pointed out) between his study and her nursery. It is known that his wife was frigid and he was too devout to have a mistress. If anything did happen, Antonia certainly 'forgot' it. Perhaps she invented her expulsion from the convent as a stick with which to beat her father. So strong were her feelings about him that in the one passage of the diaries where she obscenely abuses him her handwriting deteriorates into a childish scrawl.

Closely connected with her father was the problem of her writer's block, for which she considered him responsible. Diary entries over the whole fifty years refer to her ability to start a new novel and her inability to continue it. She once wrote, 'I have a superb collection of beginnings.' She longed to be able to write novels with the ease with which she wrote the diaries. 'How fast, how comparatively painlessly I write [these] ... I have sat here for only one hour and a quarter and how many sheets are covered – over ten pages – over 1200 words. If I could do as much each day to my book, I would have the body there to work on in a few weeks.'

The third subject that constantly concerned her was religion, or to be more precise, Catholicism. In the course of the diary we see her slow return to the fold after her long lapse, a period of fervour during the Second World War, and then the equally slow return of doubts, which her painstaking reading of the Old Testament did not allay.

In places, however, the diary *is* a writer's notebook, in the conventional sense. That is to say, it contains sketches of people and places that the writer can call on for use at a later date. There are descriptions of the English countryside in particular, and of Germany and Spain in which she seems to be consciously filling in a card for a card index section entitled, 'Backgrounds, countries, various'. Few of these descriptions were actually used since the events her novels described took place before the start of the surviving diary. According to Antonia, one episode from the lost 1927 diary provided material for a short story. It was entitled 'Mon Pays c'est la Martinique', 1927, and described a holiday love-affair between Sabine, a young English girl, and a boy from Martinique. The setting was the Mediterranean coast of France. Antonia considered the story, her first, a failure, and it was not published in her lifetime. Events in the diary did, however, supply her with material for at least one published short story, 'The Moment of Truth', which is based on a holiday with Tom Hopkinson in Brittany.

Antonia White's diaries are not exclusively for the literary. Life keeps breaking in. A discussion on the literal truth of the Old Testament is cut short by calculations for paying Harrods' bill or planning tea for a burglar. However trivial her subject her pride as a craftsman never allows her to write less than well and her honesty drives her to see the ridiculous in herself as well as others. A critic reading these diaries in manuscript has declared, 'They are more important both as literature and as a record than I had believed possible. They will enlarge humanity.' Most people, on reading the last page, will brush aside a tear for a woman who, though far from perfect, fought a lonely battle against the demons without and within, and never lost her earlier curiosity about this world and the next. Her comment on any particularly unfortunate event was, 'But it was so *interesting*.'

There remains the question of whether the diaries should have been published. Certainly Antonia White constantly read and reread them herself. Not only did she go back over the past year's entries at each year's end, but she often read much further back, frequently amazed to find how little her preoccupations had changed, or, worse still, that she had absolutely no recollection of making certain entries. Occasionally she was pleased by what she read. More often she made remarks like 'They're all alike, the *dreary* things,' or 'It is extraordinary glancing through these last pages. They really seem to have been written by someone insane.' During these rereadings she occasionally made corrections or added footnotes. She also gave the diaries to other people to read. She lent Dr Carroll a volume and read extracts aloud to Ian Henderson on one occasion, and to her friends Eric Siepmann and Mary Wesley on another. She once left a volume around for Tom Hopkinson to read during his affair with Frances Grigson (the wife of Geoffrey Grigson), and was surprised that he wasn't nicer to her afterwards.

Antonia did herself consider publishing the diaries. Among her papers is a typed section of the 1937 diary (identified in the text as 'Revised Diary'), describing her holiday with the Group Theatre, sometimes known as the 'Grope Theatre', at Summerhill. It differs significantly from the original diary for the same period. She has added a description of the celebrated educationalist, A.S. Neill, aware that it would interest readers, and cut down on a private adventure.

The question of whether or not Antonia intended her diaries to be published is finally answered by the entry of 24 June 1964. 'I ought perhaps to have put in my will that they should all be burned at my death. On the other hand, if anything of my writing survives, other writers might find things of interest to them in it. And perhaps other Catholics – and people interested in religion. Or in psychology ... I think the only thing is to tell Sue the whole story and leave her to decide.'

My decision has been that they should be published, believing that, until someone writes a biography of Antonia White (my sister and I only wrote memoirs), these diaries must stand as her memorial.

Chronology

1899   Birth, 31 March
1908   Convent of Sacred Heart, Roehampton
1914   St Paul's Girls' School
1917   Governess to Lattey family
1919   Academy of Dramatic Art
1920   Acts in *The Private Secretary*
1921   Marries Reggie Green-Wilkinson and moves to Glebe Place, Chelsea
        Commences Diary
1923   Marriage annulled
        Three-week relationship with Robert Legg
        Certified insane
1924   Jim Dougal and abortion
1925   Marries Eric Earnshaw Smith and moves to 55 Paulton's Square
        Ceases to practise as a Catholic
        Job at W.S. Crawford's advertising agency
1928   'House of Clouds' appears in *Life and Letters*
1929   Birth of Susan, daughter of Silas Glossop
        Death of Cecil Botting
        Divorced from Eric Earnshaw Smith
1930   Marries Tom Hopkinson
        Moves to 18 Cecil Court, Fulham
1931   Birth of Lyndall
1933   Publication of *Frost in May*
        Leaves W.S. Crawford's
1934   Visits Hayford Hall. Meets Emily Coleman and Djuna Barnes
        Tom's affair with Frances Grigson
        Holiday in Brittany with Tom
1935   Starts psychoanalysis with Dr Carroll
        Group Theatre holiday at Summerhill
        Leaves Tom and moves to 105 Oakley Street, Chelsea
        Job with Michel St Denis's Theatre School
1936   Moves back to 18 Cecil Court without Tom
        Affairs with George Barker, Eric Siepmann
1937   Job with J. Walter Thompson
        Affairs with Ronald Moody and Basil Nicholson

1938   Affair with Ian Henderson
       Moves to Cornwall Gardens with Susan and Lyndall
       Analysis ends
       Divorce from Tom
       Enters nursing home in Devonshire Terrace
       Fashion editor of *Sunday Pictorial*

1939   War.   Stays with friends at South Mimms and Marshfield
       Children evacuated to Tom's parents in Westmorland
       Death of Christine Botting

1940   Return to the Church
       Lyndall to live with Tom and Gerti
       Both children at boarding school
       Return to London to Linden Gardens, Notting Hill
       Job with BBC

1941   Writes 'The Moment of Truth'

1943   Job with SOE (Special Operations Executive)

1944   Moves to 29 Thurloe Square, then to 13 Ashburn Gardens,
       Kensington
       Three in a Room staged at Oldham

1947   Susan goes to Oxford
       Eric Earnshaw Smith marries Georgina Horley
       Affair with Benedicta de Bezer. Early diaries destroyed.
       Analysis by Dorothy Kingsmill

1948   Lyndall goes to Old Vic Theatre School, lives at Ashburn Gardens

1949   Denyse Clairouin Prize for translation of *A Woman's Life*
       Death of Hugh Kingsmill

1950   Publication of *The Lost Traveller*

1951   Susan at Maudsley Hospital with depression
       Susan turned out of Ashburn Gardens, marries Thomas Chitty
       (Hinde)

1952   Publication of *The Sugar House*
       Lyndall goes to Rome
       Four novels translated from the French

1953   Birth of Andrew Chitty, first grandson
       Tom Hopkinson marries Dorothy Kingsmill

1954   Publication of *Beyond the Glass* and *Strangers* (short stories)

1955   Lyndall marries Lionel Birch

1956   Libel action against *The Sugar House*

1957   Publication of *Minka and Curdy* for children
       Reconciled with Susan

1958 Translates several Colette novels
1959 Semester at St Mary's College, South Bend, Indiana
1961 Moves to 42 Courtfield Gardens, sells Binesfield
1965 Produces typed versions of first four chapters of two sequels to
      Beyond the Glass: *Clara IV* and *Julian Tye*
      The Hound and the Falcon published
      Commences writing autobiography
1966 Lyndall starts relationship with Count Lorenzo Passerini
1970 Publication of *Living with Minka and Curdy*
1972 Death of Eric Earnshaw Smith
1975 Thomas and Susan walking in Europe – April '75 to Sept '76
1977 Meets Carmen Callil of Virago
1978 Virago edition of *Frost in May*
1979 Moves to St Raphael's nursing home, Danehill, Sussex
1980 Dies, 10 April

ONE

1958–1961

In 1958 Antonia was fifty-nine, and living at 13 Ashburn Gardens with Leslie Earnshaw Smith as lodger. In 1959 she spent a semester as writer-in-residence at St Mary's, South Bend, Indiana, USA – a college run by nuns. On her return she moved round the corner to 42 Courtfield Gardens, which was to be her last home. She took her cats, Minka and Curdy, with her.

Translating from the French now became almost a full-time occupation. In 1958 alone she translated a quarter of a million words, including much of Colette. She attempted by this means to earn short periods of respite in which to continue her fifth novel, provisionally entitled *Clara IV*. The first four chapters of this were published after her death in *As Once in May* (1983). They described Clara's adultery with a young Austrian when on holiday in Salzburg. Clara (Antonia) was married to Clive (Eric) at the time.

Antonia's younger daughter Lyndall had become engaged to Lord Edward Montagu, who had recently been discharged from prison where he had served a term for homosexual offences. The engagement was eventually broken off. Shortly before these events Lyndall had suffered a severe attack of hepatitis, followed by appendicitis.

Antonia's elder daughter Susan, her husband Thomas Chitty and their two children were all in Kenya from 1958 to 1960.

1958

1 Jan How much I had to be grateful for in 1957. First and foremost the reconciliation with Sue. Who wd. have dreamed a year ago that I should spend Christmas 1957 with Sue and Thomas† and my grandchildren? It was heavenly and I don't need notes to remind me of it.

Work . . . it was all translation, end to end. Today begins 3 months 'freedom' to work on the novel. I am afraid my feet are cold, but I must try and take it easy, as I did the little cat book (*Minka and Curdy*, 1957]. Think of *Elaine* [Lingham]† when writing it, not Emily [Coleman]† . . . Emily (bless her) paralyses me, though it's the *last* thing she'd wish to do.

Lel [Earnshaw Smith]† still here; a fixture and I have quite accepted it. The rent dilemma solved all but the signings: alarming of course but must do my best and trust God . . . my notebooks and desk diary for '57 seem endless frenzied calculations of figures. I *must* try to ease up on this. The great thing is to get the novel [*Clara IV*] going.

6 Jan   I did begin to try recasting Ch.I on Jan 1st. The trouble seems to be . . . it flows all over the place and I don't seem to be able to control it. Everything suggests something else. I seem incapable of deciding what's relevant or what's irrelevant, what should come here and what later on.

5 Feb   What I have done of Ch. III . . . pages of it . . . is hopeless. I think maybe I've got some wrong *conception* about Austria. Isn't the point that in Salzburg and St. W. she was *on her own*? and she literally never *has* been on her own.

Later   It seems absolutely beyond my capacity, this book. I gave up from blankness, disgust and tiredness, lay down for ½ hour, tidied a cupboard; did some washing: read a little of Suso's letters. He [Henry Suso, fourteenth-century German mystic] *does* frighten me: he makes the spiritual life seem impossible for anyone who isn't a saint already. I just get deafened and frightened by all the big words.

Every soul is so different. It does seem I'm meant to write novels. And that inevitably means being interested in human relations, and the surface of things. I do NOT *want* to be preach[ed] sermons.

It is no good sitting staring at this paper and smoking.

Now just think round the book as if you were telling Elaine about it; forget the sense of being unable to write.

There is Clive and there is Clara and their extraordinary bond. There is her sense of freedom, her 'amusing' life, her 'delivery' from religion and her father. BUT there is also:

1) the sex question which has become a series of meaningless affairs.

2) art more and more appreciated but always as the *onlooker*.

3) the advertising life and the night clubs and the parties. Now what, to revert to the sex life, did I *in fact* do? There was first Yvon. Rough sequence:

1924   Italy. Eric.† Alan [Walker]†.

1925   Marriage [to Eric] and honeymoon

1926   Versailles

1927   Yvon and, in the autumn, Brian [unknown]. *But* there was also Ian Black,† Géry [Forsythe].

1928   Edo

I really led *two* lives with Eric. He wouldn't come to parties except very rarely. We went to theatres, concerts, films.

2 Feb   Today has really been like one of the bad old days. This morning, though Mrs L[inturn, cleaning lady who took over from Jessie Entwhistle] is away, I did more housework than I needed to. I felt too guilty to go straight on to the Colette. Result I have done nothing but idle with aching eyes. I have washed clothes, had the gas man etc. I have looked at some old notebooks because for a moment I thought I'd found one of the operative year. They were interesting because of Versailles and a description of Paris in – probably – 1926.

Certainly I have now got so much into the habit of translating that it is extraordinarily hard to launch with conviction into anything of my own.

'Dodges?' Writing it in the first person? I think it's too obviously a 'dodge'.

11 Feb   The jam-up continued and I have not gone off on to the trans. *And* there is sloth, fear of the huge LABOUR involved. However the thing has got to be done. I can also remember the 'dead-line' is for my benefit, no one else's. The only person who suffers if it isn't done by Oct. is myself. It is touching, as in this letter from a stranger this morning, about *Beyond the Glass*, to realize that my novels mean something to people.

13 Feb   So exhausted after my session with Malcolm Williamson [the composer] yesterday over the ballet that I have deliberately done no work today. I am very tired indeed: it has been mounting for many days. There is some excuse for it. Last year really was endless slog against time on translations. Deliberate slacking for a day or two nec. Too tired even to translate.

16 Feb Mania for reading flat ads in Sunday papers goes on: Suppose I saw, '6 room Mais. in Kensington overlooking garden square. 2–3 sitt. rooms (one 25 × 15); 3–4 bedrooms; also large attic. Except. light and sunny back and front. Large bathroom, quite good kitchen. Splendid cupboards inc. 2 airing cupboards. CHW and part CH. Resident caretaker who deals with dustbins etc. for 10/- a month. Rent inc. £350 a year. No premium. Two rooms just completely redec: rest in quite good condition.' Wouldn't I jump at it at present astronomical rents? And I HAVE it. So stop this balleyhoo.

17 Feb There is NO immediate crisis if I behave sensibly. I have been a little extravagant about the house, that lamp etc. The real thing is *great* self-control now.

Clothes as everything else, don't fuss, fret and fume. Beware of both false economies (buying bits and pieces) and extravagance. Provided an outfit suits you and is immaculately tidy . . .

21 Feb Must not go *too* crazy on painting up the house. Above all not use it as an excuse for not getting on with the book. A couple of hours a day is legitimate: it can be done slowly . . . not *rushed* at in my usual way.

'Saint' [short story] was in *L[ife] and L[etters]* in 1931. Did I write it *after* I married Tom?† When did I write 'Strangers'? 'H[ouse] of C[louds]' was almost certainly written late in '29 or early '30. My father† died in Nov '29 so there was NO question of Tom then. That all began at *Christmas* '29 and I think we went to a dance on New Year's Eve. So 'H[ouse] of C[louds]' was quite definitely not written before my father died.

Now, for new readers, we have got to know one or two important things. That Clara was married to Archie, that she went mad, that she was formerly a Catholic, that she had one shattering love-affair. The obvious difficulty is to convey all these things *naturally*.

How was I *really* feeling in 1928? Vienna was fine. Salzburg not as bad as I am making out . . . there was Hellbrunn etc. No, I think I have got something wrong in the conception of these first chapters. But *what*?

Forget the literal facts of your own life for a moment. Think entirely in terms of a novel.

24 Feb Try altogether a more relaxed approach. Try and get interested as you do in decorating. I *have* to admit that in some ways it will be a relief if L[el] goes, provided he's happy at Morden [retirement home]. He is *very* sweet and considerate and in many ways I shall miss him.

26 March I have taken nearly 4 weeks off and had my orgy of redec. This week it must be firmly ended and forgotten. I have lost all this time I intended on the novel. Forget that too for time being. Get back to as orderly a life as poss. now. Concentrate on Colette. That must be finished by end of May. Money from now on must be positively hoarded. For clothes, shortening only: manage with what I have. 1 corset later on, possibly a hat.

31 March My 59th birthday. Queer to think I am now as old as my father was when he died. A *happy* birthday: present and telegram from Lyn† and tonight Sue and Thomas are taking me to a film. First time for SEVEN years I have seen Sue on my birthday or she has even acknowledged March 31st.

I meant to spend the morning on Colette and celebrate the day by getting back to the desk. But 2 lots of flowers, a telegram and Lyn's lovely scent had to be acknowledged. The flat is finished and looks lovely. Now I must get back into harness and work *hard*. I'm out of the habit of desk-work! I wrote letters WHOLE of Sunday – must have written about 3000 words! Keep desperately striving to catch up and clear decks for an *orderly* life! Don't suppose I'll really *settle* till after Easter . . . Easter Monday will do those horrid I.C. [Income Tax] returns and get them out of the way.

26 July My main preoccupation is, of course, what Lyndall will do about E[dward] M[ontagu] and, even more, whether she really does have this idea – as anything more than a *very* faint possibility – of becoming a Catholic. The whole of July has really been taken up with this problem and with her illness. I do love her so much: wish I could really be some use to her. I *can't* advise her about E.M. (even if she'd listen!), it is impossible to know whether that marriage would work, even if she went into it whole-heartedly . . . and she is anything but wholehearted at the moment. It is her old familiar pattern, getting involved in something she thinks she wants, then finding she doesn't want it after all. She is v. honest with herself, for all her lying to others. The trouble is, as she begins to realize, she has no centre in her life, though she is full of good instincts. It is extraordinary how, at my age, one's children are so important that it is impossible to recapture the state of mind when one's 'love life' seemed so desperately important – as, of course, it does to them at their age. I definitely am older than my father was now. And my life will probably not be very different from what it is now until I die. Three more books to translate by the end of the year. My own book? Goodness knows when. Everything seems to go in the business of just making a living . . . The quantities of letters I have to write is exhausting. I do not want to be ungrateful. I love my friends – but most of them have more leisure than I have! I *do* sound ungrateful; I don't want to be. I have *innumerable* blessings. But, even at 59 one has foolish fancies. It's as well to admit them and laugh at them: a book that is both good and a success . . . some kind patron . . . 'pennies from heaven' . . . At least I would rather see Lyndall a Catholic than have comfort and success for myself. It is terrible what I deprived my children of through my own desertion of God.

Later   I have got so used to Lel being here. 18 whole months. I *think* I shall be relieved when he goes and certainly *every* evening is too much . . . BUT there were some very lonely ones before. He is out tonight: I *could* even do a page or two of the book IF I passionately wanted to. I cannot presumably have lost *all* capacity to write . . . and presumably I once had *some*, if not as much as I hoped. Reading these notebooks . . . or rather this one . . . they're all alike, the dreary things, I am struck by how much Lyndall resembles me – far more than Sue. Lyndall suffers from a huge gulf between what she feels, at some moments, capable of, and impotence when it comes to doing it. I think we both need another *person* to give us confidence, yet live in dread of being *found out* in our inadequacy.

Probably I'm *far* too self-conscious about the whole thing –

terrified of writing badly, with the result that I write WORSE than badly. Why not just WRITE as Eric says?

16 Aug All the usual fretful calculations: certainly made more difficult by not knowing about L[yndall]'s wedding . . .

* * *

In September the offer came from St Mary's, South Bend, Indiana, sister to the male college of Notre Dame. Sister Madeleva, the principal of St Mary's, was a self-styled 'poet, saint and scholar'.

* * *

12 Sept Still the suspense about L[yndall]'s wedding. I WISH she would let me know — if she knows herself! Edward must have left Rome by now . . . as things stand I am supposed to go down to Beaulieu to meet his mother on the 22nd.

My other 'nag' is this extraordinary proposition from Sr. Madeleva.† After 2 letters I *still* don't know whether this is a temporary or permanent job she is offering. I don't feel I want to go to USA for more than 3 months.

I somehow *did* write that story for *Observer* Competition. 10 days' *real* hard labour. But I *did* it, that's the main thing. I shd. say *most* I could hope for is one of the £20 prizes.

9 Oct Odd how careless even a good writer like C[hristine] Arnothy† can be. All *Le Guérisseur* [*The Charlatan*, 1959] happens in just over 2 months . . . during which a 'long-unwatered' widow has time to be advanced in pregnancy, a poor man becomes immensely rich and a well-known doctor (he doesn't get going till November!) by Christmas has developed cancer. And so on.

18 Oct The little Spanish priest said to me this morning that Holy Communion was the best means of making progress in spiritual life. My Communions seem so tepid and mechanical yet I am sure Our Lord takes the mere going as a sign of good will. He said 'Be happy and kind, remember you are a friend of God, a daughter of God.' I loved that.

This business of Lyn and Edward Montagu goes on as unsettled as ever. Horrible and silly publicity – they've both had to lie.

I have taken on yet another trans. Yes, I need the money. But that undone book still looms. The labour of producing that short story was unspeakable. It reduced me to rags. Thank God I did produce it. I think it came out 'good of its kind'. It had nothing to do with my first idea, the real experience of going back to Bedlam. That just wouldn't come off as a story. What did come off was something rather frightening, rather well done, a condensation of the experience of years in a purely imaginary form. Top slick maybe. I can't judge. No one has seen it but the typist.

The need to earn money has made it impossible to do anything but trans. and they come in a steady flow for I am getting a name for them. I think I have done 19 now. I don't think I *really* want to go to America, anyway not yet. I wd. awfully like to get that novel done first. It is no good counting on winning even £20 in the competition. America would be profitable: *might* be interesting.

If I were talking to a sympathetic listener about this book what wd. I say it was 'about'? It wd. seem that Clara has escaped from all the old bonds. How about 'The Invisible Ring' for a title. Possible, I think. There is the marriage that is not a physical marriage; the escape from the father that is no escape, even when he dies.

1959

9 Feb A good many things have sorted themselves out since that last entry – nearly 4 months ago. Lyndall is not going to marry Edward. I think this is a good thing. The new prétendant is the son of David O. Selznick, the film producer. Edward lost no time: has already announced his engagement to another girl.

I am definitely going to America. It is incredible how inefficient, though charming, my employers are! Last August, expecting me to arrive in 4 weeks' time, not even saying how long for, what salary – blissfully unaware of travel problems, formalities etc. Have had great difficult (in Jan) booking a passage for *next* September. Now they have not filled up the 'petition' right so I have had to send it back to them and it may take weeks. Lucky I got started early!

The problem of who will be here to look after the flat and pussies mercifully solved – Shirley [ex-lodger] and her husband. Huge relief.

I have decided to do the abortion [*Dougal*] book after all. This doesn't solve *my* problems for it will be *very* difficult. But I am now sure it is right for the sequence. It is the only logical lead-up to Clara's marriage to Clive.

The money situation has mercifully and unexpectedly eased because of this new act which, this year anyway, means I will get Daddy's royalties free of income tax.

Denyse [Sawyer]†'s book [*L'Aube*] after 3 months maddening frustrating delay (because of John Raymond) has been taken. I am so glad. I have got that (very long), and *Claudine en Ménage* to do by the summer. Can't take on any more. Am still tired and not working well. *So* many letters. I clear them and on they come again. Darling Emily – I *love* to have her letters – is a trifle like V[irginia Johnes]† except E. really *means* one not to answer! BUT she nearly always slips in a question wh. requires immediate answer! So much correspondence – sometimes unnecessary, as with their muddle today with Notre Dame. I wish they'd be a little more explicit about what exactly I'm supposed to do there! Still it's no good worrying. Look forward to it in many ways . . . the practical organization a bit bothering. I try not to fret and fuss too much.

At all costs must avoid taking *mornings* off. With a good *morning's* work done the day goes much better. The Day of Recollection [at the local convent] yesterday – though good for me, I know – was tiring.

8 April   I have still not finished *Claudine*. After tonight at [Neville and June] Braybrookes',† I think I must aim at *seeing* no one and writing *no* letters for a week.

21 May   Have finished Colette and am launched on my last – Denyse's. V[irginia] J[ohnes] has exploded again, rather seriously. I said something about it to G[eoffrey] and D[enyse Sawyer]. They were sweet. G. determined to help me. So I am going 'to tell them all' on Sunday week. I have been looking through old journals to try and get it a little straight in my mind. This has been going on since late '52 or beginning '53. And the 'persecuting' phase since early '56. Now it is concentrated on her having been ruined by the A[nonymous] D[onor] business. The second theme is the wickedness of my books and how priests say they should never have been written. She strikes me as no better at all. If poor Fr. V[ictor White]† hadn't had this accident I shd. consult him. With all dear Geoffrey's goodwill, I am not sure that he will see all the difficulties. The *disturbance* is worse, the mental misery she causes me, the constant interference, the attempt to stop me from working. Her subtlest weapon is her assertion (backed by Raymond [Johnes]) that when I 'abandon' her she gets in a terrible state and takes to drink. Sometimes, when she's 'quiescent', Raymond rings up (or she gets him to) and it starts all over again. I don't think it's much good tackling him. He's a pretty broken reed — naturally the poor man only wants peace.

28 May, Corpus Christi   Well, well, well, here's a bombshell! My dear G[eoffrey] and D[enyse], obviously with the kindest intentions, write that I must stop the 'Clara saga' altogether and suggest their idea for an entirely new novel for me to write! *This* alas couldn't be more utterly alien to my kind of work. Frankly I *can't* understand how two people so sensitive, intelligent and obviously genuinely fond of me *could* have suggested either stopping the series or substituting this manufactured banality for what I was planning. Just as I was beginning to simmer — in the tiniest most tentative way — about the D[ougal] book . . . what irony! These two — rushing to come to my rescue over V[irginia] J[ohnes] — playing *her* exact game. MUCH worse than V.J. I don't feel impotent — I feel *castrated*. Serves me right for going about bleating for affection and understanding. Their suggestions — especially G.'s 'improvements' — ending with the 'heroine' being offered a huge American contract and becoming 'world famous' are so damn *stupid*. And yet they talk with such love etc. of the diaries (fool that I was to show 2 notebooks).

Their idea of the sort of book I ought to write — especially Geoffrey's — just leaves me gasping. It doesn't even begin to be a 'theme', not for *anyone*. Poor darlings, they're obviously enraptured by it. Oh dear! The obvious thing is to ignore it but they've planted this poisonous dart in my consciousness.

1923   Poor little rich girl first sung by Delysia!

29 May   Going downstairs last night, found a letter from V[irginia] J[ohnes] in *typed* envelope on the old themes. At least the Sawyers' bombshell has acted as a counter-irritant. I felt almost *fond* of poor V.J.! Late last night I wrote to Elaine wh. appeased me a little.

This morning I feel a little calmer. I don't quite know what line to take on Sunday: am afraid of losing my temper, saying too much and hurting them. G[eoffrey] doesn't mean to patronize and interfere, I am sure. It all comes from goodwill. But he doesn't really understand a writer's problems. Part of him is always trying to 'muscle in' – he does it with Denyse – and see a book as a commercial proposition, with an eye on 'rattling good yarn', film rights etc. I have no objection whatever to the competent commercial novel. You just can't mix the two things, that's all.

6 June   The Sawyers couldn't have been sweeter last Sunday: I think I got them to understand.

I begin to feel restive after this long bout of translating. *L'Aube* will be the 10th on end. Always working on other people's work . . . Enormous amount of tidying up. You see darling D.'s amateurishness when you get down to translating her!

I've had an unusually social week and am tired, though I enjoyed it. E[ric] and G[eorgie]† to dinner, dinner with Rooney Pelletier [BBC colleague], Jonquil Anthony [author], etc on Thursday; the Millers [unknown] on Friday. I certainly enjoy social life, though I pay for it next day. Must try and stop smoking so much.

Worst of dinner parties – just as you're having a really interesting talk as I was last night with that young clergyman you are switched to someone else and have to reappear just as interested in Formfils brassières! That tiresome incredibly conceited young cousin of Mark [Bence-Jones]'s† was there. Her novel has actually appeared so all the evening we got nothing but 'my agent', 'my press-cuttings' etc.etc. I shall read the book out of curiosity. I guess it will [be] 'clever' and vulgar. She is still under 20. She may, of course, be remarkable.

Eric has been staying here this week. I wonder if G[eorgie] will see reason and stop these house-buying ideas at least till she's got a new job.

I never really have time to talk to Eric. If the 3 of us are out together and we begin to 'warm up', G[eorgie] always starts some silly red herring – about the dangers of air travel or the awfulness of working-class people and ruins any possible conversation.

Fussing should I give a party. I ought to, I know. Maybe better wait till I return from USA.

30 June   Last night I had a real crackerjack of a dream. Sue and Thomas appeared, both friendly. T. in fact more so than I have ever known him. They then said rather apologetically that, being in London only for a few days, they had asked one or two of their friends to come round to the flat. I didn't mind though I was totally unprepared and untidy . . . People – mostly young – began to arrive in numbers: obviously S. and T. were throwing a large party. I became really worried about the drink situation. It would be absurd to waste my few carefully preserved bottles of claret – they wouldn't even have been nice for there was no time to chambrer them. Obvious thing was to send T. and S. or go myself to a local wine shop and buy some cheap wine. But I had only £2 in my purse. The party was now growing fast and becoming enormous. Sue kept vanishing into the kitchen and efficiently producing food – quantities of it – including great bowls of strawberries and cream. They had somehow managed to transform the flat; had hung lots of their own pictures on the walls, produced a typical young-bohemian party atmosphere. It was obvious that the £2 would go nowhere. Thomas and Sue had no money on them and were obviously trusting me to produce drink somehow. They were so busy producing quantities more food that obviously neither could go out to the wine shop. The only solution was for me to go out, buy all the cheap drink possible for £2 and bring out every bottle left in the chest. But every time I tried to move, either to go out to buy stuff or even to get to the chest, I had one of those queer prolonged pre-orgasms that I have in packing-anxiety dreams and was too exhausted to take more than a step or two, then had to sit down. When finally I woke up, still in the throes of one, I could hardly believe my good luck in being rescued from this impossible situation.

9 July   First moment I've had for days. The grind at hot pace in boiling weather has been awful. Day after day, sweat pouring off me as I write frantically against time. Only about 80 pp. more . . . the amount of re-writing I have to do! She [Denyse] has talent, yes, but my goodness HOW much to learn! Slapdash – pompous at times – no idea how to manage a story. Does she *want* to learn? I begin to wonder. A sweet creature but a bit spoilt by an adoring husband. And Geoffrey – how much does he *really* know about writing?

Just as I sat down to get a few precious minutes 'alone with myself' Georgie rang up, burbled on for 20 minutes.

What an amazing year this has turned out to be. Money problems almost miraculously solved for the moment. More decent clothes than I've had for years – and in September off to America.

I really feel I NEED to get right away and that this is a God-sent opportunity. If I am EVER to do any more work on my own, I have got to have a breathing-space, even from my dear friends!

In 2 months from now, I shall be on the Atlantic.

The Hidden Face [Life of St Thérèse of Lisieux, I.F. Gorres, 1959] excited me . . . that extraordinary relationship between St Thérèse and the Mother Superior, Marie de Gonzague. The nun who had failed herself from lack of discipline disciplining the novice with apparent harshness because she *saw* what was in the child. T[hérèse] longed to be attached to her – Gonzague, for once, did NOT exploit it. She co-operated in making the saint she could not be herself. Somewhere that theme is mine – whether using the original or transposing it into an entirely different setting – the first thing that has struck a chord in me for years.

Eric is too 'young' for me now in many ways, or rather he's stopped developing, withered in some ways. Much of his talk and behaviour seems purely automatic now. I know something's alive in him still, but less and less communicable. I don't think he's really interested in anything but his own situation.

Emily [now living near Stanbrook Abbey] is irreplaceable and I love her. But I couldn't stand the strain of the incessant communication she would like. I like to stare and think, not have to produce an articulate opinion on everything and [be] asked all the time 'What do you mean?' 'Why did you say that?' 'Describe her exactly' – 'Why did you never say that before?' and 'You never TOLD me' (though I often have!). Because, though darling Emily MAKES you talk, FORCES you to talk, stares at you with avid eyes, you cannot be sure she has heard what you said – or taken it in. Her mind moves in a solid block; quick allusions, assumptions that she'll 'get' what you mean without spelling it out word by word are wasted. Anything that distracts the block is ignored or else the block heaves round and opposes the poor butterfly with all its guns. *Mem*: Be grateful, for goodness sake. Try and have a *scrap* of humility and patience and a *great* deal of gratitude, you mean, carping beast.

27 July   Thank heaven, *L'Aube* is finished. 90,000 words. Tonight I feel immense relief, almost calm after having been almost insanely on edge for weeks. I think tonight I shall not wake up and be awake mentally arguing with Denyse. For this morning at 8.20 I spent an hour and a half writing that letter. I had put it off, not wanting to hurt. Lately it had become an obsession, this sense of being suffocated and – unconsciously, I think – exploited. Mercifully I made no reference to their – however well-meant – quite *awful* suggestion for my next novel. One point I have firmly made. I will not accept *any* 'commission' on her royalties. Otherwise they will imagine they can buy me – and they can't. I rashly undertook to do this thing. I have only myself to blame for having landed myself in the longest, most gruelling task of all my 22 translations. She will probably never know how glaring the faults of this book are. *She* is willing to learn – *could* learn, I think. But it is probably best to let her flounder on: she may well become a best-seller of the Vicki Baum [author of *Grand Hotel*] type. She is not going to get me as a tame fairy-godmother. *What* a fool I am – the old 'domineering woman' cropping up again. After the humble 'prepared to wait years', the angry 'I had set my heart on its being out next Christmas'.

I re-read 2 of Tom's stories – ['How We Bought the] Lord Angus', 'Happy Returns'. HOW good they are! Denyse doesn't yet begin to KNOW what writing is. The deterioration of Tom's work in the past few years is tragic.

28 July   By now she will have got my bombshell. I am completely impenitent. Geoffrey will comfort her for any pain it causes her. But I am *not* willing to accept G as a literary arbiter. I quite like him but greatly prefer her.

Forget all about that. *Quietly* begin reducing all the mass of practical stuff that has to be done before America.

29 July Nothing from the Sawyers.

30 July Still nothing from Denyse. I have sent a reply-paid telegram. My fear is that, if she comes, she will bring Geoffrey with her for protection . . .
Later Telegram from Denyse: 'Returning scripts today. Regret impossible to come. Denyse.' She's obviously furious. I am shaken and annoyed: obviously she is too. But I don't think she has any conception of the nervous strain that book involved. Those niggley 'suggestions' – on top of that 90,000 words – were the last straw.

2 Aug The situation is still uncomfortable. I am to blame for having been too intimate with people who don't really understand what I'm talking about. I fear that her tendency to sententious sentimentalism is ingrained. She keeps putting out organ stops and treading on the pedals. And she *cannot* keep the scene clear and sharp in her mind. In dialogue she will suddenly go off into some pompous, artificial speech, utterly inappropriate to the occasion or character.

3 Aug I really think I must now dismiss *L'Aube* and all that from my mind.

8 Aug I am still quite absurdly tired. But this is, I suppose, natural. It would probably be more sensible to go out for a long walk. But I am too tired to make the effort. I had a pleasant afternoon with Denyse. We were both perfectly honest. She sees what I mean about G. . . . I told her what struck *me* as weak in *L'Aube* and possibly in her writing. I think she agreed with a great deal.

Someone said on the wireless 'worry is hard work . . . and unproductive.' That is certainly true.

9 Aug In assessing one's own character, do one's first 'sins' indicate trends? I think they must. Mine go back v. much to 'desire for approval'. First I remember (4) is lying out of fear . . . When I'd scribbled on the wall, I flatly denied it. It wasn't *at all* a 'clever lie'.

Then a few small stealings (between 7–9) all (except the 'gaudea-mus' book which I desperately wanted to read and return out of fear before the loss was discovered) for 'social' reasons – wanting to

'stand well' (I felt *terribly* inferior, even at the Froebel in spite of being
top in work) – the assegai, the stamps, the lie about the cricket tie to
get money for 'standing' Dorothy sweets. Funny I *don't* remember
the things my parents told me about my rages and refusing to
apologize to Lizzie [Cook]. I'm sure they were true! I *do* remember
my 'independence' (4) not wanting to be carried by Tidey [the driver
of the local cab at Partridge Green] as if I were a baby . . .

My 'ambitious' side now can be divided into insane vanity and (I
think) reasonable desire to do some good work. The vanity part is
wanting people to know 'who I am' . . . viz the author of a *very* small
number of books which have received *some* – very limited –
recognition. It sometimes causes me to behave *abominably*, lose my
temper and make an utter fool of myself.

* * *

Antonia sailed for the USA on the *Liberté* at the beginning of
September. She soon became a close friend of one of her students at St
Mary's College, Lyn Cosgriff (now Lyn Isbell) whose family owned a
bank in Salt Lake City. It was Lyn who took her to see the Notre Dame
football team play.

* * *

6 Sept   Almost incredibly, I *have* left and am in the waiting-room of
the *Liberté*. It really is like a floating hotel, except for the cabin I share
with 2 other elderly women, one a laundry manageress named
Queenie Page . . . a very hearty lady who is determined not to leave
me alone, insisted on being at my table etc. etc. It is v. difficult to give
her the slip; she pursues me everywhere. I heard Mass in the cinema:
odd sitting in plush stalls, with a string quartet playing Beet. slow
movements and Schumann's *Reverie*. Served by a steward in uniform.

14 Sept, St Mary's   Still no time to catch up.

18 Sept, St Mary's   Impossible till now to get a moment to try and
record any impressions of USA. Thank God for my quiet 'carrel' in
the library – the *only* place where I feel alone. I can't smoke here, but
it's worth that.

   New York   We were packed into the ship's cinema for 2½ hours waiting to be let off. Suddenly my name was called, there was a tall, pretty girl waving to me (Ann Reinecke) and, to everyone's jealousy, I was hustled out ahead of the others. An enormous Irish cop . . . couldn't have been less than 6ft 4″, revolver on hip . . . smuggled us off a back way. So I set foot in America under police protection. Ann was marvellous, found a tame customs officer and I got through fairly quickly . . . all told about an hour in the customs shed.

Train light, elegant colours, amazingly wide choice of food. They actually gave me and the two nuns an orchid apiece (a real one) in a cellophane box! Food madly expensive and *not* madly good.

I did not sleep well as my roomette was over the wheels and I felt bruised all over . . .

A vast car met us at S[outh] B[end], everyone seems to have vast cars here. We drove up a tall avenue and there at last was St Mary's (it was now about 8 p.m.). Grouped inside the porch of Le Mans were girls in white singing to welcome us. Charming. They are the 'Julians', picked band of hostesses. On the blackboard was chalked.

> Welcome to Sr. Madeleva
>   Sr. Aloysius
>   Antonia White

Charming girls seized my luggage and I was shown to my room. It was *very* prettily arranged [but] I don't really like living in a basement with windows so high I can hardly reach them. It is also v. hot there and extremely noisy. Streams of students flock past all the time and their recreation room is overhead, piano, ukulele and singing . . . delightful but distracting. I wander restlessly about trying to find a peaceful corner. This morning I am writing out of doors with a kind of bed-table contraption I bought in S. Bend and this is the best so far but it's very windy. Anyway I'm getting some air which I feel I need. It is a lovely morning, soft west wind. The crickets (cicadas) are singing in these very English-looking trees . . . strange Mediterranean sound . . . the first thing I noticed here. The people who live here don't hear them. But it's just outside my flat and it's pleasant . . . the girls going past all the time in the pastel-coloured 'golfers' they wear as uniform on week-days. All fresh, mostly pretty, charming in their rose, yellow, turquoise-green and white well-cut shirtwaisters. Much prettier than in their Sunday clothes.

26 Sept   This is only an experiment to see if it would be possible to write in bed – almost but not quite.

Maybe the simplest is the best: just propping it up on the whole case.

Pep Rally   The cheer-leaders shout the various rhythmic calls . . . conducting and working up the crowd like an orchestra.

'N-O-T-R-E D-A-M-E (spelt out) Notre Dame, (repeated 3 times crescendo, rising on *Dame* . . .

After an hour Lyn and I got out into the lovely warm summer night which felt *cold* after the appalling heat inside. But it was wildly exciting, a trifle alarming, these preliminary beating of the war-drums. *Very* tribal. In the arena the students' brass band played, splendid rhythm: great silver tubas, glockenspiels, cymbals – Then the team filed past . . . I thought nothing in their future lives could equal this glory and wild acclamation as football players for N[otre] D[ame].

27 Sept, Game

'Get 'em again, get 'em again,' *HARRDER . . . HARRDER . . .*

'The Ref beats his wife, the Ref beats his wife' or worse still: 'His wife beats the Ref'. . .

There is any amount of knocking down and falling on people in heaps . . . indeed it looks like some wild game of human ninepins. I sat there in pouring rain, drenched literally to the skin (I had to take off every stitch, even my bra was soaked, when I got back and have a hot bath) but I wouldn't have missed it for anything. It is extraordinarily exhilarating and the excitement, one feels, isn't just worked up, but simply directed. The Pep Rally seemed a little artificial, even sinister but once you get out into the open, with this vast crowd of enthusiastic youngsters and a real game in progress, the effect is quite different. Everyone is happy and excited, you all rise spontaneously at big moments and clutch each other . . . it is a mass experience and oddly refreshing. I felt wonderful, once I'd had a bath and changed . . . serene and cheerful. And I thoroughly enjoyed eating a 'hot dog' out of a bag in the stand, though my feet were icy and my cold clammy clothes sticking to my skin . . . as I say, I wouldn't have missed it.

America fascinates me and I just don't know where to begin trying to record impressions of it. I have one simple trouble . . . my life is so taken up and 'dissipated' for I can't go anywhere without someone waylaying me and talking to me or carrying me off to talk to someone else.

12 Oct The place is like a big English park. There are blue jays and cardinals (haven't seen either yet, only some pigeons). Squirrels in the trees, once saw a gopher or a chipmunk, little striped animal that popped down a round hole. Typical sound is the melancholy musical hoot of the cars. Very few flowers, some petunias, salvias, geraniums, fine zinnias – climate very variable. Until recently very hot, like summer. Brilliant transparent blue sky. Frequent violent thunderstorms in evening.

On Saturday I came back from South Bend to find a kind of ballet going on on the front lawn. Girls in gay sweaters and shorts and bright stockings or leotards playing a kind of football with Notre Dame boys. What made it odd was that with their 'tough' clothes the girls wore full make up so that it gave the effect of a stage chorus.

15 Oct The animals on the beds. You look into the bedrooms of these 18–22 year olds and on almost every bed is a huge toy animal, many new, many from nursery days. Nothing like St Mary's exists in England. In some ways it is like a Roehampton for older girls, with many differences. The girls wear make-up, have boy-friends who invade the campus at week-ends. Nuns and students are on friendly terms, you see nuns eating ice-creams at the student parties, listening to the girls at the 'informal social evenings'; they eat with them in the dining-hall. But there is pretty strict discipline and supervision. Smoking is allowed in certain rooms, but no alcohol of any kind, even beer, even at dances. This means the faculty may not have any alcohol on the premises either. I am told that if a girl were suspected of having a drink she would be expelled at once.

I think they *are* from their sophomore (2nd) year, supposed to be specializing in something. However there seems to be a bewildering variety of subjects in which you get 'credits' and I can't believe the standards are high. This American restlessness, constant change, constant 'development', above all constant being talked-to or discussing in groups seems to me to destroy all possibility of concentrated work.

19 Oct   We went over to St Joseph's hospital to see Marion [unknown] the other night. It is a huge modern building whose foyer looks exactly like that of a luxury hotel. There are glass show cases full of vases, presumably for sale – great comfortable divans and soft diffused music . . . symphony type . . . playing all the time. Something faintly sinister and 'loved-one-ish' about this.

My 'podiatrist' Dr Smith is a negro. Expert beyond anything, never gave me the faintest twinge of pain. Almost at once, he launched on the subject of smoking, said it was a sin, 'defiling one's temple'. Christ and His Apostles never smoked. Drinking was a sin too, so was dancing. I do not know what sect he belongs to. Some people here think he may be a Jehovah's Witness. He seemed pretty sure I would go to hell as there is no salvation except through the Bible.

26 Oct   I have really got to take myself in hand. Have spent *far* too much this month and must begin to think of next year. The more I can take back to England, the more peace of mind. Also I must begin to think seriously about the book.

* * *

After her semester at St Mary's Antonia went to spend Christmas in the southern states. She was in search of the birthplace of Julien Green.†

* * *

22 Dec, Savannah   Almost 2 months since I made an entry. At least one thing is clear to me now: if I ever come back to America it will not be to St M[ary]'s. I would not have missed all this experience but the life at St Mary's does not suit me at all.

Charleston is fantastically beautiful. Huge white – or pink – or blue or green – but mainly white Georgian houses with verandahs and pillared porticoes. Down by the Savannah river, lovely shuttered Georgian houses. In the rich planters' houses in Charleston the servants' (slaves') quarters are separate small buildings. The town was strangely deserted; we drove through miles of these glorious houses, set in big gardens, with narrow lanes almost like little Roman streets running between them . . . Sherman behaved like Cromwell, burning down houses and even churches. J[ulien] Green's house in Savannah was his headquarters. Green, an Englishman, rented the house to Sherman to spare the Georgians the shame of having to house him. It is a strange house, ugly really, with . . . narrow Gothic windows . . . Oddest of all, the staircase which you expect to be a broad sweep is narrow and 'mean' – barely 3 ft wide I should guess. It goes twisting up in almost a furtive way from the main hall. I don't wonder J. G. has a 'thing' about staircases.

We went to Tomatly that J[ulien] G[reen] mentions in *Sud* [a play]. The house has gone, replaced by a modern one owned by a rich polo player who uses the place only for shooting and raising horses. Thousands of overgrown acres, huge trees dripping with Spanish moss.

(Pause for usual calculations. I should say $200 shd. see you through till you sail.)

30 Dec   Impossible begin record south . . . little negroes on skates and new bicycles after Xmas day – cowboy hats, red coats. Endless hospitality, parties, dropping in, enclosed society – everyone knows everyone in the right circle. Genealogical talk. Intermarriage – some divorce – good works.

Julian Hartridge detests his 1st cousin Julian [sic] Green. Says he is ungrateful – J.H's father spent thousands of dollars paying for J. G. at Virginia University. Says J.'s books are like a wet Sunday afternoon in Bonaventure (famous Savannah cemetery).

1960

Antonia returned to England at the beginning of 1960 with the firm intention of starting a new version of *Clara IV*, which she began to write that March.

4 June   May be 2 reasons why I cannot get this book started right though I have done over 2 months hard work every day on it – not counting all the other times – and there are now about 100 pages of rejected drafts – mostly of 1st 3 pages.

1) the interval of doing nothing but transl. for so long.

2) psychological . . .

In daily life, since America became 'focus' last summer, both there and since I came back . . . extravagance. Buying far too many clothes etc. I now have too much of everything.

I keep revising, revising, revising, until I've no idea which version is the best of a paragraph, even a sentence. I don't know what I want to say and I don't know how to say it.

I suppose the crows are coming home to roost because of all the things I have left out.

23 July   I have of course missed the deadline. Did the unconscious want to miss it? There must I think be some inner conflict besides the technical one. I get the childish tearful feelings over any 'success' story or any 'new beginning'. Was profoundly depressed by [meeting] Frank Freeman† – the sense of a man who feels he has failed and covers it up by his old pose of omniscience – all those funny stories which all really say the same thing: I am the most original, honest, intelligent, witty, wise man of my generation. He looks so old, so eaten up from inside.

I suffer absurdly from not being able to discuss the book. Moll [an ex-actress, Alec Guinness's secretary and a recent friend of Antonia who had come to live in the basement at 13 Ashburn Gardens], of whom I am extremely fond, cares much for me, not in the least for my writing. Wyn [Henderson]† shook me by bringing out the old one about 'liking *Frost in May*' best. She gave me the idea of not having really read the others. One simply cannot *depend* on other people like this. One *must* learn to be lonely.

People like me. People want to see me. They know I am interested in them and their problems. Sometimes I feel pulled all out of shape and physically as well as mentally exhausted by them. I long *absurdly* for someone occasionally to be interested in mine – the writing ones I mean.

3 Sept   For the first time in 9 years Sue was natural here, wandering about the flat, wanting to look at it, compare it as it was when she lived here. I gave her presents of anything I thought she might like to have. Curious how I spend so much time with Moll. Her boringness ... bless her heart, she *is* a bore because of this compulsion to recount the *minutiae* of everything ... is I am *sure* due to a terrible loneliness. The older I get, the *sadder* I find people and the more courageous. You listen to someone boring you, yes, to tears and yet you love them. I think of Moll's transfigured face when she looks at a baby. I notice this odd thing over the last 10 years ... people terribly wanting my friendship and SUCH different people – all *women*. Hadn't struck me before. Not *one* new man in my life except . . . Lel! He most definitely needs my friendship because I'm the 'safe' woman! The *hard work* I put into it! to know how much I shd. let myself be devoured and pulled out of shape. Perhaps God means one to hold on to NOTHING . . . but of course to Him.

My mixture of masc. and fem. *is* very marked. Outwardly I seem to get *more* feminine as I get older.

Do I miss a man around? YES.

Dr. said that on the first night of insanity I talked *in a child's voice* about my money box.

26 Sept Yesterday was the anniversary of my father's birthday. He would have been 90. Once again I had the same trouble with the book. I sat down at 11 ... When I looked up, it was 4.30. I had spent $5\frac{1}{2}$ hours – absolutely unproductively.

28 Sept There are plenty of obvious things I ought to do here and now, quite apart from the book but I am in one of those flaccid will states – I am, after all, 'ordered' to do the Arnothy translation [*The Serpent's Bite*, 1961].

30 Sept This morning after that absurd author's party where I was mistaken for Antonia Ridge [a broadcaster], then Noel Streatfield, then congratulated by Henry Andrews [unknown] on my charming book about *The Three Rivers of France* [by Freda White] I woke up feeling rather cheerful, thinking how exquisitely comic life is. I almost felt like writing a funny article. In the end I raked up 'Week-end Neurosis' [published in *Punch*] which I really did think quite funny and thought I'd send it to *Mademoiselle* [American magazine].

1 Oct   It is silly to be depressed by the incessant rain and dull weather. It has been one of the worst summers I remember.

3 Oct   I find I *am* still worrying about 'exposing' my father in this [book]. 'Thou shalt not uncover thy father's nakedness'. In church this morning I remembered that strange temptation when I looked at my father's dead body to which mercifully I did not yield. I don't really think it was a wish to do something wrong. I cannot analyse it. Perhaps I wanted to see for myself that my father was a man like other men.

Have mercy on me, oh Lord, for I am *weak*. I want to trust God and I seem unable to. Probably the best thing is to abandon all this self-questioning and get on with the translation. I have to keep telling myself silly things like 'Fr. Victor . . . Elaine . . . Emily . . . I think I should write it.'

One thing is sure, the two most important things in my life . . . the Catholic religion and my father. The only time sex presented itself to me in the simplest, most straightforward way, wanting the man, wanting children by the man, was with Robert [Legg]†. I then 'disappointed' myself of that by going mad. When I look back on the fantastic mess of my life, my one hope is that God can make something of it. This need to *love*.

3 Oct, St Thérèse of Lisieux   A sweet letter from Emily saying she is sure my 'genius' hasn't been taken from me, that this is just a 'trial' and 'all these things will be added' and '1000 fold'.

BEGAN PIQUE-NIQUE. SHOULD BE ABLE TO DO IT IN 6 weeks.

6 Dec   A few days ago reached such a pitch of complete impotence and frustration on the book that I have decided to give up altogether for a week or two . . .

It may be just age and a real failure of mental powers.

Frankly, I feel no *urge* to write anything at all . . . not even the American notes. I have become so mentally lazy . . . nothing hits me hard enough to make me *want* to do something.

8 Dec   Went to a Pet Show and to see film of *Sons and Lovers*.

Am deliberately 'doing nothing' . . .

Less tight behind the eyes . . .

13 Dec For once, except for having 22 parcels to wrap, the plate more or less cleared.

I thought I wd. start doing an hour at the piano every day.

16 Dec I practise five-finger exercises for an hour a day and mean to keep this up.

I am now v. glad I took in Giorgio [new lodger]. He is a charming boy . . . a little importunate like a child but it's probably a kind dispensation of the Lord's that I shd. have this young thing about, needing to be talked to, shown how to cook, wash, etc.

19 Dec This 'battle of the cards' etc. Have sent over 100 and done up about 25 parcels. One shouldn't grumble I know; it is the season of goodwill and sending a greeting to people one hasn't seen for years but it IS a burden . . . I had the impression that I'd given quite a lot in 'charity' this Christmas, but apart from Lel's £5, it's only about £15.

I *should* be able to manage till Jan 8th without cashing another cheque.

I need NO CLOTHES.

It's been, on the surface, a pretty unsatisfactory year . . . because of the jam-up on the book. Extraordinary how one tells friends this and in the next breath they are asking 'Inspiration flowing?' and 'When's your book coming out?' and all these really *idiotic* questions.

20 Dec Always a little melancholy before Christmas. This year for the second time I'll be with Sue and her family and that is the most wonderful Christmas I could have. I miss Lyn very much. I don't know how many years it is she and I were together at Christmas and it is 2½ years since I saw her. I suppose we all find it hard to realize that we and our generation are getting old and there are few of one's parents' generation left alive and they are ninetyish! Yet it is almost odder to think of anyone being 90 . . . i.e. 30 years older than oneself. Or to realize that it is over 30 years since I was 30 . . . 32 years since Sue was born . . . 31 years since I married Tom. So much of my 'life' was crammed into the years between 21 and 31 – madness, 3 marriages, both children born. After that, this huge stretch of nearly another 30 years when my life has been this curious isolated thing.

I suppose my life is no odder than many people's but it *is* rather an abnormal one. Particularly all these years of living alone when I think I would have been happier sharing a life with someone. I cannot, even now, imagine any man to whom I could have been a real wife.

27 Dec   I had a lovely Christmas with Sue and Thomas and the grandchildren . . . and of all people – Lyndall. I didn't recognize her!!

I tend to let this bad writing failure overshadow everything else. I suppose I really AM beginning to 'feel my age'. I can't 'take in' things as I used to. I prefer old books to new.

I try not to be depressed by Moll's incessant talk of Alec Guinness, his success, his offers etc. etc. Is it pride that makes me not want to equate myself with Moll – i.e. a 'has-been' who was once reasonably good, but *not* first class in their line, and who now ekes out a living as best they can?

WHY is it, that deeply touched as I am by people's affection for me, I so much want them to care about my work too. Seeing so much of Moll brings this home to me all the time. It is idiotic of me because Moll has practically NO real knowledge of writing. I ought to be grateful that she is fond of me as a person.

I get on with people nowadays, yes. But oh, the strain, the agony, the wringing exhaustion of *boredom* in some conversations . . . or rather enforced 'listenings' that I endure nowadays . . . conversations that aren't 'exchange' (which is a delight) but simply being a receptacle for endless, boring repetitions . . . Maybe in my time I've inflicted that agonizing torture on other people and am being paid out now!

28 Dec   . . . the prospect of Lyndall arriving doesn't liven me up: perhaps because she's always such an uncertain quantity that she'll probably just dash in, change and be off somewhere. I'm in that silly state where trifles assume enormous importance – like G[iorgio] not having thanked me for his tiny Christmas presents which I *know* is sheer oversight.

1961

3 Jan   Typical of me that I've started two notebooks . . .

7 Jan   REPEAT. TRY HARD TO MANAGE TILL END OF MARCH ON WHAT YOU HAVE NOW. FORGET ALL ABOUT MONEY THAT MIGHT COME IN.

10 Jan   Finsit [financial situation] is very bad indeed, *if* this [John] Lewis £29 is right but I think it can't be as much as that. It *could* be £20: they must have forgotten to send me the bill. Darling Emily sent me £3.

12 Jan   Stop fussing about the mystery bill for £29.

15 Jan   Somehow you must break this habit of sitting paralysed at your desk, smoking and scribbling endless versions of one sentence. You *feel* that smoking helps you to concentrate but there's fairly good proof that it *doesn't*. You were able to concentrate perfectly well on teaching without smoking. It is now becoming a VICE . . . something you can't do without as a drunkard can't do without alcohol.

19 Jan   Well at least I know the worst about FINSIT. The £29 was right – it was Peter Jones and accidentally charged to Lewis. This shd. teach me not to buy things recklessly on account. *Many* things (though mainly hats) I have bought that I did not REALLY need.

21 Jan   At least something seems to be moving in the 'deep freeze'. At least I can stop 'post-watching' for news from Chicago. Dan Hayes [American publisher] has left for Doubleday. He has had NO luck with my stories . . . all I can be SURE of even now (and it's a good deal more than I hoped) is that I might get at least £450 from Daddy's royalties. Faint possibilities of a lodger.

4 Feb   Is translation in any way responsible? A little, I think. Being now so used to having my material provided and simply having to re-shape it, I feel lost at having to provide my own.

* * *

Antonia finally decided that she must move from 13 Ashburn Gardens, and bought the lease of a fourth-floor flat a few hundred yards away at 42 Courtfield Gardens. To raise the necessary money she sold Binesfield, the cottage in Sussex which had belonged to her father's family and which she always loved.

* * *

4 March   The great crisis is now on. Let us say I move in June . . .
Various thoughts [about] 42D Courtfield Gardens.
PRO
Situation
Price (no borrowing)
Cheaper outgoings
CHW
Resident Housekeeper
All those marvellous fittings including new fridge in kitchen
Fitted carpets etc.
Much easier move
Excellent cupboards
CON
Pokiness of bedroom, dining-room bathroom
Narrow and dark passage
No basin in bedroom
PROS definitely win

23 March   It is a queer thought that after the tremendous upheaval of the last month, selling Binesfield, selling every possession I can part with, piano . . . clothes, books etc . . . I could after all have a new lease here. But in '64 it would arise again and perhaps be worse.

Ever since I saw 42 the second time it has become a kind of obsession, how much I wanted it. Tonight for the first time, I have a feeling that I shall probably get it. And, for the first time, I feel a little sad. I shall miss shabby roomy old Ashburn Gardens which has been my home for 18 years and where so much, good and bad, has happened to me . . . a whole big section of my life. Except for Perham Road [her childhood home], I have never lived so long anywhere. I feel now, after the first excitement, a little melancholy. It seems God

wanted me to make this big move *now*. The way the whole thing
began a few days after the end of Emily's novena; the panic, the 'false
dawn' of Rosary Gardens, then the extraordinary series of 'coinci-
dences' and 'luck' over 42. There are weeks of suspense still but some
big change has taken place in me. It is in an odd way almost like
preparing for death . . . the knowledge that if I buy 42 and settle there,
it is my *last* home on this earth. Tonight I feel sobered after the
intoxication of the last few weeks. 42 is like going to another country
though it is only in the next street.

One great thing is that it has broken the horror of the book jam. It
was, I see now, a HOPELESS book. 42 seems in a way 'too good to be
true', too luxurious and 'well-appointed' (naturally I love that!) after
all the makeshifts of 13 A.G. I would feel almost prosperous and
elegant: I would have to 'live up to' its cleanliness and general
atmosphere. It is small, after this; concentrated, you might say.
Funny to have someone else's carpets and curtains but they are *very*
nice and *what* a saving of time and effort. I am delighted the Chambers
want Binesfield. Only hope that sale goes through smoothly.

29 March   So FIRST JOB now is to finish FILING. When that is done, all
the files can go in the attic . . .

AIM at starting Colette [*Claudine and Annie*, 1962] on THURSDAY
week, i.e. April 6. UP TO MIDDLE OF MAY there should be a lull and no
more of this frenzied rushing about . . .

There should not be any more big upheaval till middle May when
we HOPE we can really get started on planning the move etc.

Among other things I have acquired an entire new bedroom suite!
I wd. still be about £260 down (but wd. have a lot of fine new
furniture – which could go wherever I *did* go).

4 April   I think the great painting orgy [Antonia was repainting to
leave the flat nice for the new tenants] should not take more than a
week. It now comprises:

new   4 tallboys
old   cake-stand
        Landing cupboard
        dressing-table
        study table

kitchen object
Bathroom cupboard.

7 April   This chaos should last only a few more days.

I think today move my 'office' into G[iorgio]'s sitting-room as dining-room is uninhabitable.

9 April   From Tuesday on, I must settle to a quiet routine of work and finishing the painting jobs a little at a time.

3 May   Have now 17 days before I can go and do anything myself at 42. This time is VERY precious and must be used to get ahead with Colette.

From now on, Colette takes precedence of domestickers.

7 May   It is JUST possible I could manage without an overdraft. It is *miraculous* how the money has come in. £125 from Lyn and Phyllis . . .

When all is done, it should be a really lovely and very comfortable little home, ideal for my purposes, for the remainder of my life.

14–20 May   For these next three weeks you MUST try and do 6 pp. of Colette a day . . . It is not necessary to hang the passage pictures till you have finished Colette.

IMPORTANT NOTE CONSULT LYNCH ABOUT ELECTRICIAN.

15 May   What I dream to move into . . . curtains up . . . lampshades on, shelves lined, cats' trays waiting.

What do I dream it will look like? Passages much lighter.

The kitchen clean and nice and gay with blue and white curtains up and all the new veg racks etc.

Dining-room   A shade less pokey. New furniture, anyway.

Griselda [the lodger]*'s room*   Nice curtains anyway. White furniture.

Study   REALLY nice I hope . . . mixture of old and new but all *clean* . . . 3 new chairs . . . new curtains . . . divan cover . . . new pictures . . . chandelier . . . new lamp shades and ornaments, white tallboys.

Bedroom   Clean curtains, white furniture.

Secretly I think it's going to be the most attractive home I've ever had.

24 May A fortnight today I shall wake up in Courtfield Gardens.

21 June I have been at 42 a fortnight yesterday. I *am* still in a kind of dream. Hard to realize that all the strenuous work and the worry of the past 4 months are really over.

I still tiptoe about as if it weren't really mine . . . just 'lent' to me. Ashburn Gardens is already unreal as if I'd never lived there. Not one nostalgic pang did I feel when I went back. It was simply a large bare flat that might have belonged to anyone.

I suppose what makes this unreal is that I haven't yet had a normal working day in it: I am just crazed with domesticity. Yet all the astonishing things that have happened ought to convince me God *wants* me to have it! I will never know what I owe to my friends' prayers and generosity . . . think of Phyllis, so poor herself, giving me that £100.

Of course what makes it seem unreal is the money I have poured out on it. I must have spent about £800. And, miraculously, I seem able to pay for it by selling all my old stuff and raising an overdraft.

I have literally *bought everything I wanted*. I don't think I've *ever* done that before all at once! Even things like glass and cutlery.

29 July I am in confusion about work . . . what to try and do in the brief interval between one translation and another. I have been too busy, ever since I finished organizing the flat, to do anything but hammer out that awful 'synopsis' (it took me a fortnight) to catch up on Colette. On the C[olette] I often spend hours on a single sentence, work even harder on it almost than if I were composing something of my own. I feel a desperate need for an interval of doing nothing . . . except *brood*. I wonder if I really have lost the capacity to write anything of my own . . . or, at any rate, another novel in the Clara series. Apart from the 8 months slaving on the abortive one last year, I have made innumerable attempts at the other . . . the Eric one [*Julian Tye*] . . . which I now tentatively think of writing and of which I have actually made a synopsis.

The new flat is having a curious effect on me. As it were, I don't know if it is 'right' to give in to it or not. A feeling of a new beginning, a break with the past . . . a different way of life. I think selling Binesfield and buying something that suits me has something to do with it. I still feel guilty underneath at this assertion of independence . . . of my father, of course. The thing is how to *use* it best.

Should I, in writing, jolt myself out of the past and come into the present? How often I have said that series was like a millstone round my neck. Yet I can hardly leave it suspended at the end of *Beyond the Glass* – it just doesn't make sense. But if I tried to write about St Mary's [Indiana], what form could it possibly take?

30 July   I think there is no harm in thinking about this St Mary's book. Both Sue and Lyn Cosgriff are very anxious I should write it. I must finish Colette and then do the *Month* articles. After all, if I don't do St M.'s soon, it will fade. The other will keep.

31 July   I still feel timid, even a little guilty about the flat . . . it is so clean and charming and 'well-appointed'. Cornwall Gardens was a joy to me too . . . and it lasted only 8 months.

I do see the hand of God in it . . . all that time of frenzied anxiety trying to find somewhere – anywhere at a price I could pay and then suddenly this turning up, exactly what I need.

The hand of God was certainly in my going to St Mary's. It was a complete break . . . a real new experience that made a sharp impression. Yet when I came back, I fell back into the old stale misery about writing and had the most impotent year of all.

I know I am unable to 'invent'. I can only write about what I know. The underlying theme *would* be 'mother and daughter' which interests me *far* more now than man and woman.

13 Aug   Already, here, new bad tendencies arise to be curbed! Suppose I could afford to do without a lodger . . . enlarge the dining-room . . . It is foolish because it is totally unrealistic: it is going to take considerable management to live here even *with* a lodger, with the bank overdraft to pay off, big expenses (like my share of redoing the staircase) liable to occur with very little warning . . . my income is, as usual, quite unpredictable. It has, in fact, dropped £20 a month from the 'basic' (Tom's money goes to pay off overdraft which will take $2\frac{1}{2}$ *years* i.e. to December 1963) and I no longer have the Binesfield rent.

I have heard now that Doubleday will take me on. That means I really must do this book [next in the Clara series] and if possible by next spring. The book I outlined for Doubleday may, perhaps, one day be written but my instinct does seem to be that the American one should be done first. At least it might get away from that terrible sense of staleness I have every time I try to write about the other time of my life. Partly, I think, because I myself have changed so much since I first began to write them.

18 Aug Sue's 32nd birthday. I am still exhausted – and in what one might call a bruised, convalescent state after going to see Géry Forsythe [an ex-lover] yesterday. Something like 35 years since I have seen him. Géry who has now had 20 operations, 10 for cancer, 10 for something wrong with his stomach and kidneys. Unable to walk without help, his hands semi-paralysed, his face strangely swollen and pitted, his voice a mumble, yet unmistakably still Géry. Immensely brave, forcing himself somehow to get about. We met in a pub . . . I had expected to find him in bed at home. Drinking too much. An appalling life for him . . . lonely (though he has a wife) 'nothing to look forward to', practically immobilized. And yet somehow underneath the same ebullient, restless, dissatisfied, eternally young and self-centred and frustrated Géry, desperately needing, as I see now I am old, to be loved and not, perhaps, capable of loving . . . at any rate of not entering into another person's thoughts or feelings . . . perhaps no lonelier now than he ever was. And yet lovable, if someone had had infinite patience with him. I certainly could never have been that person. He was touchingly pleased to see me and – characteristically – never asked one single question about what had been happening to me in 35 or more years. It was a strain trying to hear what he said and follow his erratic jumps from one subject to another . . . he was always like that. You never had a *conversation* with Géry in the old days. He doesn't love his sons or his wife . . . G. said he couldn't read any of my books because they were all R.C. propaganda. I've prayed for him every day since I heard he was ill. He says he has no friends. One of his tragedies is that he wanted to be a writer and, as he rightly says, it was too hard work! He isn't cruel in the way [Eric] Siepmann† is, but he *is* cruel, I think, as a child is cruel. But he hasn't got Siepmann's brain or Siepmann's powers of concentration. That curious softness and flabbiness was always there even when he was young under all the exuberant 'golden giant' – and he struck me as far more 'real' than he was then. He is *terrified* of being serious about anything.

I did not mean to write in here about Géry. I mean I don't think I need anything to remind me of yesterday.

Of course I will have to use characters I have known etc.etc. But suppose I start by thinking, what is the theme of the [American] book? I think it is TEMPTATION. *St Mary's itself*. Now that obviously started as *something*. Devoted women with a much broader outlook than could have been common in the USA then. Then the insidious beginning of competition. The Alumnae association. Bigger and more impressive buildings. The need to attract more and more students. Finally, to pay debts and keep up the show, endless campaigning for money. In the end *St Mary's* becomes at once a fetich in itself . . . a legend, like Sister Madeleva.

The situation of X can be very much my own, a novelist of 60, forced to do endless translating to make a living. She has perhaps been married and had her marriage annulled by the state but not the Church. What is *essential* is that she has a daughter and is estranged from her. Anyway, X has reached a stage of pretty thorough frustration in work and in life.

Over there, of course, she finds this 'substitute' daughter [Lyn Cosgriff]. The crisis is when she discovers the girl wants to be a nun just when she herself has 'seen through' Sister Evangelica [Madeleva].

I think probably the best thing to do is forget about EVERYONE and just make a start on it. They are all too much in my hair. TRY *for once* to get away from the whole approval and disapproval business.

20 Aug   Re-reading that short story, I think I *can* still write, even though I *feel* as if I couldn't.

1 Sept   All the sense of MUDDLE starting up again. Financial largely my own fault: I hoped against hope Harrods crediting me with £43 was right. AND I have been extravagant. I seem *incurable*.

There is only *one* urgent thing now. Just sit down quietly and try and get on with the St M. book. It will soon be autumn – Phyllis says 'not to make a chore' of this book, just do it as an 'exercise'. Of course that isn't quite as easy as it sounds. I *can't* help being conscious of the fact that I am committed to write a novel – 6 years overdue now – and that every single attempt has been a failure.

. . . 'just clasp His hand and go blindly on' . . .

2 Sept TO SUE AND LYN WHO ENCOURAGED ME TO WRITE THIS BOOK AND TO PHYLLIS WHO MADE IT POSSIBLE . . .

4 Sept The circumstances are that you are committed to write a book. You have been paid, in fact, for work you haven't done.

7 Sept I tried here and there dipping into *Justine* [by Lawrence Durrell] and found it conveyed nothing whatever to me except the feeling of that city . . . it seemed to me so pretentious and over-elaborated that I felt no desire to read it 'properly'. It may well be my own stupidity: I often feel I *am* becoming stupid. I simply do NOT understand what Durrell is trying to convey in this mass of verbiage. I have a suspicion that it's all *inflated*, that there isn't anything real underneath. It is supposed to be a modern masterpiece . . . not one of these characters lives for me. I also get surfeited easily with this eternal obsession with sex. When Colette writes about sex, I *believe* her. I suppose I feel Colette has a centre . . . that she's real. I don't agree with her but at least I understand her. Maybe I just hate inflated styles. Every now and then Colette does, I think, inflate hers. Difficult to judge, in French. How can *I* tell if I know French better or worse than Raymond Mortimer [literary critic] and can judge her style? Durrell is supposed to have a wonderful style: I personally find it appalling.

14 Sept The financial situation is really serious. I don't see how I am going to get through to the end of the year. It is my own fault; I have been, as usual, extravagant. I think I will have to begin the Colette [*The Shackle*, 1964] in a month's time. I definitely do NOT want to do this *Mer Rouge* book . . .

PUT NOTHING FROM NOW ON [department store] ACCOUNTS.

17 Sept   Yesterday was a really bad day again . . . like those awful days when I was trying, for 8 months, to do the Dougal book. I sat for hours reading over, trying to revise, only making it worse than ever. In despair I rushed round to Moll. She let me talk quite a lot. In the end she made quite a good suggestion: begin with the woman packing, then have a flashback to how it all came about. I CANNOT break the habit of going back and revising, seeing what is bad, trying to make it better, changing it all, then coming to a paralysed stop and starting all over again. The old awful sense of impotence *and* the pressure of time.

19 Sept   A dream about Fr. Victor in which, vividly lifelike, he was wandering about my room. During his visit, to my annoyance, I fell asleep and woke up, very apologetic. He said he had been looking about for some sign of what I had been writing and how I was getting on. As there was none, I obviously wasn't getting on – as is the truth in fact! He seemed disappointed but sympathetic. He seemed, as in life, to want me to get on with the book.

Today I am going to try and look on it as 'manual work' like painting. In painting one *longs* to put on the top coat at once without preparing the groundwork and putting on an undercoat. I must try and look on this rough draft as the groundwork, the undercoat . . . The fact is I am terribly out of practice and have just got to get my writing muscles supple again. It *is* partly the habit of translation: revising each sentence as one goes. My problem is simply how to *spin* some raw material to work on. I am going to try the experiment of putting the cigarettes out of reach so that I don't just go on lighting them automatically. To smoke one will be a deliberate act.

26 Sept   Somehow I have got 17 pp. done – all mess and scribble which I have posted to Phyllis [Jones]†, forbidding myself to look through it. I did [it] in 5 days . . .

3 Oct   Have been working hard the last few days on this revision of 'Happy Release' [unpublished short story]. I now see this is a very big task . . . Any idea of being able to work it up into a 'quick sale' to make the money I badly need to keep going is not really feasible.

6 Oct   Two days ago I heard of the sudden death of Lyn Cosgriff's father. He was killed at once in a car crash. Apart from the fearful shock to her, I do not know what effect it may have on her whole life. By the same post a depressed letter from 'my' Lyn in New York and hating it . . . I worry about her. She *can't* go on drifting like this. She isn't even really running away from 'The Fiend' [an Italian admirer] since she has given him her address and he rings her up all the time. If only a *decent* man would fall in love with her and she with him. Perhaps six months of having to fend for herself with no rich admirers around might do her a lot of good.

I have decided it is no good tinkering now with 'Happy Release'. It would be a very big job to make it any good. I must just try and ignore the money scare – serious though it is. The best plan seems to me to alternate Colette and the American book. Thank goodness Phyllis likes the first chapter. I am too like Lyndall myself – hoping for something outside to solve all my problems.

11 Oct   Tired tonight. It is a shock, Griselda's having to go in a fortnight. Just when I am really desperate about money, too. She was an ideal lodger and it may be difficult to get anyone, let alone the right one. I wish Elaine would come but I've no idea what her situation is at the moment.

Today I made my will, which is a relief. I had to get things straightened out now I have the flat. Of course, I've nothing to leave except copyrights which may be quite worthless.

I can't see, at the moment, how I'm going to get by for the next 6 months. I think I am keeping more or less within the £10 a week limit but there are all these debts and extras to pay out.

If I could get a lodger at £4. 14. 6. a week . . . Everyone tells me I don't charge enough and maybe they're right. But it makes a lot of difference having the right kind of girl.

18 Oct   It worries me that they still haven't finished [wallpapering] the stairs after nearly 4 weeks and proceed at a snail's pace, putting on about one piece of paper a day while the stairs get dirtier and dirtier.

A theatre has become a penance. I am dead-beat today with the effort of trying to see and hear *Becket* [Jean Anouilh's play about

Henry II]. Quite unsuccessful. Faces out of focus, speeches almost inaudible. Old age.

19 Oct   St Theresa says that, in Communion, Our Lord never fails to give to us in ways we do not know and that, as we do not know what to ask, it is best to leave it to Him. My difficulty is to realize, I mean *really* realize, that religion is the centre of my life, not writing, personal relationships, security, anything else. The 2 positive commandments of the New Testament are *far* harder to obey than the prohibitions of the Old!

In ordinary daily life, I have to keep reminding myself over and over again, in the most trivial ways, that one's childish wish to sweep everything away and start perfectly fresh with everything new is impossible and absurd. The whole art of living is to make do with what one has. This becomes more and more obvious as one gets older and finds things slipping away – energy, hearing, eyesight etc. Involuntarily, I still find myself thinking as if I had a long future ahead. I wish to goodness I could do that American book and do it decently.

20 Oct   I had a curious dream last night. I was being married to Virginia Woolf! I often have this dream of being married to a woman but this was peculiarly realistic. It appeared to be 'love' on her side ... I was sad at leaving my little flat, though it was to live in far more elegant surroundings in the beautiful house in Gordon Square, inhabited by other 'Bloomsburies'. I was rather nervous of *them*. They were obviously looking one over critically. However I managed to say spontaneously something they thought 'amusing'.

24 Oct   'Extra room' dream again . . . seemed to belong to Cecil Court [the flat off Fulham Road where Antonia lived when married to Tom Hopkinson] (it usually does). This time a handsome panelled circular room, a library, with carved arched recesses. It was let to two rather disagreeable queers who used it as a bookshop.

I suppose my principal vice is always *wanting things to be other than they are*. Like Lyndall! I just don't *realize* how lucky I am to have this home in my old age. The only thing is I can't help worrying how I'm going to keep paying for it. Only one answer – by my own efforts! I took over 3 hours on ONE difficult sentence in Colette yesterday. It is silly to worry about the future – we live on the verge of being destroyed by atom bombs anyway . . . Absurd problems like the intolerably slow progress of the staircase – in its 5th week now – affect me. My *frightful* impatience! And still no news after 7 months of the rebate, or after a fortnight, of the £50 loan. I am making a novena to St Jude for Emily's finances, Moll's and my own.

29 Oct   Ian Black died on Oct 26th, very suddenly. I went down yesterday and spent the day with Eric and G[eorgie]. I have found myself thinking more and more of Ian since he died. And, inevitably, of my own death. I catch myself thinking 'I will do this and that – if I can – perhaps in 3 or 4 years time' and then realizing I will possibly be dead and it is absurd to plan for the future.

Spending so much on organizing the flat and really getting everything I needed gave me an absurd illusion that somehow I had become richer, which of course isn't true!

31 Oct   I feel after reading reviews and listening to *Critics* [radio programme] that my work is so hopelessly 'uncontemporary'. Think instead of the handful of people whom I know like to read what I write. If I could ONLY bring myself to think of the American book just as 'something to amuse Phyllis', something which would give pleasure to Lyn Cosgriff – at a time when, poor child, she needs *anything* that would give her pleasure.

From the purely practical point of view, if the Lord would send me that £200 odd I need to bridge the gap – and if he wants me to write *The Polished Apple* [the American book, later called *The Golden Apple*] he will – the thing to do is get straight on with Colette and get that done by end of November and then get down *at once* on the novel.

1 Nov   I do try not to worry so much about the money situation. But it is frightening all the same. If ever I make a sum of money, it is going straight on deposit and staying there, to stop this sort of thing happening again.

No progress has been made on the staircase – 6 weeks since they were started and each week, DEFINITELY to be finished by the end of it . . . my story refused with polite notes both by *Encounter* and *London*

Magazine – no work offered for translation though that I do not want
at the moment because of the book, but it would be a relief to have it
in the offing. But I MUST not yield to this frozen-up feeling.

10 Nov   Still no thawing out. Complete deadlock on stairs. 2 months
now . . . Much cheered by [Roger] Senhouse's† enthusiasm over
Claudine s'en Va trans. *Entrave* half done: tired: pace slackening. This
S. African lodger is leaving after 3 weeks instead of 9. Frankly a relief
. . . a strongly oppressive influence though I barely see her: a neurotic
child. One joy . . . Elaine will now be able to come for the full 4 weeks.
There will be a gap of 3 or 4 weeks. Certainly I feel isolated here –
more lonely, in spite of the pussies, than at Ashburn G. where I had
friends in the house.

   Plan for tonight   Have a bath, supper in dressing-gown and go to
bed.

   Sat: Confession. Return books Harrods. Revise next Col[ette]
chapter.

   Sun: Write Lyn C[osgriff].

   Mon: Take revised trans. to type. Look up Bézique.

13 Nov   These deaths recently, Ian's and Lyn's father's, have
saddened me. I know my attitude is wrong and I want to get it right. I
ought to be detaching myself more and more from 'earthly things' –
and I'm not!

Later   I ought to be doing Colette. Instead, I have been wandering
round the flat, trying to 'make friends' with it, altering the position of
a chair, drawing the curtains. It needs love – like everything and
everyone. I think maybe the source of this malaise is much deeper
than money. To do perhaps with writing . . . I am thinking of all the
houses I have lived in since Perham Road. Glebe Place, King's Road,
Paulton's Square, Cecil Court, a bedsitting-room on Oakley St,
Cornwall Gardens, Linden Gardens with Ian Black, Thurloe St with
the Moodys, Ashburn Gardens (the longest of all, 17 years) and now
here, the last. And always till this year, Binesfield in the background,
part of my life.

   It seemed to me, as I took this notebook instead of the Colette
book, that something was faintly, faintly tugging at me . . . the feeling
of wanting to write something myself instead of endless translation.

But I think it was an illusion. All that comes is the old sick emptiness.

I feel other people KNOW HOW to live their lives and I don't. God does not seem to listen when I implore help . . . I need *something* very badly. To be able to write a book again, I think. To be wholly engaged in something. The long winter evenings, shut up alone, always depress me. The best thing is to go back to Colette even if I only write a page. Why can't I be like Moll who is so wonderful about not worrying about the future? I can only plead feebly that there is one difference between us. She is not haunted by this having to produce something out of herself.

Later Beryl [Hope]† rang me up and said could she have a word with me when she left the Christmas cards. The word was that her friend Dora Wilkinson tells her that Sue goes to Mass every week in the little chapel in West Hoathly and also cleans the chapel with her once a week. This is so wonderful I can't quite take it in. I have told Moll. Even if she has not got to the point of wanting to get her marriage regularized, it is wonderful that things have gone so far.

I love Lyndall dearly, I love her as my child and I long to see her and I worry over her – but she has never been so right in my life as Sue or had such power to hurt me. What I have with Sue . . . ever since she was about 15 . . . is something I have with no one else and cannot define. And even 'having her back' but not the whole Sue – for Sue-out-of-the-church is another person – there is always that unspoken thing between us.

15 Nov They want me to do *La Retraite* after June.

I miss, in many ways, being part of an organization as I was in offices. This being shut up alone, day after day translating or trying to write, with no companion, no one to talk to, certainly *is* a trial. In some ways, for companionship, I miss Tom more than anyone. Honestly, I don't know anyone who has made more of a mess of their life than I have! Both ways . . . from the religious point of view and the non-religious! Had I not lapsed for those 15 years, I might have made a good life with Eric . . . but I would not have had my children. Had I not been so foolish as to fall in love with Tom, I could have had a real life with Si [Silas (Rudolph) Glossop]† (was I capable of it?) and Sue's life would have been far happier. If I could have weathered the Frances [Grigson, Tom Hopkinson's mistress] storm better, I might have made something with Tom, allowing for his infidelity and accepting the 'half-loaf' which was nourishing in its way. Even materially speaking, with any of these three men I would have had a partial 'good life' and I would not now be alone and always in this precarious financial state!

Dear Mr Mumford [a neighbour, known as 'the Squire of Kensington'] has just rung up to say he will try and find me a lodger. So I MUST stop repining and make the best of things as they are.

Just egg yourself on to the end of the month and say: By Nov 30th Colette [*Entrave*] must be finished and the stairs *should* be finished! And be thankful that, whatever happens, at least you have enough to live on till the end of the month. Shelve Christmas presents and all that until Dec 1st. Send £10 to Harrods.

NOW get down to work: shockingly late!

18 Nov   I find myself wishing perfectly absurd things, such as that Géry or Lyn C. would come to my rescue. I can only hope and pray Daisy [Green-Wilkinson]† will send me a Christmas cheque as promised.

Among my many bad habits is finding it a nuisance instead of a pleasure to write letters to people who are ill or lonely, go to see Elsie [Morgan, Eric's cousin in Salisbury] in hospital etc. Heaven knows I do little enough for other people.

21 Nov   Today is the 50th anniversary of my First Communion. I lay awake in the night, finding I still felt bitter against Mother D'arcy for not letting me make my First Communion with the others on Corpus Christi – and I still do not think it was justified to do that – with no warning and no chance to appeal – just on the grounds that 'I talked too much in the corridors'! I would have kept silence all day rather than have had it postponed! . . . six whole months to wait. I had been wanting to make my First Communion since I was 9 and I did not make it till I was 12. I can't help feeling, if I'd been an Ambassador's daughter she wouldn't have so cruelly disappointed both me and my parents. But I have *got* to forgive her . . . and see she was God's instrument for God must have wanted me to have this disappointment . . . wanted me to make it 'obscurely' with just one other child, Lily Bunbury, on this quiet little feast of the Presentation of Our

Lady on a November day. An ironic feast for me when I think of my life and Our Lady's utter dedication. It was a very happy day in spite of everything and I want to be grateful today and try to do better these last years of my life.

22 Nov   Last night a wonderful surprise by the second post – so it came on my 50th First Communion Anniversary – an American publisher wants to reissue *Frost* and *Lost Traveller*. This really *is* a present from heaven.

25 Nov   Thank God Daisy has sent me a cheque for £50, bless her. Also Andrews [Antonia's bank manager] will allow a £50 loan on the royalties. Now I should have enough, with Colette, to pay the bills and get by to the end of Jan, even if I do not get a lodger. There is now a hitch over the next Colette, but I was not reckoning to begin that till June.

27 Nov   St Jude seems to be working nobly for me. News of a possible lodger from Spain, Eric Chapman, who may want to come for 9 months. A convert, sounds nice. It wd. mean my having to put off Elaine. I am sorry about this, but I think she will understand.

7 Dec   Darling Lyndall sent me £25 for a Christmas present. A godsend!
   The only important thing to record is that all the signs now seem to point to my trying to do the other Clara instead of the American book . . . many 'hints' coming together unexpectedly point to Clara. I am trying to clear the next 6 months for my own work, in spite of finsit.

9 Dec   Géry is worse, I think I am going down to see him on Wednesday if he is well enough. I don't think I ever remember so much death and illness of friends in one year. I am worried about still not being able to let Elaine know about coming here. She has been very sweet about it but I feel horribly guilty letting her down like this. If only this man would write and say one way or the other. Poor Curdy [Antonia's marmalade cat] is ill . . . gravel in the bladder – but the vet thinks she can cure him. I couldn't go and see Elsie because I had to wait in for the vet.

11 Dec I thought in the night it might be a good idea to continue the American thing still but in the form of rough notes. Whether it wd. be possible to write two books at once when I haven't time for one! But I don't want to forget America.

12 Dec I have had to let Elaine down about coming here on Thursday. I was so looking forward to having her for 4 weeks and I hate having to do this just when she has enough strain and worry. But Eric Chapman wrote yesterday saying he was arriving at 8.15 on Sunday night. I was to have dined with Robert Demenge† that night . . . hate putting him off because he only comes to England once a year and he asked me a fortnight ago.

With Eric Chapman coming and Colette finished, I feel a new 'phase' beginning and I *hope* a better one. It is rather a gamble, this taking on a man and a total stranger as a lodger. He is a convert and I believe in his forties. Sharing this tiny flat with a man may be a problem, especially the kitchen . . . One can't be *unaware* of someone as one could be at Ashburn Gardens. But I think the Lord has sent him to me. I have to *feel* alone when I'm working and not be conscious of someone there bored and longing for someone to talk to. It will be a relief to have no chopping and changing of lodgers as I've had this year – 3 abrupt changes.

31 Dec It certainly has been an extraordinary year, beginning with profound depression and impotence over the novel and eventually scrapping the whole thing after 8 months abortive attempts. But I think the 'Dougal' book was one that *could not* have been written. Then the violent, totally unexpected upheaval of having to leave Ashburn Gardens . . . Peace at first, then in the autumn one of my worst-ever financial crises, seemingly insoluble and miraculously solved by the Lord's intervention, via friends. Finally being taken in America, the arrival on Dec 18 of E.A.C[hapman] etc. Having done 2 Colettes since June, written (in a fortnight's 'hard') that synopsis of the Clara, and a tentative chapter of the American book on which I had decided to work in this space . . . all the signs seemed to point to Clara. And once I had decided on this, they seemed to point to it more emphatically still – e.g. R[obert] Demenge's out-of-the-blue offer of an indefinite loan of £100.

I broke off to scribble a note to Géry. That has been one of the odd things this year, Géry coming back into my life, hopelessly crippled and dying of cancer. For my friends it has been a sad year: Ian Black's death, Lyn's father's death, Kathleen Judd's death, Kathleen Raine's† worry over her daughter Anna, Barbara Jencks' [unknown] *very* bad state after her mother's and father's death, Georgie in one of her blackest depressions.

My range is very limited. It is always, for me, good to envisage a reader and I am not sure that, in this case, my 'ideal' one, oddly enough, may be Georgie. She was one of the first 'signs' that I ought to write this book. After re-reading *Sugar House*, she wrote me quite an emphatic 'conscience lecture' on the subject. In her queer way, Georgie understands what I'm 'up to' far better than most people . . . in some ways, I think, better than Emily. E.A.C.[hapman] is very nice and I think we shall rub along well. This is definitely *sharing* a flat, not 'having a lodger' for he is in and about all the time unlike my girls who used to go off to work. But it makes it more of a 'home' and I think the advantages will outweigh the disadvantages.

Here I am, free at long last to tackle something of my own and a subject that interests me in a way the Dougal book never could. After all, the whole of the rest of my life has been conditioned by what happened in 1928 and 1929, by my relation with Eric, the birth of Sue, and my fathers's death . . .

TWO

1962–1964

During this period Antonia's translating continued, along with fruitless attempts to complete *Clara IV*. Both Lyndall and Susan wrote novels in this period: Susan's, entitled *White Huntress*, was her second and was published in 1963; Lyndall's was the unpublished account of a love affair. As if to rub salt in Antonia's wounds, Schwarz, an American manuscript-dealer, paid her £60 to copy out *Frost in May* in her own handwriting.

1962

1 Jan   Made a decidedly uncomfortable start to the New Year. The roads were iced up and with my terror of iced roads and the pain of the rheumatism in the sole of my foot it took me 20 minutes to get to the chapel and I arrived just at the Credo. Moll is so sure one has actually to 'hear the Gospel read' though I was on the way up that I felt . . . *very* rebelliously . . . I would have to go to another Mass. I was thoroughly bad tempered and rebellious: it seemed to me a pure formality and that Our Lord Himself wd. have given me the benefit of the doubt in the circumstances. So I took a bus to the Oratory and went to an 8.30 Mass. It was at St Joseph's altar with an old, old priest, so stiff, probably with rheumatism, that he couldn't genuflect and had to be helped up and down the altar steps. And then all at once I saw God's will in it all. St Joseph, the good workman, always in the background but so close to Our Lord and with the spirit I *ought* to have in writing this book, whether it succeeds or fails. And this old priest, this faithful crippled old servant of God. I also thought today is the feast of Circumcision and that Our Lord submitted to the pain

of it and to *all* the minutiae of the Jewish ritual . . . and here was I
rebelling against the Church's prescriptions and feeling aggrieved at
what seemed a piece of absurd formality . . . literally one minute late.
After that I felt much better. I didn't mind having to wait till nearly
ten to get even a cup of tea on this icy morning, and somehow
managed to plod back over the icy pavements, feeling every time I
reached a crossing 'I CANNOT get over this' for I feel neurotically sick
with terror walking on ice, especially crossing a road, and got back to
42 about a quarter to eleven.

5 Jan   I must not let the first chapter [of *Clara IV*] get me bogged
down as in all the other attempts. It does seem right to do the
necessary 'recapping' through the eyes of Claude and Isabel [fictional
names for her father and mother†]. But the question is just what do I
want to establish?

7 Jan   Perhaps begin on the first Sunday of his retirement.

8 Jan   What I feel I need most is a little stimulation of some kind to
dissipate the staleness. Yet talking to people for long tires me as much
as anything else. Fond as I am of Moll, it was an agony of weariness
and boredom on Saturday, straining my ears to catch her long
monologue of things I'd heard over and over again . . . minute details
of small happenings in the Guinness ménage etc. exactly *how* and
when Seraphine jumped on her lap etc. She never wants to hear
anything about my friends.

   However I didn't mean to write about Moll and I feel a beast to be
unkind about her for she is the staunchest and kindest of friends.

   What *I* want to think about a little is my *own* fixed ideas about
writing. This impotence and frustration . . . Joy in work is one of the
greatest human joys. All I really *want* to do at this moment – 12 noon!
– is just lie down on my bed and close my eyes. I want, not to *do* the
work, but to *have done it*. At my age, had he lived to it, my father
would have been doing *nothing*, having slaved all his life. Bless him,
how he *enjoyed* his brief retirement – or would have, if I hadn't ruined
it for him.

10 Jan I have taken 2 or 3 days off from actual writing. I really was feeling extremely tired and with my strained eyes and this tiresome rheumatism in my feet very much an old crock. My new glasses arrived today and should help quite a bit. Turner [doctor] seems convinced, which I wasn't, that this painful inflammation of the sole of the foot *is* rheumatism so I can go on with this medicine which makes me feel so sleepy and stupid.

I hope I'm not being *too* extravagant having these final odds and ends done to the flat . . . new lino for the kitchen, 2 new covers to protect the chairs from the pussies – they have made them very shabby already – and a cover for my divan in the bedroom – for protection and looks. Perhaps they aren't 'brute necessities' but they will give finishing touches and they've been 'bothering' me for months. But there MUST be the end. This week, when I really felt incapable of work and had to rest my eyes anyway seemed a good one and it also coincided with the tail-end of the Sales so that I got good lino and moiré cheaper. I also bought a pair of 'reduced' snowboots which don't hurt my feet and seem to have fairly good-gripping soles for walking on my *terror* – slippery pavements. I *don't* think it was foolish.

It is odd that, even though I have now been 7 months in the flat, I still keep reading the notices outside every agent in the district. I still read on fascinated about flats in Putney, Blackheath, Wimbledon, goodness knows where, trying to envisage them, thinking whether they are nicer or not so nice as this.

12 Jan I have, almost deliberately, done nothing this week on the book. I HOPE I have not been too extravagant in buying a mattress cover . . . Last night Kathleen McClean† came to dinner: haven't seen her for 2 years and I enjoyed it very much. She has just moved too and we compared our sensations of 'last home'. It is sad when I think how beautiful she was when she was young that only her contemporaries can know it now . . . you could not guess that everyone turned and stared when she came into a room. I am trying to ease myself in to my latest 'new life' . . . making myself 'love' the flat (which I do . . . it's just 'adapting') and trying to realize that E.A.C. *is* a blessing . . . that he's sweet and kind and friendly and that it's *good* for me to share the flat.

13 Jan   I am sure it is a blessing having E.A.C. here: he is a friendly cheerful presence with his cooking etc. It makes it more of a home. It is silly to keep dreaming of the best features of any flat I have ever lived in all being combined into one – Cornwall Gardens was really far and away the nicest, except that it didn't look out on trees. It is good discipline having to adapt myself to small space etc.

Later   All too characteristically, I have spent 4 hours (or more) since I wrote the above, fussing about the flat, moving furniture in the workroom, cleaning the brass on my desk, worrying endlessly about that striped chintz. I am now convinced it *isn't* right, that stripes won't do and the print is not mauvish enough.

14 Jan   I meant to 'have a word with' E.A.C. about his inhabiting so much of the flat, esp. the kitchen with his friends but he was so disarmingly sweet and friendly I didn't have the heart.

15 Jan   I really should be ashamed of myself. I did only one page yesterday. A fortnight of my precious working months gone already. And all this morning fidget, fidget, fidget about my workroom shifting chairs and ornaments, rushing to P[eter] J[ones] to change the chintz . . . A room is just like a sentence – a change of one object, even an ashtray, can mean revising the whole thing to get the balance and colour right.

16 Jan   A most odd nightmare last night. I was with Moll at some convent function and I began to vomit and vomit, bringing up the most extraordinary things, old silver spoons, pieces of wire and metal etc. It was an odd 'displacement' for on Sunday I had been telling Moll I wanted to scold E.A.C. a little about the dining-room episode and was afraid I'd lose my temper and say too much.

19 Jan   Luckily I looked at my cheque book just now. I have been living in a world of pure fantasy the past 2 or 3 weeks. Owing to a slip in figures, I thought I had £100 more than I have! . . .

This morning I had, after all this time, a postcard from V[irginia] J[ohnes]. It announced the publication of a book of Raymond's on Japanese Art. At least it must mean she is not in a mental home.

2 Feb   I read the *very* few pages (about 3!) to Georgie last night and she liked them. A great comfort and it gave me a slight feeling of *reality* about the book. As I read them they seemed dull and pompous beyond belief but she said they were good.

I am still having this absurd trouble about *concentrating* on the book. I spend hours on it every day yet can't get it in the *centre* of my preoccupation. I keep fidgeting over possible improvements to the flat.

Yesterday a gipsy cornered me into buying a bit of junk jewellery. It will be amusing to see if March 5th which she swears will be a particularly lucky day for me is marked by anything special. I do think these women have intuitions sometimes but I don't *want* to be superstitious and ask God not to be angry with me because I'm such a feeble creature.

5 Feb   I have come to a decision about the book. I think the *only* way is to go straight on, make a huge sprawling draft HOWEVER bad and stop this endless niggling and re-starting. I have just written to Phyllis, asking her to 'conspire' with me and let me send her each chunk to type before I *start* niggling.

6 Feb   Chapter I *is* after all v. important and not mere recap. It has to do a great deal. Prepare the stage for what is to come. Establish not only Claude and Isabel, but Clara and Clive seen through their eyes . . .

11 Feb (*Our Lady of Lourdes*)   Mother Clutton's Diamond Jubilee [nun who taught Antonia at Roehampton]. For the first time I feel a little better about the book – that at last I had *begun* to come to grips with it. Phyllis angelically says she will type bits however rough. I have at least 20 pp now and have just (7.15 a.m.) thrown away a bundle of tentative ones and think I've got C[laude] and I[sabel] started on the right lines.

22 Feb   A year ago today since the news that I had to leave Ashburn G[ardens] and here I am, settled in the new flat, content with everything BUT in the same impotent misery over the book. For, having re-read those 30 pp. they are as hopeless as all those other frustrated beginnings of every other attempt to do a Clara sequel. It is just shockingly bad, that conversation.

27 Feb   I am really in a state of despair about that first chapter – and the whole book. Today Schwarz who bought various MSS etc of mine for £50-odd rang up and suggested I make a manuscript transcription of *Frost in May* for which he would pay me £35. I feel that is about all I am good for now. Nowadays I never go to a film or play, never read a book; I do nothing but potter about the flat, spend hours trying fruitlessly to do that one wretched chapter and listening at intervals to the radio. I really DO feel I am finished as a writer. I don't even *want* to write any more. There is just this terrible load of a task I have undertaken and just CANNOT do.

28 Feb   Yesterday I really did reach a point of despair. I thought perhaps I'd better abandon Ch.1 for the time being and perhaps try one later on with Clara and Clive. I read some chapters of the begun-and-discarded one about Tom [*Julian Tye*] and found some of it not bad at all. I came across them when I was looking out manuscripts for Schwarz. They put a little heart in me and I decided to try and keep on with Ch.1 and did a page.

6 March   Yesterday (March 5) I posted a rough draft of Ch.1 to Phyllis. The gipsy said March 5 but actually I finished the chapter on March 4. I longed to tell Moll last night but she didn't give me a chance: she was too busy describing in minute detail everything that had happened in her daily life at Petersfield [the home of Alec Guinness] – practically down to every meal.

10 March   Phyllis likes it, bless her. And it doesn't seem *too* bad to me. I have finally given in to Schwarz and said I will do the transcript of *Frost in May* for £60. I need the money. But he won't get it in a month as he hopes.

11 March   It is very odd, this business of transcribing *Frost in May* wh. I have just begun. I wish I could recover its simplicity and freshness – it is so much *alive*. And it has such a nice easy movement. When I think how I wrote it practically straight off, and uncorrected and the labour and the torture of writing *now*, it is sad and ironical. And how all the themes of my life are there – my father and religion.

13 March   I seem unable to get over this crazy restlessness about the flat. I still read agents' notices, imagine flats I would like better. This is absurd and even *wicked* . . . I wish I knew why I am behaving in this absurd compulsive way. It isn't obviously just that E.A.C. makes me fidgety and restless with his endless 'popping in' – I like him very much and his cheerful presence is good for my spirits, if not for my writing morale.

24 March   For 2 or three days I have worked entirely on *one* paragraph . . .

2 April   On my birthday, at Moll's suggestion, I began a novena to St Jude. After all this really is a 'case almost despaired of' and this time last year St Jude got me the flat. I had a very nice birthday . . . and yesterday E.A.C. gave a lunch party. I was a wreck after – fit for nothing.

Good Friday   This book is NOT an autobiography and in any case in every instalment it deviates from autobiography.
   I MUST think of the *novel*, not my life.

28 April   As soon as I start to write I start smoking compulsively as if *smoking* were the occupation not writing.

1 May   Over the week-end Sue suddenly said to me, 'By the way I'm back in the Church – marriage regularized and everything'. She and Thomas had their marriage regularized about 6 weeks ago. She was going to tell me on Easter Sunday but I had already promised to go to Georgie and Eric long before she rang up to ask me. It is so wonderful I can still hardly take it in.
   Before she told me, Cordelia [Susan's second child], taking me for a walk, said she went to church with Mummy sometimes. Cordelia took me into the little chapel – *very* beautiful I thought – perfectly simple and all white. She showed me a statue of Our Lady and the stations. I had the same dreamlike feeling as when I first saw the

grandchildren and I walked up the hill with Andrew holding my hand as I pushed Cordelia's go-cart. And she said people went up to the altar and had some bread but she didn't though Mummy did. The rest of the Sunday I was in a kind of trance with this secret happiness.

She [Sue] told me she had been thinking of it even before she went to Nairobi – it was having that chapel right there in the village. I always felt her faith wasn't dead only gone underground. I've been aware of a difference in her. She has been sweet to me ever since she first let me see her again but these last months – since last summer – she's been different both to me and in herself. It is hard to describe – not just warmer but more _real_. She has grown into a wonderful person – admirable mother and wife and now I feel her happiness goes deep down. Naturally I say nothing to Thomas . . . I hope and pray he will eventually become a Catholic but I do not think it _at all_ likely yet. Thomas will always, I think, be suspicious of me but he makes _great_ efforts to be nice to me and I am very touched. I respect him very much . . . I am quite content to be very much in the background and not to try for any intimacy with Sue. It is enough to see her happy and to know she is back in the church. I did not expect it to happen in my lifetime. I feel I can die happy now. And in a queer way that it doesn't matter if my writing life is over for Sue means more to me than anything else. And I feel a deeper responsibility to her than to Lyn because of all I deprived her of and all the complications I caused in her life. Darling Lyn, I love her just as much but in a different way. I suppose because there has never been such a deep, painful bond between us and I have never suffered over her as I have over Sue. I love her and _worry_ over her and LONG to see her life take some real direction. The older I get, the more my children mean to me.

Later This afternoon Collins's rang up for my address. This probably means they are sending Christine [Arnothy]'s book and maybe a letter about it. I wish I _knew_ if the Lord wants me to do this book of hers as soon as possible which of course means dropping my own. I wish I knew what was RIGHT to do at the moment.

I knelt down just now and _implored_ help.

4 May At least I have something to show for today: a few pages each of the [Loys] Masson [_The Whale's Tooth_, 1963] and the transcript of

F[rost] in M[ay]. I ought to be able to get Masson finished in 4 months (i.e. working alternate weeks on it and my own) i.e. end of Aug.

* * *

Lyndall was just home from a year in New York, and she and Susan were about to drive to Turin via the Camargue in Lyndall's new Volkswagen convertible. They spent the night before their departure with Antonia.

* * *

12 May It is extraordinary glancing through these last pages. They really seem to have been written by someone insane.

Since Sue and Lyndall spent the night here, I think something has happened. It seems real . . . my home. Having them here brought it to life. It is wonderful for me that E.A.C. is away for 2 months (provided of course that he pays me!) much anxiety over keeping the place tidy – I'm becoming a fussy old maid.

All today I have been thinking about Lyndall's book. Spent an hour or more searching through Blake for a possible alternative title. Except for lyrics (and only a few) Blake now seems to me almost incomprehensible. He meant so much to me once. How can one change so? Is it just age and growing dulness [sic] of mind?

Lyndall's book haunts me. That is the only word. A terrifying book. Wonderful things in it. What that child (for I feel her to be still a child) has experienced. *What* is the fascination this man [her Italian lover] had – I hope *had* – for her? She is like a hypnotized creature. I *can* understand it. But it is frightening. It is a miracle she has not gone out of her mind or killed herself. It comes out all the time, her lack of any centre, her desperate isolation, her sense of not existing unless involved in some violent emotion. Which I understand better than she thinks.

Typically, when I said I would like to read it, she said she had no copy. When she had gone I found the manuscript on my desk. I read it all yesterday, much of it twice. Almost impossible for me to judge it as a book; I am much too involved in trying to discover her mind in it. Certain weaknesses, faults in style etc. of course I *can* judge. The 'landscape' as she saw herself is admirable. Over and over again there are really marvellous things in it – and not only landscape. But it is a terrible picture of *despair*.

Her picture of me is highly unflattering. Is it true? I don't know . . . objectively, I think not, since she leaves out little things like my being a writer. But it is very probably how she sees me . . . or, at any rate, saw me in her 'teens. An embittered frustrated woman, devoured with jealousy of her daughter, always frustrating the daughter, angry if she is happy, only sympathetic when she is in trouble. I have few friends, having driven them away by my sour temper, am 'an intellectual with no normal intelligence' 'unable to face life', always complaining about lack of money (true enough!), arousing no feeling in the daughter but occasional guilty pity; cynical, neurotic and possessive. She draws a dreadful picture of 5 years cooped up with this monster. That at least is untrue, for as soon as Sue married, she had Daphne with her.

She told me this time she did not *hate* me as a child but was *terrified* of me. I have long ago got used to having two beautiful daughters and am proud of both of them. When I was younger, I admit it was sometimes irritating to hear the constant cry 'Fancy *you* having two such lovely daughters.'

She is, I think, genuinely 'ashamed' of me. Socially, of course, this is just childish. I am accepted for what I am. Sue . . . who has *not* been infected with Lyndall's curious touch of vulgarity or anxiety or whatever it is . . . is never ashamed of me. Lyndall lives in terror of my making a bad impression which will react on *her*. She was always terrified of introducing her smart young men to me – Dicky [Muir]†, Willy [Mostyn-Owen], Edward [Montagu] etc. She isn't, I think – I am sure – a 'social climber', but finding herself caught up in a 'smart set' both here and in Rome, was both dazzled and afraid of losing her footing.

It comes out over and over again in her book – she *wants* God and yet has this fashionable fear of 'organized religion'. I am so thankful Sue has come back before they went off on this trip. It could mean so much if they can establish their old bond again – they have not been alone together like this since Sue married . . . . nearly 11 years ago. Sue is the *one* person, humanly speaking, who might be able to help her.

I do NOT think Lyn has been corrupted by all those experiences in

Italy . . . She is a magnet for the neurotics as I was. Poor child – a mixture of Tom and myself. *What* parents! And HOW does one grow out of being in love with one's father's image?

The odd thing is that the ONLY time I remember seeing Lyndall look REALLY happy was just after she had married Bobbie [Lionel] Birch† . . . The other day when we had that extraordinary meeting with Bobbie, she was terribly affected by it. He is obviously going downhill fast . . . But why did she look like that then and never before and never since? However briefly, she MUST have had the illusion that she had found the right man. But, in that one long talk, I trusted him in spite of all my prejudice.

22 May   Eric's birthday. Yesterday he rang up to say it didn't look as if it wd. be a very happy one since G[eorgie] blazed up yesterday in one of her fiercest moods and made an appointment today with a solicitor about a judicial separation and put the house in the hands of the agents! . . . If only, only G. would not keep nagging him to do things which aren't possible. She *cannot* have all the things she wants. And you can't *command* 'fame' either. If only her novel wd. be published, she might be a little appeased.

The only serious worry is my own book. I must try this alternating with translation. If only it could be possible to finish it a year from now, at the time of the Arnothy trans. (if I do that). It *could* give me almost 6 months if I keep going at it and the translation at a steady pace and *do not waste time* as I so often do in 'fidgeting'. The transcription of *Frost* MUST be finished by the end of June.

23 May   Last night, a psycho-analyst on the wireless *at last* talked sense about 'immaturity' and quoted Christ's 'Except ye become as little children'. He said this concept of neurosis being caused by 'emotional immaturity' was extremely valuable BUT it did not cover everything. The child *is* greedy, selfish, unable to see other people except in relation to itself, violent, impulsive, demanding, unreasonable etc. BUT it is also capable of growth, wonder, experiencing new things etc. The child *must* remain in us . . .

This Masson book is very good on the necessity of wonder for a child.

29 May   All the months of contriving over the flat last year were very happy ones, being completely absorbed in working out how to eliminate and fit things together in a much smaller space. I MUST try and do the same with the book: accept the limitations of my own talent, the difficulties which have to be overcome and just try to do the best I can.

5 June   I had a heavenly weekend with Sue. It was wonderful to go to Mass with her as if it were the most natural thing in the world. Cordelia came too. I kept thinking of my father and the extraordinary happiness it would give him to see us all there. I am sure he was aware of it.

6 June   Less tired today. A year exactly since I moved here. What have I produced? Only 2 translations and 2 first chapters. The last between them represent 6 months of miserable and almost fruitless daily struggles. But I must not despair. I have been skimming through this notebook for that year. It is a fine day after months and months of cold wind and that calms and refreshes me.

18 June   At least I have finished the transcription of *Frost in May*. A curious experience. It really seemed to me rather good, especially the actual writing. Above all, it has *life*. Those few characters really seem to have life and there is an authentic feeling of the place itself. When I think how quickly and easily I wrote it! It is, I suppose, no more than a series of vivid little scenes. But I was back in it as I copied it out. What depresses me now is that I *then* seemed to 'select' automatically and *right*.

19 June   Another hopeless morning on the book, bogged down again over a single sentence. This is the worst since *The Lost Traveller*, which I worked at on and off for *fifteen years*. *Sugar House* and *Beyond the Glass*, agonizing as they were, only took two years apiece.

For nearly 8 months now, I have been on my 'own' work with nothing to show for it but two first chapters of different novels. Schwarz coming upset the whole day but at least I've done that job and got the much-needed £60.

20 June   A little honesty never does any harm . . . Regard your *job* as translating and write something of your·own now and then – if you *can*! You are a spoilt product of bourgeois comfort; you haven't the guts to live as Emily does, not bothering about clothes and such frivolities. Or as Thomas and Sue do. Fitting it in as and when between translations, after all, that was how you did *Frost*. And try to sit a bit easier to it. Forget all about 'work of art' . . . be *natural* as you were in *Frost* . . .

30 June   Wasted far too much time over a crossword. Having done my horrible income tax forms became demoralized. Bought a book on Bible study. Will I *ever* get on with the Old Testament. It terrifies me. How *does* it all fit in with evolution etc? How much is 'literal' truth, how much poetic? I've never yet had a satisfactory answer from any priest. Now I hardly know any, since Fr. Victor is dead. And priests don't *like* talking 'shop'.

I *do* believe, I do, I do. But oh how many questions I'd like to ask!! Most of all, a very simple one. IF we now as Catholics accept evolution – HOW did a good God create a world in which animals could only survive by destroying each other – and often by the cruellest means? Must finish Masson by end of July. By then I MUST surely know about Arnothy.

5 July   Spent a *very* happy 2 days with Emily and Phyllis. Today as always after going away, rather tired and demoralized.

* * *

'X' was a man serving a long sentence in Dartmoor (not his first) for burglary. His case had been brought to Antonia's attention by Mr Mumford. Antonia wrote to X regularly and encouraged Susan and Lyndall to do the same.

* * *

9 August   Too tired yesterday to do anything but write to Sue and X. X's weekly letter takes me 2 hours and quite hard work. No word still from Chapman. He owes me about £80. Emily has nobly sent me £40. The Lord is trying my patience again with this suspense over

Chapman. I broke off here and wrote to Emily. Trying, as I do, every few weeks, to explain I really can't write to her as much as she wants, dearly as I love her. Her demand for letters is insatiable (though she tries heroically to moderate it) and her capacity for writing them apparently inexhaustible. I sometimes wonder if darling Emily *knows* what it is to feel flat and tired. Apart from her incredible mental vitality, she doesn't have to do any of the ordinary things people have to do, apart from having to earn a living. Such things as shopping, getting meals, washing up, writing business letters, paying bills, coping with income tax, making and receiving phone calls, washing clothes. She doesn't even keep her own bank accounts or sign her cheques. Phyllis does it all for her. There *are* moments when I wonder if it's a good idea for anyone to live as she does, convinced of her own genius, writing and painting and criticizing (most intelligently usually) other people's work but never exposing herself to the rough world where writers aren't taken entirely on their own valuation. It was so typical of her to write to me the other day: 'You have as much genius as I have or Elizabeth Bowen or Ivy Compton Burnett'! The good writers I do know – Elizabeth, Graham Greene, Julien Green, Eva Brown – don't feel a bit like that. I don't think Thomas does ever. They all work with misery, hard labour, awful uncertainty and dryness. I do *not* think it is *entirely* the stupidity of publishers and editors that stops her work from being published. I wish to goodness some of the poems could be, because there *are* wonderful things in them. Like the beginning of that story about Phyllis – I can't see how she could ever *imagine* it was good. I suppose that one of the things that makes it hard for me to understand someone like Emily is that, with all her intelligence and acute appreciation, there is something nobly, almost barbarously simple about her. She's built on the heroic scale . . . faults, virtues and all! She probably *is* a saint in the making – but she must be the first on record who was serenely (or rather violently) certain there was no question of *her* having ever to go to purgatory. I think what I find most difficult to accept is her claim to be a 'mystic'. What little I have read of Raïssa [Maritain]†'s journal – *that* is the real, classic terrifying thing. Frankly I do *not* believe Emily's 'mystical experiences' are at all like that . . . Saints change their *desires* even on earth – their whole inner substance is changed and only heroic love of God can make them willing to submit to this terrifying change which *feels*, as you read in all the records of real mystics, like utter annihilation.

10 August   All those *hours* spent trying to say something about Jennifer Lash's book [*The Burial*, 1961] and now they won't use it because I won't say it's a flawless novel. How I hate this *inflation* and falsifying of values in the publishing world.

Absurdly tired and *funking* getting back to the book. But I think I'll try today if only for a few hours and take those burdensome letters to write at Lance and Emmi's [Sheppard, Catholic friends in the country]. At least I could write a letter there, even if I can't *work*.

Widow's Cruise [sic] dept. £3. 7. 0. this morning: royalties on F[*rost*] in M[*ay*]. Plain facts dept. This novel [*Clara IV*] has been commissioned and the advance paid. Therefore you have to try and produce it. Emily's latest idea is that maybe God doesn't want me to write and that I am regarding writing as a kind of mental self-indulgence. It is quite possible to make her understand the misery writing causes me. Don't think about writing 'well' . . . above all, put darling Emily RIGHT out of your mind.

16 August   Very tired, almost more so after my weekend, much as I enjoyed [it]. Finally made myself go to doctor about this blocked up nose wh. may be one reason for feeling so stupid. Could of course be eye-strain but I had my glasses changed this spring. Dr. said I needed a holiday. He actually gave me some vitamin pills. Smoking is *purely* a nervous habit with me – obsessional for I don't even like the taste of cigarettes.

6 Sept   X is very much on my mind but I am not going to write about him here. I hardly seem to be living at all except when I am at Mass or with other people. The latter is seldom. I like it when it happens but cannot make the effort to bring it about. Obviously I cannot go on like this, fussing about the flat and watering plants. At least that shows some results, unlike the impotent hours I spend every day at my desk.

Having no translation in hand, I have no excuse not to work on the book.

I have about enough to live on for another two months. No more
. . .

The jam up is just as bad on this as on the Dougal book – or on the
other attempts at a sequel to *Beyond the Glass*. They have occurred
every single time I try to do another 'Clara' book. Added together
they must cover a period of years . . .

However, a change of possibility came into my head at Mass this
morning – to revert to the American book . . .

My friends may *well* be right in thinking I live too much in the past
. . .

And America *did* make an impression – the first *impact* on me for
years . . .

Less claustrophobic, for one thing. And isn't it rather hard on Eric
and Sue and Silas, the other one, anyway?

22 Sept   Darling Emily sent me £50 . . . it becomes more and more
dubious if E.A.C. will ever pay and I still have no translation
commissioned. Emily is one of the people I love and value most –
unique and irreplaceable. Her passionate *interest* in literature, her
wonderful eye for the best in any work, her marvellous vitality, her
honesty, her generosity, her glorious humour, her intense loyal
devotion to her friends. She's the most *loyal* person I know. She lives
almost on the poverty line herself and gives her money to other
people. I feel ashamed when I think of the comfort in which I live
physically compared with Emily. Poor darling, she feels so guilty
about having a private income.

5 Oct – There is *some* possibility that E.A.C. may return. Though the
Finsit is so bad now, it should improve of its own accord in 18
months' time when I get Tom's money again and my O[ld] A[ge]
P[ension].

14 Oct   Still no news of E.A.C. Still no progress with *The G[olden]
A[pple]*. Still on that same 2nd page of 2nd chapter which I re-write
daily and cannot get right.

Georgie came on Friday and read me first chapter of her new
novel. *Much* best she has done so far . . .

I may have trouble finding a new lodger. The Oratory doesn't sound promising. I have put a card up at S[outh] Ken[sington].

17 Oct　Two applicants for room. But nice as that singer was it would be mad to have a professional singer *and* a piano next door to my workroom . . .

Clearing out all E.A.C.'s stuff and generally 'sweeping and garnishing' the room . . .

Nospigliosi [lodgings agency] has rung up and is sending along a nice Catholic girl.

What an ungrateful beast I am!

18 Oct　Repeat last sentence! For the girl is coming on Friday. Only till Dec 15th, but never mind. She is absolutely charming, 19, and she goes away for weekends and is at the LSE all day. And Nospigliosi connection sounds just what I need. She is Mia Woodruff [wife of Douglas Woodruff]†'s sister and I think would send me other girls – is, I'm sure, in touch with the right kind.

18 Oct [sic]　Emily sent me this extract from a letter of Teilhard de Chardin to a cousin of his: couldn't fit my case better! [Trans. from French] 'You offer God, in the midst of your dissatisfaction, the sacrifice of a humble soul which bows to an austere Providence. You are deprived even of the joy of feeling that you are resigned, that you accept, that you love, and still you want to resign yourself, prove yourself faithful.'

X's record　brn. Jan 27 1929
(age 11)　1940　Approved school
　　　　1947　Borstal (a ship) (Rochester)
　　　　1947–9　Army in Germany. Discharged with ignominy.
(age 21)　1950–52　2½yrs Correct. training.
　　　　1952–54　Oxford and Winchester [gaols] 3 years
　　　　1956–61　Canterbury and the Moor (7 years)
　　　　1961　Stafford [gaol]
　　　　May 1962　[Dartmoor] 6 years
His longest interval out was from '54–'56.

8 Nov   My situation is as bad as ever but my spirits a little better . . .
E.A.C. *did* turn up about 9 days ago with a *fairly* convincing story
that Paramount was supposed to have sent me two cheques which
would cover the balance when he came over to 'settle up' and then
return to Spain to do this film job. I'm convinced that he's tangled up
in such a web of falsehood that it is impossible to believe anything he
says. I've just rung up S.H. who tells me that his landlady in Madrid
rang up her sister to say E.A.C. owed her money and did she know
where he was . . . S.H. says he [E.A.C.] knew all sorts of 'high' people
in Spain but they've all dropped him. How right I was to connect him
with Dougal from the first. I think he's *exactly* the same type except
that he's queer and D. wasn't. I'm resolved not to let him have his
things till I'm paid.

Either I can't do the American book *yet* . . . I'm not ready to . . . or
there's something wrong with the conception. I mean it's all too
much vivid unrelated scraps to make a *novel*. And I suppose though St
Mary's and my life in USA was vivid and most strange as an
experience – it did not go *deep* enough.

I suppose the mere wanting to fiddle with the flat is a faint sign of
returning energy. This state of inertia has been appalling and the
torture of nervous suspense over Chapman. Two whole days last
week were spent waiting for a promised phone call from him which
never came.

A letter I have to answer from the Carmelites about Teresa
Higginson [a devout Carmelite; letters published 1937]. She wants
me to write her life. Oh dear! DOES the Lord want that?

I have never had such a long hiatus between translations.

But I must use my human reason too. Thank heavens I no longer
feel this agonizing suspense about E.A.C. I don't watch the post and
listen for the telephone as I have month after month. The torture that
man has put me through. I don't suppose he has any idea of the
nervous strain I've gone through since last June over this business.
The two days last week were the climax of that. Now I know the
worst about him there is nothing I can do. He will pay me if it suits
him better to pay me than not. That is all there is to be said about it . . .

Yesterday I reverted to the Clara book. I felt much more *love* for it,
even if I can't do it.

You see, I *do* want to write about my father and mother and Eric.

When Eric suddenly rang me up a week ago about G's latest explosion which really seemed final (it wasn't, as I heard a few days later) I realized how *terribly* important Eric is to me. I should never have left him. We *are* indissolubly bound to each other . . . this book could be something for Eric and for my father. It *could* be a beautiful book if I could do it right; *far* deeper and truer than the American book. It is a *lovely* subject . . . even if it weren't something from my own experience but had been 'given' me. To me it is my farewell to Binesfield. And I *must* do it before I die . . . [It] should be my tender, loving farewell to my father in *this* life: it should absolve me from the guilt which I am *sure* I feel about selling Binesfield.

16 Nov   Thank heaven, things are getting better. Yesterday Christine Arnothy rang up about translating *The Cardinal* [*Le Cardinal Prisonnier*, 1964] and Collins are going to risk doing it.

5 Dec   I will have to trust E.A.C. to pay me the £5 a week he promises. It *looks* as if he means to and I had the impression he was rather subdued and frightened. At any rate, I now know where to find him and have a signed account. It is a relief to have got all his things out of the place.

15 Dec   I *must* not spend anything on the flat except spring-cleaning.

16 Dec   I saw Kathleen Raine last night. It looks as if she really is coming back to the Church which is wonderful. She is very enthusiastic about *Beyond the Glass*. This touched me very much, coming from her and knowing what she thinks of 'women writers'. It is very good having K[athleen] back in my life: someone I can *talk* to. There are not all that many people I can. Georgie was here the other night and read me more of her book. It is going on very well.

31 Dec   I have just heard from Templegate that they have abandoned the idea of re-issuing *Frost in May* in the USA because their editors are convinced that it would be impossible to make a commercial success of it.

   Well, here is the end of another year, which from the material point of view has been quite unusually worrying and frustrating.

I think some things I have written are better than books so much cracked up as Iris Murdoch's and Muriel Spark's. After all the writer's occupational disease is vanity.

1963

10 Feb   I am beginning to feel very old, not so much physically as mentally. I often simply do not *understand* what people are talking about. I never felt at home in big generalizations; I like and always shall be drawn to the *particular*. And I shall continue to believe that the novel is a business of *characters*, not 'types', generalizations, symbolic figures and mouthpieces of particular ideologies.

14 April, Easter Sunday   Now we can rejoice again! It has been quite difficult the last fortnight not to 'anticipate' Easter as it were, because of the wonderful thing Lyn Cosgriff has done for me [Lyn had given Antonia 'a handsome cheque']. I *have* bought some new things for the flat and I have done a lot of painting and touching up. So that now on Easter morning it looks fresh and clean and all essentials are in good order. I also have what clothes I need. But that burst over, now I must settle in to work . . . First I must finish de Gaulle [translation *The Trials of Charles de Gaulle* by Alfred Fabre-Luce, 1963].

* * *

At this point Pope John XXIII was dying. He had convened the Second Vatican Council (1962–5) and his successor, Pope Paul VI, was to continue its work. It was intended to bring up to date the teaching and organization of the church, abolishing among other things the Latin Mass. The process of fresh presentation of the faith was popularly known by the Italian word, *aggiornamento*. Disagreements in the Church were echoed by a violent rupture between Emily and Phyllis.

* * *

1 June   We wait bulletin by bulletin for news of the Pope. The doctors say that this rally cannot last. Perhaps he will die tomorrow, Pentecost. Humanly, it seems heartbreaking . . . this wonderful old man who has brought this new life into the church to die before the Ecumenical Council finishes its work.

. . . this painful business of Phyllis and Emily which pre-occupies me all the time.

I am not well. Only a bad go of sinusitis and the pain is almost gone but absurdly languid and exhausted. Not to go out till fever has gone. I haven't much, but could not even make the effort to dress yet. I was of course exhausted after de Gaulle – over 2 months of starting work at 5.30 a.m. and often at 4.30.

The flat is finished too. Except for the lodger's room, it has all been re-done, mostly by myself with Gladys [cleaning lady]'s help – all paintwork and furniture repainted. I think at last, after 2 years, I feel it is *mine* and will lose that absurd fidgetiness.

If I had hoped for peace of mind – well, I can't *quite* achieve that because of the Emily business which I mill over and over in my mind – *feeling* her avidly demanding – and I am sure *needing* sympathy – and unable to give it. *Whatever* Phyllis has said or done – and after all I don't *know* – she comes out of it much better than E. does. Nearly all Emily's letters to me are full of bitter hatred and resentment and Phyllis's are so different – blaming *herself* and showing such concern that I should be 'kind' to Emily . . . There comes a point – which Phyllis has obviously reached! – when one has to fight for one's self-preservation.

2 June, Whit Sunday   I wrote to Emily this morning about 7 a.m. Quite a long letter. I said – very carefully – some of the things I feel – I don't want to hurt her when she is so unhappy but I *have* to try and make her see, if I can, that Phyllis is not entirely unjustified in exploding. Long ago, when Viola [Garvin]† used to talk of the 'slave friend', Phyllis was always the person who came straight into my mind. Phyllis has had a *far* harder life in every way than Emily and isn't always screaming about her sufferings.

3 June   Still mentally harping on Emily. I wonder what her reaction to my letter will be . . . I cannot help thinking that the Maritains [Jacques† and Raïssa] made a mistake telling her to regard herself as a contemplative. There seems to me an awful lot of false mysticism here. I am afraid I obstinately persist in thinking Phyllis, even if she has momentarily lost her faith, a much more Christian character because she is so much humbler and also so very much kinder to her neighbour. Her [Emily's] last furious letter was because Phyllis hadn't answered a note. Phyllis – in the throes of moving house, begging for a little peace . . . E. never takes these simple factors into account – as she bombarded poor Father Victor on his deathbed with those huge letters he dreaded.

The flat all newly decorated and looking lovely. *What* Lyn Cosgriff has done for me I'll never be able to convey to her. It is still unimaginable to have the collar off my neck for a while after 18 years of 'hard labour' and incessant money worries. Free to think about my own book.

11 June   J. Bruneis on modern translations of Bible: 'I have always sympathized with people who wish to understand what they are expected to believe.'

I hope I have not been too extravagant. I expect I have. But it *is* wonderful to have the flat really nice at last . . .

I had 2 sad poems from Emily, but no letter . . . this [quarrel] has been a terrible psychological shock to her and may well have unbalanced her mind . . . After all, her mother was insane and she did have this one bout of insanity after John's birth [described in *The Shutter of Snow*, 1930].

18 June   Week-end with the Bertrams† which I enjoyed very much. Barbara is one of the best people I know. I admire her and love her more and more. Tony was observing, as one can't help, that Jeremy [their son] is becoming rather trying with his insistence on talking at such length about his brass rubbings etc. And of course I couldn't help observing that J. is becoming exactly like Tony. He gave me, detail by detail, every moment of speech day, and in his room a kind of lecture on brasses. Except for enquiring after the cats, he never asked anything about myself . . . B[arbara] told me on the way to the station that Tony won't let him have other boys in the house – the mere appearance of another child at tea would be too much for his nerves! So poor J. really *needs* someone to show his brasses to . . .

Still no word from Emily . . .

20 June   I wrote Phyllis an enormous letter today. I said to her some things I have said to myself on paper. Like her, I feel 'a cold-hearted bitch' about Emily. I *know* she is fearfully unhappy and I *cannot* feel as sorry for her as she wants me to feel.

23 June   Have done nothing today. Letters seem to exhaust all my mental energies. I had to write a long one to Mary Siepmann [Wesley].† Hers to me confirmed exactly all I feel about Emily (of whom she too is extremely fond) and was a relief to me. Mary has obviously spoken a good deal more plainly to E. than I've ever dared to do and told her she isn't a saint which 'made her very cross'. She says Emily feels like an abandoned wife – which she obviously does . . . Mary says that what Phyllis is escaping from is 'involvement' and thinks, as I do, that she's very wise to get away. I hadn't realised till P.'s last letter that she never *wanted* to go to Callow End (she's so terribly good at concealing her feelings) and that Emily, indirectly, put immense pressure on her, finally, of course, seeing the will of God in the cottage being for sale. Poor Emily was very lonely and will be very lonely – no doubt of that. I think Eric Siepmann is now getting the letters I surprisingly *don't* get. Mary is quite right – that Emily has nothing to do – and will keep trying to involve all her friends with each other – I *know* it's because she loves us! She has now done the incredibly stupid thing of writing to X and telling him Mary will go and visit him in Dartmoor – without even consulting Mary. How *can* she be so stupid! Mary is desperately busy and now poor X will be taking it for granted she will visit him and be bitterly disappointed if she can't. But it's no good – Emily is *full* of good will but quite incapable of imagining other people's lives and feelings.

24 June   Just when I thought things were peaceful – or going to be – this Leslie Wilson [lodger] business. He will have to go and I am not looking forward to the unpleasant business of telling him so. I have written to John Wilson explaining why. There are limits to what we – Gladys and I – can put up with. Thanks to dear Lyn [Cosgriff], I can wait till the right sort of lodger turns up. I would like him to go at once but I think it is only fair to give him time to find somewhere else so I will make it a week from Friday.

29 June   I am now convinced that the real culprit is John, not Leslie Wilson. I am sorry about John, but the crisis has really been a blessing in disguise. It will stop this weekend business and I now feel on much easier terms with Leslie who obviously wants to stay on and has been making touching efforts to be less messy. I believe what he told me. And it *does* suit me much better to have someone who is out most of the time and does not use the kitchen.

The sight of Emily's handwriting on a letter this morning made me, I admit, feel apprehensive. It was, however, a perfectly calm, sensible letter, asking me to see a friend of Martha's . . .

Went to the cinema today with Moll and am dining with her tomorrow. It is *very* good for me to have to put up with the boredom and to remember Moll's really impressive goodness.

30 June   All I need to [do] now to bring the lodger's room a little into line is to paint the woodwork and little chest and have the curtains cleaned and the white ones washed. Also the bedspread . . .

3 July   I am still not quite sure about the Leslie Wilson situation, but I *think* he is telling the truth. John's letter carefully avoids the crucial point, so he may be the guilty one, as L. says. Anyway, if I have told L. he can stay on, I cannot very well take that back and he has behaved beautifully ever since.

4 July   Today I had the excuse of finishing off the painting of Leslie's room. That does finish off the entire renovation of the flat . . . I have cleared out possessions too: got rid of a very beautiful and hardly worn dress . . . Perhaps it was lazy of me to give them to G[ladys] and not to some Catholic sale, but I don't want to hoard . . .

21 July   It is a lovely, peaceful Sunday evening – actually like a summer one! I went to see the Linturns [cleaning lady] and the lovely gardens they and their neighbours have made. Meant to work this evening but have only arranged the exquisite roses they gave me and stared at them – they are so beautiful.

Iceberg – pure white . . .

Ma Perkins – deep pink rosette like giant rambler
Columbine – pale yellow
Pinocchio – very pale pink, small, exquisite floribunda
Goddess– white, scalloped petals bordered with pink
Fashion: deep pink . . .
Prelude – *mauve* . . . yes, really mauve

The Emily situation is still tense. She is making great efforts *not* to be angry with me but she is obviously highly offended at my suggesting even a possible shadow of an excuse for Phyllis. She sends an absurd list of all the 'geniuses' I have known which is quite beside the point . . . Humphrey Jennings (whom I hardly met) Hugh Kingsmill, Edwin Muir, Eric (who?) George Barker, Dylan Thomas, John Holms,† Father Victor, Kathleen Raine, Julien Green and Malcolm Williamson. The whole point was people who *think* they are geniuses, whether they are or not. Malcolm may be a genius but how can anyone know who is not a musician?

I never heard Dylan refer to himself as a genius.

I doubt if Barker *really* believes he is one.

I can't imagine Julien Green calling himself a genius though he comes nearer to being one in my opinion than any of the others.

As to Father Victor *thinking* himself one – the idea is preposterous. He had too much intelligence.

Kathleen at times *does* think so.

Whichever Eric she means, Siepmann or 'my' Eric, the idea is absurd.

I can't believe that either Hugh Kingsmill or John Holms would have overrated themselves to that extent.

I can only presume that what E[mily] means by 'genius' is talent, sensibility, intelligence, etc . . . She mentions, as usual, Dorothy Holms,† who, as far as I know, never produced anything whatever and was only an interesting eccentric.

It is so sad, her longing for recognition. It must be awful to believe you are a genius, pour out quantities of work and find no one who will publish any of it. The pathetic thing is that, though she is very indignant and hurt with me, she is desperately afraid of losing me too and is being extra handsome about my writing. But, alas, at the moment it isn't exactly 'self-confidence' I lack for I still persist in thinking I could [write], if only I tried hard enough.

23 July   Lyndall's 32nd birthday.

   To be well-bred means to have respect for the solitude of others, whether they be mere acquaintances or, and this is much more difficult, persons we love; W. H. Auden. Preface to an anthology of de la Mare. . . . describes so exactly the Emily–Phyllis situation.

   How much that goes home to *me* too . . . especially 'with persons we love'. I was particularly guilty of it in the past in my relations with Sue.

20 August   That bad moment waiting for visitors from the USA for dinner . . . have they got my instructions – will they find their way? The usual rush – shall I get everything ready in time, though it is only a cold supper and everything was cooked yesterday. How DO people manage to entertain often and with no apparent effort? I'm so appallingly slow about everything. True my kitchen and dining-room are very small, but I take ages over all the little fiddly bits – ice, lemon, biscuits, etc. It takes me 2 hours to do what another woman wd. do in 30 minutes or less. I expected them at 7 . . . now I've got to the stage (though it's only 10 past) of wondering if to ring their hotel. And, if I do, shall I hear the buzzer if it goes . . . Have just rung up to discover the Murphys [American friends] aren't arriving till tomorrow.

17 Sept   Re last entry. Having been *convincingly* informed that Wesley [Murphy] and her husband weren't arriving till the next day, completely frustrated. Dinner all prepared, self tarted up, no guests. Would food keep till tomorrow? Wine already open. Anyhow would they be able to come tomorrow. No. Only thing invite some understanding friend in the neighbourhood to come and eat it. Rang Moll. Would have loved to if I'd rung 10 minutes earlier but had just washed her hair. Rang Beryl and Anthony [Hope]. Had just had their supper, earlier than usual. Rang Margot [King]. No reply. That exhausted possibles. Couldn't invite B.P.s [unknown] or Dutches [from Ashburn Gardens] at last second, having never had them to dinner since I moved and owe them both hospitality. Lit another cigarette, stared impotently at wall. At 7.30 buzzer rang. Wesley and Jim. Immense relief – they looked surprised! They *had* arrived at their hotel the day before as arranged: had been in constant touch with receptionist all day.

Yesterday I did something odd. Charlotte [d'Erlanger]'s† £80 – which has nagged me again since Lyn's present – came into my mind at Mass. I felt I *must* do something about it. Daren't think how long ago I borrowed it. Probably well over 30 years . . . Even now, paying her £80 only represents ⅓ of the value of the money she actually lent me. It is no good being self-righteous about Chapman's not paying me when there was this old beam in my own eye!

I had a wonderful weekend with Phyllis. She has come back to the Church. We were able to talk more freely than we ever have in the 30 odd years I've known her. I have hardly ever seen her without Emily. I like her so, so much and admire her too . . . The pages I took her don't look half as bad as I thought now they are typed. The great thing is that P. seems to *enjoy* the thing and she somehow manages to make it at last seem real to *me*.

Phyllis prays far more than I do. I could *never* be like that – those hours of prayer. Everything terrifies me and makes me conscious of not even having the *rudiments* of being a Christian. Ought I to join the CND? I'm so lazy and such a coward. Oh God be merciful to the weak and cowardly and hopelessly confused . . .

21 Oct   General clearance of letters etc.

In next 14 months try to finish book . . . aim at minimum of a chapter a fortnight. If you cd. do 4000 [words] a week and make your deadline your 65th birthday – it *could* be done.

2 Nov   Yesterday I had lunch with Charlotte . . . hoped she would be alone but I enjoyed it all the same. A nice woman who seems to live with her – didn't get her name – and Muriel Nevile (O'Conor). She has a very beautiful house. Monmouth House in Lawrence St. The right sort of house for her. She is very thin and elegant. Her face rather haggard but *her* face still, except that her eyes which I remember as green are almost blue now. Her hair slightly reddish-brown, a little untidy as of old, combed up carelessly in wavy peaks above her narrow face giving it a touch of Medusa. Her voice, her way of speaking have not changed – the old edge and the old charm, unlike anyone else's, are all there, thank heaven. Her eyes are sad.

Under the wit and acidity, something extraordinarily sweet and one can only say *good*. She *hasn't* changed – she is incorruptible. I have been thinking of her ever since. *Is* she embittered, as I have been told? Perhaps. She has that aloofness still and that critical air – or rather an air of faint detached amusement. One is afraid of boring her.

16 Nov 3 weeks ago I said to God 'If you *really* want me to write this book, give me some idea *how* to handle this chapter' . . . I woke up after praying this at night and with the idea to do it in a dialogue with one or both aunts. Even working on this has been as painful as usual . . . yesterday I destroyed everything but one page and have added 2 which may possibly stand. But most days 6 hours will go over one paragraph. But at least this seems a possible way of *seeing* the chapter right. No one would believe the absurd amount of effort that goes into each day's work. I have never known *anything* like this impotence before . . . But it seems I am *not* meant to give up and I suppose it is my cross. In every other way my life is so pleasant and free of anxieties at the moment, thanks to dear Lyn.

15 Dec Last Sunday, having started at 5 a.m. and worked, except for Mass, washing-up and a couple of meals, till 9 p.m. I somehow finished a rough draft of the Claude chapter and sent it off to Phyllis – Have NO idea what it's like – better or worse than all the discarded alternatives. But at least I can say to myself *some* sort of rough draft of Part I is done.

I went to the E[nfants] de M[arie] meeting. Behaved shockingly, nearly burst into tears because poor darling Beryl asked me if I'd done that piece for 'Parents'. I think they'll let me off. It was absurd and shocking of me but to be asked about that when for once I felt I'd cleared up and cd. breathe (though not for long; the Arnothy proofs arrive tomorrow) I just COULD NOT take it. I couldn't attend rosary, procession, anything. It is absurd this agonized flare-up when I feel hemmed in and *driven*. Have come back too tired even to do Christmas cards. Childish and weak . . . I was nearly rude to some inoffensive 'Old Child' who asked me what kind of things I write and did I admire (name's gone – that American best-seller) Frances Parkinson Keyes? I ought not to be allowed out in public if I can't control my nerves and temper when people mention writing to me.

18 Dec Charlotte [d'Erlanger] came to dinner on Monday. An extraordinary experience. I really did enjoy it and almost believe she did too. She says she has not believed in God since her twenties . . . She does not feel it necessary that the universe should have any purpose or explanation. You feel a profound melancholy in her. She is as witty as ever. Has obviously suffered a great deal . . . She misses her husband badly still. A sense of isolation about her, as there always was.

20 Dec Still do not know if L[eslie] is coming; whether to go to bed or wait up.

Have been glancing at a book about the sources and writing of the N[ew] T[estament]. *How* complex it all is and yet how interesting . . . This state of flux is at once alarming and exciting . . . something is happening in the Church. I felt a different spirit when I came back – 23 years ago . . . the whole climate of thought has so much changed, even in 50 or 60 years, that it would be impossible to assimilate all the changes – one can only sense that God's *way* of revelation is entirely different from what one was taught.

30 Dec I think the basic cause is the difficulty of accepting being as old as I am; people like me, half optimist, half pessimist, find it difficult to live from day to day; we are always either expecting impossibly much of the future or being nervously apprehensive of it. I am extraordinarily lucky to be so well . . . My faculties haven't declined too much; my deafness is the only real tiresomeness. My slowness and stiffness in writing – well, I can only hope and pray it will wear off . . . [Dr] Carroll said long ago that I had a compulsion to *disappoint* people and there is some truth in that. But disappointing other people's expectations of me about work etc . . . that is odd, since it means so much to me to be approved of. And going back, as usual, to my father, the person I most *anxiously* wanted to please, why did I disappoint *him* . . . not want to go to Cambridge etc.etc? Insist on going on the stage – the thing he most disliked? I have no idea. But it was not till after the Roehampton episode that I inwardly rebelled against him.

I am nervous of 'New Year Resolutions'. I think, if anything, I need to loosen the screws, not tighten them. Thank God for all the blessings of the past year –and *how* many there have been – and make an act of confidence in Him for the next one. Just work quietly on the book for the time being. Not even saying anything like 'a chapter a fortnight'. Simply immerse in it, think of producing something for Phyllis who is interested in it . . . and – for goodness sake – go easy on spending now the Christmas orgy is over. There really is nothing you need, or even want. Do *try*, from now till your birthday not to put anything on account.

1964

31 Jan   This is the first day I have taken off book since I went to Sue on Dec 29th. I read Ste-Beuve on Pascal – the book M. Demenge gave me a year ago and have not read till now.

I will try and do a few things I want to do – Goya exhibition, Ruskin and his circle etc. But I dared not let up till I had done another chapter. The enormous amount still to be covered and the vast amount of material to be shaped *somehow* into a book frightens me . . . Terrifying to read of Pascal's penances. I do sometimes wish saints didn't do such dreadful things – spiked belts – and almost worse, refusing to allow themselves to take pleasure in *anything*, even the most 'innocent' things, conversation with a friend etc.etc. It is this from my childhood that has made me realize I could *never* be a saint. I'm too self-indulgent and cowardly. And I love the people and things of this world too much – animals, plants, books, pictures, just *fun*. And comfort. And clothes. And I fuss about my appearance, even at my age. If one really loved God, I suppose one wouldn't care about any of these things.

Dame Marcella† said maybe it's what I'm meant to do – grind away a few lines a day with this *appalling* sense of impotence. It really is suffering – of a kind.

The nervous fret and impotence about everything! Even asking a few people in to drink the champagne Christine [Arnothy] sent me. Am already in a frenzy of neurotic anxiety. Will there be enough to drink? Will they be bored? The lights on the stairs? Food if anyone stays on?

The agony of bringing myself to ring up Charlotte. The relief when she said she didn't like cocktail parties. My terror of course was that if she came she'd be bored.

It's no good. I *am* still frightened of her. I like her so much, but there it is. It is a relief to be able to leave things to her. I only thought of asking her because I knew S[ue] and T[homas] would like to meet her and I'd like her to meet Sue – I'm so proud of Sue!

I can't pray even at Mass or Communion. Just one long distraction.

All I can do is *try* and fight against my 'evil inclinations' – the usual one of resenting I never get even a mention among modern novelists. It is all Iris Murdoch, Muriel Spark, Kingsley Amis, Lawrence Durrell etc.etc. I feel quite different about writers I *know* to be better than I am – Graham Greene, Evelyn Waugh, Elizabeth Bowen, Ivy Compton-Burnett (yes, I'm coming round to her!). But I'm afraid I think I'm 'as good as' the first lot and am truer to life. And I'm afraid I also think I write as well as Thomas (my son-in-law) and Anthony Powell – both of whom are now practically 'modern classics'. The truth is I have a *tiny* talent which may have gone or might show a *tiny* increase before I die.

4 Feb   Tomorrow there is this little party. It is only 20 people, but it is the first since I have been here and the first since the huge one in 1955(?) which in its turn was the only one I had in my 17 years in Ashburn Gardens. *Absurd* apprehensions . . . I have been worrying, making lists etc. for over a week.

Having been to nothing in the way of films, exhibitions etc for over a year, went in one day to the Goya exhibition, the Ruskin one and enormously long film *Lawrence of Arabia*. L. of A. worth seeing for the magnificent desert sequences and interesting on Lawrence too – the iron will, the vanity, the tremendous physical courage and the inner weakness – the collapse under the physical indignity of being *handled* – not the pain: he is sacred to himself and must not be profaned. The loneliness of the man and yet the longing to be *accepted*, to have a recognized place. This is always shown as the result of his shame about being illegitimate. A good touch at the end; when he is being driven away, officially a success but knowing he has failed, the car is passed by a soldier on a motor-cycle and the last shot is of Lawrence staring at the motor-cyclist as he disappears ahead.

Ruskin exhibition fascinating . . . poor Effie! She was very beautiful. A curious drawing of her by R[uskin] a *very* cold drawing, rather dull. Someone complained there was 'not enough fire' in his eyes. Hardly surprising. One can hardly blame her for going off with Millais (there is a portrait of him, magnificently handsome and *alive*-looking) after 6 years of unconsummated marriage with R. Some of his drawings of plants, crystals, etc are very good but there is a certain feebleness in them, exact and lovely as they are. Quite the most beautiful things in the exhibition are the exquisite crystals, shells etc. he collected. Carlyle called him 'a bottle full of beautiful soda-water'. One forgets all the new territory he opened up – the world of medieval art included – in an age when painting had declined into formalism. Yet it is strange he could appreciate Turner who was revolutionary and could hardly have been less like R[uskin]'s beloved Pre-Raphaelites who are really *very* dull painters without a genius among them.

I also saw the Omega exhibition. That really *was* strange. Nothing could seem more 'dated' than what, in my youth, seemed so fresh and exciting. The fabric designs stand up best. Some of them are splendid. But when one thinks what 'Bloomsbury' stood for in my youth, a kind of holy of holies of art. Of course one doesn't see the best of Vanessa Bell and Duncan Grant here; there is a 'good' D[uncan] G[rant] of Vanessa which brings back that whole period so vividly. And one (almost academic) of Nina Hamnett. A shock to see her as an attractive young girl, when I think of the battered woman I remember. What is odd is their mania for decorating *everything* – so different from our liking nowadays for plain things. If one has one patterned object in a room, one likes the rest plain. But there, no inhibition *at all* about using any number of conflicting patterns and colours, the more the merrier. A painted table – quite attractive – but sadly chipped and battered-looking now – formerly belonging to Mrs St John Hutchinson. *That* brings back the whole world of my early twenties!

18 Feb   For ten days I have been labouring away at the next stage of

Clara's journey. Had meant to get her to Victoria in Ch. IV but the last bit would NOT come right and I finally 'cheated', as I thought, by sending it off to Phyllis – it was already very long – at the point when she gets on the train at Dover. I still don't know if introducing the two nurses [from the asylum] was right – it took one miles out of the way – but it's one of those ideas that thrust themselves in – it has done so in an earlier version (years ago) of this book and of course into that short story ['Surprise Visit', 1964]. But I *have* meant to round off Chapter IV by her finding Clive waiting for her at Victoria – an unprecedented thing for him to do.

Yesterday, after endless re-writings of here a sentence, there a sentence of the 2 pp. finally salvaged and in a complete mess, it simply ground to standstill. Last few days have been *very* bad but yesterday the worst. I smoked compulsively. Couldn't get either her feelings or the language right and it had *gone dead*. So I think it was badly conceived and somehow false. That is the worst of it; one gets a definite picture like Clive at the station and tries to lead up to it. Besides it really is high time I got Clive in and Clive and Clara together.

15 March   Something *very* important has happened. For a long time I have been having serious mental conflict about religion and for the past two months it has been acute: the old 'double think' problem, in fact the whole Catholic 'thing' – the Old Testament and even the New – the impossibility of getting a 'straight' answer to anything. Last Sunday I went to a 'Day of Recollection'. Not one *word* of nourishment did I get from the priest's talks – it all seemed words, words, words, the old clichés.

2 April   The 'very important' thing was Kathleen Raine's introducing me to the works of Fridhof Schuhon, all of which (in English) I have now bought. It is the line of thought to which I always come back at intervals – what is *behind* the outward form of Religion. Schuhon understands the Christian tradition – and, for him, this is the Catholic tradition – perfectly and I find him far more illuminating than the 'scholarly' approach of Fr. Bright . . . Schuhon is in the real tradition of the *sacred knowledge* – the 4 levels of interpretation of St Thomas and the fathers. There seems no doubt that there was an esoteric knowledge in the Church itself and still is. The great thing, for me, in this is that it makes my religion live for me again since he insists that one has to stick to one's own tradition which is God's revelation for oneself. So there is no mixing of the East and West as in these bastard cults and 'theosophies'. I was getting worried by the 'literal', historical' etc . . . the paradoxes and contradictions. But I see dimly now that this was because I was *approaching* it wrongly. Knowing that the Bible was compiled at different dates etc.etc. is interesting but irrelevant. The scriptures are *inspired* – that is what matters. All these attempts to 'bring religion up to date' are futile. It is the truth, 'ever ancient, ever new', that matters.

For a fortnight I have not attempted to work on my book. In the light of these things it seems a futile activity. Nevertheless I shall try to finish it. If God does not wish me to, that is that. The old problem – is it *wrong* to write my kind of book at all? But I think it better to try . . . hoping that at least it isn't a *sinful* activity.

Set-back over sudden disappearance of Leslie Wilson [lodger], leaving his last week's rent unpaid. I have now spent all Lyn [Cosgriff]'s gift and am back where I was. Except that I still have this £100 in 'Ernies' [Premium Bonds] . . .

Lyndall touches me very much. She has been so sweet to me during her stay. I so long for her life to be happier and more satisfactory than it is. I can't 'preach' to her, only pray for her. I like her employer Wolfgang Reinhardt [son of Max, the theatrical producer] very much but I see her point – that his negativity increases her own. She has so much capacity to love and it never seems to have been called out by the right person. She has grown up a great deal since I last saw her. She is so *lovable* and kind . . . She wept at *The Seagull*. I can see how Nina affected her: her own sense of failure. Wolfgang said to me once 'If she were humbler, she would have more self-confidence.' There is *some* truth in that but not the whole truth. For she *is* humble, I think, which must be difficult with her beauty and rather sensational attractiveness. It is more, perhaps, that she dreads failure which is, I suppose, a kind of pride. I understand *all too well* the desire for 'fame', 'recognition' etc. If she had some work that absorbed her, she might think more of the work itself and not at the recognition it might bring her. She feels, poor child, she has missed *all* the boats, marriage, career etc . . . no wonder she has no sense of security. Things *happen* to her, she becomes involved, she drifts; if she sits down to 'think things out', she becomes lonely, depressed, pessimistic and then a new adventure begins which distracts and drugs her for a time. And, of course, she has to make a living. It is *very* much to her credit that with all her chances of marrying very rich men, Dicky, Montagu, Selznick etc, she has never married for money. But I *do* see her point about Wolfgang . . . Marriage is out of the question there, but he is living an unreal life – as a rich man – for perhaps one more year. And absorbing all her time. She is aware of this danger. I am not sure that he realizes that he is, in his gentle way, eating her up.

* * *

Jacques Maritain, the French Catholic philosopher, had recently been widowed. His wife, Raïssa, also a writer, had left a journal. He was anxious that Antonia, who had met her, should translate it for an American publisher.

* * *

14 June As usual found myself re-reading what I had written. A year ago much the same – book, Emily, Phyllis. Having just spent two days apiece with both of then, I feel much the same as I did then. I am very fond of both of them. P. is *very* like me! She writes, 'I only want to love God.' Seeing Emily *was* rather a strain after the ease of being with Phyllis. Yet on the whole it went well and E. herself said it was the best visit we'd ever had. I 'stood up to her' a bit better. It's useless arguing with her about prayer and all that. Dame Marcella agreed with me that what Raïssa describes is quite different from normal human suffering, however painful, a spiritual suffering *like purgatory* which the *real* mystics get in this life. But E. of course will have none of *that*! My weakness, according to her, is that I *hate* mysticism (totally untrue!), have conventional ideas about religion etc.etc. She now tells me that getting me to translate Raïssa was a plot for the good of my soul, because she told Dame M. 'Tony hates mysticism' . . .

However translating R. *is* for the good of my soul – a mean, cowardly little soul, as different as possible from R.'s great generous courageous one. I certainly love her dearly .

I think I was right to go off from the book [*Clara IV*] and go on to

Raïssa. I pegged on till the impotence became unbearable. Sonia [Orwell] asking me for chapters of the novel precipitated it. Tempted by the idea of their being published . . . pleased anyone *wanted* my work after all this, tempted too by the money, I broke my rule and looked back and got turned into a pillar of salt. Two of the first 3 chapters seemed so awful to me that I spent a fortnight trying to revise them and it got more and more hopeless. I wrote to Sonia saying it was impossible, but, remembering 'Surprise Visit', sent her that. To my joy and relief she and the editors [of *Art and Literature*] like it.

I think God *does* mean me to do Raïssa now. It would mean so much to Maritain if it was done in his lifetime and there may not be much of that left. This *Journal* [is] a book of *great* importance for the world here and now.

My 10 days in Cornwall with Charlotte and Madeleine [Charlotte's companion] was wonderful. Did me all the good in the world physically and mentally. After all I haven't had a holiday since long before America . . . got 60 pp. of translating done.

I am *trying* to pray a little more. Dame Marcella says Prime and Compline. I find it NOT nourishing, yet but peg on – to show a kind of minimum 'good will' anyway. Some of the psalms I find *incomprehensible* – I mean the language doesn't even make *sense* to the normal mind.

Had meant to write a lot more [of diary.] Wasted time in reading through and am tired now. My hope is that I may do better on the book, once I have finished Raïssa. Meanwhile peg on with *her*. It *is* an experience, *living* with her. I *love* her, even though she frightens me. I WISH I knew exactly what she means by 'renouncing the world' and not making the *least concession to nature*. They ALL say that! I wish I'd known her in the flesh as Emily did. It was a relief to me to know she dyed her hair and varnished her nails – at least she *seemed* human!

A gem from the radio: 'built-in disincentive'.

24 June Raïssa takes all my time at the moment. I MUST finish by the end of August. Even when I have finished my part, there is all the final revision with Maritain. Slightly ominous first batch not back from him yet. I fear endless niggling corrections of the actual English (and he really *can't*, bless him, know English better than I do!). But if he's going to take so long over each 80 pp. or so, delays look like being considerable and I want to post it to USA complete in September.

It worries me that I have not yet had the chance to tell Sue about my will and this notebook. I practically never see her alone and it's a difficult subject to introduce. I know that it seems conceited to imagine that anyone might ever want to publish any extracts. And I can most truly say that nothing in all these volumes covering, I suppose, something well over 30 years (and which would have covered, intermittently, over 40 had Benedicta [not] persuaded me (wrongly, I think) to burn the first 2 – has been written with any idea of publication. They contain too much of what I am heartily ashamed of for that! I ought perhaps to have put in my will that they should all be burnt at my death. On the other hand, if anything of my writing survives, other writers might find things of interest to them in it. And perhaps other Catholics – and people interested in religion. Or in psychology. I have not faced reading them – the long-ago ones – for many years. All I can say is that they *are* a record of what I was thinking and feeling at the time. On the other hand, there are things in them which it would hurt Sue, and perhaps Lyndall to read . . . And I know they are a rather horrible exposure of myself. Yet here and there in them I think there are things which are interesting and which I have not said anywhere else. And, if I ever *do* write a good novel, which might encourage other writers who have suffered the same agonies of impotence and self-distrust. Again, I have no money to leave Sue and Lyn. If there is *anything* that can be made out of my 'literary remains' I would like them to have it. I think the only thing is to tell Sue the whole story and leave her to decide. I keep them to *clear my own mind* more than anything else. And they have helped me sometimes to do that.

What I love most in Raïssa is her passion for truth and her love of human beings. She had a real genius for friendship. I met her only once, cannot even remember what she looked like (it must have been in 1946 or 47) retain only an impression of someone *immediately* 'sympathique' and easy to talk to. I think we talked mostly about Emily. In *Les Grandes Amitiés*, the copy she gave me, she has written *Avec profonde sympathie*. It would have been wonderful to have her as a friend. But one knows her in her books – I have been re-reading *Les*

Grandes Amitiés – and I really feel I have her as a friend in heaven. From L.G.A. one realizes how immensely *gifted* she was – she had . . . a love of art, especially painting. She was also extremely musical and at one time a very good pianist, good enough to have made music her career. Most striking, of course, is her *thirst* for the truth, for the absolute . . .

Bobbie [Speaight]† said she had no feeling for nature, never went out of doors, even at Kolbsheim. One does not feel this in her books. She does not talk of it much but one feels it there, a sensitivity to the visible world. He also said that the Maritain atmosphere was a 'hot-house' one – he called it a 'hot-house' piety – that it was 'all God and each other' – and that they were all terribly upset by any criticism of them. I can certainly imagine Raïssa being a little tiger to anyone who did not appreciate her beloved Jacques. But that is her passionate loyalty to those she loved. But it *is* possible there was something of the Sitwell clannishness about the M[aritain]s. Bobbie said that Véra [Oumançoff, Raïssa's sister] was, for him the most remarkable of the three. She was evidently a great contemplative and her life was completely *hidden*. Not in the least an intellectual. B[obbie] said she was usually completely silent but every now and then came out with a remark of 'devastating common sense'. I wish someone was competent to write a complete life of the three of them – it would be one of the most fascinating stories ever written.

The other day I borrowed the key and went over the now empty 13 Ashburn Gardens. Incredible what has been done to it in 3 years. It is like a slum property. Water has dripped through upper floor ceilings which are covered with great brown stains. Here and there a wall has been daubed with magenta, the Greers' only effort to 'give it their own atmosphere'. Indescribable filth of everything . . . every room and cupboard filled with old newspapers, bottles, broken objects and miscellaneous shabby broken bits of furniture. Dust *literally* an inch thick . . . At least it has destroyed any hankering I had to live there again. When I think of the enormous trouble I took to leave it 'nice' for the Greers . . . even repainting the walls so as not to leave any ugly patches where furniture has been removed, it is ironic! It has been 'killed' by neglect and wanton destruction just as Binesfield – the Binesfield I knew – has been 'killed' by almost *too* much house-pride and smartening up.

29 July   Stella Lange [Professor of Classics, St Mary's, Indiana] over here. Have reached the slightly weary stage on Raïssa and visits etc. have held it up. Have still about 150 pages to do and still not a word from Maritain. R[aïssa] has now raised all my old scruples about the 'wrongness' of writing. She puts 'artistic creation' among the things of *this* world, the devil's world, along with 'le jeu des passions', over against the world of peace. Yet it seems to contradict her whole attitude elsewhere to art. For she was passionately *pro* painters, musicians, writers as 'spiritualizing' the world. I think I'd better take no notice.

Stella repeated something very sensible a priest had told her. In reading anything, even Gospel, only take what you feel applies to you and what you react to *calmly* – not with agitation and distress.

2 Aug   Have actually cleared my tray of all the backlog of letters, bills etc. *And* revised Raïssa up to date. All this going about with Stella had got me behind on everything. Wonderful to be clear again for the moment. By paying my bills, I have reduced myself to nothing but my £10 on deposit. But I prefer to pay them as they come in. Now, apart from O[ld] A[ge] P[ension] and Diane's rent in cash, I have nothing till I get paid for Raïssa. Have at last heard from Maritain. His revision is agonizingly slow. He asks me to send no more till Sept. He likes the translation BUT at the moment refuses *point blank* to let me use 'prayer' and 'recollection'. He would rather I left *oraison* and *recueillement* in French throughout! If you can't use the words 'prayer', 'mental prayer' and 'recollection' in a book which is entirely concerned with them, it is really rather absurd. He *admits* the words are the correct English terms but he has a violent prejudice against them – to him they are '*néfastes*' etc.etc.etc.

The other night at the Braybrookes, Neville started talking about my 'diary' – the extracts he said had appeared years ago in *The Month* ['Smoking Flax', 1950] and which he said he had never forgotten. John Guest [publisher] became very interested and implored me to lend him that copy of *The Month*. I found it – it was in a 1950 number – and, of course I knew, it was about my return to the Church (1940). I read it with extraordinary curiosity after all these years. I had believed, like Neville, that it was extracts from my notebooks. But no, it is extracts from that huge correspondence with Joseph [Peter]

Thorp.† When I had read it through, finding no account of that extraordinary business of my actual return except a brief mention of 'the hand' and finding myself against my will in the Confessional [see Introduction], I tried to find the actual notebooks of that time. I can find only 1939 and 1941. '41 refers back to my return, but I make no mention of it at all at the time: there is big gap between 1939 and 1941. It only shows how people often don't record the most important things that happen to them in their private journals.

But naturally I read, fascinated, through the scraps recorded there. Alas, I don't change much. I seem pretty horrible to myself when I read them . . . *What* a messy, muddled creature! And not improved, except perhaps on the surface presented to the world, in these more than twenty years.

What is more noticeable than any joy or gratitude is the seasickness and doubts after returning to the Church. Many of the same troubles I have now. But – at times anyway – I can 'live with them' and still, I hope and pray, have faith.

I suppose I wrote to friends at the time. 'Smoking Flax' is a pretty true picture of my state of mind. Extraordinary I should write like that to Thorp, a 'fan' and a stranger. We were always at complete cross-purposes. His difficulties were totally unlike mine and I'm quite sure he didn't know what I was talking about half the time. And being a romantic person, nearly 30 years older than myself, he fell in love with me by letter and it all became rather embarrassing.

What strikes me as odd is that I don't mention in my own brief allusion to the actual 'coming back' . . . that it meant giving up Ian [Henderson].† I talk of being in 'a period of sexual calm', of 'being willing to accept the fact of having no more sexual experience'. I presume Ian must have gone into the army. But my relationship with him *sexually* was probably the happiest I ever knew. It had gone [on] a long time, that curious affair. Though I would never have considered marrying a man 17 years younger than myself (and I didn't love him enough even to *want* to marry him) it was a very real thing in my life. I did only sleep with him once after I came back – the night he climbed through my window at Linden Gardens and I hadn't the strength to refuse. It always seemed to me that having to give up a happy sexual relationship was one of the things that convinced me it was genuine, my return. I think he may well have been away that Christmas of 1940

– possibly in India . . . But the Linden Gardens episode must have been some time in '41. The real crux came much later when he came back finally – either on leave or at the end of the war – and we had dinner together and I had to tell him what Catholicism meant to me. Because he had hoped that we could be lovers again and I hated having to hurt him. I don't think I've seen him since then. That time in Linden Gardens in '41 was the last time I ever was a man's lover. I remember asking God even at the time not to be too angry with me – it seemed so horrible to refuse someone I was so fond of and who might be going to be killed.

I *can*, with God's grace, dominate my impulses – it seems absurd to talk like this at 65. But I wasn't 65 when I came back to the Church. It isn't the deprivation of the sexual act that is so painful – it is not being able to show physical tenderness . . .

I never write what I want to in this notebook. If I know what I want to say, there is no time. Or I am too tired. Or too involved in living it. When I have a little time, I don't know what I want to say. Or there is too much for the little time.

At the back of my mind, always the book . . .

3 August, Bank Holiday Rather wonderful – a day on which no letters can come and, having for once caught up with mine, none to *write*. Writing letters has become a real burden to me, though, like Julien Green, I love to receive them! They take me so *long* to write now. I think my worst bugbears are 'Collinses'. The thought of having to write one hangs like a cloud over every weekend. I *love* staying with my friends – my 'regulars', the Sheppards, Bertrams etc. But having to write a 'thank you' letter which somehow, the more you have enjoyed it, is more difficult not to make sound insincere, is a real nervous ordeal. I sweat over it. And then of course there is X's weekly letter. I *don't* sweat over it as much as I used to. But it always seems to be due and the weeks go by so fast. One always feels he doesn't read it anyway – or rather that he doesn't take in anything you say except simple facts such as that I have a new lodger or that the boiler has burst. I don't think I've conveyed to him in 2 years the difference between working on a book of my own and on a translation – and certainly not the idea of the time and mental effort involved in either. He seems to think a novel is something you dash off in a few weeks and if you can't, you can't be any good at it. He grasps, poor boy, that writing can tire your eyes – but not that it can tire your whole self. He has no intellect at all – doesn't even know what it *is*. But a quick, sharp mind and lots of 'cleverness'. And, alas, pathetic conceit – I really think he believes there is nothing he couldn't do if he set his mind to it.

7 August   This business of *oraison* and *recueillement*.

J. Maritain categorically refuses to let me use 'mental prayer' or even 'prayer' for *oraison* and 'recollection' for *recueillement*. He attacks savagely – not me – but the English Catholic language. To Emily he writes even more fiercely about it. It is *néfaste*, it is created by priests with no knowledge of the beauties of their own language etc. To Emily, he nearly chokes with spleen . . . 'mental prayer' suggests gymnastics, the English Catholics are abominably cowardly – they are like millionaires who from meanness employ a Bantu to translate the catechism etc.

His own suggestion [keep] *oraison*.

For *recueillement*, heart-collecting (I think that was the last. OH DEAR!

If the word prayer is good enough for the saints it's good enough for Raïssa – and for Maritain. It sounds as if *oraison* were something peculiar to the Maritains.

Much as I have come to love J.M., he is very obstinate and unreasonable. Sometimes she *is* almost unintelligible . . . writes a language of her own . . . poetic (?) prose. And sometimes very bad grammar (natural in private notebooks). Most often she's compressed and elliptical.

I still find [Léon] Bloy† terribly hard to swallow. But not *one word* of criticism is allowed against him. I have no right to speak. I didn't know him. But I have read a good deal of his writing and a good deal about him and Huysmans [French, and ultimately Catholic, novelist] and his horrible behaviour to Huysmans. The Maritains thought him [Bloy] a saint . . . I'm afraid he's not my kind. All that savage abuse of people. And really saying all the time how marvellous *he* was and how unjust everyone was to him (actually his friends were extraordinarily patient and long-suffering and gave him money they could ill afford themselves). The M[aritain]s only knew him when he was old

– no doubt he was much mellowed then. I exaggerate, of course. But there really is something maniacal about him. You feel he *loathes* humanity.

All this Mélanie thing. Was *she* a saint? The Church hasn't accepted her. La Salette . . . maybe Our Lady *did* appear [to her] there . . . maybe she *was* weeping . . . we give her enough to weep about! But is that a reason to attack Lourdes? Bernadette is so utterly different.

Oh dear, I wonder how good judges of *people* the M.s were, humanly speaking. I can't help feeling a little dubious when J[acques] writes of Emily '*menant une vie de retraite et de contemplation*'. '*Retraite*' in a sense, certainly. But '*contemplation*'? Honestly, from the way Emily talks about Raïssa's journal, I sometimes wonder if *she* knows what Raïssa is talking about.

8 Sept   Actually packed up the last Raïssa this morning. It HAS been a task due to Maritain's endless notes and queries and of course ORAISON and RECUEILLEMENT. Just as I was packing the last parcel, Elizabeth Smart rang out of the blue asking if I'd interview the Archbishop of York for *The Queen* [magazine] on Thursday. I *could* just have made it but even for a much-needed £20, I couldn't face driving all the way to York the day after tomorrow and anyway I'm entirely out of practice for journalism. I need a day to myself even more than £20 (and anyway that's very poor pay for an article nowadays) so I turned it down politely. I've really been working all out the past 4 months and it was a gruelling, though 'rewarding' job translating the *Journal*. Of course troubles aren't over yet. Maritain has still to go over the last 200 pp. with his toothcomb.

I have also looked out the Thorp letters that Guest wants to see, . . . in looking them out, found this long unposted letter to Cyril Connolly so am getting Phyllis to type it as well. *Very* odd to re-read that correspondence. Odder still if it should be published. I shan't write to Nell [Thorp's wife] yet – till Guest has had a look at them. Embarrassing to ask her if she has the letters (his). In any case, I'm almost sure she hasn't. I'm pretty certain I destroyed them along with all those other papers of mine including MSS of my novels, which I destroyed in loads in the grand clear-out from Ashburn G[ardens].

Phyllis said of 'Smoking Flax' that every word of it might have been written by her. She has permanently all these doubts, feels completely arid, goes on practising 'dumbly and doggedly'. I suspected this. The only point in publishing these letters would be if they were any help to people in the same state. And I imagine there may be many Catholics who are. Odd how the whole thing came via Raïssa. Full of things I'd quite forgotten, for my life in London during the war in early '40s is the part I remember *least* about. I don't know how it wd. look with the other half of the correspondence missing. But Thorp's character comes out oddly clearly.

I am still v. troubled about Emily. This illness of hers does seem to be psychological – the doctor told Phyllis as much. Phyllis had her there a week – E. obviously gave her a hellish time. Now I get a letter from E. back on the eternal subject – abusing Phyllis – saying P. only had her there 'out of pride' etc. Really I want to *shake* Emily . . .

E. said to Phyl when she was staying there 10 days ago, 'The more you live alone, the worse you get. You organize yourself to suit yourself and no one else. Your soul is sick.' Of all the *classic* cases of projection! For this *exactly* describes Emily herself as she is now . . .

Poor Phyllis – this last year is about the only time she's been able to call her soul her own. For years she devoted herself entirely to her mother (and that *was* something, for the poor woman first lost her memory, then her reason) and Phyl was a nervous wreck at the end. Then to the Siepmanns for 2 years. And then to Emily in Callow End where E. decided it was the 'will of God' Phyllis should live though poor P. didn't *want* to in the least. And even now, she's at the beck and call of anyone who wants her. *And* Phyllis is living in desperate poverty and insecurity, mainly on national assistance.

12 Sept Curious dream . . . I found myself sitting at a long table, opposite Charlotte. The coloured man was sitting at the same table, on the same side as C. but several feet away. C. ignored him. Charlotte made the most extraordinary proposition to me. She said that she and M[adeleine] had decided to part and suggested that I should share her life instead of M. I was flattered and very tempted. Yet I had the oddest feeling that there was the faintest suggestion of Lesbianism in this proposition and that she expected me to understand this. All the while I was acutely aware of the coloured man, sitting apart, and, I knew, listening and feeling that *he* represented something much more important and that I was being disloyal to him and disappointing him if I said 'Yes.' I had this sense that the coloured man was more real, more important than she. I can't understand this dream but it had the 'imprint'.

13 Sept Godfrey Winn [popular journalist] to Kathy Kirby – pop singer: 'Are you superstitious? Have you any special mascot?' K.K. 'I used to have a rosary bead, given me by my grandmother, and wear it inside my dress. But it got lost when I was singing in Spain. I was terribly upset because we are a Catholic family.'

Fr Leonard SJ. Today at the E[nfants] de M[arie] meeting (talking of the recalcitrance against having any part of the Mass in English): 'You have witnessed an authentic miracle worked by the Holy Ghost at the Vatican Council – the Irish Hierarchy have actually withdrawn their objection to having even one word of the Mass in the vernacular'.

Behaved *shockingly* again at the E. de M. meeting in spite of *all* my good resolutions. It seems a real 'occasion of sin' to me. As usual about writing. This time with an *exceedingly* nice, very intelligent *nun* whose name I don't know and who sometimes talks to me. Was telling her about my troubles over translating Raïssa. Don't remember exactly what set me off – something about what an honour for me to be asked to do it . . . but it nettled me and I said tartly I was supposed to be fairly good at translating, having done over 30. And then she said something about the difficulties of translating and of course one would have to be a genius at writing oneself. I said something hot, silly and conceited to the effect that 'in the world' I *was* considered to be a pretty good writer – I did *not* think myself a genius – but I was fairly well thought of. Shaming to explode like that. And after *all* my good resolutions. Because she *wasn't* one of the really rather maddening ones – nuns or old girls – who ask with a patronizing smile 'Still writing?' It's true I get so much condescension and smiling patronage at these gatherings but that was *no* excuse. Anyway the nuns have never read a word I've written except *Frost in May*.

The Sacred Heart is having a Council too. They admit *they've* got to adapt themselves. This is 'aggiornamento' with a vengeance!

The really important problems will be shelved or fillibustered. It *isn't* disloyalty to the Church that makes us want her to free herself from the dead wood of bureaucracy and emerge *alive* – to face the real problems of the world which needs her so much to talk to it in language it understands. It's not a question of *tampering* with the truth but of *revealing* it more clearly. She is the Catholic church, not the *Roman* church; the Church of Christ, not of the Curia and the Cardinals.

14 Sept   Today I must start 'easing myself in' to the book. That nun yesterday – the things she said about the jam. That I am too critical of my own work. There has *got* to be some change of attitude. It's probably *humility*! Not to mind if it isn't as good as I want it to be. Especially style and all that. Not worry about clichés. Above all, for *me*, think *not at all* about 'literature', 'reputation' etc. That child Mimi [unknown fan] (16) writing 'Please go on writing, if only for my sake.' Try to *enjoy* it! Write, if you like, as if not for publication. Like this notebook, or letters.

15 Sept   I *did* actually get a page done yesterday. Ch. V is such a bundle of different versions.

Cecil King† on the wireless last night. Asked, of all the statesmen he had met, who had most impressed him: 'Kennedy. And I'm not easily impressed. Not a great man, but one who might have become great.' C.K. himself produced a more disagreeable impression on me than he ever did in life by his voice and manner – incredible pride and self-satisfaction. And *coldness*. That contemptuous self-satisfied laugh. Well, he's got the power he wanted. But I don't think he'll ever be a great man – only a *large* one with a passion for power and a very able manipulator and business man. [Hugh] Cudlipp is what Basil Nicholson† used to be to him but Cudlipp is a *real* thug. That is what he [C.K.] really admires: 'The finest journalist in the world.' C.K. . . . might have been all right if he hadn't been at Harmsworth. He isn't human any more. Only a glimpse of humanity when he said he loved the country. Margot [King] still loves him with all her heart in spite of the abominable way he's treated her. He still won't arrange to pay her alimony after two years.

12 Oct   At last I am more or less clear to have another run on the book. There have been a great many interruptions since I finished

Raïssa – going away for week-ends . . . Also having to read and criticize (to the writers) two books, one enormously long: Denyse [Sawyer]'s *Madeleine* and Christine [Arnothy]'s '*Le Saison des Americains*' – a ticklish task because I didn't think either of them very good. But of course the main worry on my mind has been Emily who is, I fear, pretty near madness. I hope the possibility of cerebral tumour can be ruled out: it *does* seem more likely that this illness is mental. She really has tried all our patience with this incessant and quite unjust railing about Phyllis and the impossibility of making her see, even for a moment, anyone's point of view but her own. And it is almost impossible not to think her increasing self-centredness and refusal to consider herself anything but a saint and a genius is partly responsible for this breakdown. What does she *do* in fact? Sits all day in her room, almost automatically pouring out poems and paintings, all, she is convinced, works of genius, reading, listening to the radio, and writing letters while food appears of its own accord at intervals and Phyllis continues to deal with all the 'practical' things she abhors – coping with money and income tax and so on.

Writing down all this – which I have written a dozen times before – is probably just an excuse for not getting down to the book, which I dread as much as ever.

Have wasted a whole morning in this stupid, repetitious stuff about E[mily]. No excuse that she's 'on my mind'.

I don't know . . . [that] she is *really* a writer: I can't help feeling she ought to have done a bit better by now considering she's been writing endlessly for over 30 years. She never seems to get anything properly shaped and finished – it's all in the raw though she throws up wonderful images and occasionally some really good lines. But to me her ear is defective and she mangles the English language. Her paintings have the charm of a child's, often, but it isn't necessarily a merit to be unable to draw – the charm fades awfully soon when you possess one and look at it constantly. But I prefer them to her writing . . . they *do* convey a kind of religious feeling . . . and [she] often achieves humour and tenderness and a touch of the medieval. Anyway it's very good for her to do them. She looks happy and earnest and absorbed when she does, a child doing something it enjoys but takes very seriously. And she listens when you make suggestions and often adopts theme. Oh dear, she is *very* lovable. She can be the best company in the world. I've probably had more laughs with Emily than with anyone I know. But you never know at what moment she's going to get offended, aggressive and even downright violent.

But she isn't petty . . . as I am. And she lives a life of voluntary poverty, for she could be quite well-off if she lived in America and hadn't given so much to Johnny [her son]. She goes without what to me have become almost necessities whereas of course they're luxuries – decent clothes, pleasant surroundings, cigarettes, hair-dressing, well-warmed rooms and so on.

I did NOT mean to sit scribbling about E. I've just wasted a day when I could have been working. No excuse that I just feel *incapable* of it. I had to go about my deaf-aid, yes. And to get that hat loosened because it's too tight. I did NOT have to dawdle about in the shop trying on jumpers. Or to have tea at Fullers. Bone idle, that's what I've been today. I've learnt *nothing* from writing all this stuff about E. except that I'm a complacent prig and probably more self-deceived than Emily.

I've already got 'notions' about the Thorp letters, that they'll be published and I'll make quite a reputation in another field. *Highly* unlikely. But of course felt quite aggrieved that Guest was away from the office when they arrived and it'll probably be weeks before he even glances at them.

The only sensible thing to do is *forget* about it. It's just one of those hope-raising pipe dreams like that American publisher wanting to re-do *Frost* and *Lost Traveller* and then crying off, or television approaching my agent about doing *Frost*, of which nothing came and I don't think I really expected it. That sweet Mimi, aged 16, writing to me about *Beyond the Glass* and saying it enthralled her and that she *loves* the Clara books and prefers them to *Frost*. Bless the child, that really *touched* me. I'd give a lot if Susan would just *once* say she thought them good. But she *did*, bless her, send me that adorable 'pep letter' some time ago to encourage me to go on writing . . .

I always keep coming back to what [Dr] Carroll said – about my unconscious drive to *disappoint* people. It is odd, because I am certainly *terrified* of disappointing people – and obviously myself too. Disappointment, for me, is still one of the hardest things to bear – I'm quite childish about it – even the most *trivial* disappointment – a parcel arriving late, a workman not turning up, an article being out of stock. I want everything when I want it *at once*.

And I still have a childish love of 'nice surprises'. I really am *infantile* still – not child*like* as the gospel says we *should* be – but plain child*ish* – a peevish, complaining child. Which I never *dared* to be in my *real* childhood. I was far more patient, sensible and *humble* then. I was genuinely agreeably surprised when anyone liked me and thought me pretty or clever. Looking back, I think I was really quite a *nice* child, content with very little . . . satisfied with what I had . . . even that old blue glass hatpin top that I thought of as the 'philosopher's stone' which could transform everything into something wonderful. And strangest of all, the crucifix that was in my Christmas stocking (and like all my Christmas stockings it contained unimagined treasures) and on which I wrote in pencil 'my nicest present' and was then filled with guilt and terrified anyone should see it in case they thought I had been blasphemous. I suppose I was 7 then and had just been received. WHAT an odd child I was – a real 'old-fashioned' kind. I hardly knew what other children were like, except from books. But I think the children of my generation were much 'older' than children of Sue's generation and that of my grandchildren. There wasn't this almost *reverent* attitude to children *as* children that developed about the 'thirties . . . We were perfectly well treated but, up to a point, ignored. So we got on with our own lives and didn't expect much attention from the grown-ups. I don't think it did us any harm – rather the reverse. We observed the grown-ups a good deal more than *they* observed us.

I see it's 8 – I must go and get my supper for Diane [new lodger from Rhodesia] wants to get into the kitchen. Good for me to have to adapt my way to hers – and she couldn't be a nicer lodger. Perhaps it hasn't been a wasted day after all. Maybe I'd better think of myself as a child industriously scribbling in the nursery – *any* trick to get going.

21 Oct Last Tuesday Sue came to tea. It was heavenly for me, she was so sweet and stayed much longer than she need have for she was going to a party. Wonderful news – Cordelia wants to become a Catholic. But I think what meant more to me was to hear Sue [talk] so naturally again *as* a Catholic – of going to Mass at the Trinità etc. She really is the biggest blessing of all of my many. When I think of those five years – and now!

She took away the Thorp letters: she wanted to read them. I've no idea what they'll seem like to her – impossible for me not to feel embarrassed . . . But it's no good my pretending: anything that gives me a feeling that maybe something I've written was worth saying, even if only in bits in a mass of unimportant, even rather silly stuff – makes me feel a little more 'alive'.

The Maritain thing *must* soon be over. I try to fight down my resentment at what I think, in many cases, *ridiculous* emendations. He's messed it up so that I seriously think of asking not to have my name put to the translation on which I worked so hard to make it read naturally. Now passage after passage sounds not only stiff and awkward but in many cases real 'translatorese'.

Emily has seen the psychiatrist and thank goodness she finds him 'intelligent and perceptive'. He has X-rayed and tested her for cerebral tumour but of course she does not know the results.

I'm every bit as insane as Emily. Having seen the Turnells' [Martin and Helen]† really exquisite new house, perfect in every detail, I *did* manage – *just* – to fight down my envy. But the whole morning I fussed away trying to think of some way of masking those ugly exposed pipes in the bathroom here and wishing it could look as impeccably neat as even the smallest and most modest of their three.

Childish, greedy, stupid, *ungrateful*. Poor Gladys confided to me that she hasn't a bathroom at all.

Later As further proof of my idiocy and childishness, I fiddled round in the bathroom, trying trays, wastepaper baskets etc. to hide the pipes. Finally I stuck a red box of tissues on them to distract attention from them, hung a clean towel to hide brushes etc. and appeased my fidgetiness not every effectively but at least cheaply.

22 Oct House of Lords party and going back with Turnells – very nice – but not in bed till 12. So I've been tired and distracted and scatty. Worse, suffering from a kind of revulsion from religion probably due to an overdose of the *Journal* and all this Maritain business. And what all this Maritain 'direction', in my opinion, has done to Emily . . . How is one to live a normal human life – because one goes on doing so willy-nilly – if most of one's activities are irrelevant and probably sinful? The awful wish that one were dead and the question settled once and for all.

However the only thing is to peg on – try again at the book even though it is absolutely *dead*. And instead of thinking of Emily, Maritain etc. remember there are other kinds of Catholics – Père Maydieu [French Dominican], Lance and Emmi, Dame Marcella. Maritain is so convinced he knows the truth about everything – no other view than his is possible. Raïssa knew what it was like to suffer from agonizing doubt.

24 Oct (St Raphael)   Yesterday, the Pope made St Benedict the patron of Europe. Thinking how good a choice this was, just now as I was drinking my morning tea, I thought I would put my book troubles under the patronage of St Benedict and adopt him as another of my saints. Since I have come to know some Downside monks and Dame Marcella, I have become more and more attached to the Benedictines. Theirs seems a wonderfully sane and solid approach.

28 Oct   The night before last I had a wonderful evening with Sue. I am still living in the afterglow of it. She came for a drink and to return the Thorp letters (which she truly liked and found interesting) and I thought she would be rushing off as usual to a party. But she asked me to come out and have some dinner. So we had four hours or more alone together and it was like the old days, only better. We were able to talk freely and naturally. It's a wonderful thing to have a grown-up daughter. But Sue is more to me even than a daughter. She is the person to whom I feel closest – to whom I can say things without having to explain. I have something in common with her that I have with no one else.

For the first time, she referred to the break. She said she had to get away, to be herself. That Thomas saw me as a rival powerful influence. What surprised me was that she said she felt 'inferior' because of having such a 'clever' mother. This seemed extraordinary to me, because *I* always felt Sue to be as intelligent as myself if not more so, as well as having many gifts I have not, including beauty.

Every now and then a look on her face suddenly reminded me vividly of Silas and I could feel again what it was like loving him.

4 Nov   It is 6.25 a.m. I am excessively tired after an almost sleepless
night (due mainly to trying Kathleen's 'pep' pills!). All past 5 days
wrestling with slow impotent agony trying to make that American
1st chapter into a story.

The last week really has been a kind of slow nightmare – trance-
like days (not exactly unhappy – just trance-like) sitting all day long at
my desk, smoking far too much, altering maybe 2 lines – changing
back – scribbling over typescript etc. In intervals I have thought –
'What *am* I up to?' Is this going on for ever – this awful burden, not
just of the story which *could*, I think be done – but the book and this
complete deadlock and feeling right away from life in a kind of no
man's land. Dislocated. Not desperate – just dull and unreal. I think
quite calmly 'Is it time I died?' Surely no one can go on for ever in this
blank meaningless automatic state – each day a replica of the last – all
day at desk, producing nothing? I feel *something* must happen – some
kind of change, explosion, even illness. A letter saying *F[rost in
M[ay]* was being remaindered increased this 'finished' feeling . . .
Later, same morning   Broke off there to go to Mass. The possible
'conviction' that came to me during this sleepless night was that I was
meant to abandon the Clara book and finish the American one
instead. (Not that *that* wd. be easy. I had the same hell with that when
I started it before. Of course I felt a bit guilty. Sister M[adeleva] was
still alive.) And the reason for not doing the Clara book (though
theme is marvellous if ONLY I cd. have handled it) was that it would
hurt Sue and Silas, and Georgie too perhaps. And though E[ric]
wouldn't mind, it meant exposing his homosexuality.

Arrived home. Adorable letter from Maritain. Suggests, instead of
both names, mine only but a *charming* note signed by him to go on
front page, which *absolutely* lets me out over the style question.

Sue's saying about the Thorp letters the only bit she'd like me [to]
take out was a reference (unnamed) to Si's shirking responsibilities. I
realize now that the Clara book wd. hurt her terribly and hurt Si. So I
may not have the *right* to write it – even if I *could* have made it very
good.

I haven't had time to think it over. But today, for first time, tired as
I am, feel a lessening of that awful burden of impotence and unreality.
It *may* be the beginning of coming to life again, knowing what I'm
meant to do and trying to do it.

No news from Guest.

Desk littered and filthy – everything in a mess – self tired, battered old and unkempt – but never mind. Things *could* get going right again. Deo Gratias. And thank Raïssa too. I think she's glad I did that job. And it was a bigger and more tiring one than I expected.

Maybe *this* is the thing for which I have had the sensation of waiting all these weeks – something *had* to happen from outside. I think I was pretty near going mad. Not sensational. A quiet decline into a compulsive, automatic, meaningless state.

5 Nov   This morning I had a note from Guest, saying he'd been too busy to read the letters yet but had had reports from 2 readers and was 'enormously looking forward to reading it himself'.

6 Nov   A *wonderful* letter from Martin Turnell for me to send to the R[oyal] L[iterary] F[und] [to which Antonia had applied for a grant], saying I was a 'perfectionist' etc. I rang up to thank him but he was in his bath and I could only speak to Helen. I've seldom been so touched. Helen kept repeating 'It's all *true*'. She said Martin was a great admirer of *all* my work. I had *no* idea of this. I knew he liked *Frost* but he's never said one word about the others. Helen kept saying 'Martin and I think you have an *exquisite* talent.'

Now my guilt about asking for a grant is relieved. I feel I have a case.

But everything seems to be coming together in a curious way to point to abandoning the Clara books and doing *The Golden Apple*.

Alice Beech [the fictional Antonia in the American book]'s past need be only what is needed for the book itself. I will be writing about what interests me *now* – not 'love' but old age and youth, parents and children, writing itself, religion, the temptation of money.

8 Nov   Was up at 5 a.m. again. It is now 6.20. Looking through 1959–60 notebook. A few notes about USA. *Why, why* didn't I make more? The usual endless money calculations . . . The old, old story – the endless impotent torture over the Clara book.

On Thursday I have to see the R[oyal] L[iterary] F[und] secretary. Embarrassing, very, and I don't think I'll get the grant.

I opened the notebook marked 'American Random Notes',

hoping to find I'd written a few rough impressions, associations etc.
It contained only the words 'soft shoulder'.

10 Nov   Spent 3 hours and 17 cigarettes yesterday staring at a blank
page and thinking where and how to begin. The temptation I must
avoid in this book is being cheaply funny. A smile, not a grin. It can't
help, I hope, being funny, but not too obviously 'comic'. A more
important temptation to avoid is being unkind to Sister M[adeleva]. I
must try and *see* her as a whole because she was, I think a very innocent
person. The point is that she has been blown up into a legend and
come to believe the legend. And she is old and tired.

13 Nov   This morning I had a wonderful surprise. John Guest rang
up to say he had had 2 excellent reports on the Thorp letters and is
now halfway through them himself. He sounded genuinely enthusiastic and says he definitely wants to publish them and that they may
well turn out to be my best book. I can still hardly believe it. Here
have I been struggling all these years to write this novel and I seem,
by sheer accident, to have written a whole book of a totally different
kind – 24 years ago!

Yesterday I had a somewhat embarrassing interview with the
secretary of the Royal Lit. Fund. He was very nice really – but, oh the
questions! I really couldn't see the relevance of some – such as the
name of my son-in-law and were my daughters in a position to help
me.

I do truly thank God for what really does seem to be almost a
miracle – Guest's enthusiasm for the letters. And now I *can* afford to
carry on for a time without doing a translation.

And I needn't feel guilty about buying those kitchen cupboards at
£7 each to store things in the passage.

3 Dec   It is amazing that Longmans *are* going to do the letters. There
is however a tremendous amount of editing, cutting and annotating
to be done. I shd. think that will take me well to end of next week. I
wd. like to have it all ready to show to Guest before I go to Sue's for
Cordelia's First Communion on 13th. 2 late nights, both involving
Kathleen Raine. Don't think I realized before what a *very* good poet
she is. She read us her last 'Greek' ones. Last night, Frank Freeman

really happy. I'd been a bit nervous, not having heard his tape-recordings, how Kathleen might react. But all went beautifully. His readings were splendid – especially of parts of Blake's prophetic books and of some lovely poems of Kathleen's. It is always a difficult business introducing old friends – I'd no idea whether Kathleen would like him or not. But Frank was at his very best. I've never liked him more – and they got on admirably . . . I'd been so nervously dreading it, too. It had taken all my courage to ask Kathleen to come, though I knew how much he wanted to meet her. I'm so glad now that I did.

The *immediate* finsit is taken care of by Longmans. I was able to turn down that *loathsome* book *La Bâtarde* [Violet Leduc].

Oh, if *only* 1965 could see the novel finished. I think it would be my last novel. I don't really *want* to write any more.

20 Dec Cordelia made her First Communion last Sunday. That was something I had never hoped to see. Sue's little daughter making her First Communion. It was all so lovely. Everyone but Thomas came to the chapel. Andrew, Mim [Thomas's mother] and A.K. [her sister, Kitty Gladstone]. Sue had arranged an enchanting breakfast table with white candles and silver tinsel, even the crackers wrapped in silver paper, like C[ordelia]'s presents. It was a lovely feast and Sue had done it all with such love and care. I had such a happy feeling of our being a family again. Thomas took it all wonderfully well. I am beginning to like him very much and to feel easier with him than I ever thought possible. Lyndall wrote Cordelia the sweetest, most touching letter. My last from her was so sad – her letters nearly always are. I love her so much and there is nothing I can do to help her.

23 Dec A telegram from Phyllis yesterday to say that Emily had an operation for brain tumour on the 21st and was 'as well as could be expected.'
Later . . . what a wonderful relief it was to find Phyllis's letter when I got home – to say the operation had been completely successful and that she could be out in 10 days, though she will have to have radiation treatment later.

Mr Mumford's prisoner, 'Tony'. His boy-friend slashed his face.

Tony bore him *no* ill-will. He said 'You can't hold such a thing against
a friend.' C. M[umford] says he is becoming almost a saint. There is
nothing for him to 'come out to'. He has spent most of his life in
prison; he *dreads* release. We both almost hope he will die before his
time is up: he is a very sick man and there is *no* happiness for him in
this world. He loves C.M. When he is tempted to one of his rages, he
clutches the rosary he asked C.M. to get him.

This certainly has been an extraordinary year for me, ending with
things I could never have imagined – the publication-to-be of the
Thorp letters and this grant of £400 from the R[oyal] L[iterary]
F[und].

THREE

1965–1966

The Hound and the Falcon, Antonia's letters to Peter (actually Joseph) Thorp, appeared in 1965. In despair about her various unfinished novels, Antonia now began an autobiography which she also never finished.

This period ended with a stay in a château in Alsace, followed by her third and final breakdown.

1965

4 Jan The whole of December was very broken: the annotating, cutting etc. of the Thorp letters . . . Extras of course, like this total stranger Anne Sanctuary who rang me up out of the blue, talked for ages, wrote enormous letters, etc. I wrote her a long one and hope I have politely dried up the flood. I suppose she's lonely. But people are extraordinary how they eat one up – a total stranger . . . really this month it's been like brushing off clouds of flies.

A woman read my hand at Fred Marnau†'s party. A very nice woman, Dolly Cooke, one of these warm, open, easy-going people (a painter) who manage their lives so simply and make their husbands so happy. I do profoundly admire women like that. She kept saying what an extraordinary head line (of course she's a generous, kindly, optimistic person) I had. 'It might be a philosopher's.' That I was very well balanced. Artistic etc. v. marked but she felt in some way I hadn't realized all my potentialities there, that this 'head' kept it down. Maybe she has something there . . . After all it's what so many people say about the writing-jam – the over-critical side inhibits me.

5 Jan Was still tired for slept till 7 and so did not go to Mass. The man arrived a day earlier to leather my desk so I was a 'displaced' person and have not yet got down to the book.

The Golden Apple must be written . . . *This* year is the important one.

T.S.Eliot died yesterday. Another of the great figures of one's youth gone.

One only has NOW.

A sweet letter from Lyndall. She sounds a *little* happier.

22 Jan   Poor Emily has now been removed to a mental hospital.

Phyllis said she was very incoherent and she certainly has delusions that she is being persecuted etc. If only they would clear up the wretched thing completely and this bout of real insanity would be completely over. The awful thing is that, horrified as I am at what is happening to her, I still can't feel as much as I would about almost any other of my close friends. Is the horrid truth that I have never been *really* fond of her – that she was a kind of phenomenon in my life . . . I have always, I think, found something a little inhuman about her – thought of her as a kind of monster – a wonderful monster in some ways – but incapable of understanding ordinary human feelings and preoccupied with herself . . . you *couldn't* be altogether honest with her. Apart from dreading her violence, she was so agonizingly vulnerable. As to her . . . one can't say nymphomania or erotomania . . . but something that seems almost to verge on it . . . that is something I don't understand. It is more like a kind of idolatry of sex – *not* Wyn's kind – a kind of obsession that seems to enter even into her religion. But then I always have hated this 'Bride of Christ' business.

7 Feb   The news of Emily continues much the same. She is quite aware of what is going on around her, but has delusions. One is that Phyllis writes her 'cruel' letters . . . She rages at Phyllis for her 'boring Englishness' – in this case P's efforts to smooth things over with the staff at the Radcliffe [Hospital].

Last night I again had this recurring dream about Cecil Court. It comes in various forms but usually there is a sense that in some way it is still mine, that it is bigger than I thought – (there's always a second bathroom) and could be made wonderfully attractive. Tom often comes into this dream. He did last night. We had decided to get married again . . . a sort of friendly, companionable marriage.

This obsession with 'homes', especially flats has been very marked since I moved. Once again I am re-painting this one. The money from those two hectically rushed *Vogue* translations last week will all go into having the bathroom pipes covered in, some tiling and getting Mr L[inturn] to repaint bathroom and dining room. Yet I keep reading, every week, advertisements of flats and dreaming idly (and I *mean* idly for it is a physical impossibility) of moving. The rest of spring-cleaning and painting have still to be done, so I don't see working routine re-established for about a fortnight. Naturally, feel guilty about this. Haven't touched the book since that *Vogue* work came − frankly as a relief! − after last terrible jam-up on *The Golden Apple*.

I've been reading this condensed English version of Julien Green's journals. All the misery and impotence *he* had − oh, HOW well I know them. Yet I think he *enjoyed* writing more than I do. I love his saying of his journals − 'telling myself all about myself'. Which is *precisely* what I do in mine! His extraordinary sudden intrusions of 'happiness' − for no apparent reason − into profoundly melancholic states. I *know* what he means by 'happiness' − it *isn't* describable. His mind and temperament fascinate me more than anyone's I know − he is the one person from whom I learn, who *confirms* things for me. Strange to read the early ones again for when I read them first I knew nothing whatever about him . . . I did not then even know that he was homosexual. Where I *do* differ from him most is that I do not have his incessant craving of the flesh, which must be such torment for him now that he has returned to his religion − so *profoundly* returned. Nor, I think, his violence. One could not possibly suspect this violence when you meet him − he is so extraordinarily quiet, calm, gentle, almost diffident. I can't bring myself to write to him − any more than he can bring himself to write letters. I have not seen him for five years. Then he was obsessed with the idea that when he became a Catholic he was not properly baptized. Fr. Victor said, yes, he was but not to tell him so: he would only develop some other anxiety.

I *ought* to write and tell him how much I loved the autobiography. He didn't send it me − the only one for years that he hasn't. I felt guilty because I hadn't liked *Le Malfaiteur* and so hadn't written to him. But I think we understand each other well enough for our friendship to persist in spite of silence. If I go to Paris again − if I ever do − I will see him, I hope. He means so much to me.

22 Feb Having to stay in bed till this attack of lumbago eases up. Seldom had such pain as when I get the real spasms.

Emily no better: due to go home today. I fear her back hair won't grow again. It is wretched for her and Phyllis says she is very depressed. The madness went off much sooner than expected . . . . Must go to bed. Writing impossible.

24 Feb Extraordinary how a little pain can alter one's life. It is not acute all the time but it affects everything I do and also makes me feel v. stupid. Not able to make any ordinary movement, even writing without difficulty. Doesn't do to think what it wd. be like if it became chronic . . . I deserve this little cross to remind me how much I have to be grateful for.

28 Feb Somewhat better today: have managed to get dressed but can only move with utmost caution. Never know when some apparently innocent movement will bring on a spasm of pain . . . I have *no inclination whatever* to write. What is the sensible thing to do? Force myself or deliberately give up? Awful guilt when I do nothing. These states of mind are of course familiar. Any physical illness always demoralizes me terribly. I feel stale, listless, poisoned all through. In these states I really feel as if I could go mad if there were no one else about the place. Simply decline into total inertia. Oh God, help me! . . . I should have tried to get on with the book instead of having this orgy – an expensive one too – of getting the flat improved and partly redecorated. I deserve to be punished! It's the old thing – this compulsive spending that I seem unable to control.

It is no good – the Old Testament is absolutely incomprehensible to me for the most part. I do not know *how* we are supposed to understand all these slaughterings and burnt sacrifices . . . I *can* see the thread running through, the people constantly turning to false gods and God constantly making a new covenant with them.

The New Testament is often of very little comfort. Christ seems so harsh sometimes – to demand the impossible of human nature. One wonders if *anyone* but great saints and ascetics can be saved?

A certain relief from *Honest to God* [John Robinson, Bishop of Woolwich] opened at random, p.57, and reading Ps. 139.

2 hrs later   And I have been reading *Honest to God* ever since – finding it *full* of light: the day has not been wasted.

1 March   On that wretched book [*The Golden Apple*]! How UTTERLY impotent I feel. Ten years now, this impotence about ALL original writing. WHY? Am I 'written out'? If I hadn't 10 years ago signed a contract for another novel, would I have even attempted to write one? Is the novel not my 'thing'? I hoped getting away from Clara might help. But it hasn't.

26 April   On Easter Sunday Thomas told me that he's seen Malcolm Muggeridge and that M.M. had sent me a message. 'Tell her she *must* write her autobiography. She could give a better idea of what the 'thirties were like than anyone else.' But I couldn't write my autobiography – too personal, too many other people involved, most of all in the 'thirties . . . There *are* things I want to record – the world of my childhood which has quite vanished. I *would* like to write about that – up to 1914, though everyone must be sick of Edwardian childhoods. Every single Sunday when I read the reviews of novels in the *S[unday] T[imes]* I feel so *completely* out of step with all that is being written and admired now. A cosy old Woman's Magazine Aunt Edna! Well, if I'm that, I'd better accept it. Some other ladies may find this book readable IF I can ever finish it.

I go through all the motions but what *do* I really believe? I find it all more and more difficult to attach a real *meaning* even to the gospels. What is *fact* about all these records? What do these ideas MEAN . . . 'being buried with Christ', 'baptized into his death', 'redemption', 'salvation' etc.? And it was all written down from memory, long after his death. St Paul's readers must have known what he was talking about. But do we?

27 April   Took whole day off work yesterday. Bought shoes, probably spent too much as usual. I *can't* cure myself of liking nice clothes . . .

Fidgeting as usual before getting down to work. Terror of failure.

On Sunday had one of those impulses to go and wander around West Kensington. 22 Perham Road even more sordid than last time. I think the shabbiest house in the whole street. All let off in floors, may be furnished rooms. Dirty curtains at windows.

I see houses in Perham Road advertised at £4000 freehold. For these days, incredibly cheap. They *could* be made good flats: can't think how the neighbourhood has come to be so run-down for all sorts of once 'mean' streets in Kensington are tarted up now and the houses sell at £10,000 or more. My father paid £600 for 22 in the 1920s. The rent was £60 a year.

Once again messing about before starting – G[ladys] wanting to show me the oven and are we to try different cleaners. Washer needed for tap. Ring up Water Board. Am much too preoccupied with the flat! Houseproud old fuss-pot.

7 May   The last days have been as bad as ever on that wretched book. I have dreaded every day. I have still only done a few pages of Chapter II. I dare not think how many months I have been vainly working on it.

Along with this, for months has gone a complete 'dry up' on religion. I continue to go to Mass every morning – try to believe – try to pray. But I feel an utter hypocrite. As soon as I try and *think* about any concept of religion it seems utterly meaningless to me.

Today Phyllis came in for an hour. She feels just as I do. 'Do I really believe all this' – and goes on 'practising'.

The only thing I feel any urge to write is this autobiography – and that only about my childhood – the sort of thing that's two a penny now.

Phyllis said 'DO IT'.

The voice of the temptress or an answer to prayer?

The last half hour she was here I felt as excited as a child waiting to get down to a promised treat.

Exhausted after she left – silly eyestrain from *listening*, though her voice is clear. The deaf-aid man says it *is* intense nervous strain listening, though I *can* hear without it.

I didn't sleep, was absolutely happy though tired. It seemed too good to be true.

Imagine it!

To do something I WANT to do . . .

And I don't think I AM a novelist. All my novels are autobiographical.

I can't 'create' characters: only describe them. I am going to do it.
TO AMUSE PHYLLIS.

22 May   Eric's birthday. His 72nd.

This has been a queer day.

Owing to this Tom situation, I got out 1949 notebook and have been reading nearly a ten-year sequence of them. The Tom thing odd. Began with a letter in March out of the blue from Dorothy [Hopkinson]† asking if I wd. send Tom a cable for his 60th birthday. I had a rather sweet letter from Tom, saying only reason he hadn't wanted any contact with me all these years was that I had been 'unjust to Dorothy'. Said he was coming to London at end of May and wd. like to see me.

I wrote him quite a long friendly letter, keeping it 'light', talking about work, his and mine, and neutral topics, said I wd. like to see him.

Letter back saying he and Dorothy had been very pleased with my 'long and interesting' letter. They were BOTH coming to London and would I dine with *both* on May 24th (next Monday). One obstacle he had to 'clear away'. The bitter injustice of my affidavit about Dorothy in Gerti's† case over the children. He had suffered very much in being deprived of A[manda] and N[icolette] (which, in fact, he wasn't). But perhaps all had been for best in long run; A[manda] and N[icolette] hadn't suffered and he and D[orothy] had been able to make 'a new life in a new world'.

This put me in a frightful quandary.

1.   I thought he was coming to London alone.

2.   As to the 'obstacle' – 'bitter injustice of affidavit' – I felt if this meeting had to be with both of them, I had to do a bit of clearing up on my side, explain why I did what I can see must, to him, have seemed monstrous.

Terribly difficult letter to write and I had to write it at once to catch him before he left Kenya. I knew of course that he would show it to D.

But I felt I *had* to say that D., in spite of her psychological gifts, had done a great deal of harm by trying to psycho-analyse us all and trying to run our lives. I also felt that G[erti] had had a very raw deal and that I felt I had to stand by her, as I was in a way responsible for the final break-up of their marriage because, believing very much then in D.'s psychol[ogical] abilities, I had introduced her to Tom. I *did* not feel it was right for the children to be allowed to spend long periods with D. and T. (no question of *Tom* not seeing them) and the idea was driving poor Gerti nearly frantic, and though I knew it meant a permanent break for me with Tom (which I did *not* want) I felt I *had* in honour to stand by G. I also mentioned as a further reason for my own loss of confidence in D. the ferocious letter she wrote me when I broke off 'analytical' relations with her, but said I wd. like v. much for us to go on seeing each other as human beings, not as 'analyst' and 'patient', or 'master' and 'disciple'.

I received this from Tom yesterday.

My dear Tony,

Thank you for your letter. This makes it clear that it is not good for us to meet since our points of view are opposite on the subject – Dorothy – on which it is essential we should at least have some common ground.

Dorothy's 'weakness' has been, not a drive for power but a drive for service – a passion for helping other people. Being myself a worldly character, I know how intense an enmity this provokes. I wrote to you as I did with the idea that fifteen years might have made some difference to your own attitude – as it has done to mine on almost every subject.

I won't go into a detailed discussion on matters long over and done with, but on one point I must speak my mind. I will believe that Dorothy wrote 'asking you (or anyone else) how you dared to consider yourself her equal and threatening you with dire curses from Baba' [Meher Baba, Indian holy man] when I see the letter. Not before.

Though there is now nothing to be gained from meeting, I do assure you that neither Dorothy nor I wish you anything but well, particularly in your writing.

Tom

So that is that. In a way it is a relief; it would have been pretty artificial, seeing them both. Yet I would like to see Tom, naturally much better on his own.

The one thing I really resent is his refusal to believe that D. wrote me that letter about Baba etc. I am almost sure I destroyed it, with the other documents backing up my affidavit when Lousada [lawyer] returned them to me . . .

* * *

Antonia commenced her autobiography at the suggestion of Malcolm Muggeridge, who thought it would help her to conquer her writing block. (She had by now given up *Clara IV*.) She worked on it for the last fifteen years of her life, but only achieved fourteen short chapters, which describe her family background and herself up to the 'eventful age of four' or a little beyond.

The account she gives of her ancestors, particularly those on her father's side, the Bottings, Jefferys and Bonifaces of Sussex, is as confusing as she suggests. Daisy and Lena Boniface were the unmarried daughters of one of the farming Bonifaces, who worked all their lives as postmistresses and in retirement were a pair of white-haired old ladies of great charm, when Susan knew them.

Arnold was Antonia's first cousin on her mother's side. Her mother's brother Howard was his father. His parents lived comfortably in St John's Wood when he was a boy and, as he was only three months older than Antonia, she was occasionally taken to play with him. He had a younger sister, Helen. Winnie Patterson was another White cousin, living in North London.

* * *

I have begun the childhood book. I am having a *great deal* of the old trouble: constantly sticking and re-writing. But I *have* produced 9 pages and am resisting temptation to re-read, constantly revise and alter. My own life – and of course, myself – do fascinate me. After all, they're the only thing I *really* know anything about at first hand. And that vanishing world, almost vanished, of life in the early part of this century fascinates me, however many other people have written of it. I love to read their memories of it too. My talent is very small, very limited – maybe this is all I can now do with it.

Odd how often, all those years ago, I say how the only thing I really *enjoy doing* is planning, decorating and furnishing rooms.

27 June   The old troubles *are* cropping up with the autobiography. Revising and going off on wrong tracks. Hours over a sentence or even an adjective. But this is partly because I am in the introductory part still which is hard to handle: my parents' previous history. Amazing how little one knows about that: have had to do quite a bit of 'research' and consult Arnold, Winnie Patterson and Daisy Boniface to get any information about Jefferys, Whites, Bottings and how the families fit together. It is difficult at this stage not to turn my parents into *fictional characters*, or to *invent* things about my grandparents in Storrington: autobiography I see now is as difficult in its way as a novel.

Social things wreck me for the day – even if I enjoy them, like Mary Siepmann coming to lunch. She has written an extraordinary book – the first part *marvellous* – the rest not up to it but with wonderful bits in it. Tremendous imagination, wonderful visual sense – marvellous on country and animals, every detail right. But it goes quite wild – you can't begin to criticize a person like that with an amazing natural gift and no logic. She just goes on inventing and inventing and changing her ideas all the time so it's full of inconsistencies, contradictions . . . I hope she does this children's book . . . She LOVES writing, bless her!! Hope some publisher realizes she has talent. Maybe a good 'editor' could get her to put *The Heirs* right.

Much depressed at a cocktail party at June [Braybrooke]'s daughter's. How hideous we all look now we are old. Stevie Smith . . . grotesque. [William] Gerhardie [the novelist] was there, leering at a little fashion model. I find him repulsive . . . always did. But Olivia Manning looked – and *was* nice . . . Schwarz [who bought Antonia's handwritten *Frost in May*] obviously *is* a crook. I should have guessed. She [Olivia Manning] sold a MS of hers to him for £25 and he got £1500 for it. She says Buffalo and Texas pay fantastic prices for MSS.

The worst of old age is the tiredness. And the terrible *slowness* with which one does everything. Time goes at appalling speed and one has nothing to show for it. I didn't realize how much one's mind slowed down as well as one's body.

8 July   Martha Johnston [unknown] of Catholicism: 'Endlessly fascinating and endlessly exhausting.'

She and Emily came the other day. Everything was fine – E. loved Martha. Emily (in spite of this terrible depression) very gay and like her old self. Until at the end of the evening she brought up the eternal Phyllis grievance. And then one was back against the old barrier. And of course the rage that Phyllis had said that E.'s religion to *her* seemed false. What CAN one say? . . . She talked obsessively of it, with *that* look on her face.

20 July The party last Thursday went very well. Sue and others wrote sweet notes to say how much they'd enjoyed it. So it was worth all the trouble and absurd nervous fret. Today no excuse except tiredness for not getting back to work on the book. Have done a little 'research' on the Storrington part.

The flat *is* a little too small, yes. Wd. be ample if I had the use of Diane's room. But I can't *manage* without a lodger. And in many ways it's nice having someone around, especially anyone as nice as D. I *am* beginning to find the stairs a little tiring.

If, in some years' time, God wishes me to have a flat with more room and less stairs, He will provide one. *Now* my job is to do some work in this one.

24 July I have sprained my ankle. So painful I had to take a taxi back from shops. Could hardly move about the flat. Witch hazel compresses and bandage have relieved it a good deal.

The book has jammed for days. Maybe today hasn't been as utterly wasted as it felt. Was being too conscientious about Storrington, my grandparents etc. I was v. lucky to have Diane here. Couldn't have gone downstairs again. And I needed witch hazel. It has really made a difference.

I enjoyed Audrey Beecham's dinner party v. much. Particularly meeting a man called Hart – professor of jurisprudence at Oxford. He talked about America and philosophy. A man I'd like to *know*. Impossible.

Kathleen Raine was there: looking very beautiful. She has a new book of poems coming out soon. She talked with great passion of David Gascoyne's collected poems, soon to appear. She thinks him one of the few real poets of the century . . . the holy innocent. His parents are looking after him. Friends are trying to get him a grant.

Extraordinary to realize that he must be about 50. I think of him as I knew him first in the mid-'thirties. I have not seen him for many years. He was very much in my life – always will be. But I could not cope with his persecution mania, his complete disruption of any normal life. It is all right for *him* to live on other people – he *cannot* cope with ordinary life on his own. But for people who have to make a living, need sleep and an orderly life it is impossible to have him 'settled in' on one. But he *does* produce good poetry. I didn't think his early surrealist poems good: I thought them artificial and manufactured. But the much later ones I loved . . .

Kathleen retains her sanity, in spite of all she has suffered. I am *very* fond of her now and admire her greatly.

She agrees with me about Emily's poetry. What is one to do? I never admired [George] Barker's work as much as Emily does. I don't like what he has become by all accounts. But there was always something false in him. The beauty was, he knew it. And probably still does.

30 August   On Friday I went down to spend the day with Daisy and Lena [Boniface]. It was a *most* pleasant day: I really enjoyed it. Was surprised to find they live in quite a large house – but they share it with Peggy (Lena's daughter) her husband and the 4 children.

Children   Andrew 21 (exceptionally nice, intelligent, undergraduate at St Andrews)

Sarah 13 – riding, brass-rubbing

Timothy 9 – *trains*

Deborah 5 – lively – demanding

L[ena] and D[aisy] delightful, just as they were. Lena sweet and serious. *Loving* people. *Good* people. Immensely more sophisticated than I had imagined they would be.

We talked so much about the old days: it was a bit of a nuisance having Deborah demanding attention all the time because we three old ones wanted to reminisce and piece things together. Their farm [at West Grinstead] was called Griffins.

D. could remember me at 5 in the walnut tree with Mr Dash! And Aunt A[gnes] when I was 5, putting my knees together when I was sitting with them apart.

I have just finished Naomi Burton's book. At first I was put off by the breeziness and facetiousness. But that is just my pride and fastidiousness. She is genuinely 'fighting the good fight' and it's full of spiritual advice for *me* personally. It's as silly to be put off by *her* language as by St Thérèse of Lisieux's. Here's someone trying to do God's will first in the middle of ordinary life – and successful career-woman.

Neville Braybrooke rang me up on Sunday to say he'd been reading *The H[ound] and the F[alcon]* all day and liked it so much that he wanted to tell me so. Naturally I was terribly pleased. Said he wished I'd publish some of my journals. But that really *wouldn't* be possible.

Must get out the writing-block. No good saying 'Start off again tomorrow, Sept 1st.' Lunch with Allene Talmey and getting hair done in the morning will kill Sept 1st as a writing day. So go to it! (And no listening to the Test Match till after lunch.)

1 Sept Re-reading notebooks: at least feel God must be *amused* by me. I'm so ridiculous. But it's awfully like watching a cockchafer spinning on a pin. Not that I ever have. But it's in Hans Andersen.

I feel as if I'd made NO progress in all these 25 years since my return [to the Church] . . .

24 Sept A little ill. But it may be a good thing. This extreme tiredness has gone on for months. Then suddenly, during a heavy cold about 10 days ago, swellings all round eyes. My usual N[ational] H[ealth] doctor was not there. Returned later, saw his partner. Some eye infection. In a week, no better, went back. To my amazement he asked how I was generally. You don't expect NH doctors to do that and he doesn't know me at all. It came out I'd been in Bedlam, my crack-up in the '30s etc – à propos of the eyes, bc. I said I couldn't work with bad eyes and writing was my job. Of course he'd never heard of me. It's always so embarrassing when they ask 'What do you write?' and you say 'novels'. I always expect them to think I'm a Ruby M. Ayres. Anyway he was terribly nice – wouldn't let me go for about $\frac{1}{2}$ hour – I was terrified I was wasting his time – tiresome old woman etc. We keep having it pounded into us on radio how we waste their precious time when there's nothing the matter with us – especially 'old ladies'. He took opposite line – staggering. This was serious, more serious than I realized. Rather think he wants me to see a psychiatrist. Unnerving to me. I thought I was – rather prided myself on being – sane now . . . The mere fact of someone asking me – listening – showing interest – was such an amazing relief – I was so grateful – I thanked him and even cried a little with gratitude.

The load on my conscience is terrible – that grant – no work to show for it.

Have been dreading Cornwall invitation – though I loved it last year and love being with Charlotte. I couldn't FACE it – the packing, the journey etc. Now if it comes, I have good excuse. I can go later to Phyllis for some days. There I CAN completely relax.

Galway [the doctor] made me go and see Miss Kane. She examined me v. thoroughly. Still suspects diabetes. Anyway cataract is no worse.

Gladys has been saying for weeks how ill I looked and unlike myself.

Well, my life IS a bit unnatural! Cooped up too much. And all these years fruitlessly trying to write between translations.

26 Sept, 12.30 at night   A curious experience today. Walked down to Cecil Court. Looked in at open door of 18. Still let off in rooms. Shabby. Depressing. Came home, tired, lay down. Then got up; on impulse re-read 2 whole vols of journals. 1937. Basil Nicholson . . . Am writing this having been to bed, slept an hour, got up again.

Extraordinary to read those 2 vols. Not only the B.N. part, but some of the things [Dr] Carroll said, for I was still having analysis. I had forgotten that I saw Basil much more than I remember. I knew it was an important thing for me; I had forgotten that it went on longer and that there was more *to* it, on his side, than I thought. It comes out as very real, in spite of the frustration. How could one have foreseen how Basil would end up? He seemed to have all the success he wanted ready to pick up. He did, I think, marry Ruth. It was a failure. I heard no more of him for years. Only God knows the whole truth about Basil.

27 Sept   I certainly have had a very peculiar life, looking back on it. What I *have* had is experience. But on the face of it, what a mess, what a failure.

How I *wish* Lyndall could be happier in her life. She is the tragic one.

30 Sept   Dr Galway said yesterday: 'You are rather up against it.' He is trying me with anti-depressants and tranquillizers and I'm to go back in a week.

Amusing result of taking *1* anti-dep. Took it about 6. by 7.30 was so sleepy had to go to bed. Fast asleep by 8.30, did not wake till nearly 7 and still feel drugged and drowsy! He says they make me 'excitable' . . . no sign yet! Anyhow it's a relief not to have to go to a psychiatrist.

3 Oct   Just the same. Feel very peaceful; not at all 'excited'. But the peacefulness is very pleasant. How odd that a drug should give one peace of mind.

15 Oct   Gladys today. 'I don't want to be nasty but you *are* getting on.'

20 Oct 5 a.m.   Yesterday Galway kept me for about ¾ hour. On the little I told him he came extraordinarily close to Carroll's findings. Difficult to put into words. That there is this tremendously powerful wicked father inside me, also that I have unconsciously destroyed my father and feel guilty about that. That I can only write if I think it is not going to be published, that I have a fantasy of omnipotence but also if I use this power it will destroy *me*.

I said to G[alway] 'I would like to marry my father and mother inside me and produce a legitimate child.' He said it was quite a good way of putting it.

He obviously isn't content to leave me just on drugs. Still has idea of psycho-therapy.

26 Oct   I have actually written in all 64 pp. – i.e. 16,000 words, further than I have got with any of the novel attempts.

I was *so* touched by Charlotte's saying on Saturday night that if I needed money, I was to come to her.

27 Oct   Saw Galway yesterday. His plan for moment is to see me once a week at his surgery for not less than 15 minutes . . .

On an impulse I took him my Carroll analysis notes and *Beyond the Glass*. Was pleased that he said he wd. read them.

Think my motive was to show him myself at best and worst . . .

He says there is a whole area of myself that has got split off and which I think of as bad, destructive terrifying etc . . . he thinks the trouble goes very far back indeed, to pre-conscious stage, actually babyhood. I had told him the first time of my tremendous reaction to Carroll's jingling the bunch of keys whereas, though I have no conscious memory of that, I must have been a baby at the time.

Next time I think I will tell him of my first conscious memory – in my cot. I could, in the book, only convey the cot, not my confused terrified feeling that the stitching on the blanket was my own toes and that they were bleeding. I could also tell him the pram one. And what I certainly *don't* remember, that as a small baby I slept in my parents' bedroom.

I think I can honestly say that my father was *not* generous to me with actual money. On the other hand he would *pay* for things for me: school fees and things I needed at school.

I think I can also say that he wanted me to be *impossibly* good, in behaviour, in work, in everything.

31 Oct   Writing to Dame Marcella today, I seemed to see *why* this has all blown up just now.

For the past 10 years I've always had translations to distract me from the impotence.

This year the first with no translation. *And* I get that grant from the R[oyal] L[iterary] F[und]. So no excuse for not doing own work.

2 Nov   Went up yesterday to sign copies of *The H[ound] and the F[alcon]*. Memory lapses. Could not remember Peter Carson [publisher]'s surname. Odder, much, that I had quite forgotten that I had already given him the addresses. Took my address book with me and was amazed to find that I had already written them out for him in full when I was last up there.

Can't pretend I'm not excited to have a book out again after so long. Came home and did typing exercise (after a rest) and then read quite a lot of *H. and F.* Couldn't help thinking it was rather good.

Very short session with G[alway]. He again stresses not to idealize him. He is NOT analysing me, so I must – or rather *we* must – keep it 'down to earth'.

6 Nov On Nov 4th, Raïssa's anniversary, I had a wonderful letter from Fr. Gregory Murray, a Benedictine, about *The H. and the F.*

Eric and Georgie both like it very much.

This morning, a charming note from Graham Greene saying he was going to read it.

Last night, a dream . . . Dorothy Kingsmill came into it, also Tom . . . Dorothy looking very pretty, as she used to look in '47. She had pushed in on my analysis, offering her services free . . . Many elements can be traced to recent events. I had met Edmée [Kingsmill, Dorothy's daughter] yesterday in the street and was struck by her resemblance to her mother. She is now not very much younger than Dorothy was in '47. About 35 to D[orothy]'s 43.

9 Nov
Home Sickness (by Cordelia, aged 10) [Cordelia was with the family in Illinois, where Thomas was teaching.]

> Will I ever go back again
> To my lovely garden and den
> To see the house and dell and pond
> My poney [sic] in the field beyond
> The things of which I am so fond
> Will I ever go back again?
>
> The apple tree close by the run
> The dog resting with day's work done
> The doves cooing in the evening sun
> Will I ever go back again?

In C[ordelia]'s letter: 'It is not accurate but when you are home-sick you are not at all accurate.'

10 Nov He [Galway] was *very* nice and friendly yesterday: we actually both laughed. He was amused when I asked for a prescription for more pills, though I think I've more than enough to last out the week. I said 'Suppose you weren't here next week?' He said

'Don't worry, I shall be here' and wouldn't give me the prescription.

This morning v. nice letter from Bobbie Speaight about the book. It's all very dreamlike.

21 Nov A wonderful notice of *H. and F* in *Cath. Herald* by Fr. Caraman. First review I've had. The book came out last Monday. Martin Turnell's should be in today's *Sunday Telegraph* and Bobbie's and Neville's in the next *Tablet* and *Spectator*. Father [Philip] Caraman [SJ] says I write best when I write spontaneously, as in *H. and F*. He also says I was unlucky to write my best book first (the old *F[rost] in M[ay]* story!!), otherwise talks of 'accomplished novels', 'brilliant' short stories, 'exemplary' translations. I wonder if people *are* right that *Frost in May* was my best novel? Naturally one likes to think that one improved in 20 years or so! But perhaps it was because of all the feeling behind it. And the same may apply to the 'Peter' letters. Again with short stories, there is usually a strong impulse behind *them*.

25 Nov In the evening, Kathleen's party for David Gascoyne . . . People were so kind about *The H. and the F*. Senta Marnau snatched it from Fred [Marnau] and says she can't stop reading it. Kathleen herself, though she's so harassed 'doing nothing but cook' with dear David [Gascoyne] staying there, said she'd read it far into the night. Strangest of all, Sonia Orwell whom I haven't seen for years, said that Cyril Connolly had drawn her attention to it. Then I had a wonderful letter from June Braybrooke, actually saying 'I think that without any doubt at all, the publication of *The H. and the F*. is one of the high-water marks in writing of our time.' Marjorie Villiers [agent?] . . . has recommended it for Fontana books. It's impossible not to be pleased and excited, yet I feel 'Did I really write those letters? Is it *me* they're excited about?' They talk of the 'power' in them – I think *everyone* has said how 'well written' they are. This is stranger still, since I dashed off those letters at top speed, often when I was very tired.

27 Nov Having had no dreams for nearly a fortnight, last night I had a real 'crackerjack'. It's going to be difficult to recapture it all. It began with my going to stay with Aunt Edith and my cousin Helen [Edith's daughter]. There was a dinner party at the house to which I had invited Noel Coward whom Helen was very anxious to meet.

During the meal Aunt Edith made herself so unpleasant to me and Aunt Georgie [Edith's sister] even more so, emptying salt all over my food and so on, that I lost my temper and walked out of the house, taking Noel Coward with me. The next thing I remember it was daylight and I was driving round the park in an open taxi. I was slumped on the floor of it and was conscious that I must be looking terribly dissipated and dishevelled. I caught a glimpse of myself in a mirror. I did not look quite as bad as I imagined but I definitely looked as if I had had a terrific night out, and had a very rakish air, still wearing cocktail-party clothes on a bright summer morning, slumped on the floor of a taxi with my hat cocked over one eye. At that moment, also driving in an open taxi, appeared Crawford and Margaret Havinden [directors of the advertising agency where Antonia once worked]. All at once I realized that I had done for myself as regards my job at Crawford's. I had been having a nervous breakdown and they had held my job open for me till I recovered. The sight of the 'invalid' in a taxi, obviously well enough to go out for a night's dissipation and looking extremely disreputable, could hardly have made a worse impression on my employers.

Finally I was in a kind of waiting-room with a group of friendly people, some strangers, some people I knew, including my cousin Arnold, Helen's elder brother. I broke off a conversation I was having and said I was going to the lavatory. It was a little embarrassing as the WC was right off the room and everyone would be able to hear what I was doing. It was still more embarrassing when I got inside to discover that the door had vanished and everyone could *see* me. My cousin Arnold, looking just as he does now, the perfect picture of a retired headmaster, gave me a very sweet smile and put not one, but both arms round me and gave me, not the usual cousinly peck but a real kiss. He himself is the perfect example of someone who never put a foot wrong, fulfilled all his ambitions and lived in a perpetual sunshine of approval. Helen, the much wilder, more rebellious one, did many things of which he did not approve. She and I have more in common than Arnold and I have. She is passionately devoted to Arnold, jealous of his wife, half envies me, and still has a certain resentment left over from childhood when, being almost the same age as Arnold, he found me more companionable than a 'baby sister'.

Though I have, it seems to me, hardly paused at all while writing this, it has taken at least $2\frac{1}{2}$ hours, nearer 3.

1 Dec There was also another dream in which W.H.Auden appeared. Cannot remember much about it except that there was a small baby in it. It had wetted and fouled its napkin very thoroughly and I could not help being disgusted, though I knew the poor thing could not help it. I said to Auden how much more tolerant I would have been had the baby been a kitten!

On Tuesday (yesterday) rather disagreeably taken aback that G[alway] did not seem as pleased as I was about the long dream of the 26th. He had unusually large number of patients waiting and was late for surgery. I went in with my notebook thinking it wd. save time to read out the dream. He said he cd. only give me five minutes and when he saw how many pp. it was, asked if I could just give him the gist.

He thought the main theme of it was resentment – that he can give me so little time each week. The disappearance of the lavatory door he thought symbolized my desire to break down the barrier between us imposed by the conditions of treatment. He said the immense length of the dream showed that I wanted to make big demands on his time.

I couldn't help feeling cast down and actually felt tears come into my eyes. I said it was rather hard to be so slapped down when I thought the dream showed I'd made progress. He said it was hard and he knew it was painful, but that if he'd let me go on feeling slap-happy about it, I'd have got into an excited manic state. He keeps stressing that I 'have a real problem' and that this illness or whatever is 'serious'.

9 Dec If it were possible, financially and every other way, I would go next year to Rome [where Lyndall lived], Ottrott and USA. I probably will go to Ottrott [the home of the Demenge family in Alsace]. I don't see how the others could possibly be managed unless the book brings in quite a lot of money.

The last time I saw G. I had no dreams to report . . .

When I went, I left my umbrella on the chair. Remembering it just before I got to the door, I said, 'The good old unconscious – leaving something behind shows one wants to come back.' He said I was afraid to take it and actually handed it to me. He was too polite to say what we obviously both noticed then. An umbrella is a good old penis symbol – and my umbrella is red, the colour of danger! If he gave it me back, I *hope* the unconscious grasps that this penis-symbol (writing power) is quite OK for me to have . . .

Carson rang up yesterday. They're quite pleased with how it [*The Hound and the Falcon*] is going. Nothing sensational – 1000 sold so far – and of course he's sorry there's been this hold-up on the reviews by Speaight, Braybrooke and Turnell. But he thinks it will go on selling reasonably steadily.

15 Dec   Take Simone Weil – I am prejudiced against *her* – more unreasonably than against Bloy, since I had read quite a lot of Bloy and nothing at all of Simone Weil, only things written *about* her. Yet Eric Siepmann sent me this wonderful thing from her: 'For it seems to me certain, and I still think so today, that one can never wrestle enough with God if one does so out of pure regard for truth. Christ likes us to prefer the truth, because before being Christ he is truth. If one turns away from him to go towards the truth one will not go far before falling into his arms.'

G. said that I was suspicious, though all was going well and I was looking so much better. Gladys says how much better I look, and *she's* a realist! And it's true – it seems too good to be true to feel so much better!

But to feel calm and well, to have coped with a flood of letters (and 100 Christmas cards) without over-strain, above all to *want* to get down to writing again – it's all so wonderfully, miraculously *new* to me. I feel like Peter Arno's new man coming out of the night club, sniffing round and asking what the peculiar smell was. 'Fresh air?' *That* is how this all feels.

30 Dec   Rosemary Davy [Roehampton 'old child'] told me the other day of an 'Old Child' of Roehampton whose address is The Rosary, Balham. She swears to it.

After the 'nothing to declare' session with G. I had one bad turn the following Saturday. Nausea, vomiting and inertia. And, of course, inability to work. I told him I felt quite calm and sensible, not

elated or depressed. He asked how things were going. I told him that
the book had been taken by Fontana.

I have been reading through this notebook for 1965. It certainly
has been a year for me. Most important, of course, the blowing up of
this psychological situation, the danger I was in without knowing it,
Galway's finding that I was on the verge of a third mental breakdown
most astonishing of all, beginning to write again. For I have done
quite a lot of all the childhood book [autobiography] since he began
his treatment.

In this year 1966 I really must make a serious effort to restrain
impulsive spending of money. I should really say to myself 'Shut
your eyes to the flat, beyond keeping it clean and tidy.'

1966

2 *Jan*   The other day Irene Handl rang up to thank me for my letter
about *The Sioux*. The book made a great impression on me which I
don't expect all my friends to share and, on an impulse, I wrote to her.
We talked for over half an hour. She calls it 'autobiographical'
because it sprang from a single unique experience in her own life. It is
one of the most remarkable and haunting books that I had read for a
long time – entirely original. Not everyone's cup of tea but very
much mine.

The Pope has made the Sacred Heart abolish lay-sisters. I had a
fascinating conversation with an old nun with gnarled hands and a
strong accent, now forced much against her will to be a choir-nun
and 'Mother Warren' instead of 'Sister Warren'. She worked as a
servant girl before she entered, for a few shillings a week, had only 2
years 'schooling' which ended when she was 11. Now she finds it a
penitential life: she was perfectly happy as a lay-sister. Recreation is
worst of all: she cannot enter into the conversation about education,
the children etc. When they were lay-sisters they had their own
recreation with their own nun in charge of them and 'could let their
hair down'. Now she has to sing office, knowing not a word of Latin.
I loved her and could have talked to her for hours.

I have at last caught up with all Christmas and 'book' letters. I can finish the Hans Andersen life which I have much enjoyed – Monica Stirling's *The Wild Swan*. Have just re-read, with more pleasure than when I first read it years ago, that masterpiece *The Daisy Chain* [C.M. Yonge]. I wish I could write a novel as good as *that*!

Must try and do the Binesfield chapter [of the autobiography] this coming week. To read some Hans Andersen stories – especially 'A Story from the Sand Dunes' and 'The Marsh King's Daughter'. It is wonderful to be able to *read* again.

3 Jan   The fact that I dreamt again last night shows that there is still some anxiety. My guess is that G. will interpret it as anxiety about the efficiency of his treatment – the rather 'cheap' hospital with few normal amenities.

8 Jan   What I find hard to swallow in psycho-analytical theory is the idea that the baby has violent destructive phantasies about its parents? How, since it has no verbal thoughts? And why? But it seems an established axiom, at any rate in the Freudian school.

I must finish Fred [Marnau]'s *The Guest*. I find it rather heavy going. I am not quite in the right mood for it though it is a strange and beautiful book – a poet's book.

11 Jan   This morning a welcome letter from Sue [in the USA] and some press-cuttings from Longmans. Two provincial papers and the *Universe* which I had not seen. All quite good. Interesting how nearly every review contains some inaccuracy. I suppose critics are always in such a hurry these days.

12 Jan   I think this violent cold *was* psychological. It came on suddenly the day after I had that dream, was much better yesterday and has almost gone since my session with G. I also feel much more 'normal' and 'firm in tone' this morning.

14 Jan   Dreamt twice of 'another flat' . . . Tom was in the dream. I returned to the flat and found Diane packing her bags. She said; 'You're losing your little lodger.' I had not expected her to leave without even discussing the situation. I was overwhelmed but too proud to ask her for the money she owed me. I said 'Why? Because you think I'm a disgusting person?'

'Yes'

'Have I ever been unkind to you?'

She said that I never had, but now that she knew I was such a bad person, she could not stay another hour under my roof. Oddly enough what seemed to shock her most was that I should talk in person to a man who was my ex-husband. She said:

'You could have afforded to telephone if you really had to speak to him.'

She went down the stairs carrying her suitcases, leaving me in utter despair.

15 Jan   In the other dream, Ronald Moody† was painting my portrait. He said that the picture was nearly finished, that I was a very good sitter and that the portrait was very good but he wd. not let me see it. Wanting to go the lavatory, I could not find one, as I expected, in the studio and supposed it must be out in the courtyard. But the yard was full of mud and builder's planks and material. There were some dirty, broken-down sheds which might once have been lavatories but were now full of rubbish and useless for my purpose. So once again I was frustrated.

25 Jan   I was not altogether surprised when Galway told me tonight that he thought I needed more prolonged treatment than he could give. He is trying to arrange something for me with the Cassel hospital in Richmond. This last week has not been good. Back to all the old trouble on the book.

9 Feb   A bad period still. Galway has got as far as writing the letter to the Cassel. He says however that it is better that I should be depressed than euphoric.

Poor darling Curdy is doomed. I may have to make the decision to have him killed. The vet says he is not in pain. But suppose the pain started at a time when I couldn't get the vet quickly? I will see how things are next Tuesday. I can't bear to write about it. I've been dreading it for a long time but hoped he might have a few more years.

Yesterday poor Mrs Coutts [the widow in the downstairs flat] was removed in an ambulance to hospital. I had rung her up the night before – she didn't sound too bad and had a friend with her. Mrs Crowe found her on the stairs in her nightdress. The poor thing's mind is so affected that it is almost impossible to communicate with her. Mrs Crowe found her flat in a terrible state, rotting food in the kitchen etc. I will go and see her in hospital and at least try and get the address of her relatives. I am terribly sorry for her but what can one do?

G. says, of course, and probably rightly, that all this reflects for me my own mental trouble – the old cat under sentence of death, the old woman mouldering away in her flat as I feel myself mouldering away inside.

Oh this *maddening* unconscious. What *is* it up to? One can't reason with it.

I had a very pleasant evening on Saturday with Denys Blakelock† – all result of a 'fan letter' from him about *The H. and the F.* (they continue to come in almost daily). As neurotic as I am in a different way . . . and a most devout Catholic.

11 Feb 'I have often thought how the dependence of old age, because of waning powers, comes full circle with the helplessness of infancy while the powers are waxing. The state of Not-Being-Able-To can be as irking to one as to the other. The difference is that the child is straining to become independent while the old one is straining not to lose independence . . . to know how to grow dependent without being a nuisance is one of the last bits of wisdom life asks of us.' E[leanor] F[arjeon].

16 Feb On Saturday Feb 12th Curdy had to be 'put to sleep'. The vet could not have been kinder. God gave me strength. He went blessedly peacefully, though it took nearly an hour, purring all the time as if to reassure me that he knew I was doing the kindest thing for him. Minka [the Siamese cat] is a little better today, but still not eating properly.

For the past fortnight, even before I knew Curdy was doomed, the depression has been very bad. I manage somehow to write letters but that is all. Denys Blakelock has been incredibly kind. So have other friends. So much sweet sympathy over Curdy's death. But under all is the real old grey accidie. Galway says it is connected with his passing me on as a possible patient to the Cassel. Every day is a burden to be got through. He says that I see myself as the old, incurable cat. But not even to be put away by merciful euthanasia – to be subjected to cruel torture.

I began to fret over past sins – had I really repented of them. Abbé [de] Tourville [author of *Letters of Direction*] consoled me. Also Julian of Norwich.

24 Feb From Mary Siepmann:

'I always remember Eric thumping the table during our instruction in Farm St and saying he would not join the Church if he [could] not have his dog with him [in heaven]. Father Mangan never batted an eyelid but said robustly 'You shall have him if you need him.'

I saw [Dr] Ployé at the Cassel on Tuesday. He kept me an hour and I am to go back in a fortnight. I disliked him at sight but when he had talked thought him v. intelligent and had confidence in him. My mouth dry with fear most of the time. Do not know if he will take me or not. Living in a kind of limbo. Manage to write letters, that is all. Denys Blakelock gives me a human lifeline to hold on to. P[loyé] decided to explore the mother side rather than the father. He thought analysis had probably coped with that. My revulsion at being inside my mother when Robin told me 'the facts of life'. He thinks trouble may have started pre-natally.

I keep producing still-born works as my mother produced still-born children.

25 Feb 'We are *sold* to God: we are caught in His net and we know that net cannot be broken' (Jeanne Bloy). Sent me by an unknown correspondent re *The H. and the F.*

26 Feb Still weary and paralysed, my eyes feel distorted as if they were askew in my head.

3 March Nothing for it but to lie down most of the afternoon. What a ridiculous existence!

4 March   Once again – 3 days running – I overslept and was too late to go to Mass. I seem to want to do nothing but sleep. I must try and 'creep up on' the book again.

10 March   Yesterday I saw Ployé again. He will take me on.

13 March   Spent the whole of yesterday, up to 11.30 pm trying to flog out a few words. Mark Bence-Jones wanted me to write for *Nothing in the City* to help sell it as a paper-back. I'm sure the poor man had no idea of the agony he was causing me.

17 March   I dreamt last night that I was married to Reggie. The recurring dream that I deliberately marry him again and almost immediately regret it. Each time I dream this, I think 'Before this I only dreamt it. Now it's really happened.'

I had tea with Olivia Sowerby, Alice Meynell's daughter. She was 17 when Francis Thompson died and remembers him well. She calls him Frăncis Thompson – as he did himself with his Lancashire accent. She showed me notebooks of his – old exercise books – with drafts of poems and poems in his own hand. Also a 'commonplace' book of things he liked, including some sonnets by Wilfrid Blunt [Alice Meynell's husband] and a surprising number of quotations from French authors. How jealous I used to be of the Meynell children when I was a child, though of course they were grown-up by then.

I had meant to refuse Mark Bence-Jones' invitation of Easter – my neurotic apprehension at the thought of 'displacement'. But I accepted. It would probably be a good thing to get away from here for a day or two. After all, I'm doing nothing here.

20 March   I did exactly 4 words on March 18th.

Poor Denys in a crisis. Eric to dinner. Yesterday much disturbed by 2 enormous letters from Dorothy MacAlister†, main theme that I had injured my father's reputation by writing about him. Wish she'd kept her disapproval to herself. It couldn't have come at a worse moment when I feel guilty enough anyway. If this translation doesn't materialize my finsit will be deplorable. So hard to 'take no thought for the morrow'. But something in me says, 'Who the hell are you, anyway, Lady MacAlister? I'm not really interested in your opinion. Other people like my work . . . people who were just as fond of my father as you were.'

28 March   A priest told me in the confessional on Saturday that I was not a hypocrite if I went on going to Communion when I had such doubts that I wondered if I believed *any* of it was true. He said 'You are not alone. We *all* have doubts.'

Muriel [unknown] suggests dropping writing altogether for 2 years. But what else could I do or attempt to do?

The translation has fallen through, American publisher has backed out. Just as well I rang up and found out. I've rung Marjorie Villiers and asked her to see if there's anything going there.

My finsit is bad but not quite as desperate as I feared. Nevertheless it is essential to earn £300–£400 before end of the year.

The H. and the F. has had strange repercussions. Long, intimate letters from total strangers. People say how much it has helped them, even how much my letters in reply to theirs have helped them.

How ironical – people thinking of me as *helpful* in matters of religion when I am in absolute confusion and darkness myself.

7 April   The doubts and conflicts as bad as ever. Worse since reading Santayana's *Christ in the Gospels* so strongly recommended by Eric. Impossible not to be haunted by the idea that Christianity is a myth. If I 'lapsed' again from belief, I think of the people I know, my very dear Catholic friends, my own daughter who might be shaken in their faith – perhaps they wouldn't be, only shaken in their faith in me. Which wouldn't, of course, matter in the least. I don't think I would *behave* very differently, even if I ceased to be a Catholic.

8 April, Good Friday.   Yesterday I re-read [George] Tyrrell's† autobiography. It is extraordinary the parallels that I find to my own case. The constant sense that he is suppressing his doubts, 'burying them alive' as he says. He is in a state of permanent inner conflict. One wonders whether he ever *really* believed. It could not be franker, this autobiography. He is ruthless about himself, ready all the time to catch himself out in self-deception, dreading mental dishonesty more than anything . . . What *is* there in me that is sound and genuine? I sometimes feel *nothing*. As if I had *no core* . . . Does a religion develop? Will Catholicism, with its claim to be the universal religion, develop as Christianity developed from and superseded Judaism into what one might call the religion of the Holy Spirit? There seem to be hints of this, even in Christ's own words – that He had to go before the Holy Spirit could come and that the Holy Spirit would make the darkness clear and enlighten our *understanding*. The whole *content* of our consciousness (and our awareness of the *unconscious*) is so different from what it was even 100 years ago.

23 April   At the last session Ployé said he had the impression that I had 'the treasure'.

Eric came last night. We talked of our recurring dream. He has exactly the same lavatory one. In the travelling one mine is all *packing*, but he always gets to the train and usually on it. But it is never going to the place he wants. He doesn't mind. He said 'I like going nowhere.'

Ployé said I was 'generous' in giving him the clues about X i.e. that twice since X's visit when I was feeling particularly disapproving of him, I . . . wrote 'me' when I meant to write 'him'. [X was now out of Dartmoor.] It is obvious that in my unconscious there is a 'burglar' who intends to live dishonestly by stealing, not working. P[loyé] also said that I may not want to get well, since that would give him satisfaction – the old thing of the parent wanting the child to produce faeces and the child withholding it.

My eyes hurt, I am pathologically tired. Cigarettes taste horrible and I don't feel well. But I think it's entirely psychological. The old symptoms . . . when I have a free day and could have been writing.

Have just read that Evelyn Waugh died on Easter Day. It has given me quite a shock. I did not hear because I was with Mark and Gill [Bence-Jones].

Extracts from my father's letters to Dorothy Seaton [MacAlister] [about] *Dolly Dialogues* [Henry James]: 'from many points of view it is the best book ever written' (May 1905).

26 April   I heard from Kathy P. [unknown] that a friend of a friend of hers, a lapsed Catholic, has returned to the Church as a result of reading *The H. and the F.*

As regards religion, slight thinning of the cloud. I go on *as if* I believed.

Copying extracts from my father's letters [a collection of which had been sent to Antonia] produced strange effect. Bound to, perhaps. He was obviously very attached to D[orothy] S[eaton] . . . his conversion at the end takes place very quickly. Did he ever suffer doubts afterwards? From that one conversation we had in Paris in 1924 it seems he did. If ONLY we could have talked 'straight' more often.

Who was the 'first love' he mentions in one letter? How much did he 'love' my mother?

How much *did* he read before he became a Catholic? Curious that C[atholic] T[ract] S[ociety] pamphlets should have impressed him so much. What does come out is his absolute honesty. Also, interestingly, his sense of inner compulsion, apart from 'arguments pro and con'. The hedonist and the stern moralist must have been in constant conflict.

I wish I had known him better. I feel a little depressed, reading these letters. In a way they widen the gulf between us. I can't help feeling he would always disapprove of me, even as I am now. But I *cannot* be other than I am. My nature is as different from him as my life has been. And he *has* no authority over me now. And, in any case, I am my mother's child as well as his. I think he often forgot that. My mother had as much right as he had to exert 'authority' over me, but she never did. And, of course, had she tried to, I should have taken no notice. I wonder how much he ever really knew her. Her behaviour after his death would surely have bewildered him! Odd, how he would retire to his club and write letters in the evening.

8 May Last night another 'party' dream. This time having to arrange a large one at v. short notice – only 3 hours – for friendly people but almost total strangers. Frantic rushing round in a taxi, buying food and wine at Harrods on account, not knowing what to buy or how much.

Ployé suggested I was trying to see too *much*, understand too much about myself. He said I try too hard, even with him, co-operate almost too well, preparing material for him.

10 May On Sunday, at E[nfants] de M[arie] meeting, [Revd] Mother Archer-Shee said she heard I'd written a very 'bad' book [*The Hound and the Falcon*], full of 'wrong opinions'. I asked her who had told her: she wouldn't say. Obviously it was a nun. I was driven to tell her that some priests and nuns, as well as many eminent lay Catholics, very much approved of it. She seemed impressed that a Jesuit (Fr. Caraman) had reviewed it favourably. She had, of course, not read it herself. I think I shall always be suspect to the Sacred Heart nuns. She said 'Of course, we are very much out of the world.' But surely, if your job is educating children, you ought to know something about the world they are going out into.

An odd dream the other night. My father was in it. He was wearing a hearing-aid and I was surprised to find it was the same kind as mine. When he took it off to prove it, he removed his whole ear.

23 June A wonderful letter from Fr. Hugh [a Carmelite at Kensington] who had traced me through *The H. and the F.*

I asked Fr. Stanley who teaches scripture (or did recently) in a seminary what is the Garden of Eden situation now? He said: 'Part legend, part historically true but the experts have not yet decided which part is which.'

An interrupted week anyway. Demenge twice, Denys [Blakelock], Fr. Stanley, Mumford, Longmans etc.

One or two odd dreams . . . Some rather suspect, medium-like woman ('Dorothy-ish'). I went into a trance, impressed these people with my psychic powers, talked a good deal I think, was aware of powers flowing through me. A man in the group levitated slightly, I saw his feet were a few inches above the ground.

I am 'marking time' as it were . . . The Gérard [Sinclair Hill, child lover in autobiography] bit is being extremely trying: keeps getting utterly false.

Have got into habit past few weeks of almost compulsively doing crossword puzzles when I ought to be working.

Fr. Stanley interesting about St. Mary's. Confirms all I thought about Sister M[adeleva]. He says she was eaten up with vanity. Also took violent fancies to people, then dropped them. He thinks she was after Lyn's money in wanting her to join the order. He was, indeed, far harder on her than I would be.

6 July   Last fortnight such physical and mental exhaustion! Work impossible. Pile of letters as usual to cope with. And people, people, people. Mrs Coutts becoming a real burden. I think she really *is* out of her mind. She lies all the time. You *can't* establish any real communication with her. She is driving everyone she knows nearly crazy with her insistent demands.

People are so good to me – say extraordinary things about how *The H. and the F.* has helped them. I feel, myself, empty, half-crazy, deadly tired, unable to concentrate on anything. I'm nearly as crazy as poor Mrs C. but put on a better show. Though I could *scream* often when I'm with people, from sheer weariness and inability to cope with social demands. Dreading Ottrott and all the organization, packing etc. Above all having to be sociable. Don't know when I've been so tired and for *so long*.

10 July   Long letter from girl in Glasgow re *H. and F* and her problems: v. interesting but it took 3 hours to answer. Got up at 5.30 and have polished off bills, drawn up 'Order of Week' and faced grim finsit – anyway on paper. Mrs Coutts shd. be all right for today: her new lodger is arriving. Must dress and go to Mass now. When back NO letters, not even clearing up, try and *work*.

22 July   Mem   Can now establish that it was *Wed 8 June* that X came to see me. He rang me up in late morning and arrived about 5.45. He rang me up the following morning (Thursday 9th).

* * *

The château at Ottrott, in Alsace, was the summer home of the Demenge family, relatives of the Grunelius family at nearby Kolbsheim. Françoise Demenge, Antonia's well-loved friend, had died some fifteen years earlier.

* * *

27 July, Ottrott   I can hardly believe that I am here. It must be six or seven years since I was in France. Nor can I believe that it is 19 years since I met Françoise.† I think I saw her last in 1949. We must have been much the same age. It is extraordinary to think that our daughters, Sue and Marie-Odile, will very soon be 37 and have two children apiece about 11 and 13. This is a fascinating house, the early part 17th century and with parts built on later by successive generations.

30 July   My bedroom is in the old part. The adjoining *cabinet de toilette* has not yet running water, only a vast marble-topped washstand with basin and ewer. To bath I go down 2 flights, passing the *lingerie*, and arrive at a super-modern bathroom. There are bare boards in my bedroom but with a rug in the middle of the floor. No central heating in this part for fear it should damage the beautiful old furniture, but there is a porcelain stove in my bedroom which would be heated by wood in winter. My window is just above the *perron* with its urns of geraniums and flanking parterres of phlox and zinnias and looks direct on to the little park and the wooded Vosges . . . It is all *très* Madame Ségur, the atmosphere of children here for *les grandes vacances*. The children themselves are enchanting.

31 July   We went to Mass at St Odile on the top of the mountain.

After Mass we went for another wonderful walk, the third, in the forest. The *mur paien* (built probably by the Celts and used by the Romans, later as useful defences for the medieval *seigneurs-brigands* in their castle strongholds) runs for miles – great rough-hewn blocks of stone piled together and once held together by wooden tenons of which you can still see the sockets. This forested mountain side is superb. When you *do* get a clear view through the trees you can see over the whole plain of Alsace, as far as the Rhine.

The towns and villages remind me a good deal of Bavaria – but one mustn't say so! Gabled roofs, timbered houses worked in patterns of dark beams against pink or green or white plaster, wooden balconies everywhere with flowers, petunias, geraniums mainly, of all varieties and very large and brilliantly coloured. Innumerable German names and notices though they are desperately trying to get rid of the German association and flavour.

1 August   I could not be having a greater change from London than I am having here. It is extraordinary having a French family life. Robert Demenge and all of them could not be kinder. Amazing what a united family they are and how well the two *jeunes ménages* and their

children get on. How much I wish Françoise were still alive. It is sad
that she did not live to see even one of her 6 enchanting grandchildren. She must have spent all her childhood here. There are charming
watercolours and photos of her as a little girl, with long fair hair and
wearing a sailor dress as children used to wear in my day.

Françoise was only 51 when she died.

I could not rest this afternoon: haunted by Mrs Coutts.

3 August   Spent several hours yesterday trying to compose a line or
two for the *livre des notes*. Amazing how hard I find it to write *anything*
to order.

Cognassier = quince tree.

I am less homesick today – perhaps because I am going home in a
week! The family *couldn't* be sweeter to me and I really am very fond
of them. The children are very sweet with me, particularly Emmanuel. My deafness really *is* a nuisance, my 'aid' doesn't help. I can only
hear when people are very near and as they are talking French, it is
more difficult.

I went to Mass yesterday in the little XIIth century church of St
Nicolas. Could hardly hear a word the priest said. My deaf-aid made
things only worse: every movement made a shattering noise but the
speech was no more intelligible, though I could distinguish Latin
from French. Strange that even the old women no longer cover their
heads.

It rained all day yesterday: today the clouds are heavy over the
mountain and there are intermittent claps of thunder.

In the village you see women washing clothes in a stone trough
and occasionally a cart drawn by an ox. You see old women with
kerchiefs round their heads carrying baskets of firewood on their
backs. Many of the local people speak a German dialect more easily
than they speak French. The gardener speaks French with a heavy
local accent but I can just manage to understand him. Everyone in the
village says *bonjour* to one.

Robert was very sweet last night doing conjuring tricks for the
children. How one trembled in case one went wrong! The children
are completely at ease with the grown ups though good manners are
enforced, especially by '*bon père*'. It is extraordinary how late they stay
up. Even the 5 year old Pauline doesn't go to bed till a quarter to ten.

She also eats every course of the ample and excellent dinner. They have their baths before dinner and dine and play games afterwards in the salon in their pyjamas and charming striped cotton dressing gowns. However their régime obviously suits them. They are all very slim and well-made and as supple as acrobats. I must say that French family life has many features we might well copy . . . Though Sue and Thomas are much the same with *their* children really.

6 August   I really am neurotic about holidays. This could not be a lovelier place: I could not be more kindly treated. In spite of which, I count the days till I am back in my old familiar surroundings. I shall have very happy memories of Ottrott and all the people here. But it is as if I could only appreciate things in retrospect nowadays.

The worst melancholy is in the afternoon: about 6 my spirits begin to revive.

This *has* been a very peculiar year as regards work and everything else – no work – or hardly any – done and no translation in prospect.

I can see it is very good for me to be *subject* to other people for a while, as one *is* as a guest. To have to assume great interest perhaps at the moment one's mind is not attuned to that particular subject.

A charming absurd village band is playing for the Ottrott Messtic [country dance].

* * *

Antonia fell and broke several fingers of her right hand soon after she returned to England. This accident was the last in a series of minor physical misfortunes that had plagued her. Before she went to Ottrott she had fallen and damaged a knee, and had cracked a rib.

* * *

6 Sept   The first time I have written anything but necessary pcs and note since my fall on Aug 20th when I broke 4 fingers of my right hand, middle one in 2 places. I had the splint off yesterday. Easier to hold a pen but fingers *very* painful. Mid one badly swollen and 1 and 5 crooked. It is agonizing to do the exercises but I do them, hoping to recover use of fingers in time. It was a bad shock that fall (about 7 a.m. on the way to Mass). I was lucky not to break my nose. The swelling has gone down though nose still painful to touch. Badly cut lip has healed beautifully. Irony it shd. happen just after the very first day I'd attempted to work . . . after my return from Ottrott in small hours of Aug 12. First week home was taken up with *huge* mass of correspondence (including 5 long and complex new *H. and F* letters) and coping with the Coutts crisis which had occurred in my absence. This involved much phoning and writing a long letter to Dr Beatley wh. took up a whole morning.

Margot King (she was so sweet and had me there all day Sat. when I got v. low after coping not too badly for a fortnight) said to me yesterday that she was worried about me – physically as well as mentally – I was so 'low'. She wants to pay for me to visit a doctor (woman) in whom she has great faith. I will go if she fixes it.

Dear Denys has been an angelic friend. Just before my accident he sent me a cheque for £100. It was a godsend at that moment for my finsit is v. bad. He has come over often, bringing food and drink and cheering me up. I *can* be quite bright and alive when I'm with someone. But I collapse after.

Fishy of course my injuring my right hand just then – when I'd *just* begun to work again. And *also* when Martin [Turnell] had just tried to get me that A[rts] C[ouncil] bursary. When he got me the R[oyal] L[iterary] F[und] grant nearly 2 years ago, I was so happy. BUT I promptly had that run of accidents and illnesses which culminated in Sept. with Galway telling me I was on the verge of another breakdown.

Even religion doesn't seem to help . . . These books about 'total self-giving' 'dying to self' etc. What is really MEANT by all that?

Margot said 'You need to be re-born.'

D[orothy] Kingsmill said the same!

But what does it *mean?* And how does one get 're-born' at 67?

Oh, my life, my life. What a mess. What a failure. And I was given good gifts. What have I done with them?

9 Sept   Tiredness worse than ever. Yesterday Margot took me to this doctor, Mary Austin. I had no idea that she wd. turn out to be a 'radionics' practitioner. Odd, after the suggestion made to me a few weeks ago by a *H. and F* correspondent. Rather disconcerting since I'm chary of these things. However I took an instant liking to Mary Austin herself who seemed eminently sensible, as well as being very fresh, clean and pleasant to look at. She is 53. It is awfully kind of Margot to 'stand' me in this. Mary A. did not examine me, only made me talk. She gave me some sensible advice about my hand. She is putting me for 3 months 'on the box'. Asked me to send her *F[rost] in M[ay]* 'to see what you're made of' . . . Georgie obviously suspected another Dorothy [Hopkinson].

My hand is very much better today: writing naturally still laborious and tiring. But I am recovering the use of my fingers, swollen and bent as they still are. Thank God for that. 3 weeks since my fall, which might have had so much worse consequences.

. . . my eyes hurt less. A big pen is rather heavy to hold though it writes better than a Biro. The exercises are certainly doing good and becoming less painful. I wonder if 'radionics' are helping?

Margot said I should be simpler. Well, at least I can try! Abbé de Tourville says 'simple, frank, humble'. Humble is probably the key word!! This year I have been offered help by *others* to an unusual degree – Charlotte, Robert, Denys, Margot, Martin Turnell. Both a wish and a fear – being dependent on others.

It is true that accepting such help has often landed me in dangerous situations – e.g. D[orothy] Kingsmill and V[irginia] J[ohnes]. But that should not make one suspicious of *all* offers of help. The *big* problem is the destructive impulse in myself . . .

11 Sept   At least got as far as looking at my MS first time since Aug 19. In an hour did no more than a minute alteration or two.

19 Sept   The last 5 days have been entirely taken up with Mrs Coutts' crisis. Ravings, phone calls, doctors, district nurses – the lot. Today I took her to the psychiatrist at St Mary Abbots. Trouble seems to be drink as much as anything . . . The district nurse says she has *never* had such an exhausting patient.

Margot told me that Doctor Austin has talked to her about me. Says I am in a very bad way but she is convinced that she *can* help me. She says I have used up all my reserves. I certainly feel as if I had! Margot is being *marvellously* kind and generous – My hand is going to be slow too. I have to go 3 times a week for the next 3 weeks for physiotherapy at St Mary Abbots. Fingers will probably never straighten but SHOULD recover the use of hand.

27 Sept   I had more trouble with Mrs C[outts] since last entry. On Sunday, after her coming up in a dressing-gown as I was half-dressed and trying to get off to Mass and staging another scene (she was very drunk having managed to get brandy the night before), I was shaking all over. In the evening Mrs C. was calmer. Only came up to beg some bread as she was 'starving'.

Yesterday I didn't go down.

Today as I was lying down, very tired after my late night with Kate O'Brien [Irish novelist] my bedroom door opened. I was terrified that it was Mrs C. Mercifully it was Nurse Downing. She went in *3 times* to her yesterday, got Dr Beatley. They had an awful day with her. At last Dr Beatley is convinced that she drinks. Mercifully there is *some* hope in sight. Head district nurse has suggested Anglican nuns who have a home for such cases.

Encouraging letters about *H[ound]* and *F[alcon]* keep coming in still. But I *can't* work – I try to but produce nothing. Can't say I feel any better from Dr A[ustin]'s treatment yet . . . I must just manage to get through a day at a time.

29 Sept   Mrs C[outts] rang up last night, very drunk, to say she wouldn't go to the home. Can they make her?

Rang Dr Austin as requested. Told her I couldn't honestly see much improvement. She asked if I was sleeping better. Shook me rather as I'm sure I told her my trouble was rather sleeping too much and always being tired . . .

Tried to read Thomas's book [*The Village*, by Thomas Hinde]: it induced the extreme depression his work so often induces in me. A critic calls him one of the most powerful and brilliant novelists of the century.

I get more and more uncontemporary as regards novels, art, music, theatre. I'm a tired, impotent old hang-over.

Mrs C. obviously affecting the psyche situation acutely. I identify myself with her – anyway one part of me.

Ployé says he was sorry he couldn't give me more time: he obviously thinks I need it. But I think we had a good session yesterday. I told him 'brain-washing' seemed a wonderful word to me at the moment. The idea of having my brain washed clear seems a delightful one. To be put to sleep and wake up fresh, clear-eyed, energetic – how marvellous!

1 Oct, 7.30 a.m.   Margot King has this incessant sense of the presence of God. She talks incessantly of the overwhelming *joy* she feels, the absolute confidence . . .

2 Oct   Last night I had one of those frustrating dreams about Silas. It was my last chance to go to bed with him, make everything all right between us . . . I had gone all the way to somewhere in the far north, in the snow, to a camp where he was living alone and he had welcomed me lovingly. When at last we were alone, my hopes were getting fainter and fainter. I wanted to have this last moment of warmth and affection though by now my Catholic scruples had come up about our making love physically. Then came up the old lavatory business. I *must* relieve myself, even [if] it took up some of this fast-ebbing time together, so as to have no physical distractions. The dream ended with the old frustrating hunt for a lavatory, losing myself in the search for one.

I woke up with a strong impulse to *write*. A short story about our real parting before he went to Canada, called 'The Last Day'. It was so strong that I nearly got up – made myself tea and sat down to brood on it or even begin it. Then I thought 'No. All you'll do is wake yourself right up with the tea, smoke cigarettes for an hour or two, not get enough sleep and be too tired tomorrow to attempt to write.' So I lay awake, I should think for a good hour, thinking about this Silas story. Should it be a long short story, almost a 'nouvelle'? Or should it be an actual novel, not a 'Clara' one officially, but isolating that particular episode? Or should it be, after all, the abandoned *Clara IV* about which I developed scruples (about Sue mainly). So now I am in an acute dilemma. Try to do a short story? Make another attempt at *Clara IV*? Or peg on with the autobiography?

Later   It is all over with poor Mrs C[outts]. The district nurse could get no reply today and rang my buzzer – I opened the front door, but the chain was up. We knew she must be in there so we got the police. They managed to unscrew the bolt. We found her dead in the kitchen, collapsed over the sink. She was last seen alive on Friday,

and when I rang the bell on Friday about 2.30 she may have been dead
already. She clung to her home and she died there. From 5—8, police,
undertakers, Mrs Wood, the Vicar, phoning relatives. I think we all
did all we could.

6 Oct All this week has been taken up with the aftermath of poor
Mrs C.'s death – seeing her executor, communicating with her
relatives, dealing with many, many phone calls, long-distance or long
in duration. Being on the spot I have had to be a kind of clearing
house . . . It's a frightening thing, watching the disintegration of a
human being.

Mother Gertrude [Carmelite nun] writes that her beloved Mother
Francis died last week. Poor Mother Gertrude! It is awfully hard,
much as one feels for her, not to feel that there is something
disturbing about this 'infantilism' in religion . . . And, oh dear, so
much else about Catholicism . . . Of *course* one sympathizes with grief
but this idolizing of one nun by another and this kind of 'holy
schoolgirl' business – I can't *help* it, I find it repellent. Piety, however
sweet, seems no substitute for mature understanding. I know these
women were devoted to the Carmelite vocation . . . but can't people
have a little understanding and not be so amazingly narrow-minded?
Those pathetically awful holy pictures Mother G. is always sending
me – oh, I know I'm being a disgusting spiritual snob – but there's
something so false and so saccharine about this kind of piety.

7 Oct Mrs C[outts] was buried today. The final confusion – the
Martyns (her cousins) never told us the place had been changed and
that there wd be no service at St Jude's. We waited till 10.15 then
found all plans had been changed yesterday.

Even now, I am not free of the business. The Exe[cutor] asked me
to keep the keys to let in gas and electricity people etc.

I had a long session with Dr A. yesterday. All very mysterious
though she seems a pleasant, straightforward competent person. She
gave me acropuncture [sic] (Margot hadn't warned me but I
supposed I'd better take it) then an hour lying down and being
exposed to various rays during which I dozed off. Felt rather quiet
and sleepy after. She said when she analysed my blood that I had only
25% of what should be normally 75% (energy?) and that she

wondered what would have happened if I hadn't come to her. She expects considerable improvement in next 3–4 weeks and says she has now got my right wave-length.

Today Gladys's husband had his operation. I hope to goodness it is successful and that he makes a good recovery. But he sounds a pretty sick man to me. Poor Gladys has had a very trying time this past month. She does her work but of course I have to spend a long time every morning listening to her – very real – troubles . . .

Only 8 p.m. but I'm going to bed.

8 Oct My hand was so painful last night that it kept me awake . . . Denys had given me some Lourdes water. I did put some on. I am afraid I found a compress of witch hazel did more good.

I have been in and out of Elizabeth's [Mrs Coutts'] flat all day. The pathos of human belongings, even old lipsticks. Indescribable chaos of objects, most seemingly ugly and meaningless, yet treasured by her, part of her life. A whole suitcase full of old photographs and local magazines – weddings going back to 1918. One could have reconstructed her whole life from them, all the changes in her looks from a short-haired child of 5 or so to the old woman I first remember here 5 years ago. She was a pretty girl. The all-too-familiar quilted dressing-gown of the last weeks, the shapeless sage-green suit hung over a chair . . . A thing for hanging clothes on in the hall, shaped like a gate and inscribed in Gothic letters 'May the hinges of friendship never go rusty.' Surprisingly, among the few books Rupert Brooke's complete works . . . I rescued the Rupert Brooke – given to her (*not* by Bill [her husband]) in 1937.

There *was* some truth in what she told me. I found photos of Swindon Hall, a big house owned by her grandfather or perhaps an uncle: local papers showing the hounds meeting in front of it. The beloved brother, too, in uniform and her father too. There was a kind of county background – rich manufacturers in the 19th century who had bought good houses and become 'prominent in the neighbourhood'. E[lizabeth] was very good to her mother who had long survived the feckless but probably charming father and the son who died at 27 of TB I *think* she said as a result of being gassed. Often wished she could have been more coherent, since she talked of little else but her past life, but one could never establish any sequence – she

would give you so many versions of the same episode and one could
never get her to pin down dates. Even her marriage she would say
sometimes took place when she was 17 or 27, though in the end she
seemed to place it during 'Churchill's War' when she was over 40.
According to Violet this last is right.

I only saw her dead body from the back. I never saw anything so
non-human: an old broken puppet that nothing could animate any
more, huddled over the sink, wrapped in 'Bill's' old dressing-gown
. . .

Where do I believe *she* is now? I go on praying for her as if I
believed what I *should* as a Catholic believe. IF that belief is true, she
has, I am sure, found peace and happiness. But how much instinctively stronger in me is the sense of the *natural* mystery of life, death,
change – of the mysterious natural, wonderful, terrible, inexhaustible, incomprehensible universe in which we find ourselves.

9 Oct 'It is time the English Catholic public were given an adult
introduction to the problems of the "quest for the historical Jesus".'
Abbot Butler OSB.

Be grateful – you *can't* be grateful enough – for the kindness and
generosity of your friends, especially Denys and Margot. Without
the latter I would by now have run right out of money. Think of all
my other blessings; my home, Gladys, Diane, Minka. Of the affection
of my friends, old and new.

8 p.m. I didn't try to work after all but wrote a long letter to
Lyndall. There is a radio talk at 8 on St Francis de Sales. Perhaps it
will do me some good! I read several pages of Teilhard de Chardin
this morning, in the same hopes. V. difficult to understand but
perhaps some of it sank in . . .

10 Oct The Francis de Sales talk didn't help me as much as a few
lines in Abbé de Tourville about simplicity. These masters of prayer
like St. F. de S. are right out of my range. I am just frightened and
bewildered by all this 'total stripping of self' etc. They don't sound
like ordinary human beings . . . I can't *really* believe God intends us to
detach ourselves from all human affections. I never did like that story
of St J[ane]F[rances] de Chantal stepping over her son's body as she
went off to be a nun.

I had an interesting session with Ployé today. Naturally I talked of Mrs C. In doing so, I realized how many parallels I found between her and my mother in her last years.

Ployé (this came up after I had told him how I had seen [Dr] Carroll some months after analysis was finished and was surprised to discover him clean-shaven and still more to discover that he had *always* been clean-shaven though all through my 3½ years of sessions I had always seen him with a little moustache, like my father) said he thought the transference on Carroll had not been completely resolved. He asked if my mother had ever 'come up' in my analysis and I said, as far as I could remember, never. He suggested that my writing side may really come from her, and I am inclined to agree ... her imaginative, intuitive side, her interest in people – quite different from my father's. And my jam on writing is not so much *inability* to write as criticizing too soon ... Terrified of getting carried away. Because of my mother's 'cuckoo' side, which is in me too. I am *afraid to let go* (the old fear which stopped me always from so many physical activities – skating, cycling, swimming etc).

My conscience – that I MUST answer letters at once – even if there is no real necessity. Torturing myself about religion etc.etc.

Margot said: 'Be simple.' De Tourville last night ... a passage about being simple, like a child, with God. Both my mother and Mrs C. for all their exasperating qualities and their childishness, had that other thing, something genuinely child*like*. My father was never *childlike* ... I felt that he only loved me when he was *pleased* with me. I was extremely afraid of his displeasure. I didn't mind my mother's: it was more comfortable to be on good terms with her but I didn't feel that the world had come to an end if she was cross with me. The way God is 'put over' to me in the Christian religion is so *much* the idea of an omnipotent being who only loves you when you *please* him and is exceedingly angry with you when you don't and, if you are not careful, will punish you not only in this world but eternally in the next.

11 Oct A story Barbara Wall [wife of Bernard Wall]† told me about going to Confession. She said to the priest, 'I have been lacking in faith, hope and charity.' He said, 'I don't want this airy-fairy stuff. Have you eaten meat on a Friday?'

I may not be able to prove the existence of God theoretically. But in practice I have had experiences which I can only see as God's intervention in my life . . . Such as my experience in the Carmelite church at Christmastime 1940. I *can* only see my 're-conversion' as an answer to the prayers of others. Fr. Hugh in particular and Father Van der Ghote (was that the name of the parish priest at West Grinstead?) [Fr. Jules van Langendonk] and perhaps many others, living or dead. And, more recently, the publication of *The H. and the F.* with all its consequences.

12 Oct Heard Krishnamurti on the radio last night. According to him, *all* religions are dope, crutches that must be thrown away . . . I could not help getting this impression of arrogance and contempt, almost that he was the only person in the whole history of man who knew the truth about everything.

13 Oct Fr. Brodrick SJ: 'Antonia's *Hound and Falcon* interested me *intensely*. I read and re-read it *three times*. She is a heroic soul.'

That is an *extraordinary* idea for anyone to have of me! 'Heroic' – of all things!

14 Oct Wickedly wasted morning. Disorganized by business with letting in gas man for Mrs C.'s flat . . . succumbed to temptation to do M[anchester] G[uardian] crossword puzzle after reading the book reviews.

Today 900th anniversary of Battle of Hastings. I suppose only the English would celebrate a *defeat* with much local festivity! The carnage of the battle was appalling, so was his [William I's] subsequent cruelty to the English. Yet after the battle he ordered his soldiers to do penance – 2 years if they knew they had killed a man, lesser time (as in the case of archers) if they could not be sure.

18 Oct It took me 4 hours on Sunday to type a letter to Hilda Graef,† trying to think out sentences and say what I meant – especially about the hypocrisy I feel going on when I don't know if I believe *at all*. When I had finished – I suppose because she is writing on Newman, I was suddenly impelled to take up the 2nd vol. of Meriol Trevor's life of Newman [1962] which has stood unread on my shelf for over a year and began to read it. I was instantly absorbed and fascinated and went on reading it for hours. I am still deep in it. For the first time I feel genuinely attracted to Newman.

Last night Mr Mumford rang up to say that X is back in Pentonville, remanded in custody and coming up for trial on Monday. I find it hard to be sorry for him: he's such a fool. He really could have 'gone straight' this time if he'd wanted to. But he obviously prefers to live this way and *prefers* burgling, and then doing time, to any other way of life. If only he weren't such an awful liar! It makes it so impossible to deal with him. I hope his wife – if she *is* his wife – sticks to him: I wonder if she knows the truth about him or if anyone does. I sometimes wonder if X *can* tell the truth about *anything*. I don't propose to do anything at the moment but if he writes to me, as he almost certainly will, I'll have to answer and maybe go and see him.

24 Oct On Friday Oct 21st I met Fr. Brodrick and spent $2\frac{1}{2}$ hours with him. I liked him immensely and felt instantly at ease with him. He said he was constantly riddled with doubts himself, often most of all at the moment of Consecration.

On the Garden of Eden he said definitely that it was a myth, though of course conveying profound religious truth. What a relief to hear this said at last. Eve drawn from Adam's side merely symbolizes the close union between man and woman. That is enough to go on with. I'm satisfied not to worry further about 'literal inerrancy' etc.

I said how impossible I found the idea of total annihilation of self, 'dying to self' etc. He said it was a very gradual process.

That the saints went on sinning and had to be 'reconverted' every day . . .

We talked of Tyrrell. He said von Hügel was his evil genius and much more of a 'modernist' than Tyrrell. He had talked to Bishop Amigo who was very distressed about the affair of Tyrrell's burial. Fr. Pollen had gone down to Storrington to see Tyrrell. T. was paralysed, unable to speak, lying with his eyes closed. Fr. P. said, 'George, do you want to be reconciled and receive absolution? If so, just open your eyes.' T.'s eyes, said Fr. B[rodrick], *flew* open and Fr. P gave him absolution. All was arranged for a requiem and Catholic burial. But the very day after T.'s death, von H[ügel] wrote a long letter to *The Times* to the effect that he [Tyrrell] would not have wished to receive the sacraments at the cost of retraction.

I have just looked up Miss Petrie's account which is quite different. She says that Fr. Pollen was never alone with Tyrrell (she went in with him) and it was she who wrote the letter to *The Times* (which she quotes in full). It shows how difficult it is to get the facts.

He [Fr. Brodrick] is in sympathy with Teilhard de Chardin. Says he was v. badly treated, not allowed to accept important university posts in Europe and 'got rid of' to China.

Of course his great love is St Teresa whom I never *could* properly appreciate, though I love some of her sayings.

Odd – he was one of the priests (the other Fr. Martindale [distinguished Jesuit]) who told Mother Archer-Shee not to make such a fuss about *Frost* – that most of it was absolutely true and that it would do them good to take notice of it and mend their ways.

Incidentally he [Fr. Brodrick] couldn't stand 'Faberism' [sentimental theories of Fr. Faber] and is all pro-Newman.

Mr Mumford rang this morning about X. He saw him in Pentonville last night – says he was like a deflated balloon. He was a *fool* to run away from the hostel: police watching him of course. Now they've got him for burglary, breaking in and stealing something like £200. His wife loves him (and he her); she said she didn't want to be 'out' when he was 'in' and said she was in on the job too (which she wasn't) and is now in Holloway. I wrote to X a little note. I hope he doesn't get a long sentence – he fears it may be 8 or 9 years. Unfortunately it's the same judge who gave him 6 years last time.

25 Oct   Have to stick in all morning (G[ladys] being away) waiting for man to collect Mrs C.'s television set.

And what have *I* done, with my time to myself? Lain down and listened to *Woman's Hour*, made tea and washed up . . . smoked many cigarettes. Frittered the afternoon away, in fact, as so often.

28 Oct   Somehow I managed to finish off the Gérard chapter . . . I fear it is very bad and rather nauseating.

On Sunday I went to see Esther Cleps [unknown] in hospital. I've been haunted by that girl ever since Mary Austin told me about her and this appalling alternative she is faced with – either to go on living in agonizing pain or have an operation which will leave her permanently and completely paralysed. All due to a slip of the surgeon's knife. It is possible she may have a gift for writing and I have encouraged her to try – which I *don't* normally do. Perhaps the whole point of my going to Mary Austin was simply to be put in touch with Esther . . . The last weeks have been fuller than ever of appalling disasters – first the tragedy of Aberfan and now the floods in Italy.

Perhaps *nothing* will ever assuage my fundamental doubts about Catholicism.

9 Nov A sudden rush of social engagements from Saturday right on through most of next week. They always seem to come one after the other in a rush like this.

12 Nov This morning the Gérard chapter came back from Phyllis with a *most* encouraging note. When I read it through it didn't seem at all bad. You'd think it had been written quite easily!!

18 Nov Esther Cleps seems to be the next person God has mysteriously sent into my life. It was almost frightening to hear from Dr A. how much my going to see her in hospital meant to her. I hope I am right in encouraging her to write. I have read her poems now. They are very moving but of course not very good.

A bit worried about my finger. Ogilvie thinks it may have been set wrong and trapped a nerve and that it shouldn't be so painful to touch anything with it after all these months.

27 Nov A most interesting evening last night with Audrey Beecham and her friend Christopher Evans, Professor of Theology at King's College. What a relief to be able to talk about religion as a subject of burning interest.

28 Nov Christopher Evans says that [St] Jerome says *unspeakable* things about women!

29 Nov In the evening I saw [Dr] Vaughan Jackson. Not entirely satisfactory as he had not got the X-rays. But from what he could judge by testing the bad finger and from what I told him, it does not look as if much can be done and that the hospital has done all it could. He will let me know. Nothing can make the finger straight again. I *don't* think the hospital made any mistake about the setting. I feel a bit more alive today, as if I knew where I was and what I must try to do: viz, the obvious. Manage as best I can in spite of the various drawbacks . . . not get so worried about all the things I *ought* to be doing – 'good works' etc. I have such a guilty conscience about doing nothing whatever in that line. I just try and cope a little with anyone actually thrown in my path.

I meant to read the *Apologia*. I don't think I will ever be able to: I think it is really a work for theological scholars of immense learning. And I have to admit my horror of a sentence quoted by Kingsley (and not denied by Newman) from N.'s 'Lecture on Anglican Difficulties – 1850' . . . The Catholic Church 'holds it is better for sun and moon to drop from heaven, for the earth to fail and for all the many millions on it to die of starvation in extremest agony, as far as temporal affliction goes, than that one soul, I will not say should be lost, but should commit one single venial sin, should tell one wilful untruth or should steal one poor farthing without excuse'.

30 Nov I was being stupid and splenetic about Newman. I must make another effort – but not just yet – to read the *Apologia*.

The most marvellous thing has happened. I can still hardly believe it. This morning I was rung up by a woman on *The Observer* – could she interview me about this Arts Council Grant? I thought there must be some mistake. I long ago gave up hope of getting the bursary. But it seems I have!! What is more, it is a sum beyond my wildest dreams. I thought it might be £500 – it is £1200! The biggest sum I have ever received in my life. I was too excited. I sat down scribbling out calculations and one or two tiny thank-offerings to charities. Heaven knows if I'll manage to write the book – but I MUST, MUST, MUST do my best.

15 Dec Yesterday Amanda [Hopkinson],† Tom's youngest daughter, rang me up to say she has become a Catholic. (She's 18.) She is being confirmed on Sunday and I am going to 'stand in' for her godmother who cannot be there. This is all quite extraordinary. Since I hardly know her, I have no idea how it all came about. Dorothy [Kingsmill]'s daughter Edmée became an Anglican nun last year.

17 Dec Extraordinary to find that Kathleen Raine is 'on the [radionics] Box'. It certainly seems to have had a splendid effect on her: she looked wonderful, in spite of having an *exceedingly* trying time at the moment with her parents (86 and 87) staying with her. She says she is out of the Church again.

I've been wrestling with *Matter in the Making* – all about the de la Warr set up and experiments. Very difficult to understand the technical side. Yet full of interesting ideas about all the unknown radiations and dimensions. I am, of course, always a little afraid of 'cranks'. On the other hand, there are so many mysterious and inexplicable things about the universe that 'science' ignores. In a way de la Warr's ideas fit in with Teilhard de Chardin's. And of course I have a horror of this new mechanical approach to nature, exemplified in such things as factory farming.

The trend towards 'rationalizing' everything in religion, trying to explain away miracles etc, is, I think, suspect.

19 Dec Yesterday, at Amanda's Confirmation, who should turn up but Tom? A man standing beside me on the Cathedral steps said 'Antonia' – and I did not know who he was till he said Tom.

A strange tea-party at Gerti's afterwards. Tom, Gerti, myself, Nicolette and Amanda. We have never been all together since Cheyne Row. It must have been '48 or '49? It is 17 years since I last saw Tom. He knew I would be there. We have had no communication since his angry last letter. He was very courteous and agreeable. He kissed both me and Gerti. He has changed a good deal in 17 years. So obviously have I! His face is much heavier, rather flabby about the jaw. He looks extraordinarily like his father. His voice is softer than ever. He looks rather unhappy, his eyes are rather lifeless. He is very guarded also . . . somewhat unreal. A hollow man. One will never be able to talk straight to him.

G[erti] told me that, at the end of his father's life, he [his father] went mad. When his wife came to see him he abused her savagely in four-letter words and the doctors asked her never to come again.

What an extraordinary breakdown in that ultra-conscientious, ultra-puritanical man. G. said that all the time he was a clergyman he hankered for the archaeology he had given up and all the association with Greece.

21 Dec   Announced this morning that Fr. Charles Davis is marrying and leaving the Church. He denies the infallibility of the Pope. It becomes more and more confusing to know where we *do* stand.

Today eaten up. X's commissions. Lunch at Claridge's with Lyn Isbell's mother [Lyn Cosgriff had married Harold Isbell] spread out till long after 4 p.m.

Lyn's mother and her new husband Dr Murphy have come to England to pick up a new car – a Triumph Spitfire. To drive it down to Dover tomorrow they have hired a taxi to go before them to show them the way.

Mrs M[urphy] nothing like as beautiful as she was 5 years ago, though very cheerful. Incredibly slim – 8 stone – terrified if she puts on a pound and goes for 24 hours on nothing but black coffee. But it makes her look very haggard. A gold box at lunch from which she took assorted pills. Husband agreeable but not comparable to Walter Cosgriff. But she's probably happier with him. Lyn sent me a fruit cake made by herself. Very touching. Mrs M. has that restless American vitality. After Walter's death became manager of a baseball team. Only woman in America. A tribute to W[alter]'s memory: it had been his life's ambition to get a good baseball team for Utah. 'I thought it better than building a little church for him.' Extraordinary family. *What* a queer day! Mrs M. always stays at Claridge's – it's so darling and old-fashioned. They unpack for you, automatically. She and her husband are off to do some ski-ing. What energy people have!

Bed, I think . . .

Georgie here the other day. The eternal theme, Eric an alcoholic . . . She *can't* make allowances for his peculiar nature. Ironically, I found him wonderfully easy to live with. I *don't* think he's quite as nice as he was then. He's driven to petty deceptions and has become a trifle dishonest. It's always about money. I'm very fond of Georgie . . . But she's wonderfully tactless and pathetically wonders why everyone doesn't like her. Her favourite contemptuous adjective is 'common'. Curious.

22 Dec   Re Charles Davis. Rosemary Haughton's† I think excellent letter today to the *Guardian*. 'Whatever happens, we are part of what is happening, the guilt as well as the suffering . . . What sort of a remnant will be left in the end we can't tell, but it is from this remnant that the new people will grow.'

23 Dec   Have just lost my temper with my cousin Helen on the phone. I *know* it is wrong of me to be so touchy. But I get so angry when people say 'La La' when I say I have money worries. She doesn't know what a real godsend this grant is to me. Anyway I've already given away about £100 of it. She herself has a regular job, a pension, shares and a brother to fall back on. Yes, it *was* wrong of me to flare up for I'm fond of Helen. She's just one of those infuriatingly tactless people. And she has a singularly irritating laugh which sounds affected but is really pure nerves, I think. I wish the amount hadn't been broadcast in the papers. Helen of course took it for granted that it was *yearly*, not just a lump sum!

Hilda Graef very indignant about Charles Davis. She thought him 'liberal' but very orthodox. She thinks he must have had a 'brain-storm'. I don't think Hilda really understands the very real difficulties of many Catholics. I think I admire her very much though; she's so brave and direct and wholesome.

24 Dec   Thank goodness the battle of the cards *must* end today. But I have 18 letters to write over Christmas . . . letter-writing has become a terrible oppression to me. I have never had a year in which I have had to write so many.

30 Dec   What an extraordinary year 1966 has been. Appalling from the point of view of work: I daren't think how few pages I have added to my book. Very much occupied with people – my acquaintance has certainly snowballed since *The H. and the F.* . . . .

What a year of doctors too! Ployé, Mary Austin, and 3 months of going 3 times a week to St Mary Abbots for physiotherapy.

Actual events very strange: all those months being involved with poor Mrs Coutts, culminating in her death. Poor Curdy's death, my fall and the partial crippling of my right hand. Last and strangest of all, Amanda's Confirmation and seeing Tom again. And the most startling pleasant surprise, being awarded the A[rts] C[ouncil] grant.

People have died this year. John Davenport, Jeanne de Casalis, Evelyn Waugh.

It is always a kind of no man's land, the space between Christmas and New Year. When I was younger I used to wish so much to know what lay ahead of me in the next year. Now I am thankful I don't.

Naturally, my one great wish for myself in 1967 is to be able to write again. For how many, many years I have had that wish. I keep being reminded of that odd story I wrote as a child, where people kept demanding the healing water the son had gone to search for to restore his dead mother to life, until not a drop was left. But when he returned empty handed, he found his mother miraculously restored to life. Perhaps I *have* to keep giving myself like this and, if God sees fit, the writing jam *will* break . . .

31 Dec This morning a letter from Sue saying that she is expecting her third child in July and will be home [from Illinois] in May instead of June. A lovely piece of news on which to end 1966.

FOUR

1967–1969

In 1968 Antonia was operated on privately for cataract at the Nuffield Hospital, Woking. Later the same operation was performed on her other eye. Both operations were successful. Phyllis Jones came up from Buckfastleigh to look after her when she was convalescing.

1967

1 Jan Read several of Virginia Woolf's essays. So intelligent, so beautifully written, yet somehow to me so disheartening. I feel as if I had ceased to be intelligent about literature and no longer am – if I ever was – a 'cultured person'. But how brilliant, how witty, how acute V.W. is – and what sharp claws she has too. I am sure she would be contemptuous of me as a 'middlebrow' writer.

3 Jan I had a nightmare last night . . . Sue, pregnant with the new baby, arrived unexpectedly back in England. Naturally I was delighted to see her and at first she was very sweet and affectionate. She was coming to stay with me till June. She also announced that several other of their friends – all mocking and contemptuous young people – were moving into the flat and going to live there with her . . . felt quite helpless. I had been robbed of all my furniture which seemed only to amuse Sue.

I don't know what it means. I suspect it may be connected with writing – being pushed aside by the younger generation as out-of-date and worthless.

What had happened the previous day? . . . On the radio there had been a mention of *Olivia*'s being brought out by Penguin in their

'Modern Classics' [*Olivia* by Olivia]. I was a little sore, thinking that when my agent sent *F. in M.* (which *has* been described as a modern classic too) to Penguin, they did not even bother to answer her letter. The dream shows that *something* had touched off a very deep anxiety.

8 Jan   Depressed at having already spent so much of the grant. What with Christmas presents and tips, 'extras' to friends and some charities, paying off my hearing aid, repaying Margot £40, taking friends out to dinner, buying clothes I *could* have done without but it seemed silly not to buy them with Fay Stephens going out of business and selling off very good things cheap . . . I went to bed early, v. tired, listened to a mediocre play, and fell asleep so depressed that I wept in my dreams. Minka kept waking me up as she has now developed the habit of doing: clawing my face every time she wants to change sides which she can do perfectly well on her own. But no, I must wake up, turn over on my back, so that she can settle on my shoulder.

   This afternoon I must go and see Hilda [Graef] in hospital, so the day has practically gone. However, Hilda goes back to Oxford on Thursday, so I won't have to go again, I think. I've been once a week since she went in – about 6 weeks ago.

29 Jan   Well, I *have* managed to keep going somehow on the book. Goodness knows how long it has taken me to do these last 30 pages.

7 March   For past 10 days break to re-paint workroom. Kathleen Raine and Audrey Beecham took a 'sortes' with a pendulum – should I ever finish the book? Kathleen's immediately and emphatically said 'yes'. Audrey's motionless at first, then revolved violently. 'Yes, but after preliminary difficulties.'

   The religious doubts worse than ever these last weeks. How *can* we *love* a God who can treat weak creatures so cruelly? The eternal, only problem as Père Maydieu said, how to reconcile omnipotence and all-goodness. And for me the appalling cruelty of nature in which creatures can only survive by devouring each other.

9 March   The workroom is done. The house next door [now a hotel] will, after all, be almost certainly pulled down. The stair-carpet still held up by 2 tenants refusing to pay 1/5.

I spent Tuesday with Clare [Nicholl]. I like her very much. I came back, of course, exhausted.

I have a mean, cold spirit. I could not share her enthusiasm for Elizabeth Myers. True, I only skimmed through a little memoir by Eleanor Farjeon. I can see she was heroic, dying of TB at 34 . . . I didn't like the writing itself in the quoted letters – I found it rather gushing and whimsical. I shrink instinctively from a certain kind of effusiveness. And the worst of these loving memoirs is that they present the subject as invariably marvellous and heroic, *all* sweetness and light and goodness. I *know* I'm being unfair. If anyone wrote that sort of memoir about me of course I should be delighted.

11 March After a frustrating morning yesterday – one of those maddening ones where you have made a definite appointment and wait whole morning ringing up the shop and workroom only to find they messed it up at their end, carpet cutter eventually arrived at 1.35 (due 10). I could not see Fr. Brodrick: the poor man is ill and may have to go to hospital.

12 March What *is* interesting nowadays is the apparent *thirst* for the spiritual – a real hunger and thirst for it which may so well be the 'spirit blowing where it listeth'. And side by side, this fearful violence, cruelty, destructiveness, a real sense of *evil* abroad in the world.

16 March In despair last night I turned to Tyrrell's *Lex Credendi*. It helped me more than anything, as it did after my return. Tyrrell is so honest. He is the one person, for me, who faces all the problems and does not just brush them aside – evil, suffering etc. and understands all my difficulties. He was tormented by them himself. But he emerges with faith and with an intense love of and commitment to Christ.

The last time I saw the doctor (Tuesday) he said there had been no more improvement in my hand. Had another X-ray. Doctor said he wished he hadn't seen it! Apparently that middle finger is pretty badly damaged. He said that in time it may become v. painful again.

I saw Mary Austin today. She has been gradually decreasing 'the box' and will stop at the end of the month (my birthday). But she wants me to go on going to her. I have had 6 months at Margot's expense: Mary thought at first that I would only need 3.

The big test — can I write again? — not faced yet. Last weeks occupied with re-decorating, cleaning etc. Relief not to have to go to any more doctors for a while — nearly 4 weeks to Ployé and 6 to Mary. Bigger relief still, a merciful lull and ray of light on the perpetual mental conflict over religion.

18 March   One of the worst days I have ever had on the book. At least 6 hours, without even one sentence added. Only maddening efforts to revise a *few words* of that Binesfield chapter . . .

28 March   Holy Week is always a restless time. I went to the liturgy as usual but I was only 'on the surface'.

1 April   Yesterday I was 68, the age at which my mother died. Had I known her now, how much more interested in her *as a person* I should have been. I should have *wanted* to know about her life, what she thought, what she felt. I suppose I have changed in that way, in wanting to understand other people.

Denys and Renée [Blakelock]† gave me a feast last night: it was a delightful evening. I always love going there or having Denys here. I agree with Clare about Renée, that she is a 'rare person, unclouded and serene'. And so wonderfully warm and kind. I really love her.

3 April   Suddenly, about 5, I was impelled to take down Aldous Huxley's *Perennial Philosophy* which I have not looked at for goodness knows how many years. I read — I admit dipping in here and there for what particularly interested me — for about 3 hours — utterly absorbed. The parallel between the Eastern mystics and the Western is so extraordinary that one simply cannot doubt that they are talking about the same thing.

Cordelia's poem (age 11?)

> The rushing, the brushing, the wind in your face
> The thudding of hooves
> And the quickening of pace
> Not so clear in your gaze

Blocked and dulled by a haze
You feel the horse move in a kind of daze
You are numb to the feel of the ups and the downs
The twists and the turns, the curves and the rounds
You feel only the thud of the galloping hooves
And the regular jolt of the horse as he moves.

7 April, 5.30 a.m.   Thank God for Father Brodrick. I spent 3 hours with him on Wednesday. I have never had such warmth, kindness, understanding and support from anyone, I think, certainly not from any priest. He really seems to understand all my doubts and says he hangs on himself by the skin of his teeth. He truly *loves* people. It is extraordinary to feel oneself loved.

He dealt summarily with the young, obviously well-meaning priest (Fr. Kelly) who wrote me that letter which had such a shattering effect. His efforts were like hitting one on the head with a hammer to cure a headache. Had I been alone that day, it wd. have reduced me to a terrible state and I am still a bit shaken. I'd be only too glad to take Fr. K.'s totally impractical advice to 'take a job'.

12 April   Yesterday, astonishingly, I produced 3 pages – more than I have done for months. True some of it was old draft reworked. I let myself 'waffle on' without correcting, though it kept going off the track and I had not put in what I meant to put in. This coincided with the arrival of my new distance glasses. Any connection? It is certainly a relief to be able to see the world clearly again.

There was a great change in Lel [Earnshaw Smith] . . . when I saw him for our birthday dinner [near his retirement home]. He looked old and bent, could hardly drag himself up the hill and has also been having heart trouble. I am lucky to be as well as I am.

Fr. Kelly's advice was not sensible . . . but there was something in his 'Cut out perfection'. I am *not* a genius with great powerful creative impulses and rich imagination. I have a very small, limited talent . . . I have an ambition to be something more than a writer at 'Women's Magazine' level. As a result, for something like 17 years, I have produced nothing but one not very good short story and the beginnings of novels etc.

As regards religion – I just hold on in the simplest feeblest way –

supported by the faith of *others*, like Father Brodrick's. I feel that my beloved Abbé [de] Tourville must have been very much like him.

I think I had a goodish session with Ployé this morning. He gave me a full hour and even talked quite a bit in the last part. I *think* he regards the inability to write as the main trouble, as I do.

I talked of my troubles over trying to breast-feed Sue. He thought I had never mentioned her before and quite likely I haven't. He wanted to know all the circumstances of her birth . . . I said I had lost the ability to cry. He asked me if something inside me was 'crying' – I said it certainly was! Just as I was going I remembered my recurring dream – that I have a baby and have forgotten about the poor little thing. It is shut up in a cupboard somewhere . . . In the dream it is not always a baby, sometimes it is a kitten.

Money has never come up in this analysis as it did all the time with Carroll. Yet money is of huge importance to me – witness its endless recurrence in these notebooks.

I think I must have felt deprived of something important in childhood for money to have such excessive importance to me. Yet, if it had been the thing I valued most, I could have made much more by sticking to advertising. I had a big chance at Crawford's if I'd chosen to take it – but I couldn't treat it with the passion, the almost religious reverence the advertising pundits do.

What *did* I feel deprived of in childhood? What I notice most about my grandchildren was that they felt free to ask for something if they wanted it. It simply would not have occurred to me to *ask* my parents for anything, especially my father. My mother might have been more sympathetic but I always knew she couldn't give me anything, having no money of her own. My father could be very generous about things he thought I *needed* – also about presents – but I was never *asked* what I wanted and I would not have dared to suggest what I would like. My appalling guilt when I ran up a debt of 1/6 and got the money out of him by a lie. Even when I was grown-up I never told him about this episode.

26 *April*   On Saturday I had a wonderful evening with Charlotte – alone. Have only done this twice since she reappeared in my life. She interests me more than anyone I know. I have immense *respect* for her mind. It still seems to me the best of any woman's I know. I think it is

rare for women to *think* in the way that she does . . . She reminds me of
Eric. When I said I wished she had written, since she is so gifted for it,
she said, just as he does, 'Someone has got to be the audience.'

9 May   Last night I had that recurring dream about being reconciled
to Silas. This time, when I had given up hope, we did embrace.
Usually I wake realizing it is too late: it can never happen. I wonder
why I go on having this dream so often in the last months. Perhaps
not surprising yesterday. Sue arrived in England and it was Si who
met her at the airport and drove her to West Hoathly.

After the childish elation of having managed to write a trivial little
article, I am wrestling again with my book. I sit nearly all day at my
desk, smoking far too many cigarettes, listening to radio, doing a
crossword puzzle, reading a little perhaps, breaking off for an
afternoon lie-down. What ridiculous routine.

Read Margaret Drabble's *Jerusalem the Golden. Very* disappointing
– I thought very poor. Up to now I've thought her good.

19 May   Sue is coming for the night. It was wonderful to see her
again last Friday. She looked radiant, incredibly young, hardly more
than 16. She was very sweet. I longed to have more chance to talk to
her. I wish I could have a few days of her to myself – there is so much I
would like to talk over with her and hear *her* talk about. Both my
daughters are a delight to me and I love them.

19 May [sic]   It was wonderful having Sue for the night. There is no
one I more enjoy talking to. Apart from all her charm, good looks
and intelligence, she still thank goodness has this peculiar quality that
she had when she was a girl – what I used to call the 'streak of
platinum' – and which I can't define. It is a kind of severity or
integrity – something which makes me value her judgement – and
did, even when she was very young – more than almost anyone's. In a
way it is like the peculiar quality, also indefinable, that makes
Charlotte a unique person in my life. Charlotte's is just the same at 70
as it was at 13 or 14.

Sue said that Thomas says that he wishes he had a sense of the
supernatural but that it is something he has never had.

23 May   I was much touched to have a note from Charlotte in Cornwall saying that I was 'on her mind'. It took me 2 whole hours on Sunday morning to write a short note in reply. I wanted to say how much I enjoyed that evening but rejected word after word for fear it sounded too gushing. But I was so touched by her letter – she loathes writing letters even more than I do. She even began 'Dearest Tadpole'.

30 May   Georgie rang up and talked for an hour and a quarter. A most extraordinary conversation; she wanted to know all about my religious doubts and of course nothing could be more difficult to try and explain on the telephone.

I did manage to do a little work after, though it *was* a very long interruption. G. is odd in that way when you're working – but then most people are.

Another letter from Mother Gertrude this morning. So kind, but oh dear, so very nearly dotty. Hilda's book on T[eresa] N[eumann], German girl who received the stigmata in the present century: *The Case of Thérèse Neumann*, 1950] was a fine bit of research and showed what *she* thought of Teresa Neumann. I've always thought her a bit fishy myself. But Maritain was truly impressed by her. You get these anomalies all the time. And things like Fatima and La Salette. The Pope went to Fatima for the 50th anniversary of the apparition a few weeks ago. Thank goodness apparitions aren't articles of faith. And look at the tremendous spread, encouraged by every Pope, of devotion to the Sacred Heart, based on the vision of St Margaret Mary.

31 May   It was so strange meeting Teddy [Wolfe, painter] at Marjorie Villiers' party after all these years. I don't think I had seen him since – I suppose it was in the 1930s. When he did that drawing of me his studio then was that very one where I went out of my mind in 1922. I liked the pictures very much – amazing what a range he has and what rich exuberant colour. Richard Hughes was there. I'd never met him before. I could talk about *High Wind* [*in Jamaica*] but of course I felt bad about not having read *The Fox in the Attic*. He must feel as I do about *Frost* – everyone connects him only with *High Wind*. Still I was glad I went to this party, though yesterday I'd really rather have tried to get on with the book. The morning was too short and much interrupted by Gladys with accounts of her brother's illness. I can't stop her and I do indeed sympathize but I really can no longer settle down while she's here as she keeps coming in and interrupting me on various pretexts and there is usually about 20 minutes at the end when she comes in for a general chat. Tomorrow I have to go to Marmonstein to change my will. Thank goodness I did at last get a chance to explain the situation about Elaine [Lingham] to Sue. She [Sue] definitely wants to be the only person to cope with my papers. I told her all about the notebooks. It was a relief and she was very sweet and understanding. I haven't anything to leave my children, really, but what there is or might be from books or even MSS should be fairly arranged for – Sue is the best person to handle everything.

4 June Mary Siepmann rang up just when I was going to rest. I'd been up since 5 and working several hours on the book so was very tired. But I did want to see her and she came with her son Billy. I was absurdly tired after and had to lie down at 5.30. It's stupid to be so exhausted after 1½ hours conversation. But I *had* been up a long time. Ridiculous how I hate sudden, unexpected arrivals, even of people I like as much as Mary. If only they'd let me know the day before so that I could fix things.

There can never have been so much unrest in the Church since the days of Modernism. Priests leaving, getting married, being excommunicated. Priest editors being sacked. Dominicans in trouble, especially in Holland . . . Cardinal Heenan has no use whatever for the 'intellectual Catholic' – he wants everyone to be the docile sheep we were brought up to be.

9 June Seeing Lady MacAlister yesterday *did* depress me. I suppose it was because she brought up again her disapproval of the way I wrote about my father. She had this privileged situation with my father when she was a girl: beautiful, intelligent, favourite pupil, and with quite a claim to having influenced his conversion. Though I was only a child, she *may* have envied me for being his daughter. Moreover she wanted to write and did write bits and pieces before she married, not up to much. But my father encouraged her to write.

She may secretly have wanted to go on writing: obviously impossible with a husband and 7 children. Hence, perhaps this amused air of condescension plus implied *moral* disapproval – well, *more* than implied! She has had many sorrows – 2 sons killed and one disabled in the last war – but had 48 years of exceedingly happy marriage – and what I suppose I envy anyone, a blameless, straightforward life of which *no one* could disapprove.

12 June Yesterday I forced myself somehow to write to Amanda [Hopkinson]: writing letters becomes more and more of an effort but I'd left her very good one unanswered for a month. I also made myself go to the Children of Mary. It may result in my going to this Dogma Conference as Woldingham [new premises of Roehampton Sacred Heart]'s representative. Fearful indecision on my part, of course . . . A *very* interesting programme – might tell me much I want to know about what we *are* supposed to believe nowadays. All the top J[esuit]s from Heythrop. Where Charles Davis was teaching theology!!

23 June It is no good. Trying to write gets more and more hopeless. I daren't think how many weeks have gone by with nothing added. I devote Sundays to letters – which are almost as much a nightmare as writing – or trying to write – this infernal book. I can do nothing but *begin* things. They peter out to a dead stop and I am left with an enormous block . . . With Ployé yesterday I said I just wanted to sink back – not to have to do *anything* – to retire. And yet I also hate the idea of being dependent. One part of my mind feels very much alive in spite of everything. But it doesn't know what to *use* itself on.

I drug myself – cigarettes – radio - crossword puzzles – scraps of haphazard reading. In a sense I only live for the moment when I go to bed . . . I make no effort to do anything – see films, see friends (unless they actually ring up) as if my time were precious and must be preserved, even from ordinary pleasures. But for WHAT.

25 June An odd dream last night. Reggie again . . . we seemed to be still married. He asked me to give him a pound. I did, but said 'I'm not going to keep you.' I was living in a curious bed sitting room, small, very Victorian looking . . . After I had given Reggie the pound, he walked off across the park with his arm round another woman. I gathered they were going to stay at some expensive hotel. I felt free of responsibility to Reggie and that I could leave the bed sitting room and go back to my own flat. It was a joy to remember I had one.

I spent nearly 3 hours writing to Edythe Echols – duty letter – she wanted comments on her story. I did my best: doubt if it'll help her or if she'll really understand what I was trying to say. I don't think it's any good with some people. It's like my cousin Helen who also 'wants to write'. You *can't* teach them what they haven't got. Both she and Mrs Echols haven't got a sense of *form*.

1 July   Last night again one of those 'marriage' dreams. This time I was marrying an Indian. He put his arm round me and smiled. 'Now you are getting quite used to it.' I felt absolutely confident in him as if I had always known him and we were real friends.

3 July   I had yet *another* 'marriage' dream. This time it was to Alan Walker – a new one. I've never dreamt of Alan Walker. Of course I might have married him and very nearly did. At any rate we were engaged, but I married Eric instead. Why *do* I keep having these 'marriage' dreams? This was quite a sober, realistic one; not romantic. Just two elderly people who were fond of each other getting married for companionship. Maybe because I spent so much time yesterday reading Monica Dickens' *Winds of Heaven* . . . She's an excellent 'good bad writer'. And of course it ends with the elderly lonely widow marrying an elderly lonely man.

It's 6.25. I will go to Mass after all instead of trying to work. I enjoyed seeing Hilda . . . She doesn't really understand my religious problems – how can she, since I can't express them clearly even to myself?

20 July   Miranda was born at 2.50 a.m. on 15th at Cuckfield Hospital. I saw Sue and the baby on Monday. Sue looked wonderful but I think she was feeling tired. She did not have a bad time having the baby: only 1½ hours of the worst. Miranda slept all the time. She is a beautiful baby – looks much more than 2 days old: her skin clear and not red or mottled and she already has a face. Beautiful hands with

long fingers, like Sue's as a baby. I liked Fr. Russell [a Theologian]
who came last Friday very much . . .

I saw Ployé this morning. He thought it a good sign that for the
first time I wore my hearing-aid. The whole core of my problem does
seem to be my guilt if I *don't* write and my inability to produce
anything when I do.

Tonight I thought quite seriously of breaking off the book for a bit
and writing a sequel to *Minka and Curdy*. Nothing *wrong* in this but of
course I feel I *oughtn't* to. I may be getting another translation. First
approach for one yesterday. Book hasn't arrived. Didn't awfully like
the man who talked to me on the phone . . . Felt there was something
a little queer and suspicious about it all.

24 July   Douglas McClean† died about 2 weeks ago. The McCleans
were so much part of my life. I've known them for over 40 years. It is
terrible for Kathleen. I wrote to her – what *can* one say? – and was
surprised and very touched to get a most moving and warm letter
back.

The Scottish widow who had (I think really had) known Mr and
Mrs Coutts has proved to be a 'con' lady. She conned me and, alas,
conned Mrs Rennick too. I 'lent' her £5, little knowing that poor Mrs
Rennick had already lent her £2. She was certainly good at her job!

Fr. Russell has sent me many articles of his. I don't really think
they'll help much – partly because I'm no philosopher. I feel more
and more confused about 'dogma', 'articles of faith' and all the rest.

I have made an attempt to begin the sequel to *M[inka] and
C[urdy]*. Even that is difficult. But I think I will go on and try to do it.
At least it is entirely unconnected with religion.

26 July   Unexpectedly had to cope with 3 letters about religion. A
distressed one from Amanda who is in an acute state of depression.
This involved a long letter to her and a short one to Father Brodrick
who could perhaps help her. The third was to an unknown lady . . .
She wrote me 6 pp. after reading *The H. and the F.*, describing her own
– obviously sincere – experience of 'finding the Lord Jesus' and
certainty of Salvation. She is anti-Catholic. Firmly convinced that
there is no purgatory but that those who refuse Jesus Christ will burn
for ever in hell.

What are my main troubles? The problem of evil, of course. How could it ever arise? In Catholic theology, the devil was the highest angel, intellectually far above any human being, *knowing* God. How if God were infinite goodness and truth could this being deliberately rebel against Him?

This glib assertion 'suffering is the result of sin' – what does it MEAN? It seems patently untrue. Animals do not sin but they suffer ...

The whole doctrine of atonement. Does Christ ever even mention it? *Or* original sin? The idea of punishing wretched weak creatures (who CAN suffer) for offending a God who by definition cannot be injured in any way by their 'offence' and is incapable of suffering ...

Is God *only* interested in 'morality'? It is awfully hard not to feel that Santayana may be right – that the Catholic religion, *all* religions are 'inventions'.

27 July   Nothing for it but to go on 'as if'.

Interesting that Marx definitely said he was *not* an atheist.

14 August   I'm not going to the Dogma, mainly owing to a series of absurd muddles on the part of the Roehampton Association. I cannot help being relieved. With my deafness etc. it would have been almost impossible to cope with discussion groups . . . I spent nearly all yesterday reading Huxley's *Perennial Philosophy* again. It must be one of the best books ever written on religion. Without looking at the names, one could swear that a passage *must* come from an Eastern writer and it turns out to be a Christian. I think it helped me more than any Dogma course.

I always come back to the Garden of Eden. I do not think people really grasp yet the difference that the fact [we] are now, after nearly 2000 years of having to believe it as *literally* and *historically* true allowed to believe it a symbolic myth makes to the whole of Catholic theology. It is interesting that nowhere in the Gospels does Christ refer to Original Sin – only to *sins*. But of course the *content* of the myth is true, that in this world man has lost his true relationship to God through his desire for autonomy and fallen into utter darkness and confusion from which only God can save him, if man is willing to co-operate.

There was a 'portrait' of Evelyn Waugh on the radio. Some rather frightening things. There was no doubt that his Catholicism was genuine and meant much to him. In becoming a Catholic, he certainly thought at the time that he could never marry again. Yet how extraordinarily, even savagely uncharitable he could be and how he seemed to cling to the outward forms. It is hard not to think he regarded it in some ways as a kind of aristocratic club in which the 'peasantry' were tolerated but on no account the vulgar middle class. He *could* of course be wonderfully charitable and patient in his giving any amount of time and trouble to Moray McLaren to get him on his feet again as a man and a writer. His friends certainly loved him, in spite of his cruelty. Yet what arrogance! One tells a story of how some American woman said at lunch how much she liked *Brideshead*. He said '*I* like it but who cares if a common, boring American woman like you likes it?' And he was entirely unrepentant. I think Nancy Mitford describes how at lunch in Paris to which she had invited a young French writer who was an ardent admirer of E.W.'s he was so abominably rude to him that both the writer and his hostess were reduced to tears. Afterwards she said to him, 'How *could* you behave like that? I thought you were a Catholic.' He said: 'I should be much worse if I weren't.'

Ian Fleming's wife described a fortnight he spent with them – in Jamaica? – during Lent. E.W. insisted on a lobster for lunch every day (difficult to procure). It had to weight *exactly* 2 lbs – no more and no less. He was furious if his evening meal consisted of only 2 courses instead of 5.

19 August   I saw this notice in Earl's Court on a Volkswagen mini-bus:

Wanted Girl to share large room with student (male) and after-wards go round the world in this VW. Girl must

1) Have a pleasing personality
2) Show consideration for others
3) Have a passionate interest in 'biological urges'

NO MONEY REQUIRED

31 August   I go to Ployé today. As so often the night before a session I have an obviously 'psychological' dream. I was with a party . . . the hostess took us to an exhibition, one of the exhibits was a model submarine. It lay at the bottom of a kind of swimming bath and to get inside the submarine you had to go down a steep iron ladder. I went down rung by rung into the depths. At one point there was a gap in the rungs and nothing to tread on but a kind of handle, like a stop-cock. I called up to the man behind me about this. I said 'It seems a kind of pump handle and I wonder what happens if you tread on it, perhaps it turns something on or off.' I know one suggestion that either he or I made was that it cut off the air supply to the people in the submarine.

1 Sept   Ployé certainly *was* interested in this dream . . . I told him how extraordinarily the unconscious used actual happenings as a basis for a significant dream. We have no hot water because the tank on the roof went dry owing to a ball-cock jamming and the gas heater cracked the cylinder of its boiler as a result.

He interpreted the whole thing as a pre-natal trauma that at some time in the womb the supply to the foetus through the umbilical cord had been cut off – 'a matter of life and death' he said, which would cause acute anxiety. From the first both Galway and Ployé have had the idea that my trouble went back to some pre-natal experience which has always seemed very strange to me but they may be right.

Anyhow this idea of a blockage or jamming is always how I describe my writing trouble and the accompanying anxiety is of course acute.

In all this talk about the plumbing I said how glad we were to find that it did not need a tremendous job to locate and cure the trouble, as it was quite a simple operation to deal with the jammed ball-cock.

On the way home I tried to think what could represent the 'ball-cock' that had got jammed. The first word that came into my head was religion . . .

My eyes which have been behaving very well lately are suddenly sore and inflamed. No doubt the dear old unconscious again, since it was a particularly bad bout of this 2 years ago which made me go to the doctor and started up the whole psychiatric business. Presumably they're trying to stop me working today . . .

4 Sept   My eyes *did* clear up. I wrote several pp. on Friday in spite of them and yesterday they were all right again. So it *must* have been the dear old unconscious.

I have misgivings about H. [publisher]. I've never had anyone so slippery to deal with in spite of all this 'bonhomie'. I'm tempted not to do it but I need the money. I've never had so much trouble with a publisher over a translation.

Elizabeth Maclaren [a student friend] came to see me yesterday. An enchanting girl, highly intelligent and pretty as well. She is going to do a 3-year theology course at Edinburgh having already done philosophy and classics. She wants to work 'in Church in the world'. I could talk to her absolutely frankly about religion – her difficulties are just the same as mine. She told me that she had never experienced *fear* of God. Also that if God is the tyrant he is so often represented to be, she would not *want* to 'save her skin' by kow-towing out of fear of going to hell. I found her *much* more help than people like Fr. Russell. It was really refreshing to meet someone so genuinely eager for *truth*.

6 Sept   I had lunch with Anne Morgan [Eric Earnshaw Smith's much younger cousin] yesterday. I admire her very much. She has a very hard time looking after her two old parents doing a part-time job and desperately trying to get on with her painting. We talked about art – also religion. We *all* seem to have the same difficulties nowadays. She was saying how much 'Williams' rang her bell. I thought the one article that really rang mine in *The God I Want* was by a Williams. I find it is H.A. Williams.

Yesterday I managed somehow to finish that *M[inka] and C[urdy]* chapter. I did what I haven't done for months, probably years – I sat up till 10.30 determined to finish it. I'm worrying if it's poor – it probably is. The thing is that I finished it and have written about 60 pp.in 6 weeks.

Last night I had another marriage dream. This time my husband was Basil Nicholson. It was an extraordinarily happy dream and strangely realistic. Basil was just like himself in his best moods, dry and cynical in his manner, with his harsh croaking voice, but genuinely affectionate. I said 'You aren't committed for life; I'm so old that you ought to be able to marry again in five years at the most.' He said thoughtfully, with his friendliest smile 'No, I think you ought to last at least eight.' I felt wonderfully happy and at ease with

Silas Glossop, Susan's father, in later years in his flat in Warwick Square

Susan and Cordelia, aged two and a half

Lyndall Hopkinson in Rome in the early '50s

Thomas Hinde, in Sussex, at about the time Antonia first met her grandchildren

Left: Andrew, aged ten in West Hoathly. *Right:* Cordelia, aged four in the garden in Nairobi

The Great Donkey Walk. Thomas and Susan Chitty set out to walk the breadth of southern Europe from North-West Spain to Smyrna, a distance of at least 6000 kilometres. *Left*: Jessica with Hamilcar, the donkey she rode. *Below right*: Recorder trio in the Appenines. Andrew, left, Miranda, centre, and Cuthie, a visitor. *Below left*: South of Cahors

Antonia at a wedding in
1950 with friends
(unknown)

Sr Madaleva, Antonia and
two pupils at St Mary's
College, Indiana

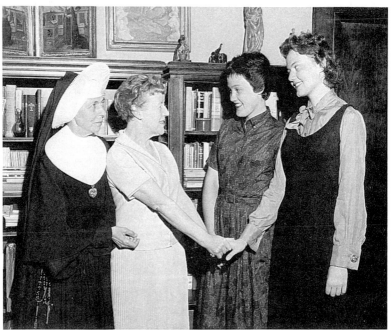

Antonia in her room at St Mary's

Antonia aged sixty-five, at Courtfield Gardens, with Minka

One of the last photographs of Antonia, by Thomas Hinde, at Courtfield Gardens

Novelist
Antonia White
(Eirene Botting)
1899–1980
LIVED HERE
1899–1921

The plaque in Perham Road, Kensington, put up by the local council

Susan Chitty, photographed recently by a neighbour, Jenny Ripley

Susan at a party given by David and Periwinkle Unwin in the 1970s

him and looking forward to our life together. There was no sexual approach in the dream but we were certainly going to sleep together – it was not to be a *mariage blanc* . . . He even suggested our going into a church together. Characteristically he would not kneel beside me but told me where to kneel and then went and knelt somewhere else. Basil was so absolutely like himself in the way he talked, looked and behaved. This is very rare in these marriage dreams. He once said to me 'You have no sense of self-preservation.' He could have said the same of himself.

26 Sept   I went to see Fr. Brodrick this morning. He and Amanda have struck up a great friendship. He wrote to Clare: 'Her soul is as beautiful as her body.' He looked very frail himself . . .

He kept saying my troubles were 'emotional'. But I don't think this is so. It is dogma that worries me. He did admit that it's very difficult nowadays to know what the Church *does* teach. He also keeps going back, as Hilda does, to my having been taught it all too rigidly.

We were really on happier ground with Keats whom he *loves* and says was a non-Christian saint. What I love in Fr. B. is that he recognizes the good wherever he finds it, whether in or out of Christianity. I told him how much I liked what little I've read of H.A. Williams. I was delighted that he said *The True Wilderness* was marvellous.

I said, should I confess 'doubts'? He said, not to confess them, just what I feel and know to be sins, uncharitableness etc. and make an act of contrition for the sins of my past life. He thinks it's 'so good' that I go on going to the sacraments. Dear man! He thinks the best of everyone! He thinks I am so brave because I went through the blitz in London. I told him that it wasn't nearly so upsetting as the inner assaults in the bad days of mental breakdown. But he does encourage me because he's so *good*. I am tremendously attracted by goodness, especially when it goes with understanding and love and . . . no other word . . . holiness. He makes people like Eric, for all their intelligence, seem shallow.

28 Sept   Ployé agreed with my association of 'religion' with the jammed ball-cock in the 'tank' dream. Also pointed out what I'd obviously already noticed – the male sexual symbol. Suggested that the pre-natal shock might have been during sexual intercourse between my parents when my mother was pregnant. He asked quite a lot about the writing jam. I told him again, since it came up about the trouble with my first 'novel' and my father, also about Tom and *Frost in May* and how jam since then comes when I've done a few chapters, as at first 'novel'. Also association of writing with loss of love (Tom, Sue) and feeling something bad comes out in my writing wh. will alienate those I love. I said some of the obvious things about religion – that Catholicism was 'forced' on me at 7 by my father – also about the 'brain-washing' of a convent education. I feel I never had a free choice as regards religion. Also that I suffer, and always have, from constant anxiety. Obviously not always acute but even if things are going well I am never wholly free from it: even if I'm happy, I soon feel guilty. Catholic training obviously greatly increased this anxiety.

I wonder now if the episode of my father coming home drunk some time in the first year of their marriage that my mother endlessly told me about, so it must have made a great impression on her, had something to do with my supposed pre-natal experience? He might well have had, or tried to have, intercourse with her then. I *think* she said it was at Christmas time, though I'm not sure [Antonia was born on 31 March].

7 Oct   Did manage to finish and revise Part I. Interesting woman came to see me yesterday: Anne David, Frenchwoman who returned to Church after reading Tyrrell and is now devoting all her time to studying him and writing about him.

9 Oct   Miranda was baptized yesterday. She behaved angelically all through and seemed to take a most intelligent interest in it all. The priest, Fr. Jerome OSB was so sweet and gentle with her. Thomas actually came and behaved beautifully though he kept his head averted during the actual baptizing. Isabel Quigly and Charles Hodgson were the godparents and I think Cordelia was deputizing for Amanda. Mim and A.K. were there too. We had a nice family tea-party after. Fr. Jerome came and stayed several hours. I liked him very much – could talk to him quite easily about the Eternal Problem. I'm glad he approves of H.A.Williams too.

Sue is so adorable with the baby. Her face is absolutely radiant when she looks at her. And Thomas is so sweet with her too: he holds her so confidently and firmly and she so obviously feels absolutely secure and happy in her father's arms.

I travelled back in the train with Charles Hodgson. He has made great friends with Si. He told me that Si was talking of me only the other day with real affection. I think Charles was telling the truth for he was very circumstantial and said things which only Si and I would know about in our past. I was very touched.

I could not sleep when I got back. Lay awake for 2 hours, then got up and smoked till after 2 a.m. Bad nights are mercifully unusual for me these days.

11 Oct   I begin to dread letters from Hilda Graef, much as I like her. I wish we could tacitly drop the subject of religion. She keeps assuring me that I still cling to what she calls the nuns' stupid teaching. What she does not realize is that it was not just 'the nuns' who presented Catholicism like that; it was the official teaching in every Catholic school and from every pulpit. I am not as theologically ignorant as she thinks – after all I've been in close touch with people like Fr. Victor and Père Maydieu, read a great deal, spent 2 or 3 years on St Thomas [Aquinas] alone.

25 Oct   A curious dream last night . . .

I was being married – of all people – to my childhood love, Gérard . . . the dream dovetailed into another recurring one, that of going back to live with my parents at Perham Road, but as a grown-up person, more or less my present age.

27 Oct   Another odd dream last night: a very vivid nightmare from which I was very glad indeed to wake up. I dreamt that I murdered both my grandparents [her father's parents, who lived near her childhood home] and I felt I must confess it. I thought it would be easier to tell my mother first. We were having tea in some hotel and my father was momentarily out of the room. I said to her: 'I've done something dreadful and I must tell you about it.' She said 'Not here, people might hear you, wait till we're somewhere quieter.' I wished she would have let me tell her there and then and get it off my mind. I also thought that it might be discovered. I remembered that there was another door to the room, leading into the kitchen, and this I had not locked, so that someone might go in and find the bodies. Again, if they were left there, they would begin to decompose.

19 Nov   Finished revising the last MS pages of *Minne* [by Colette, translated as *The Innocent Libertine*, 1968] . . . The whole job (266 pp) has taken 74 days . . .

20 Nov   What *do* people believe in their inmost minds? If God is omnipotent, could He not reveal himself in a way we *could* understand?

In spite of all this, the sense of Christ being *real* persists. I go on feebly trying to pray.

I just cannot concentrate for hours a day on prayer: I am quite incapable of it. If I were truly spiritual, I could.

Switched on wireless just now and interesting account by a woman of a session with the Maharishi. A friend took her to a hotel where he was holding interviews. An Indian boy took her name and address, told her the usual offering was (I *think*) £5. She was horrified, having only £2 on her, and 3 days to go before her next pay-packet so she finally left £1. Boy looked disapproving.

The M. received people one by one. The room was heavy with smell of sandalwood. He held a single flower. She said he had a mane of hair, looked very kind, seemed a gentle, good person. He questioned her about herself, then told her to go to the Meditation Room and concentrate on a single syllable for ½ hour.

Med. Room was in darkness, except for one blue shaded lamp. About 40 people there – mostly office workers. Total silence. She meditated on her one syllable: found usual clutter of thoughts disappeared and she went into a kind of semi-hypnotic trance and had to be tapped on shoulder when her half hour was up and she had to go back to the M. and report. He told her to keep it up daily, that through doing so she got in touch with deep spiritual source in herself and could combat 'negative influences'.

She was half convinced, half sceptical, did try to meditate on her own for a time but not regularly: eventually felt it was dangerous without supervision.

For 2 years afterwards she regularly received begging letters asking for either money, a house for the M., free services for household chores or typing.

N.B. Why do all religions come from the East – I mean the spiritual kind?

The West seems to have produced only primitive and practical ones – the gods of Valhalla, the heroes etc.

23 Nov I had a wonderful evening with Sue – too short, of course, for we only talked for about 1½ hour over dinner, but it was so lovely to see her. Somehow we got on to religion. I said, too much I feared, about my doubts – even that I sometimes felt it would be more honest to leave the Church. And I said much what I said to Fr. Brodrick, how it would be so distressing to people I love – Sue, of course, most of all – and perhaps shake *their* faith. Sue says *she* cannot pray either. But like me, she does have that moment of mental peace and conviction at Communion.

Most interesting about Andrew [aged fourteen]. In America he went every Sunday, entirely on his own, to the Episcopalian church. Now he is interested in Catholicism. So he is being instructed both by the local Anglican vicar *and* by Fr. Jerome so that he can compare and make up his mind. Fr. J. comes every Sunday and he, Sue and Andrew have a talk and discussion and A. asks all the questions he wants. The boy is *so* intelligent. I should love to listen to these discussions. Oddly enough, friends of Sue's are trying to interest her in the Maharishi . . . You meditate every day on one word and that puts you in touch with 'the Kingdom of God within you'. After that you go through the day able to do everything you normally do successfully. Suffering is unnecessary. Someone in the audience asked about Christ's suffering. The M. said that Christ did not know that suffering was unnecessary.

Sue felt it all very fishy . . .

It is the same in idea, in a way as Ouspensky etc. but obviously much simplified.

27 Nov Kathleen Raine actually met the Maharishi a year or two ago. What impressed her most was that he was 'so full of joy'.

Ployé and Austin today.

18 Dec It is a wonderful thing having children and grandchildren!
Sue and Thomas and all three of them came yesterday and we had a
lovely, muddly kind of anticipation of Christmas. Nothing could be
more unlike my prim old-maidish normal way of life: everything all
over the place, the baby being fed and changed, catch-as-catch-can
picnic meals . . . Cordelia and Andrew sang carols and Thomas sang
with them. They are an enchanting *family*. Thomas is marvellous
with the baby, handling her and feeding her most expertly and Sue is
so adorable with her, so radiant and tender and so careful about
everything to do with her welfare. And the two elder children are so
sweet with her – they really love her. No wonder she is such a happy
baby. She's so intelligent too – quite extraordinary for five months. I
can't imagine any better parents than Sue and Thomas. These young
modern parents who share coping with the baby and the domestic
chores are really splendid . . . Sue and Thomas put me to shame when
I think of my own selfishness and cowardice. It is wonderful to see
Sue so radiant and *fulfilled* – after the bad start she had in life and her
many troubles. I wish I could see Lyndall as happy. She is so sweet
and generous – sent me a huge cheque and a magnificent pair of
gloves for Christmas. But there does seem some hope that at last she
has found the right man, though I fear it is doubtful if they can marry.

28 Dec This morning, having just polished off those Christmas
letters, some 15, there comes a letter from Mr [John] Broom,† just as
last year! Well as I wish him, I did rather hope I'd shaken off *that*
correspondence! And here he is again, a good deal nearer becoming a
Catholic being instructed by a severe, but he says unmistakably holy
priest, who advised caution, not being convinced yet that B. *really*
believes in the Incarnation. And of course poor B. is once again in
mental tumult. How I sympathize with him!

30 Dec Somehow I managed to write 6 pp. to Broom. I sympathize
very much with his difficulties but it is the blind leading the blind. A
priest now suggests he may have a vocation to the priesthood.
  Reading through this year I realize how really awful the writing
jam was in the first 6 months. Still I *did* manage to do 60 odd pages of
M[inka] and C[urdy] before and after translating. I did finish *Minne*
ahead of time and must now try to do same with *Chandelle* [*The*

Candle, Thérèse de Saint Phalle, 1968] – have done about 50 pp. Both these books real chores – poor, boring stuff – but the money is a godsend.

I'm getting used to being old and not worrying too much about ambition to be a good writer. Mentally, the religious conflict is the most trying. I like ordinary things and people and cannot be *really* attracted to saints.

31 Dec   I have spent the last day of the year reading Kathleen Raine's autobiography. It is one of the most remarkable books I have ever read. Her nature *is* very unlike mine: I am altogether a more earthy and literal kind of person and not a poet, still less convinced of being a 'high-born' soul. If I have anything to criticize it is *perhaps* what seems like a contempt for the ordinary person.

1968

1 Jan   It is terrible that it [Kathleen Raine's autobiography] cannot be published yet. At first it made me feel there was no point in even trying to go on with my own autobiographical book: it seemed so trivial compared to K.'s. Yet now it oddly encourages me.

6 Jan   I have heard this morning that poor Lel died on Dec 29th. He has been a person in my life since those two years he spent with me in Ashburn Gardens. I had to tell Eric. He had been half-expecting it too, but I could hear he was shaken. He was very fond of Lel in the old days. He probably feels responsible, as well as sorry, for he did rather neglect him. Luckily I think Lel had got over his resentment against Eric (some money trouble I couldn't really follow).

18 Jan   Ployé today. I have never seen him so pleased: he seldom shows any feeling. It was at the very last moment of the session – I was actually putting on my shoes and his next patient was waiting. I'd talked mainly about the fear of slipping on ice, letting myself go in any way, Kathleen Raine's reference to me in her book as being so careful in my movements . . . as if I were carrying a glass, afraid to break it. We didn't seem to be getting anywhere much. Miscarriages and abortions came in somewhere: he related them to my unfinished books as I do too. Sleep came in too – once again this time I nearly dozed off. Always before, he's said 'sleep if you want to' but I've felt it wd. be wasting his time.

I said there was an image that had always haunted me . . . the traveller who must not lie down in the snow and sleep or he will die. His face brightened almost schoolboyishly; he made red lines by his final note. He said 'Now I know what you're up against: you really *want* to go to sleep and die.' I said *eagerly* – '*Yes* – beautiful oblivion.'

21 Jan Wonderful to see Lyndall yesterday after nearly four years. I don't feel altogether happy about this new man [Count Lorenzo Passserini†]. For one thing, he is not free to marry and there are complications about possible annulments. For another he does not want children, though very fond of them. Also he is 24 years older than she is. Also she says he is a 'muddler' and has no definite profession or interest – that he is 'like a child' and needs 'amusing' all the time and that she has to 'nag' him. She *looks* very well, thank goodness, and very young. But she still has these migraines, though not so often.

In the night I had really severe cramp. A taste of real pain. One feels utterly helpless with it. How would I ever endure severe *prolonged* pain? L[yndall] says her friend's sister has had 2 years of agonizing pain with cancer and no drug can relieve it because of the side-effects. It's no good: how can God allow such terrible suffering and the Church forbid euthanasia? It does not forbid killing people in war. Or capital punishment.

26 Jan Curious dreams about cats. In the first one both Minka and Curdy were dead and their bodies were in a lidded basket, covered with dirty rags, some stained with menstrual blood. Then I seemed to die myself. I came to, as it were in heaven, but it was a very simple childish heaven, like earth, only pleasanter. I was very relieved about this and thought 'There was nothing to be afraid of after all after death.' Minka and Curdy were there too looking young cats again, full of life, with their coats clean and shining as if newly washed.

20 Feb   At last I've finished that awful Thérèse de Saint Phalle translation. The book is both preposterous and feeble: incredible what *does* get published nowadays.

Now I have no excuse not to get on with the cat book. Funny cats have featured so much in last dreams.

Last week I went with Denys to dine with a woman (Dorothy Alexander) whom I met years ago with Malcolm Williamson and a friend of Denys' called I think Wm. Glender-Pöl. This young man formerly in BBC had had a violent conversion, tried to become a Dominican: left. He is now going to marry D[orothy] A[lexander] but doesn't seem to worry at all that she's divorced and they can't marry as Catholics though he seems very devout. He is living with her at the moment.

10 March   Last Saturday an enchanting young nun, Sr. Hélène Thériault (White Sister) came to tea with me. She's actually written a thesis about my books!! Looks 20, is 29. A radiant little thing, full of life and warmth – very unlike most nuns. She doesn't appear to be worried at all about dogma etc. She simply says 'I'm committed to a Person.' She says that if, in the end, she found she'd made a mistake – she's been a nun some seven years I think – she'd go on being one because she thinks one should stick to a thing once committed to it.

I happened to buy *Universe* and *Catholic Herald* this morning. Have just read both. Result, extreme depression . . .

Have written another chapter of my little cat book. As difficult to write as everything else. But mean to finish it, even if it's a silly little book.

Childishly, as in my years out of the Church, when I wrote up the names of Keats, Flaubert etc. on a panel because the 'dedicated' writers were my 'saints', I have to think of actual Catholics, living or dead, to 'hold on to' . . .

14 March   I'm in the middle of annual orgy of redecorating and spring-cleaning. Of course that makes the rest look shabby. But it's not possible ever to have whole flat done at once so I must be sensible and be glad that at least some of it looks nice. Of course I'm getting through money much too fast and could not really afford spending about £50 on the flat when I am down about that because of no rent from Diane for two months.

19 May   I made myself go to a Day of Recollection today. Dom Peter Flood OSB. A real die-hard. In the question box I put my eternal trouble about the Garden of Eden, saying that it did seem to be being taught now that the story was not literal historic truth. He answered emphatically that this statement was condemned. It is dogma and *de fide* that the Garden of Eden is *literally* and *historically* true . . .

8 August   Stuck still worse with Ployé at last session . . . And my deaf-aid batteries were run down.

28 August   I had dinner with Charlotte last night – one of my great treats. Madeleine was tired and went to bed early so I had a long talk alone with Charlotte. Extraordinary how, in the 40 or so years that I never saw her, she remained a key person to me, constantly appearing in my dreams. No one has this peculiar importance to me that Charlotte has and has had ever since I first knew her when she was 12 or 13.

She has some quality in her whole self, some edge, something incorruptible that puts her apart from everyone else.

She said if she were still a Catholic, she would be a 'die-hard'. She really is Santayana's 'Catholic atheist'.

Last night I had one of the recurring dreams . . .

Tom had come back to me and we were in that mysterious flat which is partly Cecil Court, but much bigger, with more rooms and that curious second bathroom. Susan and Lyndall were in the dream and we were very happy we were to be all together again. They were about 12 and 14.

I was so happy.

I am of course worried about this cataract operation – it still seems v. unreal to me – especially the after-effects. I don't seem to regard it as making me eventually able to see better but as upsetting my present vision to which I am more or less used, bad as it is, and making it v. difficult to focus with one 'good' eye and one bad one. Still I'll have to go through with it. And of course I'm worried about money (even with Lyndall and BUPA).

I want desperately to try and finish the cat book before it. But oh, oh, oh! *Never* have I had a worse jam than I have had for weeks and weeks on re-doing the last pages of *one chapter*.

It is what happened in every case: the autobi[ography], the Eric novel, the American one and now this. A complete jam up over some apparently trivial thing.

The Eric book – trying to get the little breakfast scene right (the cat in at the window).

The American – getting the woman over to the window where the nuns are sitting and describing the room.

The autobi[ography] – the scene in the kitchen.

Minka and Curdy – cats after move.

It is CRAZY. The thing suddenly petrifies. Or in re-writing new ideas occur – then I see they are wrong, after perhaps having written several pages. My desk will be littered with perhaps 50 versions scribbled over and revised, left there *in case* a few words might be salvaged. Yesterday I actually rescued a crumpled page from dustbin [in basement area] and thought it more promising than some versions . . .

Ployé seems unable to help at all. Anyway he may have to give up the treatment as they are putting him on to in-patients. Yet I am determined to finish it *somehow*. It seems no one can help me and I can't help myself. It is awful how much I smoke . . . about 40 a day. I don't 'enjoy' it – it is a real compulsive addiction.

I do a crossword puzzle, guiltily. I eat or have tea, I start reading and go on too long. I may start work at 4.30 [a.m.] and suddenly after what seems less than an hour, it is 7. I hardly go out. I listen compulsively to the radio. Money worries, of course, too. I have made awfully little the last 2 years. But for that grant, I'd be sunk.

And of course the eternal wrestling with religion in my head.

30 August I lay awake for an hour or two during the night, feeling very isolated. Not exactly depressed but very much alone, glad of the living presence of Minka, purring when she woke and making curious little grunting noises in her sleep. (I thought of the rather alarming 'Sound Poems' I had been listening to before I went to sleep. I tried to 'pray'. Saying the 'Our Father' very slowly – 2 breaths to a syllable. Then words seemed impossible. I just lay, trying to be 'aware'. Also trying to accept what remains of my life. Certainly some fear of the operation and the after-effects. Suppose I lost my sight? Millions of people have to endure blindness, but how would one 'manage'? Death cannot be all that far off now – I am 69.

* * *

Neville de Courcy (sometimes Nev or Toby) was the elegant 'bosom friend' of Cecil Botting's undergraduate days at Emmanuel College, Cambridge in the 1890s. After the two young men went down they continued to correspond. Neville died young. His descendants now live in New Zealand, and Antonia corresponded with them. They sent her Cecil's letters to Neville: later (see page 248) Neville's letters to Cecil were discovered at Binesfield.

* * *

6 Sept   I have spent an extraordinary day, glued till my eyes were sore over my father's letters to Toby de Courcy between 1889 and 1898. They really were the most devoted friends. He says somewhere that he did not want to make new friends after Cambridge – that there were no other men he felt really 'in tune with'. Toby was his *beau ideal* of what a man should be: he says so in so many words. And that he identified him with Colonel de Gray in *The Egoist* [George Meredith]. Daddy really did love him – he often writes 'My own Toby'. There is a most touching letter on April 17th 1898, on the eve of his marriage 'my last bachelor letter' – 'My best of friends . . . I have reserved it for you since it is most fitting that it should be written to him with whom all that is happiest of the life I leave behind has been spent . . . Oh Toby, the letter you wrote me I value more than all the presents I have received.'

The letters are tremendously full of comments on books and pictures. Their mutual passion for Scott and Meredith, particularly, of course, Meredith. They were both mad about Kipling too. He didn't think much of women writers. Had a horror of 'the new woman'. Pater, of course.

He talks much of his weakness of will . . . his love of the gaiety and good food of France. Also of his inertia. Obviously he had terrific fits of depression – he always told me this.

Extraordinary how int[ereste]d he was in pictures. He gives long accounts of the Academy every year to Toby. I remember his violent prejudice against Cézanne, but when he saw some Cézannes with me in Paris in 1924, he was enraptured.

So many things like me – depression – torment of conflicting opinions – feeling of being all bits and pieces and having no personality.

He confesses (*v.* secretly) to Nev de C[ourcy] that he is secretly engaged to my mother . . . 'a charming girl just back from Germany who talked Pessimism'.

He talks of 'my people' (but only to 'remember' them to Toby) and never describes Granny and Grandfather or any of his family except to say that most of them seem unable even to read. He says the Dulwich house [where his father ran a grocer's shop] is Lilliputian and in a slum.

A fascinating collection which makes me wish the impossible – that I could have a REAL talk with my father as another human being.

A really horrifying interview in *The Guardian* with John Braine – apparently ardent Catholic. His new novel sounds pretty revolting. 'The new hero sleeps around much more and touches of lesbianism and homosexuality are added to the supporting characters.' One really gets a bit weary of the current formula . . . There were some good things in *Room at the Top*.

23 Sept Obviously cataract operation is haunting me – so hard to know what *real* after-effects are. Am tired and depressed: natural. Had a lovely day with Sue and family yesterday.

Should I give up writing altogether and just chance getting translations? These last 2 days reading, fascinated, V. Woolf's *The Years* wh. I hadn't read before. *How* marvellously she writes – or rather *paints*. A beautiful, but utterly frustrating book. But she creates something out of that very frustration. We don't know ourselves, we don't know others.

But how does that all fit in with religion? My eternal, eternal, more and more insoluble problem and conflict.

It is awful to say it, but so much in Catholicism is positively *repellent* to me. More and more so. It is most of all this insistence on sin, Christ's atonement, the angry Father who will condemn to hell those who are not 'saved'.

It is strange that I somehow believe in the Real Presence. When I go to Communion, *that* always seems real for those few minutes.

What did Christ Himself believe? *Did* he really exist on earth? He wrote nothing, any more than Socrates did.

And what have each of us in ourselves but a point of awareness? . . . how can we select from all these and say firmly 'This is *true*'? All we can say, this has happened to me, I have reacted in such and such a way.

8 Oct Tomorrow week I go to Woking for the cataract operation. Nervous, of course. Dear Phyllis is being an angel: coming to stay near me in London. Went to hear Malcolm Muggeridge last night at St Anne's S[ociety]. Was disappointed. He was supposed to talk about what hindered him from committing himself to the Christian faith. We got little beyond his usual diatribes against the modern world. He seems to have a firm personal belief in Christ. When asked why he didn't commit himself one got impression that he just couldn't join Anglicans or RCs because he disapproved of so many of them — that they weren't Christian *enough* for him. Said he knew nothing of theology. This was pretty obvious. He seems awfully *contemptuous* of everyone. Don't awfully like this new Malcolm . . . Ascetic now, vegetarian, no drink . . . said the Mass seemed to him utterly meaningless. He's such a public figure now, one couldn't, I think, ever again have a private talk to him. He was very sweet to me and greeted me quite affectionately. I would like to know what he *really* thinks. Gerard Irvine's mother stood up to him splendidly in defence of the young. Talked a lot about the vanity of the young: I could NOT help thinking of the vanity of the old! His last words to me were 'I'm a kind of Gandhi now.' I think Gerard Irvine and the Archdeacon of Westminster were a bit disappointed in his talk.

I get more and more confused myself. This women Maureen Murphy, Father Hugh's friend, is all I *can't* be – 100% Irish Catholic with utter faith and all the 'devotions'. Yet it's all so *absolutely* genuine. I was touched that she sent me a 'Get-well-Mass card' and is having a Mass said for me on 17th. And a beautiful photo of Fr. Hugh dead. *There* was a good man if there ever was one. Why can't I be like Maureen Murphy? I don't, never could, 'despise' all the 'Catholic thing' – the Sacred Heart, devotion to Our Lady and so on. One half of me can take it *all*, happily.

On Sunday it took me over 4 hours to write a letter to Thomas.

Was seduced this morning to reading bits of *Beyond the Glass*. Found *very* much to criticize in it – LOTS of bad things: a few good. It sprawls badly and some of it is really feeble. Hopelessly clumsy that telephone conversation with Archie. *The Sugar House* and F. *in M.* are really the only two decent ones as regards tautness and shape. Some of my short stories aren't bad. Would still like to write something decent before I die.

I couldn't live without some sort of spiritual preoccupation. I found it for many years in art and still do. I lived for years on Keats' letters. Almost anything can start it off. Even yesterday came near it. A perfect windless autumn morning . . . the rusting leaves of a chestnut tree. I just stood staring at the tree in pure delight . . . each leaf differently marked.

Finality of death, whether there is an after-life or not. Catholicism makes one passive after death – one is *finally* judged and can perform no more *voluntary* actions. In heaven I suppose one could will – and could only will *good* – what joy!

9 Nov   I had the cataract operation on Oct 17th i.e. 3 weeks ago . . . Today I went shopping for the first time on my own.

First 3 days one is helpless: nurses feed one. Soon allowed out of bed but must be propped up night and day, not move head forward . . .

When came home should have been helpless without Phyllis, mainly owing to not being allowed to put head down and blocked-out right eye. Had to count stairs and feel with heels . . .

Now in interim stage waiting for what is decidedly frightening e.g. cataract lens wh. so magnifies that you can't judge distance.

I shall be one-eyed for rest of life, for the left eye will have a lens you can't see through. But even if I could afford it, I don't think I cd. face the ordeal again.

Have managed not to smoke for 3 weeks . . .

Reading isn't too bad but writing *is* hard – you can't see what you've written.

Of course I'm worried how I'm going to earn my living.

10 Nov   Sight affects everything I find: even the ability to think.

13 Nov Calmer and more sensible again. Simple routine. Puzzle. Necessary letters. Bit of Italian. Typing exercise. Rest in afternoon and early bed.

This morning looking for an Italian grammar, came across the little book about Père Lamy [twentieth-century visionary]. Started reading it again. Of course all my old troubles flared up. These visions of Our Lady.

Lamy worries me rather about minutiae. He would not hear women's confessions unless they covered their heads. Would rather not offer a flower to Our Lady than pick one on Sunday. Is one to cut away all these 'pieties' and 'devotions' which do form so much part of the whole Catholic thing?

Maureen Murphy is steeped in these 'devotions' – Carmelites going straight to heaven if they die on a feast of Our Lady (Fr. Hugh died on that of Our Lady of Mt. Carmel) or 'if not, on the following Saturday'.

17 Nov What are my real difficulties over THE question? Suppose I had not been inculcated with Catholicism in my childhood? I would have learnt the Greek myths as myths. I would have known that the Greeks and Romans had gods and believed in them but that people no longer did . . .

This age probably the very first in which religion is very widely supplanted and no belief is universally held in a nation. Greatest phenomenon Marxism – an ideological orthodoxy as dogmatic and binding as a religion but with *no* supernatural basis whatever. There is also humanism, but this derives most of its ethical values from Christianity.

18 Nov My aunts knew women who could 'charm' warts away. They also mentioned a broth made of boiled mouse for whooping cough.

19 Nov Fr. Anselm has just announced his intention of visiting me tonight. I am as terrified as if it were the Gestapo.

20 Nov Fr. A[nselm] is a very nice man indeed: could not have been kinder . . .

I made a great mistake, in alluding to my Garden of Eden troubles. He said he wd. have to consult and think it out and would write to me. He then went on to say that Adam *did* live a long time (900 years). So we were back just where we were . . .

I said – what is quite true – that in spite of all my scepticism, I was still convinced of the Real Presence. His face lit up. 'Then you haven't lost your faith,' he said. I said, 'But that very fact torments me – my belief in the Blessed Sacrament. Because going to Communion in my dispositions makes me feel I may be receiving it in mortal sin.' He assured me fervently that I was not in mortal sin – that I must go on going to Communion.

He also said, like Fr. Brodrick, 'Perhaps your difficulties are emotional, not intellectual.' I said, as I've said to Fr. B. before, that I truly don't think so.

22 Dec   A trying time. I had got used to managing with the left eye during the long delay for the cataract glasses. Now, in a way I am worse off than before the operation. New glasses not only blot out left eye but right now sees things so magnified and distorted that I feel giddy, and totter about, feeling everything rushing at me. So I juggle all the time with FOUR pairs of glasses. Terrifying. Especially stepping on and off curbs.

I have been labouring away again at *M[inka] and C[urdy]*. All the old trouble.

The eternal religious problem keeps on and on.

I cannot help feeling the whole doctrinal structure is based very firmly on the literal Adam and Eve, the fall, original sin, the atonement to an offended God, salvation only through baptism, the divinely guided Church, the inerrancy of scripture, the possibility of eternal damnation and all the rest.

And, curiously enough, all the attempts to 'modernize' it only make it less convincing.

We talk of 'preparing for the coming of Christ' at Christmas – and the Christmas story, angels, shepherds, the kings, the manger are so embedded in our imagination and so lovely and dear that even if they never took place as the Gospels describe them, one cannot bear to part [with] them. Yet, on the Church's own admission, Christ is already here – in what sense does He 'come again' at Christmas or resurrect again at Easter?

I am quite lost with all these new jargons. The key words of praise now seem [to be] 'erotic' 'revolutionary'. The dirty words 'bourgeois' 'Victorian morality' (i.e. Christian morality) 'unaware of social issues'. 'Society' has now become a kind of abstract god or devil.

1969

8 Feb I did manage to do another chapter of *M[inka] and C[urdy]* in 2 or 3 weeks. I did not send it to P[hyllis] till yesterday because the last page of the previous (typed) chapter wanted changing. The result was the most insane niggle of all. I spent 10 whole days over the last few *sentences* . . . If I *know* what I want to say, I cannot manipulate the words, no matter how I twist and turn them around and labour at them. I can see that translation has made it all more difficult. It is having to spit it all out of myself, instead of working what is already there. I've been so much of a tram all these years that I am lost and terrified being a bus.

9 Feb Yesterday Helen [cousin] came to lunch and stayed to 6.15 milling over her short story. I fear it really is hopeless – she *cannot* compose a story. It's not that she's stupid. About pictures she is really intelligent. It is an awful labour trying to work with her because she has a bird-hopping mind and keeps going off into total irrelevancies. Of course what is behind it is loneliness and something in her that has never grown up and wants impossibilities.

I'm just as bad as she is, still expecting something marvellous to happen out of the blue.

22 Feb Recurring dream again . . . Alan Walker (I *think* he has featured in this dream before). I wondered, just as I would in real life, how I would put up with Alan's peculiar character.

Eric has had more influence on my mind than anyone in my life, even my father. And he never aroused any sense of guilt in me, as my father so painfully did – and still does. And, of course, my father had all the weight of religion behind him – and has left that insoluble problem with me. It is useless to speculate what my life would have been if my father had not become a Catholic.

The lapsed Catholics who interest me most are all 'cradle Catholics' – Charlotte, Enid Starkie and Kate O'Brien – all three exceptionally attractive characters and of great honesty and integrity. Enid and Kate are very gay but obviously not 'happy' – they are both alcoholics . . .

25 Feb Ployé suddenly said there was something he wished to discuss with me and had meant to leave it until the end of the session, but had decided to say it now. He said that he now had so much work with the in-patients that it was becoming almost impossible to deal with his out-patients. The inference was obvious. I said I was quite willing to try and manage on my own. He seemed very much relieved and said he was very glad I felt that much confidence. I said it was a shock, but not too bad a shock. He made it obvious that he didn't feel that the treatment was finished – when I said 'It is like an unfinished story' he agreed. I can't tell yet if the writing jam really is beginning to break up (this is the one thing I personally wanted more than anything from the treatment). I am much better in other ways as regards anxiety, depression etc.

Ployé seemed more agitated than I was. I used the expression 'over-worked' at some point. He took this up – was I implying he wasn't up to his work – in other words not an efficient doctor? I said no, that didn't 'ring a bell'. He really seemed very agitated – his voice was nervous and edgy. What obviously did worry him was having to break off the treatment abruptly like this, instead of gradually running it down. What do I really feel? A certain relief perhaps at not having to go all that way any more. A certain shock at its coming sooner than I expected, like the cataract operation. A bit of pride in 'accepting a challenge' and intending to cope with it as best I can. And of course a certain disappointment, a sense of 'unfinished business'.

In the afternoon Gerti [Hopkinson] came to see me. I enjoyed seeing her. It is years since we had an intimate talk. I have not seen her at all since Amanda's confirmation. Gerti surprised me very much by

saying she wanted to know much more about the Church. She said
she could not reconcile Amanda's deep religious faith with her
behaviour – i.e. having this love affair with a married man. Lyndall
said that Amanda was going to Confession and Communion when
she was staying at the Palazzone [Lyndall was now living in Italy with
Count Lorenzo Passerini] and all the time sharing Peter [Binns, her
tutor at Warwick]'s bed. She told L[yndall], I understand, that the
priests said 'it was quite all right'. This *totally* baffles me!

30 March   I shall be 70 tomorrow. Lyndall has come over for my
birthday and it is wonderful to see her.

Poor Minka isn't at all well. Arthritis and some kidney trouble.
The vet is *very* good and thinks we can give her a pleasant enough old
age. She's on various pills, vitamins and a strict diet but she isn't at all
a well cat and I fear she is declining. She is after all nearly 16. I'm
depressed rather . . . general feeling of decline all round . . .
everything seems an effort. No Gladys now and no new body in sight
so the flat is declining too as I only do the minimum housework.

4 April (Good Friday)   I had the most wonderful 70th birthday
imaginable. On Sunday a lovely feast at Sue's with Lyndall, Thomas,
the grandchildren, Isabel Quigly and Amanda – *all* giving me
presents and the celebration candle on the table. Thomas had cooked
a magnificent curry. Then Mim and A.K. gave me a birthday tea
complete with cake.

On the day itself, I opened Lyndall's mysterious present. Not only
a huge bottle of Rochas perfume but an incredible gift – £20 a month
for a year. Really, that child's generosity! I feel ashamed to take it
after all she did for me last year. I was so thankful to hear her say that
she really does seem happy at last in this country life in Italy. She has
had so much unhappiness all her life and she has such a melancholic
nature anyway. She still cannot realize that she is beautiful and gifted
– she has *no* confidence in herself. She says she has all my faults –
perhaps she *has* some of them. We do have the same sort of difficult
temperament . . . On Monday, much as I enjoyed going to the theatre,
I would gladly have spent the entire evening just talking to Sue and
Lyn: it was so wonderful having them both together which is such a
rare treat and for me now the peak of happiness.

2 May   Only to record that I have actually finished *M. and C.* – at 1 p.m. today. The first book I have finished for more than 10 years . . . The original *M. and C.* took, I think, 2 months.

Things look brighter. G[ladys] has decided to come back for 2 mornings a week. Wonderful. I have a good chance of getting a trans[lation] from Anthony Blond [the publisher, a friend of Lyndall]. Awfully long.

8 May   I have derived immense comfort over the Eternal Question from Gollancz's wonderful anthology *From Darkness to Light* which I am reading conscientiously in order, a little every day. Amanda gave it me for my 70th birthday and I can't say how I bless her for it. Really my 70th birthday seems to have been a turning point and gives me new hope and confidence.

I suppose, as regards religion, it comes down to the old thing, that I cannot take Catholicism as the *only* vehicle of truth. But the consensus of so many witnesses of so many religions – and of pagans too – does seem overwhelming.

I am reading an excellent novel about priests. *Three Cheers for the Paraclete* by Thomas Keneally – an Australian.

9 May   Began *Chevalier d'Eon* [translation for Anthony Blond].

3 August   I have been so busy with the *Chevalier d'Eon* – still over 100,000 words to do – that what with that, and seeing more people than usual, haven't attempted to put anything in this book: not even to register that a fortnight ago today the first men landed on the moon.

8 Sept   I have started again, and this time am determined to finish, reading the Old Testament right through. It is the most puzzling book imaginable. Once you get to the Wilderness and the Mosaic prescriptions, God seems interested in nothing but the most elaborate prescriptions (in the minutest detail) for his own worship and visiting his wrath on everyone who disobeys the slightest one. All those burnt offerings, sin offerings, trespass offerings etc. Aaron's sons are struck dead for offering the wrong kind of incense. He commands a man to be stoned to death for gathering sticks on the Sabbath etc.etc.

Presumably much of the 'Wilderness' is meant to be historical. But it is very difficult to reconcile with the idea of a nomadic tribe wandering in the desert.

What did they pasture all those cattle, sheep and goats on that they owned in such numbers and were always sacrificing?

And where did they get all that water for the incessant ablutions and purifications?

Mixed in with all the savagery of the taboos and retributions are exquisitely tender and *human* stories like Joseph and his brethren etc. as psychologically and humanly true as you could find. And some very horrid ones, like their inducing the young man who wanted to marry Dinah and his associates to be circumcised and then slaying them all on the third day, 'while they were yet sore'. I remember Bertrand Russell was so shocked by this one.

This week has seen the most extraordinary change I have ever known in the Church's ritual. It would have been unthinkable even a year ago in the Western rite and it was slipped in unobtrusively in the local convent I go to a few days ago (Amanda told me it only needed permission from the Bishop). We now go *up to the altar* for Communion. (In the past, women weren't even allowed in the sanctuary during Mass except nun sacristans and brides at the Nuptial Mass.) We take the Host in our hands (like the Protestants) whereas we were strictly forbidden to *touch* it with our hands – in fact we were taught we must never bite it, just let it get moist enough to swallow, though we could use our tongues if it stuck to our palates. And then we pick up the Chalice and take a sip. We were never even allowed to *touch* the Chalice, even when empty (except again for sacristans and, in case of fire, a lay person might rescue the holy vessels) let alone drink from it . . .

Mrs [Edythe] Echols was here a few weeks ago. Extraordinary changes at St Mary's [Indiana]. The nuns wear ordinary dress and even make-up and go in for slimming. They are also allowed to drink.

26 Oct   I am into Kings II now. The violence goes on as ferociously as ever.

I have finished the *Chevalier*. 138,000 words. Just over 5 months.

My eyes slow me up badly about going anywhere: I only go out the minimum because of my sight and crossing roads. Never even think of going to a cinema, picture gallery etc.

When a bit cleared and straightened – everything such a RIDICU-LOUS effort now! – must be brave and get back to the autobiography.

28 Dec   Princess Beatrice Hospital.

Shall have been here a fortnight tomorrow with pleurisy and pneumonia. Was rushed here in an ambulance on Mon 15th. Still not allowed up. Much better but absurdly weak and tired. Everyone has been so kind: Phyllis has come up and is staying at flat. Mercifully I finished the *Chevalier* before the deadline.

It's an unexpected blow. I had for a long while been feeling very tired; it was a big effort to get out and do the shopping and bring the stuff up all those stairs. Now I will have to face explanations to about 50 people but not yet.

My faith seems thinner than ever . . .

FIVE

1970–1974

Antonia started 1970 with double pneumonia to add to her increasing disabilities. Thomas and Susan were in Boston, USA, where Thomas was Visiting Professor at Boston University, and Lyndall had moved to Tuscany with Count Lorenzo Passerini, who was to become her second husband when the Italian divorce laws were changed. Both sisters were on the point of coming home when Antonia recovered. Lyndall rewarded her with a holiday at Cortona. Susan produced Jessica, a fourth and final grandchild, and by the end of the period was planning to cross Europe on foot with the family, assisted by donkeys.

1970

2 Jan   Am due to go home this morning. 3 weeks since I was first taken ill . . . Curious institutional interlude of suspended life. It seems ages since I left the flat. Phyllis came all the way from Devonshire . . . will stay in nearby hotel and in flat till I'm a bit more able to manage. I don't feel ill – no pain now, not even a cough, but absurdly weak. It will be quite strange to be home. Haven't even worn ordinary clothes for 3 weeks.

20 Jan   Have been home now as long as I was in hospital. A funny sort of half-life. It was wonderful having Phyllis for the first week. She had to go back a day earlier for the dreadful business of poor Eric Siepmann. He died a few days later of the overdose of barbiturates. At least he was spared the slow living death of Parkinson's Disease which wd. have been intolerable for him and Mary. He was terribly depressed since he knew he had it. Whether he meant to kill himself or not, we don't know, but the hospital is treating it as suicide. The inquest has been adjourned. We hope they *won't* give a verdict of suicide, for the sake of his 16-year-old son. Phyllis is amazing . . . And no one was ever more ruthlessly critical of herself: she really believes herself to be an absolutely worthless person; selfish, hard, cynical etc . . . she despises people who like her because they must be fools.

I'm convalescing quietly. They said it would take some time. I can get as far as Gloucester Rd. but not manage shopping. The *enormous* labour of having to write so many cards . . . to explain why I hadn't sent Xmas cards. Sue and Lyndall too touching: telephone calls from Italy and Boston, even wanting to come over. I was deeply moved. Tom [Hopkinson] actually wrote to Phyllis, suggesting coming to visit me in hospital – but I was home by then. – but such a stiff, formal little note – 'As you know, I have had no direct contact with Antonia for many years' etc. And Si rang up one night – I actually SPOKE to him – first time I've heard his voice for nearly 19 years! He sounded just the same.

In hospital I went to Confession and Communion. I was v. weak and wept a little. The old priest said 'We aren't expected to do more than try,' and 'We shan't be able to pray properly till we get to heaven.'

25 Jan   Today for the first time since Dec 11 smoked compulsively. All these 3 weeks since I came out of hospital I have smoked at the most 5. Today I smoked 15 while writing that letter to Lady MacAlister. Once again in her letter, though assuring she did not wish to distress me, she brought up ALL the inflammatory topics that paralysed me before . . . that I ought to burn my work instead of publishing it.

10 Feb   Terrible trouble over the autobiography. A whole week wrestling with one revised paragraph about my grandfather's family . . .

* * *

After five years on the autobiography, Antonia was still struggling with her family tree. She had visited Zillah Tickner, a cousin on the Botting side, the grand-daughter of Charles Botting. Charles was her great-uncle, a brother of Cecil Botting's father. He had been the tenant of Upper Chancton Farm, where a famous hoard of Anglo-Saxon coins was found in 1866. The British Museum permitted Zillah Tickner to keep a few of the coins and Antonia had been shown them.

* * *

17 Feb   Have made myself write to Zillah, and Lena [Boniface] to try to do a bit more sorting out of the family.

I think I will have to simplify all this for the sake of the book since these details don't really matter.

20 Feb   A nice Mrs Gotch came to see me on behalf of the R[oyal] L[iterary] F[und]. Something about a 'Bounty' – some mysterious honour and some cash – which Janet Adam Smith has most kindly recommended me for this year's Civil List Pensions being already awarded. I don't know what it's all about but it's very nice to be considered to 'have done some service to literature'.

31 March   My 71st birthday. Several people rang up, which touched me: a drifting, aimless day like many lately since I temporarily dropped the hopeless effort to get on with the autobiography. For 6 weeks and more wrestling with it. Now that Lyndall has so sweetly invited me to go to Italy for a birthday present, I really AM going: on Thursday, April 9th. Overcoming my neurotic dread of travel, worse than ever since cataract op[eration]. I have got new passport, planned clothes, rung up BEA etc.

Civil List pension didn't come off . . . I have spent rather extravagantly: rooms painted, clothes for Italy.

I continue to read a bit of the O[ld] T[estament] first thing every morning. Very depressing.

* * *

Antonia now spent a few weeks with Lyndall and Renzo in his palazzo outside Cortona, built by Renzo's ancestor, Cardinal Passerini, in 1525.

* * *

6 May   A week tomorrow since I returned from Italy. It was wonderful to see Lyndall and I am very glad I made the effort. All the same, in spite of the beauty of the place and the pleasure of seeing Lyn, I was ridiculously homesick. I was worried about her too. Apart from her broken wrist which, after 2 months, is still almost without movement and gives her constant pain, she looked ill and tired and does not seem at all happy. Lorenzo has turned out to be yet another disappointment. Devoted as he is to her, he is not *at all* the 'tower of strength' she hoped for but makes incessant demands on *her*: he is curiously childish, capricious and irresponsible . . . I could not, of course, expect to see so much of her as when I was in Italy in 1954: that was a *really* happy holiday which this wasn't altogether, though I did enjoy it in spots. Lyndall had a great deal to do, working on these houses – on a ⌐uide Book, coping with the horses and constantly having to be on hand to entertain Italian visitors who dropped in. We did have quite a lot of intimate talk when we were driving to and fro from Cortona, the 'Casa Chitty' [a farmhouse Lyndall was converting for Thomas and Susan] etc. One lovely day alone together for several hours when she drove me to Monte Pulciano and Pienza.

I felt rather ill most of the time; the chill of the vast rooms at Il Palazzone after the warmth outside gave me a bad cold for most of my stay. I felt decrepit, tottering about on the uneven floors and rough paths.

My happy homecoming was marred by the sudden unexpected appearance, after 18 months, of X. It was really nasty and shook me, though I've got over it now. He looked and behaved very oddly, told me what I am now pretty sure was a pack of lies about a job in Liverpool, averaging £35 a week, having parked his car (Triumph) outside the house and explaining that the unusually shabby clothes and old tennis shoes were his 'driving clothes'. He asked if I still had any of his scraperboard drawings. D[iane] was out and I went into her room to fetch them. I found them almost at once: couldn't have been out of the living-room more than 3 minutes. When I came out with them, George was in the passage. I said 'I've found them; let's go back into my workroom and look at them.' He said 'I've brought a drawing for you. I'll just pop down to the car and fetch it.' In a flash he was out of the flat, I waited 5 mins, 10 mins, 15 mins. He did not return. I went on with my tidying up, for I had not finished unpacking and was longing to go to bed. I then found that £6.12.0 D[iane] had left for me on the mantelpiece had vanished. I waited up till nearly 10.30 (X had arrived at 9) and though D[iane] was still out and I couldn't put the chain on the door, went to bed. I reasoned that if he'd stolen from me, he wouldn't be likely to return. All these years he has never actually stolen from me. I suspect he is either on the run, or planning a 'job' and that he was wearing his burgling clothes.

7 May   Italy is strange: in some ways dead. The great splendid empty churches which feel more like museums. No one was ever in them praying unless Mass was actually going on. I am sure that when I was there 17 years [ago], there were always people praying in them. They felt curiously *empty*, even when the Blessed Sacrament was there. When I went to [local] Mass, except on the Sunday when the church was crammed for the Priest's jubilee – 13 priests, a bishop and at least a 100 girls in blue veils from the local convent school singing, there were no more than 6 or 7 in the congregation.

I felt 'piety' towards Catholicism when I was there, as for an old love. I *cannot* recapture a sense of reality about it.

Bobbie Speaight was here for an hour on Monday. Maritain has now decided to get an entirely new English version of Raïssa's *Journal* made by someone called Mrs Bowker and a contemplative nun. I wrote saying I gladly renounced all my 'rights' in it and did not want my name to appear.

Bobbie says Teresa [Newman, his step-daughter] is now married to her ex-Dominican. Although he has been properly dispensed, they still have not bothered to 'regularize' their civil marriage. One just doesn't know where one is with Catholics these days.

23 July   Ever since I last wrote in this notebook I have been toiling every day at ONE paragraph in the autobi[ography]. Clare [Nicholl] *implored* me to stop altogether for the time being.

It is an extraordinary feeling to have relinquished the effort for the time being. An amazing feeling of calmness . . . that feeling of physical pressure behind my eyeballs has gone. I have read several chapters of Antonia Fraser's excellent *Mary Queen of Scots* since I came back. The *incredible* feeling of *time to myself*. How I bless Clare.

Mrs Plank rang up to say Hilda [Graef] has only a month to live. The cancer is spreading everywhere. The liver is affected now and she is sick all the time. I hope it will be less than a month. She told Mrs

P[lank] she would be glad to go and that 'she has her faith'. She told her she would like to see me and I am going to Oxford on Monday. Because of feeling 'free' I did not get into my neurotic frenzy, but calmly looked up a train. I think all this started only a few months ago and then it went with terrible speed. Of course I've seen her since – I'd forgotten. When I went up for Enid [Starkie]'s memorial service. And then she seemed much better and they thought they had arrested it.

Lyndall's birthday today: she must be 39. It is amazing. And Sue nearly 41.

29 July   I do not think Hilda can live much longer. She was very, very weak but mercifully not in pain. I only stayed a few minutes. She gave me a message to give Mrs Plank about returning Mary Ward books etc. to the nuns at Ascot. She said that she wanted 'Spitz-koepfi' buried with her – the cushion that is a 'person' to her. 'Spitz-koepfi' was on the windowsill, dressed in 'his' best pink robe, feathered cap, pearl necklace and toy guitar. I wonder what she thinks of as she lies there.

31 July   The only thing that seems to me *really* wicked is cruelty. But I have become very prim and shockable in my old [age]. The accounts of such plays as *Oh Calcutta* disgust me. So does the appalling vulgarity of many things on the BBC. Also the perpetual dirty jokes about sex as if nothing else in the world were funny. And the prevalence of sex in almost every novel one reads reviews of as if nothing that was not erotic was of the least interest. It is so drearily monotonous.

7 August   Hilda died this morning.

10 August   [Dr] Mary Austin says I'm absolutely exhausted and *must* stop for at least a fortnight.

12 August   Leading a very queer sort of life. So many people have moved, some no longer feature in my life: quite a few are dead. One's address book at various times is like a record of one's life.

In spite of having many dear friends, I am really rather isolated. There is no one to whom I can tell *all*. I suppose this is true of everyone. Of course one can confide one's practical troubles to one's friends, but not really one's mental, and above all, religious ones. My Catholic friends would either be pained or unable to understand or both.

I suppose the person with whom I could be most intimate now is Sue. But distance, and her own concerns, make it impossible for us ever to have more than an occasional hour or two together.

15 August   25th anniversary of Sue's baptism. What a wonderful day that was. And how sure I was then of the truth of the Catholic religion.

16 August   I have been tidying up files, sorting photos and letters etc. Also doing what I can to make things easier for Sue to clear up when I die . . . at my age obviously one won't live all that longer and probably all the main things in one's life have happened and one will just go on muddling along as best one can, not expecting much and thankful that things are no worse.

I admire other people so much – especially people who have made such good use of their lives, as Hilda did. I was given some talents and I made so little use of them . . . my mind is a rag-bag. No concentration or perseverance or self-control . . . is my writing worth persevering with? I suppose if it gave even one person pleasure or interest it is. And it seems to. But, in itself, it is so trivial.

19 August   Had dinner last night at Rugatino's with Fred and Senta Marnau and Corinna [their only child]. I must try and remember that restaurant: it is so good and not ruinous. Dear Fred spontaneously offered to drive me down to Woking for my [second] eye operation.

Extraordinary the frightful accents one hears on the radio, especially from people connected with education. I don't mean 'regional' accents, but shocking cockney vowels, like the old-style 'board-school teacher'.

I re-read Rosamond Lehmann's *The Swan in the Evening* [about communication with her dead daughter]. This time I find the writing occasionally a little overstrained but the impression of absolute genuineness and honesty remains. It took tremendous courage on

her part to write it, knowing the milieu in which she has lived. I
would call it most definitely a 'religious' book.

21 August   Funny days: practising typing which I enjoy (as I do *not*
enjoy writing in this big bumpy notebook).

Tomorrow lunch with Moll. Really too much social dissipation
this week. I find talking with her a bit of a strain and tiring. It really
amounts to listening to her long and frankly rather boring stories
about what goes on in the office, the parish etc. She never wants to
listen to my boring stories in exchange!

23 August   I did quite enjoy seeing Moll . . . so happy with her roses
and her re-decorated room. I do admire her contentment with
everything. I couldn't gather what a very long story she was telling
me was about. She talks so low (just as she does in restaurants where
she is always terrified of being overheard and telling me to keep my
voice down) and also puts her hand over her mouth so I have to make
wild guesses at what she is saying . . . and her recurrent 'To cut a long
story brief'.

Came back very tired, but sat up till 9, reading 2 things almost
simultaneously in the crazy way I do – books picked at random from
the shelf. Lubac's *Atheist Humanism* – some marvellous pages on
Dostoievsky whom I'll just have to read again – and a biography of
Virginia Woolf. Have gone on with the latter today. The great
heroine-writer of my youth. She will always interest me extremely. I
still feel *To the Lighthouse* is her one real masterpiece. And of course
she was mad too – more officially mad, in a way, than I am. I
understand very well her intense sense of the thousand things
pressing on one's mind simultaneously which one can never capture
when one writes. She is very much of an 'impressionist' as a writer.
Yet this enormous accumulation of detail and speculation – marvellously observed – can be fatiguing: everything dissolves and
becomes, as it were, brilliantly nebulous and one is left stimulated yet
unsatisfied. Only in the *Lighthouse* do I feel she reached a point of
stability and that there are bones under the exquisite flesh.

A very disagreeable woman in some ways, ultra touchy and vain.
But only about the *reception* of her work. Utterly humble about the
work itself. Cruel and malicious too, yet one would have succumbed

completely to her charm. And how beautiful! Her relations with V. Sackville West curious: odd she should have admired V.S.W.'s writing so much! I can't help finding it mediocre.

26 August   Absurd how tired I am today after Kathleen Raine to supper. Not by Kathleen – that was a joy, seeing her, for there are few people I love to see more. But I'm so slow and inexpert about all the business of cooking and serving a meal that preparations take me practically the whole day and the washing-up all the next morning . . . She is really the only person, with the possible exception of Margot King, I can talk to about certain things. She has some very remarkable communications from Gavin Maxwell through the medium of Mrs Twigg to whom Rosamond Lehmann had sent her. Kathleen is the only person who really understands my difficulties *from inside*.

I had a most extraordinary dream last night after seeing Kathleen: I think she affects me 'psychically'. In the dream, my father appeared to me naked. A great colossal naked figure. *Most* extraordinary. No sense of embarrassment on my part and certainly no sexual association. He was massive, more than life size, like a primitive statue.

Denys rang up today. Talked for over $\frac{1}{2}$ an hour of *nothing* but his recent illness: minute details of every pill. Not even a perfunctory enquiry about me. This has been so in every conversation we have had . . . even before his thrombosis. I have to listen even to the details of the exact placings of the buttons on the surgical stockings.

Yesterday one of those beastly obscene phone-calls. The poor maniac must have spent 6d (for it came from a phone-box) to mumble 'I've got my hand on it and it's six inches.'

Hope this *Sunday Express* man doesn't ring up again. I always lose my head when 'interviewed' on the telephone [about the *Chevalier* translation] and answer questions people have no right to ask.

4 Oct   The operation is very close now: Thursday 8th. I am absurdly nervous about it: much more than the first one. I now know what the long tiresome aftermath is like. Everyone is being so kind. Denys lending me the money, Clare making me a present from a windfall she couldn't need more. Kathleen Raine wrote me a most beautiful letter, hoping the operation might restore my inner vision and creativity. If only it would!

Bobbie Speaight has just sent me his autobiography, *The Property Basket*. He may often be a little inaccurate and slipshod, but he writes well and vividly and above all with this verve and confidence which must make writing an actual pleasure for him instead of a penitential task. He also has no false shame; there is something delightfully innocent about what, in some people, would look like 'intellectual climbing'. There is a scholarly side to him too; he has really soaked himself in Shakespeare.

7 Nov   Four weeks since I had the operation on my left eye. The infection seems to be clearing up now. It was a horrid experience but the eye is getting better (I have quite a bit of sight in it now).

Annoying thing about this is that my right eye is not seeing as well as before with the cataract glasses so I am too nervous to cross roads and can't go out alone. Miss K[ane] says this is probably due to tension. Thank heaven for Lyn's promised £100.

Trying to find the most comfortable position for hand-writing on the sloping desk. Now have changed over! I think other is better and involved less head-bending as I can push it further from me.

8 Nov   Same trouble trying to decide what is best angle. Truth is I can't really see properly to write at any angle.

9 Nov   Today I really do begin to feel better. Can even see a bit with the left eye.

All my friends, as well as Sue and Lyndall, have been so kind.

10 Nov   Phyllis said she has a religion of her own which she fitted into the framework of the Catholic Church. I suppose the same is true of me.

Craving for a cigarette, have just lit 1st for 5 weeks. Luckily it tastes *so* vile I don't think I *can* smoke it. Moreover it is really dangerous to light for I can't see how to either with or without glasses. It came on badly (the craving) trying for first time to get back to that eternal jammed paragraph (mother's face) in the autobi.

Looks as if I'll be *forced* to give up smoking!!!

11 Nov Have just spent all the time over my early morning tea reading through that extraordinary book of prose and poetry my father wrote out so lovingly as a birthday present for my mother in 1894 – the year they became engaged, when he was 23 and this was her 23rd birthday. Quotations from all sorts of rather unexpected poets for him; Gray, Shelley (*Prometheus Unbound*) Byron, Burns. Prose rather mysterious. Are the unsigned things by himself? The extraordinary things are mother's additions in 1934 and 1932. 3 peculiar verses – 1 obviously referring to Gabriel Meyjes [a man her mother was infatuated with, who later became a priest] and the other 2 to men she was in love with after my father's death. There they are, written in her big handwriting (with a coarse nib) on 2 blank pages opposite the things my father had copied out so lovingly for her, in his exquisite small neat handwriting. It is like a kind of vandalism.

In '34 my mother was 62 or 63. She was seriously in love with Gabriel Meyjes. Not really with O[swald] Norton, though she had an affair with him. Her vanity was fantastic, yet utterly innocent.

Honestly, I do not think anyone could have had an odder pair of parents than I had.

23 Nov Went to church on my own yesterday and shopped this morning. I am absurdly shaky on my legs still and daren't venture out without a stick.

Mentally dreadfully confused: I can't think anything out: really almost a softening of the brain. I read voraciously (have just re-read *Dombey and Son* in a few days) but dread the effort of writing anything, even a p[ost] c[ard] or an entry in this notebook. The thought of having to do *anything* – ring someone up, write a letter, 'poisons' my whole day.

28 Nov I have just been re-reading Julian of Norwich. So much consolation if one could accept it. But my great stumbling block, as ever, DO I really believe in Christ and the Christian faith? In Julian herself always the reference to 'all men that shall be saved' meaning of course those in the Church – the elect.

29 Nov Another wasted day. Having meant NOT to do the Mephisto crossword, I did it. Is this compulsive solving of meaningless problems a way of escape from attempting to solve real ones?

The practical one I really want to solve is of course the writing one. My analysis with Ployé was left half finished: at the point where I had had one eye only de-cataracted. It was physical eye-trouble that started the whole business of my being sent to P[loyé].

After this partial analysis I did manage, with great labour to heal the writing jam enough to write the *M[inka] and C[urdy]* book.

Will the acquisition of this 'second eye' have any effect on the writing jam?

Suddenly trying to remember when and how I wrote my short stories. 'The Saint' was before *Frost*. Can't remember where it first appeared. 'Life and Letters'? 'The House of Clouds' certainly did. I *think* I wrote it for Tom to have something to read to him. 'The Rich Woman' appeared somewhere; no recollection where. *Horizon?* 'Moment of Truth' certainly did: but it was written over something like 8 years. 'The Exile' (orig[inally] 'The Mystic') in some paper Tom had something to do with: can't remember what. 'Strangers' some weekly: can't remember which. *New Statesman?*

Couldn't write a short story now. Funny, I used to like the form.

Helen (my cousin) rang up at this point and chattered for some 20 minutes so if I had been vaguely on the track of something I have lost the trail and will go to bed.

13 Dec Poor Denys died in his sleep a few nights ago: a merciful thing for him perhaps as he was in a state of such neurotic depression that life was a misery for him and must have been for Renée too. A truly appalling shock for her. Renée is a saint . . . a day or two earlier she'd rung me up to say he didn't feel up to the Christmas plan he'd made in October. Of course I quite understood. I was prepared to spend what would have been a rather melancholy Christmas day all alone here.

21 Dec I have now heard that the verdict at the inquest was that Denys died of 'alcohol and drugs' self-administered. If he did commit suicide he must have been in such a mental state that he couldn't have been responsible . . . Dr H. had told him to increase his dose of chloral; he had taken chloral for years. But he was also taking various other things prescribed by other doctors and the combination, plus the fact that he was drinking more than usual may have been fatal. I find it hard to believe that Denys, who had such agonizing scruples about committing 'mortal sin' would have deliberately committed suicide. He suffered terribly from acute claustrophobia. He alternated between extreme gaiety and self-confidence ('Mr Playgent') and black melancholy. He was terrified of his black side, 'the tiger'.

Hilda's death has not affected me in anything like this way. We have had this curious intimacy for only about four years but he has been like a kind of brother. Lel was too, in a way, but we had very little in common. We made the most of what we had and became very fond of each other. He [Lel] too was deceptively cheerful: he twice deliberately tried to commit suicide.

22 Dec In the Mass now there is no space for *silence*. I was struck immensely not just by nostalgia, when I went to that Latin High Mass in September, [but] by how much it had lost in the bald version we have now. All the slow reverent ritual gives one time to appreciate the mystical significance of the Mass. And even the very admirable preoccupation with the injustices of society and the ardent 'revolutionary' priests seem to be putting too much emphasis on what one might call the 'material' side of Catholicism – or perhaps the 'love of one's neighbour' at the expense of the love of God. And how some of these people *hate* their neighbour, especially their fellow Catholics who don't agree with them.

31 Dec It has been a sad year as regards the death of friends. Eric Siepmann, Enid Starkie, Hilda Graef and now, most unexpectedly, Denys Blakelock. But a wonderful one as regards the kindness and generosity of surviving ones. Living has become so appallingly expensive and more rises in the cost of it are at hand that one needs more than three times as much to live on as before the war or even in the first years after it.

1971

8 Jan   Today I am going to knock off from that bloody sentence and not touch the brute for a few days.

I have had very vivid dreams lately, in very clear colour but apparently nonsensical. Last night's was more comprehensible for Denys's death has been much on my mind and all the time during the Requiem Mass I was thinking of him in that big square coffin (Moll remarked on its size for a small man, as Denys was) and thinking how appalling it would be for him, with his acute claustrophobia, if he were conscious of being in it. Mercifully that was impossible for, even if he had not left a proviso in his will for his heart to be pierced, the autopsy could only have been carried out on a corpse.

I continue to read a daily chapter of the Gospels as part of my 'serial' reading of the whole Bible which has gone on for some time now – best part of a year.

26 March   Unable to bring myself to write in this notebook till now though it is several weeks since I had the wonderful news that I've been awarded a C[ivil] L[ist] P[ension] of £250, and still more wonderful that it is retrospective to March 31 1970, so that my financial problem for this year is miraculously solved. For no translation work has come in for 18 months – longest blank ever – and there is no sign of any.

All this time, as before, on the autobi. Same endless frustrating daily niggling.

Have to be a little careful of the 'class' business: do not want to hurt family feelings. What irony that I thought it would be easier than a novel! I had meant to take it to 1914. If I get as far as 1908 and going to Roehampton, it will be a miracle!

Dear Lance Sheppard is almost certainly dying, if not already dead. He had a stroke a week ago, has never recovered consciousness and Emmi's note today says there is no hope. Lance was one of the best and nicest men I ever knew and his and Emmi's marriage the most beautiful thing in the world. If anything could convince me of the *rightness* of the whole Catholic thing it would be their marriage. I love to think of these *real* marriages *so* few of them . . . Tom and Sue's is a real marriage too but it is hard for Sue their feeling so differently about religion for he has no religious awareness at all.

15 April   Dear Minka died today. My last cat.

11 May   Clare [Nicholls] died on Saturday May 8th of lung cancer. I cannot take in that she is dead. It was so unexpected for until last week we only thought it was pleurisy.

One becomes more and more oriented towards death. All the last 3 friends who have died were younger than I am. Their problems are solved once for all.

30 May, Pentecost   Though the priest at the Convent was a total stranger, I made the effort to ask him to hear my confession. A most unusual experience. I came out with my eternal faith troubles. To my intense surprise he said what no other priest has ever said to me. He said 'In my position, I can't advise you to leave the Church. But the most important thing of all is to be true to yourself.' I didn't confess any [of the] usual sins and I said to him 'Shall we not call this a confession' and he agreed so I did not get absolution. It was an extraordinary experience and for the moment gave me an amazing sense of relief and liberation. He said what I needed was a good talk with someone but I explained there *was* no one and how Fr. Brodrick kept telling me I was all right but that was just because he was so charitable. This young priest was the first who really seemed to see my point.

11 June   Jessica [fourth grandchild] was born on Sunday June 6th. What a relief that it is all safely over! I couldn't help being worried about Sue this time.

On Sunday when I went down to this absurd Francis Thompson Soc[iety] affair there was a nice woman there called Hattie Meyer who turns out to be fiction editor of *Woman's Realm*. Result, I have spent 4 days doing *nothing* but try and think up ideas . . .

3 hours to write a note to Rhoda Dawson [schoolfriend at St Paul's, the artist Rhoda Bickersdike] who wrote to me out of the blue – haven't seen her since 1918!!

I sometimes wish I'd never been brought into and up in the Catholic religion.

It was a *true* choice for my father. It wasn't for me. But I can no more escape from it all than I can restore the lenses to my eyes or straighten my broken finger.

23 August 'With the approach of death I care less and less about religious truth. One hasn't long to wait for revelation or darkness.'

'Many of us abandon Confession and Communion to join the Foreign Legion of the Church and fight for the city of which we are no longer full citizens' (Graham Greene)

His autobiography (only 2 chapters have appeared so far) is fascinating. His real horror is *boredom*. Once he had a perfectly good tooth out just to escape boredom. 'A few minutes' unconsciousness was like a holiday from the world.'

How well I understand that horror of boredom. One thing about being in the asylum – I was never *bored*. (Odd: one isn't bored in dreams either.)

1 Oct Two almost miraculous happenings in last few weeks. Dear Phyllis – heaven knows she can't afford it – sent me £100 and now Lyndall has angelically sent me £100 for a Christmas present. The awful thing about Phyllis's is that she said it was what she'd have spent on this visit to Spain she longed to get out of. Now she writes that she *has* to go after all, so she won't have saved the money and can afford it less than ever. I feel guilty about the generosity of my friends: over and over it's the poor ones like Phyl and Clare who insist on helping one.

I've been reading Ranke's history of the Popes. Fascinating but alarming. All this discussion about justification by faith. People tortured and burnt for not believing the right formula.

Poor Graham [Greene], how I sympathize with him. How touched I was that he sent me his autobiography with an inscription.

I love and revere my Catholic friends. I wish I knew what *they* really believed, though.

5 Oct Still no word from Françoise Basch [French author]. Have just rung up Peter Carson. Whole situation sounds very vague and unsatisfactory to me. Seems she's just shopping round for a translator and Carson is leaving it to her. Was a bit huffy and upstage about the whole thing with Carson. Still, wouldn't let him know how badly I need the work.

Am in a curious betwixt and between state, not quite knowing what to do. Have nerved myself to go to the Bence-Joneses for the week-end.

Jessica's baptism was very beautiful – yet even that seemed remote and unreal because of my inability to feel any real faith.

12 Oct   Spent week-end with Mark and Gill Bence-Jones. I like them both very much and was much taken with Nicholas who called me 'Big Ears' because of my deaf-aids. However much I've enjoyed a week-end, writing my 'thank you' letter is torture. It took me over $3\frac{1}{2}$ hours to compose a brief inadequate note to Gill.

18 Nov   The Basch thing fell through after 5 weeks of suspense. But thanks to dear Isabel Quigly there are two hopes . . .

Elaine [Lingham] came again the other day. She's awfully interested in the autobi.

19 Nov   The religious problem for me really does seem to me to be complete loss of *faith*.

20 Nov   At this point last night I broke off and re-read the whole of the introduction to St John's Gospel in the Jerusalem Bible. It is very good and illuminating and I felt rather ashamed of my carping criticisms.

I listened to account of the Synod of Bishops on the radio last night . . . Paul VI. He seems to listen to what people say, but never to act on it (of famous birth control encyclical) . . . Barbara Ward† was very noble and starry-eyed, pleading for rich nations to be less greedy and self-seeking. All perfectly right of course, but how is this ideal of peace and justice to be achieved in this fearfully complex and imperfect world? She is *so* good herself yet, oddly, her life has brought her a great deal of material comfort and success. Sue says she and Robert [Jackson] are separated: poor Barbara, it is the price she

pays for her fame. She always *was* 'unlucky in love'. To be the darling
of the clergy isn't any compensation for that.

23 Nov   Nasty financial shock. Will have to pay £80 income tax on
the retrospective C[ivil] L[ist] P[ension] for 1970–71.

I had supper with the Bernard Walls on Sunday. They are really
very nice. Barbara v. sweet: curiously naive in some ways. Odd that
Marjorie V[illiers] gave them the Julien Green trans[lation]
[*L'Autre*, 1973]. They seem surprised themselves, not knowing
Julien Green's work, and Marjorie knows I know it well and she also
knows I badly need a trans. Still, mustn't be vexed and anyway it
doesn't sound a good Julien G.

Have been reading with much interest Isherwood's *Kathleen and
Frank* – very new way of doing an autobiography-biography.

13 Dec   Thanks to dear Fred Marnau, I *may* get a grant from the
R[oyal] L[iterary] F[und]. Looking through old notebooks, I discovered to my horror that I had £400 from them in 1964. I had
completely forgotten this. I knew I had had 2 from them over a long
period but could have sworn the last was before I went to America 12
years ago whereas it was only 7. It is really alarming how much I have
depended on grants, generous help from Lyndall and friends. I am
becoming a parasite. I *do* try to work, but even with translations
(none for 2 years) I don't make enough to pay my way. All those
hours I spend on my wretched book produce nothing.

1972

2 Jan   I spent New Year's Day still catching up with all those letters
I'd meant to get finished on New Year's Eve. Today I *must* tackle the
most difficult one – to John Broom – who has written an immensely
long letter about his having, after 5 years of hesitation, become a
Catholic and says *The H[ound] and the F[alcon]* had something to do
with it. Yesterday I was self-indulgent, bought the Times and did the
crossword . . . also read the greater part of Pritchett's *Midnight Oil*

which I finished this morning (6.30 a.m.) before getting up and going to Mass. I was fascinated by it: the best thing of his I've read.

I went off in the middle of the book to look at the jacket of *Beyond the Glass* to see what V.S.P. had said about my writing. It was very flattering.

17 Jan Much has happened since last entry. On Jan 13th I got 2 pieces of news, one very good, one very bad. The R[oyal] L[iterary] F[und] was wonderful: far more than I dared hope for – £400 for 5 years – but Georgie's news about Eric took all the pleasure and excitement out of it. Now that he has had the operation [for a stomach ulcer] and the doctors seem fairly pleased, one hopes the worst anxiety is over but I keep thinking about him all the time. I saw him for a short time in the hospital yesterday and it was a shock. I didn't recognize him in the ward at first: I thought that old white-haired man who looks a little like him couldn't possible *be* Eric, but it was. He looked so deathly pale and gaunt and so *old* – ten years at least older than when I last saw him only a few months ago. I'd never seen him as a really *old* man before . . . one couldn't realize he was 78 until now. There *is* mercifully good hope that he'll recover. It's hard to understand G. She is distraught. Yet even now she doesn't seem able to do what *he* most wants . . . to get out of hospital and back to his own home and familiar surroundings. Yet the very day after he was taken to hospital she started seriously negotiating for a new house and is trying to make them put him into a convalescent home. She talks wildly that there's a jinx on their present house – nothing but 'death and disaster' . . . that if E. returns to it, he will die there. She has [only] just spent quantities on wonderful re-decorations.

25 Jan Eric died on Jan 19th two days after I wrote the above.

I can't write about [him] yet. I think, of course, all the time about him. Being able to cry this morning somehow helped. It was the first time I'd shed [tears] since it happened. He was the most important person in my life – and unique. All those other people, Si and Tom, with whom I was in love, of course, meant much but my extra-ordinary relationship with Eric – it lasted over 50 years – was something quite different and entirely on its own.

26 Jan   She [Georgie] *did* truly love E[ric] in spite of all her bitter complaints about him; the tragedy is that they could never really adapt themselves to each other. Eric's peculiar temperament *could* not change and neither could hers and they exacerbated each other all the time . . . In some ways it might have been better if they *had* separated: she would have remained always someone whom he loved and wanted to see much of and, with the constant friction removed, they would have enjoyed the best of each other. I was lucky in that sex did not come into my relations with him. I think I was a great fool, when Eric asked me to marry him again during the war, not to say 'yes'. Ian [Henderson] did not mean anything serious to me, only a happy sex relation . . . I still had some idea (though I was 40) that some day I would be able to have a normal marriage and didn't want to commit myself. Soon after, Eric began to fall in love with pretty girls (he actually proposed to 'Maggie' [unknown]) and then came Georgie, the only woman in his life with whom he was ever able to have sexual relations, their marriage, and the tragedy of the dead child which had such disastrous effects on both of them. There is no doubt that G. has had a tragic life.

   We were talking about the little party after the cremation: it was traditional, she said, and E. would have approved and I agreed. I think it did her good. She seemed *much* better in herself last night. Then she said that E. had always said the funeral lunch in *The Lost Traveller* was one of the best things I'd ever done. Later last night I re-read it and it did seem to me quite good. I was up very early this morning, soon after 4 and have been self-indulgently re-reading bits of the book. Some I thought quite good, some dreadfully bad.

12 Feb   The Moodys were here a week ago. I find it much easier to talk to Ronald now . . . Best of all, his wonderful *warmth*. He is one of those people who get better and better as they get older. He was truly moved by Eric's death; he cried on the telephone. He has this warm, comforting physical presence like Fred Marnau. When they envelop me in a big affectionate hug I feel happy and cherished and not so isolated from human contact. R[onald] said he had lost his copy of the 'H[ouse] of C[louds]'. I lent him *Beyond the Glass*. Of course that immediately drove me to re-read it. Some bits at the beginning and the end really *are* bad, but the rest is quite good I think. The Rousseau thing [translation] as I now know, is off . . . it is really a relief. It is such an enormous book and I would have got very weary of living in Rousseau's mind all that time, for I find him exasperating and not illuminating. He really is a colossal bore with his persecution mania and endless complaining and self-pity. What do I do all day? Smoke, try to write that wretched thing (average 3–4 hours), read desultorily, listen to the radio. See a friend now and then . . . write such letters as I *have* to, shop, get my meals, totally unproductive life.

Later   I rang G[eorgie] as she had asked. She is very anxious I should do the novel I started long ago – the sequel to *B[eyond] the G[lass]* – about myself and Eric [*Julian Tye*]. I have decided to try . . . Phyllis by a miracle found she had a carbon – looked in a folder and there it was.

It would be an *appallingly* difficult book to write at the best of times. One of the hardest parts, I think, Silas.

Also what to *omit*. The abortion?

Remember you do not *have* to put in everything that actually happened in your own life.

1925 married Eric

1926 Daddy retired

1927 Yvon [from Martinique] – Brian [unknown] – Ian [Black]

1928 Edo [Austrian]. Demoralization – meeting with Si, by Christmas knew I was pregnant and told E[ric]

1929 Sue and my father's death.

14 Feb   I have spent a most curious day, sorting through Si's letters from 1928–1930 and re-reading a great many of them. They are so touching, many of them and bring him back so vividly as a young man. We could so seldom give each other what each of us wanted most *at the time*. I should have taken more interest in his work, even in the Birmingham days. When he went abroad, we couldn't enter into each other's feelings. He couldn't understand how I was feeling, left alone to go through all the beastliness of the [Eric] nullity suit, being pregnant, having to go through all the business of having the baby, much as I wanted it, with Si in Canada. And the cable that never arrived. He sent one to Addy's [Adelaide, a family friend] address and it was returned 'not known'. Goodness knows why. I couldn't understand how *he* was feeling when he lost his job. All his letters show real concern for me and for our future. He was tired, anxious, worried, working fearfully hard. I thought he'd stopped loving me. The letters show clearly that he hadn't. He suffered from terrible depressions, even in the Birmingham days. In many letters too, he says how ill he feels.

Very strange to find a letter from Frank Freeman – obviously written a few days before Sue's birth – from France. He must just have married Joan [Souter Robertson, who later married Jacques Cochemé] and was radiantly happy:

'I am so sorry I cannot be with you and in at the life at this important time.

Is the moody Silas behaving intelligently?

I am afraid you will always find him somewhat undependable at fixed times – but he is always all right in the end.'

15 Feb   The typescript [of *Julian Tye*] came today. Some of it is *shockingly* bad: endless repetitions in the clumsy attempts to re-tell the story of *B[eyond] the G[lass]*. Conversation between Claude and Aunt Leah *terrible* – almost all must go.

22 Feb   I have been reading Mary Barnes' amazing book about her madness [*Two Accounts of a Journey through Madness*, Mary Barnes and Joseph Burke, 1965]. Nothing has struck me as so important a book for years. How I wish Fr. Victor could have read it. Eric too. I must buy it when it is second-hand.

Last night a queer dream. I was not conscious of any sexual desire but was deliberately planning to have sexual intercourse with, of all people, Bobbie Speaight. We were both conscious that it was a sin, being Catholics, but were going to do it all the same, in almost a light-hearted way. I said I had had no sex for 5 years. Why 5? It is in fact over 30. I do not remember the actual intercourse, but in the dream I woke, quite sure that it had taken place. I was going to Mass with my father that morning. Would it be wrong to go to Communion? I seemed in some doubt in my own mind whether this sexual intercourse had really been a mortal sin, though of course it was technically. I decided I ought not to go to Communion but realized that if I did not my father would know I had had sexual intercourse with someone. Luckily someone offered me some grapes and unthinkingly I ate one or two. Then I realized with relief I had a 'respectable' reason for not going to Communion. I had broken my fast so my father would think *that* was why.

5 June, 7.30 a.m.   Have just re-read whole of this notebook. 3 months since I have written in it. The situation is exactly the same. Hopeless jam on Ch. I of the E[ric] book – trying to revise *one* tiny bit which seemed all right when it came back typed from Phyllis and I read it to G[eorgie] who liked it v. much. But now jam as bad as on the autobi. And everything I have written about religion still applies. I see no way out. Writing letters still as impossibly difficult. Almost every night have vivid complex dreams, apparently irrelevant, but extraordinarily detailed and realistic – seldom about people I even know. But the scenes, the clothes people wear, even the food we eat are all as realistic as in real life.

Later   What silly things depress me. Gladys wants 50p a week more in wages. i.e. £3.20 for 2 mornings a week. In the end I said yes. She suggested a compromise of 25p but I knew this would not really satisfy her. I hope to goodness this will. It means she will get nearly 8/- an hour . . . Poor G[ladys] she is always complaining of her lot and certainly her husband is a trial to her, apart from his illness. But she *is* a one for grievances. She is very envious – not unnatural, I suppose, since my life seems so easy to her.

16 July   She [Georgie] seems, I think, *somewhat* better in herself. What she is undertaking to do in this new house is still enormously complicated and I imagine very expensive. She seems, in a curious way, to care much more about E. now he's dead than when he was alive. She now has the idea of going to a medium . . . it might be her 'introduction to the light'. I met a woman 2 or 3 years ago who had become a Catholic via spiritualism.

17 August   Extract from 'Parish Newsletter' (Carmelite).

About Assumption and Immaculate Conception. 'It would be utterly repugnant to contemplate the divine nature united with flesh and blood that was stained by even the slightest sin.'

Started Simenon [translation of *La Cage de Verre*, 1973] June 10th, *Finished* August 17th. Just over 2 months, about 40,000 words.

22 August   New Parker. But like the Sheaffer, it is really too thick for this paper. This is the old Parker, finer but rather scratchy. The Flight is still the best for looks, though scratchy. It is probably best to accept fact that new Parker is really the best all-purpose one, if I write a bit more slowly.

All this nervous buying of pens is of course absurd. It is a vain hope of somehow being able to write the autobiography – abandoned in despair for so long.

The last two nights I have dreamt of the sea. I was with Lance and Emmi Sheppard. I knew Lance was dead, but in the dream, he was somehow there, and the hotel was somehow also Capel Cottage. In it they had two children – about 9 and 5, a boy and a girl. The children too knew their father was dead but they talked of 'Papa's room' as if he were still alive.

13 Dec   Notices in Newsagent's:
   Coloured ex-mistress seeks new position
   Exotic Dominatrix
   Attractive young male and female masseuses available in your home.
   Sue has all Kingsley's letters to his wife [Susan was engaged on her biography of Charles Kingsley, published 1975]. In one he hopes heaven will be 'one long copulation'.

17 Dec   Phyllis went yesterday. It was lovely to have her but so wretched that she lost her bag with about £30 in it. And after she had given *me* £50 of her Elva legacy.

I had a passionate dream about G.Y. [unknown] last night. It was a wonderfully happy dream but I was much shaken and shocked at myself when I woke up. Is one never too old to fall in love – however unsuitably? The unconscious never lies, according to Ployé, and the unconscious made it very plain what it desired . . . too grotesque – a fat old woman who can't see without her cataract glasses! I thought I was past all that. Not even the faintest stirring since Benedicta – and that was nearly 30 years ago. Only in dreams – and it is always Silas (until last night) and then it is really the past for Si and I are as we *were*, not as we both are now. But this was the present and I was, as I am now 73, and G.Y. his age (23 or 24 I think), and it was sex I wanted with him, not just cosy friendship and affection.

Christmas Day, 7.30 a.m.   Have just been opening parcels with much the old pleasure of childhood. My friends are so sweet! A week today, thanks to Charlotte I shall get these marvellous new hearing-aids. Hearing has become a real strain lately: often impossible when I'm with more than 2 people. Parties are really a nightmare. It was almost hopeless at M[arjorie] Villiers' last night. I couldn't hear what Moll was saying except that she was raging about the new girl at Harvill. It has become a real obsession.

I listened to Midnight Mass from a Catholic church on the radio. It was very moving – great warmth and enthusiasms and young people singing – 'traditional' and 'folk'.

I still have enormous difficulties about believing . . .

I am worried about Georgie. She talks of suicide. Talks of such odd things – such as that she's no good because she doesn't know Latin. Now she talks of Eric as a kind of super-being, almost a saint. I wish I knew some way to help her for she *is* dreadfully unhappy. But you somehow can't 'get through' to Georgie. One always seems to be at cross-purposes with her.

1973

1 Jan   Waiting with childish impatience for the man to arrive with my hearing-aid – already getting neurotic because it's 11.15 and he was due at 11 . . .
Later   It has arrived . . . I long to test it. Saturday at Sue's will be a fine opportunity.

It has been a strange year, saddened early on by Eric's death . . .

My friends have been incredibly kind to me and I have acquired 2 new ones, Elizabeth Sprigge [author] (my exact contemporary [at St Paul's]) and G.Y. who is only 21 and 2 years older than my grandson.

Nice things happened. Lyn [Isbell] and her husband's visit in the summer – and Lyndall and *her* husband's (she and Renzo married this year) in November.

The religious situation as puzzling as ever. Am just re-reading Santayana's *Reason in Religion*. The beauty of the language sometimes lulls one into a kind of trance. And of course, one is too ignorant to be able to contradict him. All the same, I remain profoundly affected by him – all due to Eric of course.

Rather strange: Elizabeth Sprigge told me the other day that she has just become again a practising Anglican. She went to Communion a few weeks ago and had a wonderful sense of 'belonging' and 'being accepted'.

5 Jan   Interesting to meet Shirley Hooker the other day. She was one of my students at St Mary's; a very pretty and gifted girl, who has been a Holy Cross nun ever since she finished college. What changes in a nun's life nowadays, especially in America. She is writing a thesis on Spenser and Shakespeare for her Ph.D. She has become a real scholar. She says there is a drug problem in the Catholic colleges. Strange facts: Catholics in America are allowed to go to Communion in Greek Orthodox churches: strictly forbidden over here of course.

This new generation of nuns – she's the first I've met – is really extraordinary – and I must say impressive. Very much 'in the world' yet not 'of it'.

29 April, Good Friday   My 'liturgical' birthday as I was born on Good Friday 1899. Two days ago I had a letter from Longmans which looks like resulting in a *huge* translation of a book about Smollett. I wonder if I am really 'meant' to try and write anything more of 'my own'. I am getting old: my contemporaries are all dying ... Elizabeth Bowen and Noel Coward died recently.

I don't know whether Gladys will eventually return . . . Her husband's unexpected death a fortnight ago was a terrible blow.

Re-reading W[illiam] Janes' *Varieties of Religious Experience* with the same conviction of the genuineness of the experiences and the same revulsion (I can't help it) from the appalling penances and the 'love talk' – adored 'Bride of Christ' idea – of St Gertrude and St Teresa. Yet I cannot, like the humanists (I was just as revolted by George Melly's cheap 'old man with a beard in a white nightshirt' gibe on the radio yesterday), reject the whole idea of the supernatural . . .

But when I think of the fervour and *real* conviction I had for many years after my return – oh, how terribly I have fallen off. For a long time I went to daily Mass or at least several times a week. Now I only go on Sundays and Holidays of Obligation and these 3 days in Holy Week. I only say sketchy morning and night prayers. mainly for *people*. I find the rosary *impossible* and any form of prayer terribly difficult. I lie awake sometimes for an hour or two in the night, *trying* to think about God. Yet I am perpetually preoccupied with religion.

Easter has always been a peculiar time for me – ever since my 15th birthday fell on Easter Sunday and that terrible scene with my father. How absurd that we could never have discussed it. I did once try – I was then getting on for 30 – I said 'Don't you think you made too much fuss over that novel of mine?' His face went stiff and all he said was 'I prefer not to discuss it.'

23 June   For 2 months now I have been working on the vast Smollett translation [*The Novels of Tobias Smollett*, Paul-Gabriel Boucé, 1976]. Many other difficulties – having to work by correspondence with Boucé in Paris: his amazingly good knowledge of English in some ways a drawback. He's very nice, amusing and intelligent. Ironically, just as I'd accepted the job, came an offer to translate Voltaire's *Life of Charles XII of Sweden* – a job much more up my street, with no 'collaboration', not nearly so long. B[oucé] is terribly long-winded and repetitive – (awfully careless grammatically sometimes) and sometimes far too elliptic and even self-contradictory. But, naturally, like any writer he's in love with his own style. Sometimes these minutiae of criticism seem scholarship run mad. I keep thinking of that scientist 'who brought to a high pitch of perfection the rectal inoculation of lice'. Yet one of the huge reliefs of the S[mollett] trans[lation] was being let off the rack of working fruitlessly daily on the autobi.

Gladys had just forced me into paying her more. Now she's forced me to £4.50 a week – for 2 of her much less than scheduled 4 hour mornings. Her husband's death has naturally upset her but she has really been rather naughty, telling lies behind my back about me to Diane. She *is* a tricky character. Said she was leaving – then ½ hour later returned to say she wanted to stay. Frankly my heart sank. Inconvenient as it wd. be the relief at the thought of her not coming –

her endless complaints and little trickeries are upsetting . . . could do perfectly [well] with only one morning a week but that is hard to get nowadays.

Georgie has seemed more cheerful lately: likes her job at Penguin etc. But on Thursday she turned up at ½ hour's notice. Seemed quite all right, grumbling about workmen's inefficiency, has got her knife into another girl at the office. Then suddenly burst into floods of tears . . . saying she wants to die, life meaningless without Eric. The bursts come on so suddenly – one doesn't know what to do. But oh, I wish Georgie (for her own sake) weren't such a *complainer*. When Eric was alive, she complained endlessly about *him*. Now it is the workmen, Joan Cochemé, her great friend Joan (forget her name), the girl at the office. She is *always* running down people, even if she's fond of them, as I know she is of Joan Hornsey. I daren't think what she says about *me*.

5 July   Boucé is arriving at 9 a.m. this morning and spending whole morning here. It really is a life-work.

26 July   Someone in USA has written to me asking for any personal reminiscences I have of Norman Cameron. Hunting through old notebooks (for I think it was in 1938 I saw most of him) I found endless pages about B[asil] N[icholson] with whom I was then desperately preoccupied. They brought back all that very queer period of my life when I was being analysed by Carroll . . . reminding me of things about myself which I don't like remembering. I suppose Carroll *was* right about my being so aggressive and destructive. I *feel* as if I'd 'improved' a bit.

* * *

David Gascoyne had probably introduced Antonia to the works of Nicolas Berdyaev when she visited him in Paris in 1938. Berdyaev was a Russian émigré, though not a White Russian, who wrote on philosophy, politics and religion.

* * *

I am re-reading Berdyaev's *Freedom and the Spirit*. I forget how much that book meant to me – when? – in the late 1930s, I suppose. It seems to mean even more to me now – the most helpful thing I've read on the great vexed religious question for a long time. Berdyaev helps me more than Santayana because he *believes*. 'Eastern' Christianity is much more sympathetic to me than 'Western'.

Boucé asked me to send him *The H. and the F*. Inevitably I was tempted to read a lot of it. I seem to have been a lot more 'intelligent' and articulate 30 years ago.

29 July   Two days off Smollett. Managed to transcribe some of the Norman Cameron notes. Difficult to remember the chronology. In those enormous old journals I don't often say when I went to a particular job. Yesterday Cassidy (Victor?) the man who is writing a life of Wyndham Lewis came to ask me for what I could tell him of Alick Schepeler. It seems W.L. wrote to her over a period of 20 years. It must have been very hard to *like* Wyndham Lewis. On Thursday Authors' Soc[iety] A.G.M. long and stormy, where a man called B. Johnson, representing W[riters] A[ction] G[roup] was so offensive and abusive that Elizabeth Sprigge and I felt like breaking off any connection with the W.A.G. Today Amanda [Hopkinson] came to tea. Extraordinary girl, but I'm very fond of her. She has had a third miscarriage. Physically she is extremely delicate and has been so from birth but temperamentally extraordinarily tough. She is always engaged in innumerable activities; has just written her thesis for her MA and is taking a job as a social worker in September. She has been running a crèche for deprived children. All this while keeping open house for anyone who turns up – people in trouble, students etc. Susan is shocked by what she considers her neglect of her own child, Rebecca, and outwardly it does seem that she is pretty haphazard about her, but I think, in her own way, she is very concerned for her. I was relieved to hear that the *ménage à trois* has broken up and that she and Peter seem to have found that they really belong together.

Her relations with Gerti are very bad again. Gerti sounds unhappier than ever, enclosed more and more in her suspicions and criticisms. The only person she seems to be really happy with is Nicolette's little son Martin whom she adores. She is terribly lonely, says she has never had any happiness in her life . . . yet there is a good deal of happiness she could have had if her own nature did not fatally prevent it. I asked Amanda about Tom. He is completely absorbed in

this [Meher] Baba thing. Gets up at 5 every morning to work on the
Life of Baba, which he and Dorothy are writing together. For ¾ hour
morning and evening practises his breathing exercises – the equiva-
lent of prayer for Baba devotees . . .

4 August   Fifty years today since I came out of Bedlam.

Wages in 1929. Elspeth [Glossop, Silas's sister] got £3 a week as
receptionist at *Vogue*: Corin [Bernfeld] £5 as knitting editor . . . 1/- an
hour was considered high for a charwoman . . . 30/- a week for a
trained children's nurse . . . Furnished flat in London 30/- a week . . .
My father's maximum salary as Senior Greek Master at St Paul's was
£600 per annum . . . Hardly anybody except the rich had a car. I think
Si was the only person I knew who had one – a Baby Austin. You
could buy a house in Paulton's Square for £1000.

9 Sept   Gerti is very ill, having been operated on for brain tumour.
All the suffering the poor woman has been through seems to have
been unnecessary. Had she never recovered consciousness after the
fall, she would have died painlessly. Her mind is very much affected.
A[manda] has come back to do her months 'notice' for her mysterious social work and will then go back to Austria [Gerti had taken a
flat in a castle near Salzburg]. Poor Gerti, one hates to think of her so
far away and entirely in the hands of doctors and hospitals. I feel
guilty about ever having introduced Tom to the Kingsmill.

Today I went to see Frank Freeman's picture show – I think it is his
only *real* show after 50 years of devoted effort to painting. The
pictures are very mixed but some I thought really *had* something. A
lovely drawing, done when he was only 26. *He's* another genuine
original . . . And six adorable grandchildren. I must say my friends do
have the most beautiful and intelligent children and grandchildren!

14 Oct   Dear Caroline (our ground-floor call-girl) advertised herself
as 'New young masseuse, specializes in relaxing and stimulating
treatment'. Now she's left here, I wonder what highly-respectable
Mrs Given-Wilson [who moved into her flat] will make of the calls
she receives.

  'Large chest for sale'
  'Versatile Girl seeks New Position'

'Dog-Trainer. Obedience Tests'
'French correction given'
'Lovely young coloured governess – strict disciplinarian'
'Games Mistress seeks new pupils'

18 Nov Smollett the most troublesome thing I've ever had to translate . . .

Have discovered why my eyes get so tired: the left eye needs new lenses.

10 Dec Renée Blakelock died on Nov 30th. It was a great shock when someone I don't know rang up. When I last saw her about 2 months ago she had not been well. She said it was 'nervous indigestion'. However she went off to Spain . . . When she got back the doctor put her into hospital for an 'exploratory examination'. What they found was inoperable cancer and she was dead in less than 3 weeks. I wish I'd known she was in hospital . . . But we have no mutual friends. I truly loved Renée. She remembered me in her will – incredibly generous. Her requiem was very beautiful – Latin at her request – not at all like Kathleen Raine's mother's which Fred Marnau called 'an insult to the living and the dead'. There was a *depth* in Renée and a great strength under all that sweetness and gaiety.

31 Dec The most saddening thing of all this year has of course been Renée's death. Every year now one or more of one's friends goes; it's part, inevitably, of having lived into one's own mid-seventies. And, inevitably, one wonders when one will die oneself, and most of all, *how*. Being an awful coward, I hope it won't be a very painful way. And for my own sake and Sue's, I hope I won't become a horrible, helpless burden. It is so wretched for poor Gerti to have been through all she has with that brain tumour and to know that, almost inevitably, it will grow again. I do not know if she realizes she is doomed. One wonders if Tom feels *anything* about her being so ill and almost certainly dying. But ever since he marred Dorothy he has become so remote and inhuman . . . he really cares only for Dorothy, who has literally *possessed* him. If she died before him, I believe he would really be unable to go on living.

Of course this year has been so entirely devoted, since April, to

Smollett that I hardly seem to have had any life of my own! It is unnecessarily exhausting, due to that jaw-breaking and redundant style and, though Boucé is pleased with the results, I'm working *against* my natural grain all the time. The one good thing about Smollett [is] that it has brought me a real and very delightful friend in Boucé himself, one of the nicest, most '*sympathique*' men I've met for ages. We can at least laugh a lot together over our extraordinary collaboration, which I couldn't do with Maritain!

1974

27 Jan   Increasingly conscious of there not being many more years left and wondering when, where and how it will end. As Bobbie said at his 70th birthday party on Jan 14th (that extraordinary party where poor Teresa's ex-Dominican husband threw his employer at the Richmond Fellowship down the marble steps and she had to be removed in an ambulance), '*il faut préparer sa mort*'. I begin to feel the physical effects of old age much more than I did even a few months ago. I am very tottery now when I walk and the daily effort of climbing five flights of stairs with a heavy shopping bag is a real ordeal.

9 Feb   A severe shock this morning. D[iane] informed me she was leaving for good on Tuesday – 3 days time! – and going back to Rhodesia. Not the faintest hint of this had she ever given me. I said 'This is rather short notice.' She said rudely 'I don't have a rent book so I don't have to give you any notice.' I had been considering getting a new carpet for her room and the man was actually here this morning measuring and estimating. I told her, thinking she would be pleased. She simply said 'I dare say your new lodger will be.' Her behaviour has been very odd lately, almost hysterical at one moment, perfectly rational and amiable a few minutes later. Last week, after one of her rages about the noisy parties upstairs, she said she was not going to pay me any more rent.

After the bombshell, my knees went on shaking for nearly an hour.

When I'd got some control of myself, I thought what an enormous relief her going would be – to have the flat to myself and not be worried with her endless complaints. I also think she's showing symptoms of something like a mental breakdown. Apart from her rages against the girls upstairs, she suddenly shows violent animosity against her two parish priests and I am to say she is out if they ring up.

11 Feb Although no signs of packing, I think she is going tomorrow. I said to her yesterday (the only words we exchanged), 'I suppose you won't be going to the law-courts tomorrow and won't want to be called.' She said she would be going to the courts in the afternoon 'to clear things up there'.

17 Feb Diane did go on Tuesday. She had been here 11 years!! The relief of having the flat to myself is indescribable and I hope I can go on keeping it so. I have had lodgers, both here and at Ashburn Gdns, for over 20 continuous years. 25 I think, for I certainly had Pat in 1947. Since then Daphne, Denise, Shirley, Smith, a French girl, Giorgio, Lel, Griselda, Wilson 1), Wilson 2), a South African girl, Chapman and Diane. 14 in all! I'm going to have the luxury of a new carpet in the spare room (my room, no longer Diane's!) which I was going to get for D. It is full of threadbare patches and is not improved by her having made a conspicuous burn on it (which she didn't even bother to mention).

7 April Much has happened . . . including Diane ringing up two weeks ago to say she had come back to England, and was the room still free? I said it was, and had the greatest pleasure in saying I proposed to keep it so!

Last Sunday was my 75th birthday. On Tuesday Sue came and spent the night here – for, of all fantastic reasons, to interview me for *Harper's*! And on Monday I had been telephoned by *Adweek* for reminiscences of my Crawford days! Sue recorded no less than 2 whole hours of our conversation. Goodness knows how the poor girl will manage to boil down that huge mass of material into an article – and she has only a few days to do it in. But she is amazing the amount of work she gets through in incredibly difficult circumstances with

Miranda and Jessica and everything to cope with. Poor Lyndall is
very depressed as usual. I wish to goodness she could have a little
more of whatever it is that makes one somehow make the best of
things.

I went back with Sue to Bow [Cottage] on Wednesday, for my
'official' birthday celebration. It was marred by serious worry over
Andrew [mistakenly arrested] in Delhi . . .

9 June I spent 3 weeks in May with Lyndall and Renzo. I came back
exhausted and remained so for a week but am very glad I made the
effort. Lyndall and I had two wonderful days in Venice which was
even more beautiful than I expected. It was easy to get away [from]
the tourists in St Mark's Square. Lyn is a marvellous travelling-
companion, she knows all sorts of odd places where there are
wonderful pictures – like the little church with the Carpaccios. Our
Pensione (one where Ruskin used to stay, opposite the Giudecca) was
near the Accademia. We were only a few yards from Peggy Guggenheim's palace but we had so short a time in Venice that I didn't feel
like ringing her up and wasn't in the mood for Modern Art. Besides
Venice, the two things I enjoyed most were seeing [Count] Umberto
Mora [Head of the Italian Institute, London] and his lovely house
again, and meeting Iris Origo [Tuscan author]. After reading her
book I really longed to meet her. I was amazed to find she'd read all
mine. The gardens at La Foca [near Pienza] are the most beautiful
I've ever seen and all created by herself and her husband. She is an
incredible woman – a great scholar, a first-class writer and involved
in the most magnificent charitable work for orphans and handi-
capped children. She has adopted a little Vietnamese orphan, an
enchanting little girl who looks radiantly happy. I longed to talk to
her for hours but we did manage to talk a bit at intervals between her
talking to Lyn and Renzo in Italian. She knew Santayana well in his
last days at the Blue Nuns convent in Rome. The last time she saw
him he said 'I'd like to show you what Reverend Mother has just put
in the chapel.' It was obviously a typical 'devotional' statue but he
didn't show it her in any spirit of mockery but with the utmost
simplicity as if it pleased him as much as it did Reverend Mother.

Lyndall was terribly sweet to me – and, indeed, so, in his way, was
Renzo . . . But I worry about Lyndall. She is in a perpetual state of

nervous tension, sometimes driven to tears by the endless frustrations of her life with Renzo. He really is an impossible man to live with – so selfish and irresponsible and demanding. She doesn't really *want* to leave him and certainly not to live anywhere except Italy. She says she has become dreadfully irritable and bad-tempered and she makes desperate efforts to be patient with Lorenzo who really demands the impossible of *her* and makes no effort to understand her. She *has* always tended to complicate her life and part of her *does* enjoy this complication.

I had a strange time there – spending hours alone in my beautiful room, reading Iris Origo's marvellous *Images and Shadows* which I must buy, Augustus Hare's fascinating autobiography – I want that too, most of I[ris] O[rigo]'s *The Last Attachment* (Byron's Guiccioli) and *Merchant of Prato* and half C. Woodham Smith's *Queen Victoria*. Anyway it couldn't have been a greater change from my normal routine and it was a wonderful respite from Smollett.

* * *

Emily Coleman had been living in the USA at a Catholic Worker Farm on the Hudson River in New York State, and during that time occupied herself almost entirely with painting.

* * *

15 June   Yesterday I went to a Requiem Mass for Bernard Wall. It was a Tridentine Mass, organized by dear Fred Marnau, who is Chairman of the Latin Mass Society – perhaps a little fanatical about it. It was a strange experience – somehow rather disturbing. I did not realize how used I'd become to the vernacular Mass. Much as I miss the Latin and think much of the English translation abominable, there seemed something in the Tridentine Mass that one missed – the sense of participation. There was a rather sad sense of clinging to the past just because it *was* the past. And, like the priest, we all seemed so *old*. Most of us had enormous trouble getting down on our knees on the steps of the altar (no rail, because now, much to Fred's fury, Communion is always given standing) and even more getting up from them.

This morning I heard from Phyllis that Emily died on Thursday last . . . the feast of *Corpus Christi*.

It will be a great blow to Phyllis – Emily has been one of the main people in her life (perhaps *the* main one, apart from her mother). It is 40 years since I first met Emily and until she went off finally to America about 10 years ago, she was a very important one in mine. She was a unique person with *incredible* vitality – fierce, passionate, generous, violent, wildly unreasonable . . . Phyllis said that in these last years she'd changed a good deal and was no longer firmly convinced that she was a saint and a genius. 'The Kingdom of Heaven suffereth violence and the violent take it by force' – I always used to think that applied to Emily. It was very difficult for her to understand a weak, vacillating, try-to-see-both-sides-of-a-question person like me and I nearly drove her mad with my 'English conventionality'. She did sometimes, as Djuna [Barnes] said of her, 'pile up on one like a lifework'. One of her famous and impossible demands to me was 'Write me *everything* you think about art, sex and religion' which I *certainly* couldn't comply with! She was somehow more than life size, with enough vitality for at least half-a-dozen people. Right to the last she attracted people. Poor 'Joe' adored her and devoted himself completely to her in her last illness. My one fear is that Phyllis, with her terrible sense of guilt, will feel she ought, after all, to have gone to America at Easter.

11 August   A long time, as usual since I wrote in this notebook. I finished the Smollett trans.

Boucé came the other day . . . Dear man, he truly seems anxious I should get on with the autobi. and is full of all the usual suggestions to break the jam. He says I talk so well, why not 'talk' the book into a tape-recorder? Yet I *know* this to be impossible – talking and writing are totally different things to me.

I miss Eric's splendid mind sadly. It really was 'a thoroughfare for all thoughts' as Keats said.

8 Sept   The Voltaire [*The History of Charles XII, King of Sweden*, 1976] is being nearly as trying as Smollett. In fact almost more so, as his syntax is v. difficult and his style elliptic. Also it involves perpetually stopping to look up place names, people's names etc. in heavy volumes, atlas, Larousse, [H.A.L.] Fisher's Hist. of Europe. And it is very hard to find a suitable style, even when one is quite sure what he means, which one often isn't.

Every Sunday (today is one) I waste the morning over Mephisto – a kind of compulsive masochistic 'treat'. It is truly *shocking* all the time I waste. All those masterpieces still unread on my bookshelves! My finsit, absurdly, has never been so good . . . I hardly see anyone, except when I go over to Elizabeth [Sprigge]'s for our pleasant supper and crossword sessions. I do miss my dear friends, especially Eric and Renée. The only people I can *really* talk to now are Susan and Phyllis. Elizabeth to a certain extent, but we don't talk much, because of the crossword puzzles. But she's an awfully nice new friend to have. Georgie I really *don't* have much in common with as a person. I don't find myself thinking 'how lovely it would be to see Georgie' as I do with Sue and Phyllis – and others far away, Lyndall and Lyn Isbell. Boucé is the person I've most enjoyed talking to for years: he livens me up with all his warmth and gaiety.

The other night I dreamt of an amazing party given by Sue. The fun, the excitement, the novelty of it were incredible. I kept thinking 'what happens next *must* be an anti-climax' but it never was. At the end we went outside together and there was a marvellous landscape – trees in full summer foliage in the background and snow in the foreground . . . almost like a Cecil de Mille historical epic. I suppose a compensation for my extraordinarily *un*adventurous present life.

I dream a lot about Eric and Georgie. Rather disturbing dreams. They show how deeply I must have resented that marriage. The other night I dreamt that Eric had come back (in my dreams he always wears the clothes he was wearing about the time of our marriage, his mauve suit, cream shirt and black Borsolino) and *this* time G. seemed to have disappeared from his life and we were going to live together again. But he announced, to my intense disappointment, that he had taken rooms at 'All Souls'. It was quite a while after I woke up that I realized that 'All Souls' was a very significant name for what he was going to be!

My relationship with him wasn't exactly 'love' but a kind of mental blood-tie . . . There was nothing we would not say to each other though we were so unlike. I really married him in order *to be able to see enough of him!* Georgie is really a very unhappy person and she might have been a very happy one. I suppose her main trouble is envy and it's a painful one to have, because one is *never* satisfied with what one has and is always wanting more. Also I think she wants the ends without the means. I'm a nice one to talk!!

* * *

Thomas and Susan spent most of 1975 and 1976 walking from Santiago de Compostela in Spain to Salonika in Greece, taking Miranda and her younger sister Jessica (born 1971) with them on donkeys. Andrew (22) accompanied them and Cordelia (20) joined them during university vacations. On the journey first Miranda and then Jessica fell off their donkeys and each broke an arm. Susan came home for a month with Miranda and Thomas with Jessica. Their book, *The Great Donkey Walk* (1977), describes the journey.

* * *

31 Dec   Months since last entry. Suddenly impelled, having just read David Gascoyne's journal, to look up what I had written about him at that time . . . What I write about him tallies with much he writes about himself. We certainly did have a most curious bond and I am touched that he recognizes it in his *Journal*. I was of course very much in love with him at that time and in his *Journal* of 1938, finding himself in the same condition (with a man) that I was with him two years earlier, he says that he realized what I must have been through. I would half like to write to him about the *Journal*, but he is so hedged round by this Judy woman. She now sees herself as Wife of Famous Poet. I can't imagine what she made of the *Journal*. The one moment when I saw him alone during that crazy meeting in a Knightsbridge hotel in the summer I said 'Are you happy?' He said gloomily: 'NO'.

In my own small world, one's friends dying . . . This month Elizabeth Sprigge . . . Cyril Connolly, not so much a friend, but one of the 'landmarks'. Poor Kate O'Brien – but a mercy, after having a leg amputated. One thinks all the time 'who next?' The idea of Sue being away for 18 months from the end of April makes me inevitably wonder 'Will I be alive when they return?'

Goodbye to 1974.

SIX

1975–1979

During the last five years of her life Antonia became increasingly frail and she can hardly have been cheered by the fact that Susan was in hospital several times in 1977 with severe depression. She did however meet Tom Hopkinson again, and Silas Glossop for the first time in decades, and was reconciled with both of them and their wives.

Helen White became a serious cause for concern. She was the younger sister of Antonia's revered cousin, Arnold White. They were the children of Uncle Howard, her mother's brother. Helen had worked in a bank all her life, but had vaguely artistic ambitions. When she retired Antonia found her a job in an art gallery and helped her with her rather bad short stories. She lived in a flat in North London and played a lot of bridge. Neither Antonia nor Arnold nor the health authorities seem to have realized that Helen was suffering from senile dementia.

1975

5 April   Well, I *have* finished Voltaire – on 29th March. I feel dispericraniated. Have been translating without a break (except for my holiday in Italy a year ago) for a year and nine months. Complete mental upheaval over Lyndall's plan to move me to a flat. So sweet of her, but when I saw the flat knew I could *never* live in it. Mercifully she decided against it, but it's taking me a day or two to calm down after the shock and nervous apprehension.

11 May   Returning to the autobi. as frustrating as ever. Niggling literally for days over one sentence in Chapter II. All this 3rd person part about my parents' families *terribly* difficult.

Lyndall in hectic search for a house or flat to buy in London, all incredibly complicated . . . I could only listen sympathetically to each fresh problem as it arose. She seems very mistrustful about having any business dealings with Sue (I had suggested that I thought Sue would gladly let this flat to her after my death if she really needed a home in London). I think it rankles that Sue never even thanked her for renouncing her legal right to inherit under my father's will. I nearly mentioned this to Sue when I saw her just before they all went off on the Grand Trek on April 29th but thought perhaps better not. I had no idea that Sue had never thanked her. But it all happened at that time when Sue refused to have anything to do with me and Sue may not have realized that Lyndall was making a very generous gesture! Had she been as 'grasping' as she thinks Sue is, she could easily have refused. I don't really think Sue is 'grasping'. I am rather worried about Sue and what seems to all of us this crazy expedition. I think she is pretty apprehensive about it too but too good a wife to discourage Thomas from something he has set his heart on. She looks tired and strained – no wonder after the rush of the last months – the publicity over her book [*The Beast and The Monk*, 1974], getting another one finished against time [*Charles Kingsley's Landscape*, 1976] – all the packing up and preparation for the expedition . . .

26 May   I have spent a strange week-end reading the Nev de Courcy [see page 196] letters that Mrs Chambers found at Binesfield, sorting them out and making some extracts from them. I shall send them to his son. Touching that they kept each other's letters. The last of Daddy's that Nev kept was the one written on the eve of his marriage. Nev knew it was the end of the golden period of their friendship – though it was silver to the end of Nev's life. I don't think Daddy knew of the posthumous son though of course he knew of de Courcy's marriage.

My father *did* make great friends with his pupils who loved him – Gollancz, Barney Salmon, Compton Mackenzie . . . (must try to read Charles O'Malley as Daddy is supposed to be like Monsoon). Nev incredibly idealistic about women, but enjoys 'civilized flirtation'. Think they both wanted to be writers. They both write v. amusing letters and so *young* . . . Imagine any young man of today, visiting his best friend for the first time after his marriage, apologizing for wearing 'blue serge' instead of a frock coat.

20 July Have just spent a week with Phyllis, which I enjoyed very much. We watched cricket on TV and did crossword puzzles and I did NOTHING except read Patricia Highsmith. When I got home I picked a book at random from my shelves. It turned out to be Père Falaize's *Lettres Spirituelles*. I remember how much it moved me when I read it many years ago during my 'good' period after returning to the Church. He was that young Dominican who was miraculously cured of cancer at Lourdes and a week later it returned and he died, after terrible suffering, in 1942. Re-reading it has impressed me as much as ever with his *radiant* sanctity. I marked several passages when I first read it: they shame me now for I truly believed then.

31 August Today I have spent hours desperately writing to Thomas who has sent me his new novel *Our Father* [1975]. I feel impossibility of establishing any bond with him over his books . . . there are many obviously good things in them – sharp observation, ear for dialogue, sense of atmosphere, climate etc. But leaving aside what I find (I can't help it) disgusting physically in his writing, all that fucking, shitting, vomiting etc. they still have this oddly inhuman quality. How he hates people – especially women. In life he certainly has this cruel streak. Yet he is also very kind – and very popular with his friends. Sue says she would be desperately lost without him . . . Why does he have this need for mistresses? Is it all just lechery as his books suggest?

This expedition. Hard not to see a tyrannical imposition of his own will on others in it. Impossible not to feel sorry for those little girls, especially Jessica, being made to put up with such hardships. And Cordelia, forced to march when she was feeling so ill and exhausted. WHAT is Thomas trying to prove to himself? Oddly, in this apparently crazy character in *Our Father* – Hugh Burkett – I suddenly recognized a person like Basil Nicholson – bitter, revengeful, contemptuous, yet vulnerable – needing love and yet destroying it . . . He is the most *real* character in the book. The monstrous Wilma is really *too* much to accept. What extraordinary husbands my two daughters have! At least Sue is much happier with hers. I wonder how this intense experience she's undergoing with her family will affect her. In some ways I wonder whether Lyndall for all her deviousness has more self-knowledge than Sue? I love them both so much – and more and more.

1 Sept   Made some sort of feeble response to Frances Smith's letter. It is hard to know how to deal with these 2 women, F.Smith and M. Ward who wrote to me years ago after reading my books. I'm sorry for their problems but feel hopelessly inadequate to cope with them. I wonder why I am a target for neurotic ladies.

   Fr. Mulvey [the parish priest at West Grinstead] really a little annoying, not yet acknowledging the £50 for my grave or saying whether he had booked it.

8 Sept   Spent several hours reading Jung's *Phenomenology of the Spirit in Fairy-Tales*. Fascinating. I have always been fascinated by fairy tales and mythology. I *very* dimly see how if the Garden of Eden story is taken as a myth it is extremely profound.

   A few days ago I began to re-read Katherine Mansfield's *Letters*. At first, I was v. critical about them: tiresome whimsicality, artificiality, gush: then much of my old feeling for her returned. Her amazing courage in face of constant pain and illness. Her genuine integrity about writing. Her *genuine* desire to know the truth and face it. I've fairly soaked myself in K.M. the last few days: re-reading the short stories too. How tremendously she influenced me in the 1920s . . .

9 Sept   Jeremy [Bertram] paid me a short visit on Saturday. He has now definitely decided to become a Diocesan priest and is off to Rome in 3 weeks to begin his training. I felt a little depressed about him this time. As if he had *shrunk* in some way. I suppose he has made the right choice. I hope so. But he did not strike me as happy.

15 Oct   I'd love to hear from Sue in Cornwall, but no news is presumably good news about Miranda's arm. Anyway I hope to see Sue at the end of the month before she returns to that alarming expedition.

16 Oct   Kathleen's party was a joy. The Marnaus, Ramon Nadal and his wife, Philip Sherrard and – of all people – Segovia!! An adorable courteous old gentleman with a fine pale face and enormous thick-fingered white hands. It was a wonderful evening, only marred by my deafness . . . I wanted *so* much to hear everything Nadal and Sharrard said since they were talking of things so passionately interesting to me. I was glad to hear Nadal talking about Santayana and even agreeing with some of my tentative remarks.

21 Dec Yesterday I had a long letter from Lyndall, telling me, to my amazement that Sue had got back to Italy to find that Jessica had also broken her arm. She insisted that Thomas took J. back to England to make sure it had been properly set, which he did. And he has been here over a month, with Si and Sheila, without my having the faintest intimation of what had happened. They went back to Italy last week. I suppose he assumed that Sue would have written and told me. In the meantime Sue, Andrew, Miranda and the donkeys have been staying with Lyndall and Renzo. I've *no* idea where they are now, so cannot write to Sue. I wrote to Sue at La Ripa [her house in Tuscany], when I thought she was there, but don't suppose she ever got it, though presumably Thomas did.

The whole expedition now seems crazier than ever. Lyndall said Thomas was determined it should be continued to Turkey in the spring, though *not* with the children riding donkeys. However A.K. said last night that she'd heard (for the first time!) from Andrew and that he and Sue are going to do their utmost to persuade Thomas not to proceed to Turkey, but to come back from Italy in the autumn of 1976. *No one* but Thomas wants to go on with this absurd and dangerous expedition. They can't come back to England because they've let Bow Cottage. And goodness knows what effects it will have on the children especially Miranda, who misses her school and companions of her own age (Jessica is too young to be a real one for her) and has probably suffered even more psychologically than physically from her broken arm (which *still* isn't quite usable again). Sue said if she hadn't agreed to go it might have wrecked their marriage. I wonder if all this isn't far more likely to.

Poor Lyndall is having a worse and worse time with Renzo. He really sounds as if he is going mad – all these crazy suspicions and accusations and this mania about his health.

31 Dec   As regards my personal life this year has been Sue and Lyndall year. Seeing L. so often and S. so unexpectedly delightful – but what troubles for both of them – Lyndall with Renzo and all the complications of the flat and Sue with the two disasters on the expedition.

At Marjorie [Villiers]'s party on Christmas Eve I met a woman (didn't catch her name) who most strangely had known both Elaine [Lingham] and V[irginia] J[ohnes] and her husband. Both two latter are dead. Elaine sounds rather too 'exaltée' – our experience of her had been rather the same. Both greatly attached to her and both finding her disappearing when she had become indispensable and always changing her job. This woman said that V.J. was drinking heavily. That would explain much, but not all. It seems that Raymond's antiques turned out to be valuable when they were sold after his death. So I don't think they were in penury, as she made me feel.

1976

10 April   The other day Esther [Hopkinson, Tom's sister] came to tea. It must be 20 years since I saw her. She is an *admirable* nun and truly religious and a delightful person as well. I got news of all the Hopkinson family from her. She'd stayed with Tom and Dorothy in Cardiff and was much happier about Tom than when she saw him last. They [Tom and Dorothy] are both still deeply engaged in promoting Baba and have just been to India. Luckily Tom has plenty to do now he has retired: lecturing etc. He lectured on 'Journalism' to the Anglican Carmelites of which Edmeé [Kingsmill] is a member. Esther says Edmeé has settled down very happily now as a Carmelite, after a difficult beginning.   .

Yesterday I went to see Zillah Tickner in Croydon. Must be well over 60 years since I last saw her. She will be 85 on April 19th. She now has one room in the Whitgift almshouses . . . has to do all her own cooking on a minute electric stove. She is mentally *very* alert but looks v. frail physically.

I plied her with questions about Mulberry House, Cheriton etc. Naturally she wanted to talk about Winifred [Patterson] and Winifred's children and grandchildren and show me snaps of them (only one that really interested me was of my father as best man at Winifred's wedding). Amused that she never asked me a single question about myself. Oddly enough she'd seen a picture of Sue in Sussex paper and knew about the expedition. Have no idea whether she knows anything about my life since I grew up. Her mother (Ada Tickner) was very fond of my father (her first cousin).

17 April Much in the last few [days] to be thankful for. Dear Renée's £1000, without which I don't know how I'd manage this year with no translation since a year ago and none in sight.

6 August Huge gap. On Aug 4th Sue returned ahead of the others. Bobbie Speaight's book on Mauriac to review for *The Tablet*. Three whole weeks of agonizing. Yesterday I was in such despair that I was tempted to send the book back to John Cummings with grovelling apologies. Bless Sue! I told her this and she said that this was just what I *must* do, and I have. Moreover the angel child has actually written to Bobbie explaining I have done so and why.

2 Sept Still very shaky after the experience with Helen. Tuesday was a nightmare from 9 a.m. till I somehow got her to Liverpool St and on to the 3.30 p.m. train. She seemed quite herself in the train and until after dinner at Arnold's.

I don't know *what* is the matter with Helen. Yesterday morning at Arnold's back in the same state. Refusing to get out of bed: babbling obsessively about the flat etc. There are moments when it almost seems as if it were *deliberate* – she has a cunning, mischievous look as if she were a naughty child, determining to give the grown-ups as much trouble as possible. Yet there's no doubt she's in a state of extreme depression and anxiety. The chaos in the cupboards and drawers of her flat is unspeakable.

4 Oct Had not realized it is a whole month since the Helen trouble started. Latest development is that she did finally, after much difficulty agree to keep appointment with psychologist last Tuesday but on the way to get a taxi tripped over a paving stone and broke her wrist.

12 Dec This constant trouble with Helen. I get furiously impatient with her endless and constant telephoning.

The most unexpected and saddening death this year has been that of Bobbie Speaight. I find it hard to realize he is dead – he was so full of energy. I wonder what *he* really believed about Catholicism.

16 Dec Terrible phone-call from Helen last night. I wrote to Arnold this morning. I was shaking all over with nerves, just as I do after a bad Cromwell Road crossing. This trouble with Helen has really dominated my life ever since September.

18 Dec The Helen situation worse than ever. The last 3 days she has rung me up 2 or 3 times daily. Yesterday was the worst ever. She rang up in the afternoon screaming and laughing hysterically. Maria [Spanish cleaner] was here so I promised to ring her back, which I did. She was a shade more rational – not hysterical – but all the old story, state of flat, no food, hadn't got up, couldn't go to Arnold for Christmas because 'looking a fright' etc. After 20 minutes I begged for release. She said could she ring me up again when she got up. She did so at 6. Implored me to go over there. I said I really couldn't. I elicited that she had at least some tins in the flat and could make herself some soup. I managed to get off the hook by saying I had to make a phone call, which was true. I wanted to ring Arnold . . . The poor man is being subjected to the same treatment. Almost a relief that he too has had the screaming hysteria. I cannot see any solution except that she should go for a time to the Marlborough Clinic hospital.

More of Deuteronomy this morning. The laws laid down by Yahweh are incredible . . . a virgin raped in the city to be stoned to death along with her seducer because she did not cry out.

'A man that is wounded in the stones or hath his privy member cut off shall not enter into the congregation of the Lord'.

20 Dec Two calls from Helen yesterday. She did go to the bridge party on Saturday. But she was as bad as ever on Sunday. Obsessed with the 'untidiness' of the flat, but refuses to do anything about it. Screamed.

24 Dec Mercifully Helen *must* have gone to Arnold's [for Christmas.].

1977

1 Jan I had a lovely Christmas with Sue and the family and was put up in great luxury by A.K.

Peter [Samuel] Hoare† died last year too. And Wyn Henderson.

Thank goodness my younger friends, the Marnaus, Mark [Bence-Jones] etc. are not only alive but full of vigour.

4 Jan Last night I had a peculiar dream about Eric . . .

Eric himself was definitely talking to me as he might have done if he were still alive. It was as if he were truly in contact with me, but as a spirit from another world. He impressed on me that the only important thing was to preserve one's 'integrity' as an artist, no matter what sacrifice it cost.

19 Jan *Five* phone calls from Helen today. Arnold has rung up the Marl[borough] Hosp[ital] doctors. They came to see her this morning. She screamed at them . . .

I had dinner with Kathleen Raine last night. Oh, the bliss of being in that quiet beautiful room!

The anniversary of Eric's death – 19th Jan 1971. It is incredible to think he has been dead six years.

28 Jan The Helen situation got worse and worse. On Thursday 20th she blackmailed me into going over there. I refused to go into the flat but consented to lunch with her at a nearby restaurant. She behaved reasonably but was furious that I refused to go back to the flat with her. Said I had promised which I certainly hadn't. I managed at last to escape on a bus. As soon as I got home she started ringing up again.

The next day, Friday 21st, I had all that trouble with the fridge, which had to be removed by the fire brigade.

Dear Phyllis's almost daily letters, since that awful Saturday when H[elen] came to lunch and made such appalling scenes, screaming and banging on the street door, have been a wonderful comfort and moral support. So has Beatrice Given-Wilson who rushed out into the passage when H. was banging on the door and screaming and tried vainly to make her stop. When, at last, by ringing up Arnold and getting *him* to persuade H. to go quietly, she *did* go, Beatrice made me go down to her flat and gave me coffee and brandy. I really needed that brandy for I was shaking all over. Ironic touch of comedy – when I got back up here about 9 p.m. the phone immediately rang. It was Helen saying she had left her gloves here! Those lost gloves have been a recurring theme in her phone calls ever since – almost one of her major grievances along with the untidiness of her flat, the (imaginary) fatness of her face, the condition of her hair, her shortage of clean clothes (or any clothes 'fit to wear' though she has plenty – her underclothes I can well believe are very dirty) and all the farrago I get every time she rings. Obviously there *is* something seriously the matter with her mentally but *no one* can cope with that, except one *hopes* the psychiatrists, if she'll let them.

29 Jan   Arnold rang up this morning. News almost too good to be true. Helen actually *did* go into the hospital on Tuesday night.

The silence, welcome as it is, seems almost strange, as if a perpetual noise one had been used to hearing for months had been suddenly cut off.

1 Feb   Phyllis's generosity is incredible. Yesterday a second cheque for £20 from her – to contribute to the cost of the new fridge. I feel mean to take it for she is worse off than I am but this reckless generosity is part of her nature.

I do hope and pray that Arnold's operation tomorrow will result in a cure. It is impossible not to fear that it is for cancer. How many people I know or know of have died of cancer in the last few years – dear Renée, Meum [Stewart] and Alick [Schepeler], Gerald Barry, Beatrice G[iven]-W[ilson]'s husband, Fr. Vincent McNabb, Robert and Françoise Demenge, and many, many more, including I think, Cyril Connolly and John Davenport. Auntie Bee would have died of it if she had not mercifully had a stroke and Father Victor if he had not had a heart attack and Enid Starkie too. Clare Nicholl too died of it and Anthony Hope. Poor Emmi [Sheppard] has had two operations already and things look very bad for her. Barbara Ward was given six months to live about 2 years ago but has amazingly – perhaps miraculously – had an intermission [sic]. Hilda Graef, after having made a successful recovery from a mastectomy, died soon after of multiple cancer.

3 Feb A relief to hear from Catherine that Arnold's operation showed that he did not have cancer but an ulcer. It will be a still greater relief if he survives the critical period after the operation. Eric also had 'a satisfactory' operation for a gastric ulcer, but he died a few days later . . .

5 Feb Delightful surprise yesterday. Lyndall and Renzo have made one of their sudden dashes to London and will be at their London flat [Harley Gardens, Fulham Road] for a fortnight . . .

12 Feb Still no word from Helen, though she must almost certainly be home by now. A[rnold] had said they weren't 'solving her problems'. Surprisingly, she was lying in bed most of the day, just as she did at home. C[atherine, Arnold's wife] said the psychiatrist seemed to have 'got it across to her' that the only person who could help her was herself. Poor Lyndall had bad news from the gynaecologist yesterday: he insists that hysterectomy is essential and wants her to have the operation at once. This is impossible for her because of Renzo. But I *hope* she will come back and have it done in March. She is really having a terrible time, poor child. *Nothing* seems to go right for her these past few years.

I felt ashamed of bringing up my perpetual obsession when she has such serious troubles of her own. She couldn't have been kinder. She is absolutely convinced (says she has been for some time) that I should give up these hopeless attempts and chuck the whole thing for the time being.

15 Feb   It seems that Renzo can hardly live much longer. She is wonderfully patient with him but he is terribly difficult and demanding, poor man, and she is under great strain. She saw Mrs Wood, who, before they discussed business (the flat) said she had urgent 'messages' for her. Whether it is thought-reading, and not communication from spirits, Mrs W[ood] must be a remarkable thought-reader, for she said things which were very much in (and on) Lyn's mind . . .

She [Lyndall] says if R. dies, she would like to get away from Cortona altogether – the atmosphere there has become painful and menacing and move to somewhere near Siena – in the horse-breeding area – where she could buy an attractive house far more cheaply. Mrs W. says that after that things will go well for her and she will be happy. I think Lyndall has behaved heroically since R.'s illness this time last year. She has devoted herself to him absolutely, at great sacrifice to herself.

16 Feb   Dear Fred Marnau has just rung up to ask me to dinner with him and Senta – just the 3 of us at their flat, which is what I like best – on Friday. This is very comforting.

In despair, since I cannot think of anything I want to write, or am capable of writing . . .

17 Feb   Lyndall managed to get over this morning. She brought me quantities of food – enough supplies for several days. She had the bright idea of getting in touch with Mary Austin, who saw her, and can arrange for [her] to have the homeopathic remedies Lyn so much wants. I think this is a great relief to her mind, as she is very nervous of [Dr] Reiss's drug treatment.

Did not attempt to write today. Washed garbage pails and counter tops. Fear all those little black specks are mouse dirt, not tea-leaves. Have seen two small mice in past few days, one in workroom, one in kitchen.

Still no word from Helen . . . Does that mean she is still in hospital? or, better still, that she is back home and able to manage her life again? More probably, still in hospital. But that is good – it should mean that at last she is being more co-operative.

21 Feb   Have re-read Cyril [Connolly]'s *The Unquiet Grave*. Very disquieting! Brings up all the old problems of art and religion. Religion hardly an 'old' problem for me but a perpetually present one!

26 Feb   Last night I dreamt someone asked me who I would want to be with me when I was dying and I replied unhesitatingly 'a good old Irish priest'. So some part of me obviously *does* believe, though I am so riddled with doubts on the surface. I understand Amanda very well!! She 'wouldn't feel at home' anywhere else, nor would I. She doesn't worry about taking lovers and so on.

28 Feb   It began in Oxford. I had been to see Viola Garvin, who delayed me so long that I feared I would miss my train. However I got to the station and was just able to catch it as it was about to leave. Victor Gollancz was on the train. He asked me to marry him. I was hesitant about saying 'Yes' for I hardly knew him but I agreed. We were both old. I liked him and with him I would have security and no more worry about money. I told him how much I admired *This Year of Grace* . . . I presumably said something about the nice things he'd written about my father in *Letter to Timothy*. G. said, with a twinkle in his eye: 'But there was another side to the dear old boy' – obviously implying that it was a slightly reprehensible one – though he did not seem shocked, only amused.

   In real life Gollancz was brought up as a strictly orthodox Jew and suffered much from the burdens imposed on him. When he grew up, he abandoned the Jewish religion but became profoundly interested in Christianity though I don't think he ever became a Christian. Undoubtedly he had an extremely religious temperament as *This Year of Grace* – one of the best autobiographies in the form of quotations from poets and mystics – proves. Was his situation in some ways comparable to my own? But why *did* this curious dream seem so important to me at the time?

* * *

Antonia and Silas had both lent paintings to the John Tunnard exhibition at the Royal Academy. The private view seemed an excellent occasion for them to meet again. They had not seen each other since before Susan's marriage in 1951. Silas and Sheila by now lived (and still live) in a converted farmhouse on the moors above Penzance.

* * *

1 March   I hope to goodness Sue can come to the Tunnard private view on Friday and give me moral support at the meeting with Si and very likely Sheila too – after more than 25 years . . .

4 March   Lying in bed, I managed for the 1st time for ages to say the rosary. The Sorrowful Mysteries. It made me realize all too well how shockingly superficial I've become about religion. I didn't want to think about deep things. Because it's a fine day for once I was glad just to be alive and felt happy. It's no good – I love ordinary life and am a frivolous person.

5 March   All my apprehensions were unnecessary. Si could not have been sweeter. Sheila did not arrive till much later – and she was quite friendly. It was wonderful to see Si again. We managed to talk quite a lot in spite of the crowd. He has all his old charm and the poet is still there underneath the 'eminent' and successful man. He wrote the memoir of Tunnard in the catalogue. I did not know what close friends they must have been. Si must miss him terribly – the one person of his own kind in his Cornish life. The die-hard of whom Sue warned me showed now and then, but Si was in his mellowest mood – I could almost tease him about it. I was so excited by this meeting that I could not sleep. I got up twice in the night and sat smoking and reading the Tunnard catalogue for an hour. I did not get to sleep properly till after 3.30 and have got up at 7.15. The Tunnard exhibition was wonderful. The picture I most longed to possess was one of several that Si has – a marvellous one of herons. I told Si how much I loved his sequence of poems after the Butterworth débâcle. He has been looking them up again. I'm so thankful that that side of him is not dead. I think there is no hope of ever having a long talk with Si, just the two of us. But that does not matter. It was so wonderful to see him again and I think it made him happy too.

7 March   Rashly I rang up Helen. She sounded as bad as ever, even worse. Says the hospital is very angry with her. The people in the other flats are complaining more than ever – the screaming, throwing things about etc. In the hospital she says they were furious with her for staying in bed all day. Keeps saying she 'has broken her contract' with them and 'lost her last chance'. She is supposed to return to the hospital tonight. Of course she says 'she can't'.

8.30 She's just rung up for 3rd time. Now we're back to all the old stuff about having no decent clothes etc. Now she's rung up for the 4th time.

8 March Today is the memorial service for Colin King [youngest son of Cecil and Margaret]. Helen rang me up 6 times in all last night . . . I went to St. James' at 12. But the church was empty and no sign of any service. Suppose I must have misread Margot's postscript.

10 March Terrifying electricity bill for £54.75. I am getting quite paralysed by the perpetually rising cost of everything. Don't think I *can* really manage Sue's idea of writing stories for Jessica . . .

15 March I really am in a ridiculous state of mental confusion and indecision. What have I done all morning but read heaps of recipes – all much too complicated – in the effort to provide meals for Phyllis who is perfectly satisfied with quite easy things and 'convenience foods'.

17 March Today hasn't been much better. Sue rang up yesterday to ask how I was getting on with stories for Jessica. I had to tell her I had tried in vain to think of one . . . Yesterday I made myself cook a risotto, which filled up an hour and might make a possible meal for Phyllis. How I long for her arrival on Monday!

21 March The Bible becomes stranger and stranger. I am now in Chronicles. The Kings have their own 'seers'. Some of the prophets are musicians and inspired by music.

25 March I dreamed about my last days with Silas before he sailed for Canada. It seemed a possible theme for a short story – *if* I can ever write again.

4 April   Because I went down to Bow [Cottage] yesterday, didn't do
Mephisto (Azed *too* difficult this week). Have wasted whole of today
on it. Was a little depressed at Bow yesterday; Sue obviously not well
yet and terribly tired. Longed to tell Thomas he ought to let her have
some help in the house . . . Sue has heard from Cordelia that Lyn and
Renzo are selling the Molino [converted watermill below the
Palazzone, where they often lived] and moving to a flat in Bologna.
Also that Lyn has bought a new horse. Why? ALL very mysterious like
so many of Lyndall's actions!

On Friday I went to a cocktail party given by Maria Tugendhat
[mother of Christopher Tugendhat] – who seems very nice. Of
course have no recollection of meeting her before. She lent me a book
The Noonday Devil by Fr. Bernard Bassett SJ. Afraid it isn't going to
be my cup of tea . . .

Sue and Thomas gave me the Paul Ferris *Dylan Thomas* for my
birthday. P.F. asked me to contribute scraps of reminiscence. They
come out bad and inaccurate. I get rather weary of this mania for
writing more and more books about Dylan. I don't think I'll enjoy
this one much.

I've read Isherwood's *Christopher and his Kind* – feel ambivalent
about that one too. Much preferred *Kathleen and Frank* and *A Single
Man*. Certainly he is desperately trying to be honest. It is perhaps hard
for a woman to understand some aspects of the homosexual world,
though I came to understand so many of them through Eric. The
world of the 'boy-bars' and male brothels obviously has a tremendous attraction for them. I find Auden a more sympathetic character
than Isherwood but I *do* like the particular 'so' sense of humour and
have always liked homosexuals and male ones, with the solitary and
glaring exception of Benedicta, better than female ones. And except
in fantasy – which I haven't indulged in for some 30 years or more – I
don't have peculiar appetites – nothing as simple as straightforward
lust. Don't think I've ever gone to bed with anyone with whom I
wasn't to some degree 'in love'.

5 April   Managed at last to get to Harrods by tube. Once again
nerve failed me to get on to the escalator [after a recent fall] at
Knightsbridge, but someone kindly helped me on. Even so my knees
were shaking when I got off. Absurd this neurosis which I don't seem

able to overcome. The old gentleman I was waiting behind at the library desk turned out amazingly to be Brian Hill [homosexual poet]. If he hadn't spoken to me I doubt if I'd have recognized him – he looked so much older than when I last saw him 2 years ago. Not having my hearing-aids on I could hardly hear what he said. But he can still see out of doors without glasses, though going deaf. Poor Brian, he has angina, a painful foot and lives in dread of becoming immobilized. Waiting in the bus queue I was amazed at the endless procession of ugliness, even in the young. They call this the 'affluent' society and never were there more advertisements for beauty aids, but never have I seen so many shabby, ill-dressed and unattractive people. Brian at least was well-groomed and 'civilized'. I know I looked pretty awful myself, of course, but one does at my age and I *can* make myself look passable when I try.

Arnold's second operation shows that he has cancer of the liver . . . Helen is not to be told. She rang up 3 times this evening. There are so many people I feel so much sorrier for than Helen – Arnold, Emmi, my cousin Winifred, now almost blind and so courageous about it. I'm so *incredibly* lucky myself with so little physical disability.

6 April   In despair after the calls from Helen, rang up the Marlborough and was lucky to be put through to Dr Rollings (?). He says there is nothing wrong with her mentally. She is lonely and bored, but quite a lot of all this behaviour is play-acting.

14 April   Helen situation has become worse than ever over Easter. Four or five telephone calls a day. The first this morning was at 7.30.

16 April   Amanda says that Tom has had to go into hospital for suspected cancer of the thyroid.

20 April   Helen rang up in the morning. I was so shaken that, when I set off for my shopping-round I could not face the prospect of crossing roads, my knees were trembling so, and I simply walked round the square and came home again.

22 April   She rang up no less than 9 times yesterday. Eight of the calls were as usual incoherent – animal noises . . . but in the last one at

8 p.m. she talked quite rationally and audibly and I suggested she should buy some new underclothes (the state of hers being one of her obsessive themes).

27 April   Lyndall has become fascinated by a book written by an old professor she met in Bologna – *Una Finestra Aperta nei Cieli* which she says has changed her whole life and made her 'see the light'. She has given me a copy. It is an amazing book about the after life and the communications from the departed are very convincing and by no means irreconcilable with Catholic ideas. She herself had had communications through this old professor (Arturo Elettra) from Jenny Nicholson [daughter of Robert Graves] and from Iris Tree which seemed to her very authentic, in the way they express themselves.

Yesterday she told me of an extraordinary experience she had in Bologna. A gipsy woman accosted her in the street, with the usual request for money. L. gave her 500 L and walked on. The woman ran after her and said: 'There is something I have to tell you.' She said that someone had put a curse on L. L. said she didn't believe in curses. Gipsy asked if she believed in God. Lyndall said yes, but not in curses. Gipsy was v. persistent. Said she wanted to find out whether the curse could be removed. L. was naturally intrigued and curious, especially as her contact with Elettra had left her in a strange state of mind. Gipsy asked if she had a thread of cotton on her. Eventually L. found a piece about 4″ long hanging from the seam of her jeans and broke it off. Gipsy asked her to tie 3 separate knots in it, which she did. She then told her to roll the thread into a ball and hold it, then to say 'I believe in God' and breathe on it twice. L. did so. She told me it was the first time she had ever said openly and with complete conviction 'I believe in God' – not just in a mysterious 'something'. Gipsy then told her to unroll the thread again. *There was not a sign of a knot*!!

29 April   Sue came to tea yesterday – looking and feeling much better, thank heaven.

4 May   I have finished by far the most interesting and convincing (to me) of Lyndall's 3 books. Cumins and Tolsvig's *Swan on a Black Sea*.

Am not doing very well with Jane Sherwood's *The Country Beyond* which I find too complex and difficult to understand.

Plain, elementary Italian grammar is a useful antidote.

11 May An extremely interesting letter from Toke Townley [a copious *The Hound and the Falcon* correspondent] about how a new type of 'behaviour therapy' has cured him of years of being unable to act on the stage. Up to now he had always thrown up his part during rehearsals from neurotic fear of facing an audience.

14 May Irony. Just after first call, phone rang again. Sure it was H. I said angrily 'Who is that'. Faint voice which I thought said 'Helen' replied. But it was *Emmi* – my dear Emmi, whom I've been so worried about. When I think of all Emmi bears – so cheerfully and heroically – it is harder than ever to put up with Helen's incessant whining.

18 May Helen situation no better. This morning she sounded worse than ever, sobbing, screaming and saying 'expect the worst' if I wouldn't go over there, which I refused to do.

19 May I've given up hopes of a translation. Spend my time desultorily doing Italian and reading Lyndall's books on spiritualism . . .

23 May H. started phoning me at 7 a.m. and rang up twice later. I rashly went over at her urgent request. She was wearing a coat over her underclothes and no stockings and had not brushed her hair, though she had varnished her nails. During tea she talked relatively sensibly. Just before I left she suddenly started snarling, making hideous face and tearing up paper, but I felt this was a deliberate performance. She actually offered to come and see me across the road to the bus which she did very competently. No sooner had I got home than she started telephoning again.

24 May Apart from Helen, I've spent the whole day reading Rees-Mogg and Crookhall's *The Supreme Adventure*.

I did make a half-hearted attempt to do a little on the autobi.

25 May   Just as I had started to eat my supper, phone rang again. I expected of course it wd. be H. as voice was faint. Mercifully I realized when the woman said 'Is that Antonia?' it was poor Bridget Speaight,† sounding distraught, ringing up from Campion House [the Speaights' house at Benenden, Sussex]. She is suffering terribly poor thing – feeling the full impact of Bobbie's death now. She is coming to London on Tuesday.

My brain has become so addled that I can't concentrate on anything, even doing an Italian exercise. I am shamelessly listening to the European Football Cup, Liverpool v. W[est] Germany, from Rome. I really am becoming mentally exhausted by H.'s incessant and ruthless demands.

28 May   This morning I started a letter to him [Dr Rollings] about 6 a.m. My hand was shaking as I wrote but I managed to write it. As I was signing it at 7.15 a.m. Helen rang up. I protested furiously, swore at her, and refused to listen to the usual complaints. I caught the first post this morning and put an 8½d stamp on it, so he should get it on Monday morning. Beatrice [Given-Wilson] was very comforting and said if I can hold on till the meeting on Tuesday, things *must* come to a head.

31 May   Bridget has just rung up to say she'll be here about 4.15. At least that solves the tea problem. I *had* got everything prepared in case.

1 June   Helen turned up at the meeting looking amazingly well-groomed; hair fresh from the hairdresser, nails professionally varnished, smart check coat, shoes and stockings.

Dr Snowden, Rollings, and a male social worker were there. Dr Charkin her GP was to have come but didn't. Police did not send a representative, not being able to spare a man. Olga and her boy friend and the girl from the flat below and her father spoke for the tenants who not surprisingly find the incessant screaming worse than ever. Also a very nice man, the proprietor of the corner shop where she has almost daily been creating havoc. The tenants were furious.

Snowden said she was definitely not insane and could not be put in a mental hospital unless she made a definite attempt at suicide, instead of merely threatening it. I had told Rollings in a private talk with him before the meeting, that the telephone calls had kept increasing until they reached the record score of 17 the day before the meeting.

Well, I came home at last at 9 p.m. with the feeling a huge weight had been lifted from my mind. Helen really *did* seem to have come to her senses and be prepared to behave reasonably.

What a fool I was!

Naturally I was prepared for a call this morning and it seemed a hopeful sign that it did not come till 11.45 a.m. To my horror we were back to square one – all the usual old stuff.

What *is* to be done with this incredibly slippery, untruthful and ruthlessly determined creature who will stop at nothing to get attention focussed on her?

3 June I was out seeing Ronald [Moody]'s sculptures at Commonwealth Institute from 6–9 last night, so if H[elen] rang then I was out.

4 June Since Lyndall's last visit, I have been reading the books she left. I find much in Jane Sherwood's very baffling, particular[ly] the insistence of her 'communicators' on the necessity of reincarnation and the theory, which I find difficult to follow, both in her book and Crookhall's, of the various 'bodies' – physical, etheric, astral and apparently a 4th (spiritual?) especially as they give different names to them. I am having great difficulty in following the arguments and diagrams in *The Country Beyond*. The *Finestra* which made such a deep impression on Lyndall and which I have promised to read I find heavy going – partly because it is so repetitive and partly because, though one believes utterly in Elettra's sincerity, it is hard to believe all he claims to have been told about the after-life on other planets after death.

The result of reading all this has made me feel that Catholicism is the best path to follow through this jungle . . .

One of those uneasy 'flat' dreams last night. My mother was still alive and we were looking for a flat to take together. I was shown over it by Mrs Kirby, the long-dead caretaker at Ashburn Gardens.

I am *very* glad Arnold rang me up last night. Now I feel free to write to him, if necessary, about Helen.

I wonder how many calls I shall get from her today . . .

Oh dear – I've just switched on the radio. To my shame it was a passage from Julian of Norwich. How awful I am. I *should* be more patient with Helen.

5 June   H[elen]'s last words to me were 'I shall *scream*' . . . She has just rung up babbling and screaming worse than ever. Yet not only did she go to tea with the friend but another one of her bridge friends came in to see her and had taken the trouble to suggest she might do some work in July in connection with an exhibition at the Tate Gallery. It is *impossible* to please Helen. One of these friends had also suggested she might go and stay at guest house in Sheringham. Helen screamed 'I don't *want* to go to Sheringham.' In fact she was talking so wildly and incoherently and screaming that it was impossible to understand her.

8.25   Phone rang twice. First time there was nothing to be heard but dialling tone. Second time H. screamed in a crazy voice 'Tony – Tony – Tony' and rang off. Has just rung again – once more only dialling tone. What is she up to?

I rang up to find out. She answered loudly 'Hello – hello – who is that speaking?' I said 'It's me, Tony: Is that you, Helen?' She went on saying loudly 'Hello, hello, who is that speaking.' These last 4 calls are really the behaviour of a lunatic.

1 o'clock   Have just rung her number again. After a few rings, she asked 'Who is that?' I said 'Is that Helen?' Now there is dead silence.

7 June   Although I was not in between 10 and 5, watching the Jubilee [25th anniversary of accession of Elizabeth II] procession on TV with Beatrice [Given-Wilson], it is now 8.15 and there has been no phone call.

10 June   The barren fig tree remains a mystery, for 'it was not the time of figs'. It is like those repulsive stories of Jesus's childhood in the apocryphal gospels in which He uses His miraculous powers to play cruel tricks on people. Those stories were current in the Middle Ages and are depicted in paintings.

Fascinating talk by Jack de Manio on extraordinary religious cults last night.

He mentioned Meher Baba. Baba never spoke but used an alphabet board and later, I think, sign language. When he did speak, it was to be the greatest event ever known. He died without speaking, but his followers of course believe that he survives and the word *will* be spoken. He believed himself to be God (as Dorothy certainly did, though she later denied this) and Tom is undoubtedly a fervently convinced disciple.

11 June I have got on to Olga Hersner [Helen's neighbour]. Extraordinary result. Helen is perfectly all right! Has made friends with some other woman in the flats and they go around together to the pub etc.

Something very odd is going on. I wasn't altogether satisfied with Olga's story. About 7.15 I rang Helen's number. After a few rings, a wild voice which did not sound quite like hers, more like some rather drunk woman, yelled 'Hello – hello – hello'. I said 'Is that Helen?' Then phone went dead.

12 June I've spent the day, very stupidly, ringing H.'s number. I can't get her out of my mind. I doubt if there's been any real improvement in her state, even if Olga is right that she's been going out and about with some woman she's made friends with at Charlbert Court.

13 June Something very odd on *Woman's Hour* today. There was a discussion about mentally disturbed people in flats who caused trouble to their neighbours. Two cases were cited . . . the first must surely have referred to Helen. The woman who spoke (I strongly suspect it was Olga) said the person was a 'lonely old woman' living in a flat in North London. The woman (who lived opposite) said that outbreaks of screaming and 'animal noises' disturbed all the neighbours who called in the police. Later the 'lonely old woman' had a fire in her flat. Her only relative, a brother, who lived far out of London, had sent her to be treated by a psychiatrist. There were too many resemblances to Helen's case for this to be mere coincidence. And if it was not Olga herself speaking, I am sure the material came from her. For Olga always makes a point of H.'s 'loneliness'. Moreover Olga works on a free-lance basis for the BBC.

14 June   Just as I got back from the Translators' Ass[ociatio]n party, Arnold rang up. Helen's phone is working again and he had spoken to her. She has even been screaming again.

26 June   I got back from Phyllis on June 22nd to find a letter from Arnold and one from [Dr] Rollings. Rollings' was dated the 16th and said H. had been behaving so badly in the flat that he had no alternative but to re-admit her to the Unit.

27 June   I had an extraordinary day yesterday with Fred and Senta who took me to the pilgrimage to West Grinstead [the church of Our Lady of Consolation]. It was very moving. I came back exhausted but very glad I had gone. Afterwards they drove me past Binesfield so that I could look at the house again.

28 June   Had quite a fright yesterday. About 6 suddenly felt so ill with a feeling of heaviness in my head and sick giddiness that I panicked, wondering if I was going to have a slight stroke! I lay down and after an hour or two the horrid sensation passed [Antonia suffered a slight stroke a year afterwards, see page 283].

29 June   Out of curiosity rang up agents about ground-floor flat at 61 Courtfield Gardens. It had been sold: 90 year lease, price £21,000, but needed 'modernizing' and complete redecoration. Even if I could face moving it would be out of the question. The only drawback to my present one is the stairs. I fear nearly all my precious deposit will go on the huge bill for redoing the outside and inside of the house.

I wish I could find some solution to the immediate question of what I ought to be doing with my time. Yesterday I looked again at those 2 chapters of the autobi. – my mother's life-story before her marriage and my first visit to Binesfield. I could only stare hopelessly, as so often, at the mess of handwriting and typescript and see no way of getting them right.

18 July   I go on wasting time shockingly – the whole of yesterday, when not listening to the Radio or reading *The Observer* spent over Azed [crossword]. And smoking worse than ever.

30 August The Helen situation has reached crisis point. The Marlborough people are not convinced that she is incapable of living on her own (she is not certifiably insane but suffering from a kind of premature senile dementia) and are trying to get her to go into a local Old Folks' Home. What is to be done with her furniture etc. and *who* is going to cope with that?

31 August   V. strange seeing P[*icture*] P[*ost*] programme. Tom [the ex-editor] looking more and more like his father. [Stephan] Lorant [the first editor of *Picture Post*], though much fatter, looking much younger than 82 and as exuberant as ever. Bobbie Birch, amazingly, spoke perfectly coherently. Though obviously aged, more recognizable as his old self. Tom just a *tiny* bit self-righteous.

13 Sept   Helen problem worse than ever. The last few days she has gone back to the flat in the afternoons. When I spoke to her several times at the Marlborough she was, of course, terribly depressed, poor thing. She *hates* the idea of the home, and it does sound a pretty grim place.

Unexpected pleasure – a clergyman I've never heard of, Fred Pratt Green, reading some of his poems on the radio tonight. Book is called *The Old Couple*. I found them extraordinarily good. Tempted to write to him.

Sue and Thomas are having splendid publicity for *The Great Donkey Walk*, published yesterday ... I'm so pleased that it looks like being a tremendous success. Lovely to see Sue so excited and happy, though finding this blaze of interviews etc. somewhat exhausting. I wish something nice would happen for Lyndall.

Have been re-reading Francis Thompson. Strange how poems which seemed not at all obscure to me when I was 13 now seem very difficult. Stranger still to think that at that age I learnt by heart not only 'The Hound of Heaven' but 'The Mistress of Vision', 'Orient Ode' 'An Anthem of Earth' 'Corymbus for Autumn' and 'Ode to the Setting Sun'. Nowadays I can hardly memorize 4 lines of verse. F.T. was the *great* poetic passion of my youth – from 11 onwards. It seems incredible what a memory I had then. I learnt the whole of 'In Memoriam' by heart.

21 Sept   Helen cannot be *cured* – the arteries to the brain are partly clogged. The most one can hope for is that she gets no worse.

The three of us went to the home. In the street and in the pub H. behaved very crazily, shouting, grimacing and banging tables. At the home when we were talking to the matron and being shown over the place she behaved perfectly composedly. She and Arnold went back to her flat. Poor Arnold was getting terribly tired and told her his nerves couldn't stand her shouting and grimacing.

22 Sept   Poor Arnold has just rung up . . .

Last night I slept badly, haunted by the idea of that O[ld] F[olks'] H[ome]. No doubt a good one of its kind but how I should hate to have to live in one. No privacy, sharing a room with 2 other old ladies, a tiny cramped wardrobe, no sign of books anywhere.

Phone just rang. Only a very confused Asiatic wanting, as usual, Roland House.

23 Sept   Can't settle to anything. Sue has lent me an extraordinary book – *The Snow-White Soliloquies* by Sheila Macleod. Have been reading it on and off all morning. A *very* disturbing book – I find it impossible to understand. Must ask Sue next time I see her what *she* makes of it. It is like a nightmare to me. I can't get any clue to it. Mercifully Thomas appeared in the afternoon with *The Great Donkey Walk*, which I promptly plunged into with relief and great pleasure.

24 Sept   Arnold rang up early this morning. Mercifully he's going back today after what he says is the worst ordeal of his life. June and John [Arnold's family] were coming up today after all and will take some of H.'s furniture back with them. Oddly both he and I had cut out advertisements from the local papers about firms willing to buy second-hand furniture.

26 Sept   I went down to lunch with Georgie yesterday. She gave me a beautiful meal. She seems much more cheerful nowadays. A bit ruthless as usual about Joan Hornsey and Helen (Joan's daughter) and all the Hornsey family. Also very 'anti-black'. Can't help wondering how she manages without any kind of job. I enjoyed seeing her but came home very exhausted.

Georgie told me that Elsie Morgan [relative of Eric] has died. We don't know when. With great difficulty I managed to write to Ann. So hard to know what to say for Elsie's death relieves her of part of the burden she's borne all these years. But she still has to cope with poor Miles, now over 90 and blind. Like Kathleen Raine, Ann has been marvellous with her aged parents. I can't say how I admire them both. I do pray that I don't become a burden to Sue and Lyndall by living too long.

28 Sept Have wasted the whole morning after returning from shopping doing idiotic things – reading the *R[adio] T[imes]* and *Woman's Realm* – only bought in the hope that Sue's article would be in it which it isn't. I am as crazy as Helen without her excuse.

29 Sept What an odd day – spent partly in re-reading that strange, repellent yet compelling book *Mary Barnes*, partly combing through *Frost in May* which, to my delight, Virago want to republish, to pick up a few misprints I wanted corrected. Inevitably this led to my re-reading, for sheer self-indulgence, whole chunks of it. I really think it's rather good, though the last chapter sounds a bit unconvincing. Yet that *is* just how I remember that terrible interview with my father.

30 Sept Have finished *Mary Barnes*. Mary Siepmann [Wesley] wants me to read the MSS of her last book. Smoked many cigarettes composing an answer, warning her I find 'allegories' v. hard to appreciate. Phyllis found it hard going, I know. I hope so much for Mary's sake that it *will* find a publisher.

3 Oct Last night I saw Kathleen Raine. She gave me *The Lion's Mouth*, with a very touching inscription. I am re-reading the book; it is a remarkable revelation of a human being – almost too cruel to herself.

Arnold rang up. He has arranged to meet an auctioneer at her flat on the 20th. He seems to have managed to get someone who may clear up the flat.

20 Oct   Arnold and I had a terrible day trying to clear up the incredible accumulation of old letters, papers etc. with which every drawer, trunk and box in H.'s flat were crammed to the brim. When we finally left, exhausted, we still had not done more than half – we had run out of big plastic bags to put the rubbish in as well as out of physical strength and mental stamina. She complains of 'having no clothes'. There were 2 perfectly good coats at the flat, besides the 2 she has at the Marlborough, no less than 4 dressing-gowns, besides the 1 she has there, 6 brand-new handbags, etc. I'm looking after a few 'valuables' – a box of mixed Victorian jewellery – some charming – and 2 portraits till one of Arnold's children can collect them. NOT a day I'd like to go through again! Today all I managed to do was finish the letter to Mary Siepmann. Rest of day I just lazed and read *To Kill a Mocking-Bird* – one of the best novels I've read for ages.

Arnold is *very* tottery, poor man, but does not seem *too* ill. I liked seeing him very much – difficult to talk to him as he's deaf and won't wear his hearing-aid. We could hardly be more different and of course innumerable subjects just can't be mentioned between us.

26 Oct   Julien Green's diaries fill me with depression, much as I love and admire him. How important those diaries were to me all these years, long before I knew him. How little I dreamed that I should ever meet him and that he should count me as one of his friends. I think the last time I saw him was in 1947. How strange that in the winter of 1959 I should have been in Savannah and met his Hartridge relatives.

Last night Carmen Callil of Virago came to see me. Dark, good-looking, 39 but looking much younger. I took an instant liking to her and we talked for 2 hours. She wanted to see *The Lost Traveller* so I lent her a copy. When she'd gone I went into a bout of self-indulgence and started re-reading it myself. Must stop that now.

I've a feeling that C[armen] C[allil] will be 'in my life'. She interests me extremely. The first new person to 'come into my life' since Elizabeth Sprigge. We have a lot in common. She was at a convent school for 13 years in Australia. Said *F[rost] in M[ay]* made her cry, it brought back her own experiences so vividly. She cannot forgive the nuns for the torments of scruples, fear of hell that she suffered. Gave up her religion completely when she lost her virginity (a traumatic experience for her) and doesn't think she'll ever return. I told her about my writing block – she says it is like her 'marriage block'. We like the same books and have the same passion for cats (she has 3). She made me *want* to write again.

Later Wonderful luck. Phone from Geneva to say they want 2 more pieces translated. Also that they are sending me the money for the first one. This is a great comfort for the trans. drought has lasted so long and from what C.C. says the chance of novels v. slender as no English publisher can do one now without co-operation of an American one. And of course the re-issue of *F[rost] in M[ay]* is very comforting too . . .

6.20 Have rung H[elen] at the Newstead. Sounded better than I expected . . . *almost* cheerful in fact.

2 Nov Tremendously busy 13 days. Have done no less than 3 pieces for Geneva.

10 Nov Helen situation very bad. Yesterday last day of her official 'probation' at Newstead. Arnold rang up on Tuesday to say Matron had told him she had been violent and frightened all other inmates. They will keep her till Saturday – perhaps even a little longer – but I fear there's little hope of her staying there and she will have to go to Epsom.

After an orgy over week-end of thrillers (Emma Latham and le Carré) am now on Lyall Watson's fascinating *Gifts of Unknown Things*.

Also had a shopping orgy the last 2 days. But did fairly well thanks to Marks and Spencer [the Kensington High Street branch had just opened]. For £60 (what I received for last 2 Genevas) I got 3 jumpers, 1 sleeveless cardigan, 2 prs. good gloves, 1 skirt, 3 pairs panties and 1 pr shoes.

11 Nov Managed to finish a *very* long letter to [Gabriel] Meyjes – probably the longest I've written since Thorp correspondence in 1940 and 1941. But I really was delighted to hear from him. My mother was very much in love with him in her last few years.

If Helen does have to go to Epsom, I shall *have* to make the effort and go and see her once a month. She is so healthy physically, except

for the brain arteries, that she will almost inevitably outlive Arnold
and very likely me too.

11 Nov   Arnold and I spent some 5 hours at Helen's flat today
clearing up more and more rubbish. It is incredible the amount she
had accumulated: we filled 6 large plastic sacks from the spare
bedroom alone. She can never have thrown away *anything* – scraps of
old letters, old magazines, travel folders – it was a nightmare job.
Sacks were so heavy I could hardly lug them out on to the balcony.
Poor Arnold was utterly worn out – more exhausted than I was. I was
quite worried about him, he was shaking all over at the end. When I
deposited him at his club, he could hardly walk and tottered into it
like an old, old man; too shattered even to say goodbye to me.

I feel a bit more hopeful about Arnold's physical state; he seems to
be able to eat quite rich food with no ill effects which one wouldn't
expect with cancer of the liver.

16 Nov   When I got home, the Newstead matron rang me up. She
had had a terrible time taking Helen down to the Horton. H. insisted
on taking 2 suitcases (which she can't possibly need there) so only 1
remains in store at Newstead. Matron says H. has got very much
worse. She says there is no hope of Helen leaving the Horton. I did
not tell Arnold this when I rang him tonight but I think he realizes.
The cerebral atrophy has got much worse: she probably has only a
few years to live. She is in Ward 3, one of the 'locked wards' for the
severe cases.

18 Nov   On Wednesday had dinner with my beloved Marnaus. Fr
Ware, chaplain to the Latin Mass Society was there. There is
something rather alarming about this obsession with the Latin Mass.
Like so many Catholics I very much regret all the changes in the
liturgy, but this extreme bitterness, even violence of the opposition
to the changes – and this includes anti-ecumenism – is very disturbing. Fred really feels the new Mass is *heretical*.

What really does shock me is that priests (of the 'one of us' type)
should feel what almost amounts to hatred of the others. Fred told me
that when they went to the W. Grinstead pilgrimage last year, Fr.
Shields [a member of the Latin Mass Society] could only be

persuaded with difficulty to eat at the same table with the new young priest there, Fr. Mulvey. The Ecumenical movement has produced such a split among the clergy that it has really set brother against brother in the priesthood. I think it is the 'old' who hate the 'new' – not the other way round.

Things *are* very difficult for the ordinary Catholics nowadays, especially with the 'new' theologians like Hans Küng, with his insistence on the humanity of Christ and what *seems* to be a denial of His divinity – He is the 'ambassador and representative' of God but not God himself if I've understood *On being a Christian* rightly.

23 Nov   Extraordinary to think I may be seeing Tom and Dorothy this week-end.

Lyndall is over here: harassed and overworked as always. She is sweetly going to continue the allowance next year. She is incredibly generous.

After that bad week-end clearing up Helen's flat, I treated myself to an orgy of Emma Latham thrillers which I thoroughly enjoyed. I also bought 2 Patrick White paperbacks, remembering how much I'd admired *Voss*. Read one or two of the short stories but had to give up. I found them almost incomprehensible and so depressing as to be unbearable. I'm sure he *is* very good but I find his style very difficult and his people nearly monstrosities. He is a 'black' writer if ever there was one. Powerful, yes, but *frightening*. My stomach isn't strong enough to take him at the moment.

27 Nov   Tom, Dorothy and Lyndall to tea here. This strange meeting was at Dorothy's instigation. First time I have seen Tom in the flesh since that other – even stranger – meeting at Amanda's confirmation – which must be more than 10 years ago. (Must ask Lyndall, she remembers dates.) Dorothy could not have been more benevolent. Tom seemed genuinely pleased to see me: we talked *almost* naturally. He has spent 13 years over this 200,000 word novel [*Shady City*, 1987] which is now in his agent's hands. Agent was wildly enthusiastic about [it] but is finding it v. difficult to find a publisher. A great blow to poor Tom. Dorothy said: 'It's a very happy book – very funny – and – this will surprise you, Tony, very *sexy*.' Well, well, well!

We talked quite a lot about Benedicta. Odd coincidence: both Sue and Lyndall have recently met people who knew her.

15 Dec   Helen's 73rd birthday. On Tuesday I went down to see her at the Horton. She was, of course, as bad as ever . . . it was a pretty exhausting visit, going over and over the same old ground with her. At least the ward is much pleasanter than one could have hoped – nice colour and furnishings. The nurses couldn't have been kinder and are all wonderfully patient with her. The Staff Sister, a charming West Indian girl, had actually varnished H.'s nails for her – a very sweet and understanding thing to do. Hard not to be impatient with Helen – she is so determined to complain about everything and so unwilling to show the slightest interest in the other patients, most of whom were obviously anxious to be friendly. She keeps saying they are all low class people or prostitutes which is patently untrue.

Rather amusingly I had quite a long chat with an agreeable young man, who was being very helpful about the best place to sit and have a cup of tea, which he fetched for us. He said he had spent a long time trying to calm Helen down. I assumed he was someone on the staff – maybe a medical student or junior doctor, but Helen swore that he was a patient.

16 Dec   Very interesting evening at Kathleen [Raine]'s last night. Lecture by a young Jew (Cabbalist) on the Jewish background of Christ. Had a talk with Rosamond Lehmann. She is now living at the house in Clareville Grove which was to have been Sally [her daughter]'s had she ever returned from Java. Thetis Black and Cecil Collins [both painters] and his wife, were there too.

It has been a strange week. Bow [Cottage] on Sunday, Carmen Callil on Monday, going to see Helen on Tuesday.

19 Dec   Have just rung Helen for 1st time since I went down to see her. Poor thing, she sounds worse and more miserable than ever. Says she feels very ill too, physically. Does however admit that the nurses are very kind. I think her brain *has* deteriorated very much in the past 6 weeks. She seems to like me to ring her up, though there is nothing whatever I can say to comfort her.

24 Dec   It will be a strange Christmas Day tomorrow for I shall be alone here . . .

27/26 Dec   It *has* been a strange Christmas – quite different from what I expected. On the morning of Christmas Day, Bridget Speaight rang up to say could she and Teresa come in for drinks some time between 6 and 7. Of course said yes. Soon afterwards, the dear Marnaus rang up. Would I prefer, instead of coming to the Boxing Day drinks party where there would be lots of people (always an ordeal with my deafness) to come and have Christmas meal with them? Naturally I was delighted . . . F[red] brought me home about 6. About 7 Bridget and Teresa arrived. Bridget seemed quite all right at first, talking animatedly about K[athleen] R[aine]'s book etc. Then she collapsed into a terrible state, weeping and saying how meaningless life had become for her, her mind was going, she hated her temporary new home, she had been in a convalescent home where it was discovered her blood pressure was abnormally low. She was obviously in a very bad physical, as well as mental state. Indeed with this terrible depression and inertia she reminded me a little of Helen. Teresa did her best to comfort her. She really is in a shocking mental state as Sue had warned me. She seems terribly frail and vulnerable, though still with traces of the old, almost ruthless perfectionist and critical Bridget. She complained a little of the extreme informality of Sue's lunch party – people bringing their own food etc. But that is really the only way Sue can cope with their hordes of friends.

Today I had lunch with Charlotte and Madeleine, which, as usual I enjoyed very much. Ping Pong has gone – I was amazed to hear he was 14 –for this means it must be 15 or 16 years since I was with them in Cornwall. Charlotte has given M. a delightful little *black* pug puppy – Brutus.

When I got back from Charlotte, all I did was finish the Waugh biography. Terribly hard not to dislike Evelyn Waugh. He is so insufferably rude and often cruel to people. Certainly on the few occasions I met him he was very agreeable to me and he reviewed *The L[ost] T[raveller]* most handsomely. Last time I saw him was at some cocktail party and he told me about his 'voices' on that voyage – the basis for *Gilbert Pinfold*. The first time must have been about 1928 or 9 when he was engaged to Evelyn Gardner. The two of them turned up at Crawford's. He hoped I might be able to get him a job there. I tried but with no success. She said he desperately needed a job so that they could get married. His kindness to Ronald Knox in Knox's last years was marvellous for it demanded endless patience. Admirable too his undertaking to write Knox's biography. In some ways he was a manic depressive.

His close friends were devoted to him, though he often treated *them* abominably. I think it is his *cruelty* that I find most repellent. His Catholicism was certainly sincere though I don't like his brand of it. His last years make painful reading. One is glad he died when he did. One just daren't *judge* him. Only God knows what he had to contend with for no one could have had a more difficult nature. I think Christopher Sykes has done a *very* good portrait of him.

1978

4 Jan   Tom has been knighted in the N[ew] Y[ear] Honours List.

* * *

Susan had been commissioned to write a life of the painter Gwen John with the agreement of her legatees, Ben John and his sister Sara. Ben and Sara's father had, however, lent Gwen John's papers to Mary Taubmann twenty-five years earlier, on the understanding that she would write the biography. Mrs Taubmann, wife of the head of the Bristol Polytechnic, was a painter rather than a writer, and had produced nothing. But she was unwilling to let Susan see the papers. These, fortunately, later turned out to be of negligible importance, barely filling a shoe-box.

* * *

6 Jan   On Wednesday night Thomas rang me up to say that Sue had had to be taken to a mental home in Hellingly nr Eastbourne. She has, I know, for some time been suffering from acute depression and when I went down there on Dec 11th she was taking tranquillizers. None of the family letters from Cornwall suggested that their Christmas had been anything but very gay and festive. But when Thomas said that Mary Taubmann was refusing to part with the

Gwen John letters, I realized what a blow to Sue this would be. She had set her heart on doing the G.J. biography. In fact she told me when I last saw her (alone) that it was the one thing that would get her out of this trough of depression. She was suffering from not having real work to get down to – coping with the children did not satisfy her strongest need – which is now to write. The news that she had broken down mentally was a great shock. All yesterday I was in a kind of daze. When I went out yesterday, I was so weak and shaky that I could not walk down to Gloucester Rd. I spent the whole day reading a le Carré and waiting for the evening when I hoped Thomas wd. ring up about Sue, which he didn't. One can't phone her at Hellingly, but of course I wrote to her at once. Both he and I are a little apprehensive about shock-treatment – it seems the doctors are thinking of that. T. said that Sue had taken to lying in bed all day and refusing to get up – just like Helen. I don't think Sue has ever been *really* well since the return from the Donkey Walk.

26 Feb   Have been ill for the past fortnight. Some sort of bronchial infection. Back very painful all the time. Doctor keeps trying different antibiotics. Jackie [hairdresser] has been an angel coming in almost every day. Sue is mercifully better and is now discharged from Hellingly. She's v. kind, has been up to London twice and rings up almost daily.

16 March   Went to the X-ray about 2 weeks ago. Result mysteriously shows some middle vertebrae 'squashed together'. Mellor is mystified since I have had no accident which would account for it. I try not to get too alarmed. Everyone has been angelic, especially Lyndall who has arranged for a friend from Italy [Joan Martini] to come over and stay in her flat for a month and do my shopping. She has also arranged an app[ointmen]t for acupuncture for both of us tomorrow. And has insisted on buying me a beautiful TV set which I watch a lot.

I feel absurdly lost and drifting – v. tired and stupid. Such an abnormal life, having to move so carefully and not lift anything even a little heavy.

With difficulty managed a necessary letter to Meyjes and Andrew Field [biographer of Djuna Barnes]. People are being so kind. Wonderful having Lyndall though she must go back on Mon 20th.

She is having a worse time than ever with Renzo and is far iller than I am, poor darling.

Later   Trying writing on a sloping surface so as not to stoop too much.

19 March   On Friday Lyndall took me to a Chinese doctor for acupuncture. No obvious immediate results. Pain stabs suddenly and unexpectedly . . . Lyndall was very bad again yesterday – migraine and nausea and couldn't come. I expect her any minute now. It will be her last visit for she goes back to Italy tomorrow. I shall miss her sadly. It will be nice to have Joan Martini. It is difficult being still so very tired and lacking in energy.

23 March (Holy Thursday)   I had a very strange dream last night. I was lying in bed ill in a house or hospital opposite the Oratory. I was not in pain but there was some possibility I might die. I asked for a priest to give me the Last Sacraments. While I was waiting I saw through the window I lay facing an extraordinary cloud formation – a most vivid and clear life-size representation of Christ on the cross. This moved me so much that I was filled with sorrow for my sins and my eyes filled with tears. In this strange dream I seem to have completely recovered my faith.

Daren't venture as far as the shops yet without Joan's help (she is being incredibly kind and helpful) and am still stupidly languid and feeble-minded. I watch TV quite a lot, though feeling guilty. It was *so* kind of Lyndall to insist on giving me a beautiful set.

Have been for years such a creature of habit that rearrangement of furniture – having to take up space with TV and the trolley makes me feel 'désorientée'.

7 April   My back is v. much better. Not quite independent yet but went to Mass on my own last Sunday and have shopped once without Joan's help.

Inevitably I think much about death. I am 79 . . . Two days ago Ronald Moody rang me up to say that Hélène had had a stroke and was dead. A shattering blow for him. Gerald Reitlinger has just died.

Funny to have press interviews in prospect [for *Frost in May*'s publication by Virago] – like being exhumed . . .

(On April 19th had that severe pain and was removed to that grisly nursing-home. Managed to get home on May 1st.)

15 May   Phyllis went home. First day of managing on my own with Home Help . . .

8 June   According to Phyllis, no full stops for Mr, Mrs, and anything where last letter of full word is same as that of abbreviation. But full stops after Rev. Capt. etc. Complete sentence in brackets has full stop inside them. But if it is an aside, or something at the end of a sentence – not beginning a new sentence, then full stop outside.

Phyllis re Djuna and Andrew Field: 'If the Australian [Field was actually American] is persistent, it seems to me he will have to see John Coleman and that might cause some upsets if John gives him access to all the letters from Djuna to Emily which I have here. But, as we know, Djuna has to give permission for any of them to be published. Cannot, I think, prevent him from *reading* them if John gives permission.' [Phyllis was looking after Emily's papers.]

Very queer – this republication of *F. in M.* and all this publicity. *Observer* last Sunday and even a TV interview on June 22nd. Extraordinary letters from people who have read the book because of interviews etc.

Have got used to sharing the flat with Pippa [a hotel-management trainee] (this is her 3rd week). She couldn't be nicer and it is good for me to have to adapt a bit to other people's ways. And I *can* put Sue up on the divan in my workroom.

5 July   Unable to talk and read [Antonia had had a slight stroke]. The doctor is coming tomorrow at 12. Cannot remember even Our Father or Hail Mary. Cannot make sense of reading, not even a letter. Can't telephone. Can only stammer and am utterly incoherent. [Dr] Wilks says it a block of circulation to the brain. I think I'll have to get Pippa ring Charlotte and the dentist. It started on Monday night with a violent headache. Took pain-killer and slept. Then found I couldn't talk properly on Tuesday morning. Yet I did manage to ask if the handbag could be mended. But I couldn't make myself understood when I tried to talk to Pippa. Pippa was very kind. It was lucky that

Wilkes [sic] came that day and I plucked up courage to tell him about this queer aphasia.

7 July   Doctor came again. I managed to speak a little better. I also managed to write notes to Meyjes and Charlotte. Dr Wilks rang Charlotte for me. Madeleine rang me up later and managed to be a bit more coherent and said I'd rather they didn't ring me till next week.

8 July   To my amazement I have recovered memory of Our Father and Hail Mary. But still can make no sense of reading. Yesterday Senta rang me up. I managed to explain about not coming to the Pilgrimage. She was very sweet and told me not to try to make effort to talk.

10 July   Was very flustered at unexpected appearance of Pippa's father – difficult to explain where Pippa was at the Gloucester [Hotel] and how she had the keys.

On Friday I managed to talk quite coherently to Sue. Could read a bit of articles in the Sunday papers. The mind is beginning to work again. What luck . . . able to do the TV and the interviews. Sue was relieved that it had already been done. She thought it lay ahead but it was safely over.

13 July   I can talk reasonably well now, but find it difficult to understand what Carmen is talking about this new contract. She is coming to see me tomorrow. I will have to put on hearing-aids for shopping. Was so deaf that I couldn't understand the tobacconist manager. I cannot follow radio programmes. They talk so fast that I cannot catch the words. Almost as if they were talking another language – could catch a name here and there but not follow it properly.

Very difficult to get through the day.

Find it hard to follow Pippa's complications with the Gloucester. She may throw up the job in exasperation. Her mania for washing is extraordinary! But I like her very much and she couldn't be kinder.

Beatrice got in a panic, over Menelly [Antonia's hairdresser's: the girls used to do her shopping]. Thought they have copied the keys.

But I managed to persuade her the girls couldn't have been more honest. If a burglar *did* get into her flat in November, it was very mysterious. She has become very nervous – also very suspicious. Doesn't want to overhear any mention of leaving her flat. On Tuesday she rang me up, could she come up and tell me something but did not want to be anyone here in my flat. I think I managed to reassure her about Menelly. But would I please not to say where she lived.

15 July Pippa has given the Gloucester a week's notice. Find it difficult to grasp the complications of this hotel business. She is very angry with all the people there and feels she is being very badly treated. It looks as if she may leave here. Slight panic for me. Decidedly unsettling. Sue would worry about me being alone in the flat. No good trying to foresee what is going to happen. Just 'play it by ear'. She'll probably stay in the room for a while. Incredible accumulation of objects in that room. There would be a certain relief to have that chaotic confusion cleared up. I don't really understand what sort of job she is looking for. She is in a pretty neurotic state. Rather a relief that her father is over here.

Had a worrying nightmare about Carmen last night. Luckily I woke to find it was only a silly dream.

18 July Home help didn't come yesterday – she had a migraine. Mrs McD. [Kensington home help organizer] said she'd try to get someone. No one came yesterday or today. Managed to shop but needed quite a bit of domestic help. Felt pretty ill yesterday but coped quite well with Carmen who was most sweet and friendly.

Tried to read several of de la Mare's poems. Could make no sense of it [sic].

19 July Made 2 expeditions. Went to Smith's, bought a E. Nesbit [children's book] and a book of Patience games. Had bought a pack of cards at the tobacconist. But couldn't understand any of the Patience directions. So had to give up all attempts to play Patience.

20 July Mrs Harris [home help] turned up so was able to get Daz and bleach and change my [bloodstained] sheet.

22 July Pippa situation *very* odd. Couldn't make out what she was talking about while I was cooking on Friday evening. I had a terrible nightmare . . . Woke up about 11 p.m. tottered to the loo. Amazed to find many lights on. There was a handsome young man in the dining-room. Asked him where Pippa was. She was doing something or other in her bedroom. In the morning, Pippa had vanished. Her bed was made and her room was even more chaotic. Suitcase on bed, gaping open . . . I can't make out what she's up to.

26 July Sue came to coffee on Monday. Lovely to see her but found conversation tiring. Am much deafer in right ear even with hearing-aid full on.

Funnily enough have been able to read a French novel – Julien Green's *Chacun dans sa Nuit*. Found it easier to read French. But it was so excessively gloomy – all this preoccupation with sex-guilt and religion – that I had to give up after Part I.

Time hangs heavy on my mind – *how* can I occupy myself . . .

ITV programmes are absolute rot.

But splendid BBC 2 one on Saturday. *Royal Heritage* – Huw Wheldon. Wish there were more to come.

31 July I rang Ronald [Moody] on Saturday and asked him for drinks on Sunday. I'm glad I did. He likes to come and see me – says I'm one of the people he feels comfortable with. I was touched by this. He didn't cry. He feels very much aware of Hélène's presence. I think there is a faint possibility of his beginning to work again. He's like me – finds it impossible to follow sentences. But he tried *The Perennial Philosophy* and could follow a bit.

Susanna Day [young friend of Emmi Sheppard] is coming tomorrow for a drink. Much better news of Emmi.

2 August Lyndall *definitely* expected today but no sound from her yet. Just after 8, I expected the call to be Lyndall's. But it was Jeremy to say that Tony Bertram [his father] has died. He and Barbara were recalled from their longed-for interval of holiday to the hospital. Tony was unconscious. He died, I think, on Sunday. The Requiem is next Monday.

I had a strange call from Susanna who was here last evening for a

drink. She stayed 2 hours. Liked her *very* much but found it a strain to
listen to her properly. This call today I *couldn't* recognize her voice. It
sounded quite different. Sounded very high-pitched, almost like a
child's. I couldn't understand what she wanted to do. It seemed she
meant to come here today or tomorrow at 2 p.m. – either at her flat or
mine. I couldn't make head or tail of it. I kept saying was she really
Susanna Day but she kept saying she was. Finally I explained that
Lyndall was expected any time today and had to leave it for the time
being.

8.30   Yet another call hoping it would be Lyndall. But *no*,
Douglas's friend. (Pippa had already left.) Must tell her if she rings up
that Douglas wanted to tell her something.

Now I really will give up and go to bed!!

3 August   Lyndall did appear yesterday. They had a terrible delay
over the flight on Tuesday – a delay of 9 hours and arrived at 3 a.m.
on Thursday. Renzo came to London after all. Changed his mind 7
times in 2 days. She had arranged a perfect solution for Renzo – to
stay with [Umberto] Mora for a fortnight. Then he decided in the end
to come to London. She is absolutely exhausted. Everything that
could go wrong with the Molino, Bologna etc. has gone wrong. Now
the Harley Gardens flat has got in such a bad state that she is
thoroughly depressed. Spent her time trying to clear up the mess in
the front garden – overflowing dustbins, bad smells etc. Now even
talks of selling the flat but that was mainly due to nervous exhaustion.
Poor Lyndall, she is so overwrought and depressed that everything is
too much for her. She is in even a worse state than [when] she was last
over here. There is absolutely *nothing* I can do to help her. My life is so
much easier compared to hers.

I listened to Christmas Humphreys, the 'Buddhist' judge. But I
couldn't understand what he meant.

20 August   What extraordinary changes have taken place since
Tuesday Aug 15th! On Tuesday Lyndall arrived at teatime in utter
despair. After all the house-hunting on Renzo's new obsession, she
had found the 'dream-house' in Battersea. Planned for Cordelia and
her friend to take it. Suddenly Cordelia cried off. Reluctantly Lyndall
told the owner deal was off and owner contacted 2nd buyer. On wild

notion told L. how Phyllis longed to move and would now love to live in London, but this would be quite impossible for Phyllis. Series of frantic telephonings, first from Lyn to Phyllis who jumped at the idea, though it seemed a hopeless project for her. Lyn rang the owner, agreeable to sell it to Lyn. She arranged to pay him a huge deposit. On Wednesday Lyn and owner met at bank in the morning and the transaction was made. Agonizing suspense for all 3 of us that Tuesday night. Lyn rang me punctually at 11.30 a.m. on Wed 16th. I promptly rang Phyllis to tell [her] the splendid news.

One terrible hurdle for poor Lyn. Wretched solicitor had ignored his promises to let her know what was vital about the main transaction – can it be arranged, as Harley Gardens was, through Jersey? She ran him 5 times on Friday but cd. never get hold of him. Now the earliest hope of getting hold of him is tomorrow, Monday.

Lyn is a new person, now there is every hope of everything coming through. Renzo has been nice to her after having been intolerable before. But she is dead tired, hasn't slept properly for nights and has plenty more details to worry about. Peter [Binns] and Amanda have behaved *very* badly – what it amounts to is that Lyn has given them a car (their second one!) on condition that Lyn can use it for the very few weeks she'll be in London and desperately needs it. Peter has calmly gone off with the children for a week's holiday and almost certainly will not bother to get the necessary documents from County Hall, without which Lyn can't use it.

But the main thing we hope and pray for is that it will be possible for Phyllis to have this ideal little house. Can hardly wait till Tuesday when Phyllis comes up here for the night and we all go over to see it and meet the owner. It still seems to all 3 of us to be [too] good to be true! Phyllis says for her it will be 'like Paradise before death'. If *ever* Phyl deserved a piece of luck after all she's been through and had no hope of getting the sort of house she longed for it is Phyllis who deserves it!

21 August   Lyn is already buying furniture . . . tables, chairs, fridge etc. Before Phyl moves in, Lyn wants to do some repainting, rearranging carpets etc, with her usual perfectionism.

23 August   Slight feeling of depression and anti-climax after our visit to 82 Knowlesey [sic] Road with Phyllis and Lyn. Plenty of reasons, of course. Am v. tired today after a bad night and I think Phyl was a little disappointed in the house. Unexpected snag . . . it happened to be that day when the wind blows in a certain direction there is an unpleasant smell from some factory or brewery. Of course I didn't smell it at all but Phyl is *very* sensitive to smell. However she and Lyndall were able to have a good long practical discussion here about the whole situation and I think the plan will come off about the end of this year. All 3 of us agreed that the quantity of red paint in the bedroom was *too* overpowering. Very light and nice, lovely kitchen and bathroom (though Phyl would like a larger bath) and the little garden is *very* pretty and manageable. A little surprised that Lyndall feels *so* much in love with the house . . . she will make it very charming when she comes over at end of October and starts one of her perfectionist campaigns.

Have been awfully irritable and bad-tempered yesterday but Phyllis sweetly made allowance for me.

24 August   Saw Lyndall briefly today. We both felt the same about Phyllis seeming to be slightly disappointed, raising objections about the smell, smallness of bath etc.etc. However I convinced Lyn that Phyllis definitely did want the house and most certainly did not regard it as a duty to Lyn!! It's typical of Phyllis to be pessimistic.

Just when L. arrived, Carmen rang up. I lost my head completely – became hysterical since I couldn't possibly explain all these new complications. Begged Carmen to forgive me for behaving so badly. And she'd only rung me up to give me the wonderful news that they are republishing all my 3 books simultaneously in July 1979. Seems too good to be true. Mercifully Carmen is going away for a few days.

Am horrified that Lyn will be spending something like £1000 on furniture etc. for the house. True this is partly due to Renzo's insisting on buying a new carpet for the house – £250 – which seems quite unnecessary.

The more I think of it, the more I feel that the thought of her losing her independence is what worries Phyllis most.

26 August   Oh dear, I feel that Phyllis is extremely dissatisfied and worried about the whole thing. I *do* think she might be a *little* less gloomy about the Knowlsey [sic] house. Today she said again how dreary the neighbourhood is etc. Then of course she went to the other extreme – the house is too grand for her – she'll be in terror of spoiling something.

Lyn has just heard from Cordelia that Sue has had to go back to Hellingly. It is tragic that she and Thomas are so increasingly incompatible.

28 August   The more I think of it, the more I feel convinced that Phyllis does not *want* to move to the house. In fact I feel she thoroughly dislikes the house. Convinced that she would be turned out of it anyway – Renzo would probably decide to sell it again any time.

29 August   Last night to my great relief Lyndall understands the Phyllis situation and all her misgivings. She is writing to her today with alternative suggestions. Of course the house is a terrible disappointment to Phyl. Lyndall fell in love with it which Phyl very *far* from did! I think it's charming, but P. didn't seem to find even a good word for it. The *only* things she liked were the shower and the heated towel-rail!!

31 August   The letter I had from Phyllis yesterday seemed to confirm all her misgivings. When I saw Lyn yesterday we both agreed that Phyllis would much prefer *not* to go. We also felt that it would be better to ring Phyllis while Lyn was here so that Phyllis could definitely cry off the whole thing if she wanted to. Incidentally it would be a relief for Lyn if Phyllis now definitely wanted to cry off. Lyn had so many complicated arrangements (new unforeseen business ones). Lyn went out of the room while I phoned Phyllis. Phyllis was furious with me, she now says she definitely wants to go to the house, that I was being stupid and had completely misunderstood everything. Luckily I could call Lyn to her aid. Phyllis had answered Lyn's letter of the day before and was definitely *for* the project. They had a long talk on the phone. I'm now keeping myself well out of the way. This morning Lyn got Phyl's letter gladly agreeing to all Lyn's arrangements, though both Lyn and I had by now been sure that Phyllis would have been glad to get out of it! Oh dear, oh dear! I can only lie low and feel that Phyl will eventually forgive me for my awful blunder.

Poor Lyn has more loads of worries now than ever. She is exhausted, what with Renzo, the waiting for the solicitors, Renzo's mad idea of their taking that little car to Italy. All this delay means that she will *have* to return to London but has no idea *when*. The deal may take *weeks* or *months* to go through. She can't even see the solicitor till next Tuesday and even *that* appointment has to be confirmed.

Pippa has suddenly got the teaching job she wants and is leaving *this very night*.

Nearly 8 p.m.   Not a sign of clearing up Pippa's room! Everything in utter confusion, unwashed crockery adding to it. How on earth to get it all cleared up and packed, ready to be transported to Hounslow? Personally she is always immaculately groomed and neat, but *how* she has lived all these months in such chaos? Sue is almost *tidy* in her room compared to Pippa and up to now Sue has been the untidiest of room-inhabitants I've ever known. If I don't see her before I go to bed, shall have to leave a note for her, asking her to leave the keys etc.

1 Sept   Did all this but Pippa spent the night. Probably will stay here tonight too. Doubt if she'll manage to get it all cleared today! Further complications for poor Lyn. Now turns out that insurance isn't right for that [new] little car. Now she will revert entirely to her bicycle. At least it put paid to Renzo's wild idea of their going back to Italy in that tiny car.

Think that Pippa will be definitely off by tomorrow. If so, I can defrost the fridge on Sunday . . .

8 p.m.   Believe it or not, by soon after 7, Pippa had managed to pack all her innumerable pieces of luggage — suitcases, plastic containers, hold-alls, etc etc. Every single object, including tins of food, packets of detergents, pictures, etc. had all been taken downstairs. Even more miraculously the room had been completely tidied up and the furniture removed to its original place. I shall quite miss her lively, if somewhat disconcerting presence. She couldn't have been kinder and I cannot be grateful enough for all she did when I was suddenly struck dumb. Life will certainly be simpler without

Pippa's kitchen and bathroom activities. Yet I think she was really the nicest and most amusing of all my lodgers.

3 Sept   A pity for me that Beatrice will probably give up her flat for good, as it was ideal for me having her in the same house. She hardly ever comes here now – though she hates to part with her beloved flat for good.

Lyn has talked on the phone to Cordelia and will probably see her some time today. She said Sue came back to Bow [Cottage] for the week-end, too soon I fear. She said Sue was fine the first day but relapsed into such depression the next that they took her straight back to Hellingly. I'm sure she needs a longer rest and more treatment before she is ready to cope with normal life again.

4 Sept   On TV last night the ceremonial installation of Pope John Paul I. The Pope gave Communion to his relatives and friends and to some of his old parishioners. He is very lovable.

V. good notice of *F[rost] in M[ay]* in New Fiction Society. Much the most intelligent and well-balanced. All the notices have been good: surprised that there have been so many of them.

Lyndall came to tea. She has seen Cordelia. Bad news for poor Sue ... On Saturday a letter arrived for her saying that the Gwen John biography was off. A terrible blow for her, but Cordelia was emphatic that it was not the cause of her collapse. She was already in the bad phase, uncontactable. She herself wanted to go back to Hellingly and they took her there on Saturday. She was too withdrawn to feel the full impact of the blow. Who was responsible? Presumably the maddening Miss Taubmann who has sat on the material for 25 years and produced nothing.

I wish Lyndall's wild plan to take Sue and Jessica [aged seven] to Italy for 6 months and do the biography of [Sir John] Hawkwood could come off. Lyn has done quantities of research on it already and would give it all to Sue. But I fear it is too wild a plan and Thomas would never consent to it.

5 Sept   Critical interview with L.'s solicitor today at 2.30. She will ring me up to know the result. If she can't have the house it might in some ways be a relief to her and Phyllis. But it means a heavy money loss for Lyn. Not only would she lose her £2000 deposit but she has already bought several hundred pounds' worth of furniture. Nothing for Lyn is ever simple and straight-forward. One side of her has always been involved in elaborate intrigues. She is such a complex character. Frank as she is with me, she always retains this streak of secretiveness.

Inevitably I worry much about Sue. Things are going so badly for her just now . . . But it is impossible to know whether she will be able to weather this crisis. I do not think Thomas *can* manage to give her the understanding and support she so badly needs. Oh, how few marriages are happy. Barbara [Bertram] made Tony's happy because of her amazing unselfishness. Otherwise Emmi and Lance and the Mumfords are the only ones I can think of that were *truly* happy. Silas and Sheila's up to a point. And oddly enough, Tom and Dorothy's marriage has been remarkably successful. And one really good one is Fred's and Senta's.

1.45   No sign of carpet-fitter yet, though firm said he'd be here by 12.30 at latest. Phyllis rang very early this morning. Had tried unsuccessfully to phone Lyn, though she was there. Told Phyllis there was to be the crucial interview with L.'s solicitor this afternoon. Much to my joy, Phyllis sounded as friendly as ever. She said she was quite looking forward to a couple of months in London. Am now in some confusion. L. is frantically busy all today – solicitor, car insurance, food to buy and dinner for four. Hope to goodness she *will* find a moment to ring me and let me know the result of the solicitor's interview. Incidentally can't quite understand why she has 2 people to dinner tonight. 'Rosie' I know she needed to see about the highly unlikely Italian project but why someone else . . .

Am in utter confusion about *all* Lyn's plans . . .

Oh dear, oh dear, oh dear! I just don't know *where* I am and it is all getting a bit too much for me.

If Mick [carpenter] arranges to do the stairs at K[nowsley] St, Lyn suggests only the banisters. But I *do* think the stairs should be blocked in – *certainly* if Phyl is going to be there. Mick says it might be cheaper to make an entire new staircase. If it is to cost £80 I am prepared to do that for Phyllis' sake.

6 Sept   Very tiresome day yesterday. Waited in all day, sitting at my desk glued to the telephone. Lyndall didn't manage to ring up (very briefly) until 7.30. Solicitors seemed as vague as usual but the upshot seems that she can buy the house in her own name and that the arrangement with Phyllis still stands. I was relieved that Mick did not ring up as I was not clear as to what I was told to say to him. Lyndall was in an overwhelmed state – cd. only say a few words with cooking and dinner party on hand. Still shaking from the frightening episode. A child suddenly ran across the car, against the lights. L. managed to jam on the brakes. Child was knocked down but wasn't hurt; got up and went off.

Badly need to know what hearing-aids will cost.

18 Sept   The situation about K. St seems to be more or less solved. But Lyndall has now involved herself in all sorts of complicated new alterations to the house – gas cooker instead of electric one, new building arrangements in the kitchen etc. I can't follow all these various last minute new enterprises. Not to mention all the formidable tasks she has to do both there and at Harley Gardens before she leaves – definitely this time on Wednesday 20th. I still feel confused about Phyllis's real feelings about K. St. So does Lyndall. To me she now seems quite anxious to spend 6 months there, but Lyn says that P. never sounds at all enthusiastic. I half wish it [the project] had never started . . . I can't help feeling apprehensive – mainly for Lyn. Renzo of course imagines that Phyllis will be paying rent for K. St and the fat may well be in the fire if the real facts come out.

My new lodger, Angela Monge [Spanish girl], arrives on Sat. afternoon. Lyndall – and Thomas too – are very pleased that there will be someone in the flat as Sue is out of things at the moment. The news of Sue is rather better.

I have at last begun to read the Virginia Woolf diary . . . very interesting. Fascinating about the whole business of *writing*.

I still hope to try once again with that old book . . .

Magnificent windfall of £675 from the TV play of *F. in M.*

19 Sept, 8.45pm   Lyndall dashed in at 5-45 to say goodbye to me. She has lent me the other Guirdham book – equally absorbing. Am definitely launched on this whole Cathar and psychic healing business.

22 Sept I have been reading – in snatches – V. Woolf's extracts from her diary – It produces a feeling of extreme depression. Enough to discourage me from ever *attempting* to write again. Much better put it away for the time being. But the itch to read *something* while I'm eating makes me keep on dabbling in it in snatches and I've nothing else new to read now. Can't go on forever buying Monica Dickens and Miss Read.

Quite a busy day tomorrow. Must try not to get too panicky and flustered, trying to cope with Angela [Monge] and Maria [Spanish cleaner] on the same afternoon. Tomorrow morning I'll give myself the luxury of the *Times* crossword. My top tray is still as overflowing as usual. Never mind, I'll go to bed now, even if I haven't done the washing-up.

23 Sept Maria, Angela and Angela's obliging man friend arrived almost simultaneously. A. has masses of luggage and more to come next week-end. Maria has done all the most necessary things – remade the bed . . . thoroughly cleaned kitchen and bathroom, and even cleaned the silver.

Have been re-reading all the K. St saga. No use worrying about it now . . .

24 Sept More snatches of V. Woolf diary. Still depresses me. I can't follow her mind at all.

Angela really *has* moved in! Her room is positively a bower! Quantities of pretty flowering plants as well [as] her colour TV set. Lots of ornaments etc. She seems very happy here. It is a cheerful atmosphere, I must say. The Spanish male friend and 2 very attractive female ones have been having quite a party (very quiet) here. Rather nice with these young people around. A. is blessedly tidy . . . I think I was lucky when I answered that advertisement in the Carmelite News Letter.

Sent for a mail-order coat – expensive but cheaper and nicer [than] in Marks and Spencer or at Barkers. I do really need a new winter one. The dear old 5-year-old one is developing bald patches but I still love it and shall go on wearing it for many more years. Hope the new one will look as good as the one in the *S[unday] Telegraph* magazine. Don't know if 'rust' will suit me but I didn't want yet another brown one. Tomorrow I really mean to have another go at That Book [autobiography]. Try to get the Binesfield chapter right . . .

28 Sept   I am still very worried about the Phyllis situation. In spite of P.'s last letter in which she *seems* to want to go to K. St she still sounds pretty pessimistic, dreading the ordeal of packing and moving. I also rather wish that Cordelia and Sally [Cordelia's friend at the University of Bristol] will 'take to' the place and be glad to live there as tenants. It is very difficult to know what Phyllis *really* wants. Sometimes she talks as if she quite likes the idea of spending 6 months at K. St – but at others one is more conscious of all the many drawbacks – *so* many – the neighbourhood, the cat's reaction to the house, the muggings, her original dislike of the house which she seems to feel has *no* good points . . . And of course Renzo is only too likely to change his mind and want him and Lyndall to live there when they come to London. I think the whole thing must be finally settled between Phyllis and Lyndall. Feel I've probably done the wrong thing from L.'s point of view letting Mick block in the stairs as he's already bought all the wood. Impossible not to feel all these elaborate new arrangements – carpets, remodelling the kitchen etc. point to Renzo's idea of living with Lyndall there.

This morning I rang Carmen up to say I *would* have a shot at doing the introduction to my 3 other novels. I thought Sue would find it rather embarrassing to do, even if when she is better she would consent to do it. I suggested I might *trick* myself by doing it as if I were writing a letter to Carmen. C. was delighted . . . at least I know what in them were factually true and what were 'made up' – principally the boy's death, the scenes with 'Clara's' mother, the original circumstances of Clara's meeting 'Archie', making Archie a Catholic etc. Carmen wants me to look back at the times I was actually living – the early 'twenties . . .

What I have read of 'psychic' literature does convince me that survivors after death can and do communicate with the living. The evidence of reincarnation in Guirdham's books is too sober and too circumstantial. The whole business of the Cathars and Guirdham's firm belief that they were the true exponents of primitive Christianity is a thorny question. Indubitably the Cathars were violently anti-Catholic.

7 p.m. Have just rung Cordelia. Mercifully she seems quite happy there. Trains don't worry her, admits there's a smell. All the really trying part will be next week, plumbers etc. At present she's getting on with the painting.

1 Oct   Over yesterday and today wrote a long letter to Lyndall about my latest worries over Phyllis. Tomorrow I must endeavour to write to Phyllis. Her last one is *very* difficult to answer. It contains a furious diatribe against new Council (Conservative) in Battersea (she is of course violently anti-Tory). She hasn't a good word to say about the neighbourhood etc. It is the first time that a break between me and Phyllis has threatened.

2 Oct   I made myself write this difficult letter to Phyllis. Got up at 4.45 a.m. It took me 3 hours and 12 cigarettes. But if Cordelia and Sally, after living there for 2 months, like it and would find it much preferable to the crowded flat in Queensway, I think L. would be rather relieved if they stay there for the winter.

I *did* go to Peter Jones. Shopping was as exhausting as usual. But I managed to get a reasonably nice dress – I definitely needed a decent new and warmish daytime one for occasions like lunching with the dear Marnaus. I also bought a pretty pink jumper which will make another outfit with the skirt of the unsuccessful 2-piece mail-order one. Of course the new mail-order winter coat is a big and expensive gamble so I hope it won't be a disastrous failure.

6 Oct   Writing Carmen's introduction seems an impossible task. Even one paragraph I can't get right.

One comforting thing happened yesterday. For the first time since Sue went back to Hellingly, 2 months ago, [she] has written to me. Not only does she say that the depression does seem to be lifting a little at last, but she shows the sweetest and most touching concern for *my* welfare. I can reassure her on that point! Thank goodness for Angela who couldn't be nicer and kinder.

7 Oct   Letter from Phyllis – not at all upsetting. More mysteries about Lyndall. Cordelia rang up this morning, saying Lyndall had rung her up last night from Italy and [she] was to give me a message.

L. is not coming till *December!* But why this change? The whole idea
was for her to come in November, especially as she'd carefully
arranged for the new tenant of Harley Gardens to vacate it in
November so that she and Renzo could stay there during the final
furnishing of K. St.

14 Oct Attempts to do the Intro. in form of a letter have proved
hopeless.

What I do know *officially* is that Lyndall and Renzo are now not
coming till *January* – and will be in London for 2 months. Haven't
had the courage to tell Phyllis this new development yet. Certainly a
more serious bombshell.

17 Oct This morning Phyllis's anxiously awaited letter arrived. I
don't think she is angry. She has presumably written to Lyndall to say
that she won't be coming to the K. St house.

I rang up Carmen in despair about the Introduction. I thought she
might be back from Germany but it seems she has only just gone.
One of the other girls was *very* kind and reassuring. Also Carmen
knows all about the radio *F. in M.* project so I don't have to worry
about that either.

18 Oct Thank heaven, Phyllis would be delighted to come to the
Lindsey [Hotel] from Mon 30th – Mon Nov 6th. Oh, *what* a relief.

Hope I'm not rash taking nice Mrs H[arris] [formerly on the Home
Help Service], 'private'. Don't like to cancel Maria – so it will be very
expensive – another £6 a week. Mrs Kennedy [neighbour] says she'll
take Mrs H. for 2 hours. This extra money I'm getting from the
republications is lovely *but* it probably means tremendous income
tax. First time I've ever had to worry about making too much!!!

7 Nov Phyllis really seemed to enjoy her week in London. I felt
under some constraint about Knowsley Road [correct name]. I
hadn't realized that she really *had* wanted to go there, in spite of all her
continued objections. I think she has now interpreted it as Lyndall's
wanting to cancel the arrangement so that Cordelia can stay in the
house.

Carmen came in for a drink last night. Bless her, she'll come over one morning in Dec. with a tape-recorder and between us [we] can contrive some sort of Introduction. Other people at that Gollancz party thought Sue rather over-excited and Thomas very nasty to her.

13 Nov   The famous mail-order coat was a disastrous gamble. What with it, alterations and taxis it cost me nearly £60! I've given it to Sue – which would have been perfect on her if I hadn't had it shortened!

Last Thursday she came to lunch – first time I'd seen her for 3 months. It was wonderful to see her again. I *think* she is much better but very tired still and Thomas obviously isn't being considerate. She is still determined to do the Gwen John biography – somehow on her own – although Mrs Taubmann is now in the saddle. Mrs T. seems to have found a publisher and proposes to write the biography in a year. I told Sue that Mrs T. had seen Carmen. Perhaps I shouldn't have told Sue so. That gleam in Sue's eyes meant that Sue is going into action at once – perhaps it's a little risky in her present mental state. Maybe it will be good for her – do something to lighten the depression – but I can't help feeling apprehensive.

Ronald [Moody] came in again last night. He keeps telling me that it does him good to see me – that I am almost the only person he can really talk to. I feel *horribly* inadequate. I don't understand half what he says.

16 Nov   Glanced through that old French (18th cent?) prayer book that Boucé gave me. Those prayers almost shocked me. The perpetual preoccupation with sin – rather die 10,000 deaths than commit one sin . . . It becomes more and more *meaningless* to me. So like Alice's awakening from her dream – all those terrifying menacing figures – and the incredible relief when she discovers that they were 'only a pack of cards'.

I say the mechanical list of prayers daily. *Cannot* pray . . .

21 Nov   Sue arrived yesterday for lunch unexpectedly, having spent the night with Cordelia at K. Road. Sue fighting hard to regain her mental balance – the 2nd depression was extremely severe and she now realizes she is a manic depressive. Full of a sweet, but crazy plan for me to go and live at K. Road. Sue has fallen in love with that house. She said that Lyndall proposes to sell it: hopes that Cordelia will be able to stay there till March.

This morning very early Lyndall rang me from Florence: we must have talked for half an hour. All sorts of new complications.

1) Apparently Cordelia told Lyndall that she was definitely leaving K. Rd at the end of the year – presumably to go and live with a man.

2) L. had had Phyllis's reply to her letter. Amazed that Phyllis had been dreadfully disappointed about not going to Knowsley. She would now write to Phyllis to say that, as Cordelia was leaving *at the end of the year*, Phyllis could now come there. She is sick of all the tenant trouble at Harley Gardens and wants to have it available whenever she and Renzo come to London. So she would be delighted for Phyllis to come and live there [Harley Gardens] whenever they are away in Italy.

3) Lyndall *wants* to sell Knowsley, but can she without having to pay a huge tax?

4) Lyndall now says that she and Renzo may come to London before Christmas – at *latest* in January. Renzo now wants to come to London immediately – presumably to K. Rd – where they'd have to share it with Cordelia and presumably Sally. I give up! Lyn will have to sort it out with *all* of them.

There is a prospect (at considerable loss) of L. and R. selling the Bologna flat.

Idea of my buying Beatrice's ground floor flat really *isn't* feasible. Still I'll ring her up tonight about agent's price etc. Of course Sue and Lyndall are enthusiastic – but, apart from the stairs, it *wouldn't* really suit me when I think about it seriously. Price obviously a huge stumbling-block, even if I cd. sell this one and Lyndall would help me with bridging-loan etc.

The spare bedroom wouldn't make nearly as good a room for Angela – much too small for her innumerable possessions. And the big kitchen would really be a waste of space for me. Also remainder of lease may not be long enough for trustees to allow me to change flat D for it.

I will keep my promise to Lyn and Sue about ascertaining price etc. but I think the whole plan will prove (to my relief) quite unfeasible.

This flat suits me very well as it is and *I* don't worry about the stairs as my children do.

23 Nov Watching myself on TV was a most peculiar experience. The gap in my front teeth was horribly conspicuous, but otherwise my face looked much better than I expected. My voice sounded almost unrecognizable, but I know from the old *Critics* days . . . that one's own voice sounds quite different on radio. Mavis [Nicholson] was a marvellous interviewer; couldn't have made things easier for me. I think I was truthful in all I said – answered all her questions as adequately as I could. Pretty probing questions, but couldn't have been put more tactfully. At this very moment Mavis Nicholson rang up to say that she had been 'moved' by our television piece.

Carmen has just rung up to say that she thought the TV was splendid – that I was like a seasoned performer!

It's all so strange and overwhelming – this sudden burst of publicity in my 80th year!

25 Nov Another peculiar experience yesterday. I went to the BBC for the interview for this feature [Shaun] McLoughlin [producer] wants to do. Treated most luxuriously: car sent for me, magnificent lunch with McLoughlin and Michelene Wandon in a private room at the Langham. The studio interview was extraordinary – it lasted 67 minutes! Michelene questioned me and I talked and talked and *talked*! The studio people came in afterwards and said how fascinated they'd been. It really is all *most* peculiar – this sudden interest in me – my life, writing etc. I was exhausted after it, went to bed at 7 when I got home. It's going to be a very odd hotch-potch – this 'feature'. Myself talking (but not Michelene), actresses reading extracts from *F. in M.*, *B. the G.* and *The H. and the F.*, even possible 'sound effects' during the mad part! I liked McLoughlin very much but was more interested in Michelene, who describes herself as a 'Jewish agnostic' and who finds Gerard Manley Hopkins the most akin to her own mind. Says she cannot make the leap into faith but wishes she could. I would like to see her again.

Most unexpectedly David Gascoyne rang me up just as I was about to go to bed. His voice sounded splendid, full of confidence, not a sign of insanity. Asked if I wanted to have a word with Judy, could hardly refuse. Judy all triumphant – 'I'm an old married woman now', 'David goes from strength to strength' etc. Well, I suppose, this extraordinary marriage has worked very satisfactorily. It really is difficult to *like* her but if she is good for David that is all that matters.

29 Nov   All mysterious about Lyndall and Knowsley Road. According to Sue via Cordelia, Lyndall proposes to 'move the Italians' to K. Rd. Does that mean the ones now at Harley Gardens? And why the Italians are not to know that K. Rd belongs to Lyndall?

Did manage to get Piehler on the phone tonight – bit difficult to hear each other. All rather a flop but managed to convey that I was delighted to have a letter from one of Daddy's old pupils who had been coached by him for an Oxford scholarship in 1906 – Piehler is nearly 91! Says he's written 350 pages of his memoirs but they might be too 'frank' to be published.

Am even more 'désorientée' today than usual. Spent so much time on Times crossword (nasty one) and the incredible [Jeremy] Thorpe case.

17 Dec   Extraordinary session at BBC with Shaun McLoughlin and Michelene Wandon(?). Long recording session for this odd 'feature' they wanted to do as a prelude to the radio play.

Have spent an agonizing fortnight milling over script for *F. in M.* Trying to alter bits that don't seem right to me. Last Thursday, Kay Patrick spent $3\frac{1}{2}$ hours with me on it.

Martin [Turnell] had fallen and so severely damaged his head that he has had two brain operations. He is in St George's Hospital. It sounds pretty hopeless. Even if he recovers, he will be almost certainly a total mental wreck. One never knows when the next blow will fall on one's old friends.

Sue rang up on Thursday, meaning to come up and spend the night though she had laryngitis. Thomas rang up a few hours later to say that she had a temperature. Obviously she was in no state to come up to London for a party. She is still very excitable. Today I am going to lunch with Kathleen Raine. Much looking forward to seeing her again. Haven't seen her since all the extraordinary happenings in my life since Feb 1978 and my having now become so decrepit.

19 Dec   A trying day. Carmen's session with me this morning over the Introduction reduced me to such a nervous state that I trembled all over. She kept probing me about all sorts of things that didn't really seem very relevant to the 3 books – why I had changed Nanda's name to Clara etc.etc.

Am apprehensive about having to see the surgeon at St Stephen's on Jan 2nd. Fear it will mean that I *will* have to have the operation [for cancer of the bowel]. Wilks thinks that it needs more than the treatment I've been having.

1979

2 Jan   Saw Mr King at St Stephen's. Was kept in hospital for a week, during which cancer was confirmed.

12 Jan   Spent the day at St Mary Abbots. Seeing King and a woman doctor from the Marsden. Latter arranged for me to go to the Marsden on Tues 23rd for the course of R[adio] T[herapy] treatment to be planned.

20 Jan   Whole month since an entry in this notebook. From Jan 2–8 was in St Stephen's hospital. Operation proved that I have cancer of the rectum. After seeing Mr King the surgeon, this time at St Mary Abbots, decision that I am to spend most of Tuesday 23rd at the Marsden and fairly soon after that to have 5 weeks (5 days a week) of radium treatment. King thinks that this will make an operation unnecessary. Angela was wonderful – discovered where I was (St S.'s) and visited me almost daily. Miraculously Lyndall suddenly appeared at my bedside having come on that bus from Italy with Renzo in appalling Arctic conditions. Lyndall brought me home at short notice on Jan 8. Since then have seen Lyndall almost daily. Sue also came to St Stephen's and last week came to the flat at lunchtime. Everyone has been incredibly kind. Senta, Lillis Kennedy, Joan Harris – everyone. A strange interview last Wed . . . editor of *Nursing*

Times who wants all possible dope on my experiences in Bethlem. Sue now calls me the 'Grand Old Lunatic'.

Everything is strangely unreal and dreamy. My religious sense is deader than ever. Read voraciously – have become hooked on the 5 Peter [Paul?] Scotts dear Carmen gave me. Fascinated by, of all things, Agatha Christie's autobiography. People's kindness to me is *incredible*.

Saw Amanda today. Gerti is in a home at Leamington but seems quite happy. Amanda *has* returned to her maiden name and she and Peter live separately but are on 'good terms' and the children do not seem to be upset. Peter is fond of them.

23 Jan   Spent most of the day at the Marsden. Seeing Dr Bloom and having the course planned. Rang Sue in evening only to discover that she has had to go back to Hellingly.

25 Jan   First day of Radio Therapy treatment.

Didn't put Carmen off. She came for a drink and had a very nice and satisfactory time with her.

27 Jan   Got my hair done at 9. Thought I might as well as no side-effects yet.

Cromwell Rd. traffic lights have broken down since Tuesday and road maintenance people on strike.

Did my 'homework' on the 'Radio Portrait' script.

28 Jan   Too cowardly to go to Mass because of no traffic lights.

Had a lovely treat in afternoon. Lyndall drove me to marvellous bookshop and I bought 17 books. Am voracious for reading matter.

29 Jan   Shaun McLoughlin came at 9.30 (Michelene unable to, down with flu) and we had a fairly satisfactory session.

Ambulance eventually turned up at 2.10 and was home by 3.30.

Very queer period of my life. Centred round the treatment at the Marsden. This started on Thursday Jan 25th. Had diagram painted on my stomach in the radium room. Dismayed that I am not allowed to wash that part till the treatment is finished. Smell awful and fear it will be horrid for other people. No side-effects . . . yet – they say it will be some days before these appear. So far the most difficult thing is waiting for hours in suspense – whether or not the ambulance will come for me.

When I last saw her [Sue] she seemed wonderfully well. Only thing at all unusual was Sue, who usually arrives laden with shopping bags and quantities of objects wasn't sure if she could manage to carry 3 books down the stairs. Said she felt too weak . . . But she seemed to have got the balance of drugs right and had begun to diet, as she'd put on so much weight in Hellingly. Told Lyndall the last thing she wanted was to go back to Hellingly. And now she has had to . . . I feel utterly helpless. Thomas isn't very communicative – but it must have been a great shock to him. Cordelia is said to have gone down to Bow this week-end, so Lyndall and I hope to get some more definite information from her.

Carmen very excited at prospect of reading *Maurice Guest*. Have also told her about Emily's *Shutter of Snow*. Phyllis is trying to get hold of a copy to show her.

Re-reading *Maurice Guest* seemed to me as good as when I first read and fell in love with it in the twenties. I then launched on *Richard Mahony* which I haven't read for I think 20 years. Had forgotten almost all of it except bits of the Australian scene. Today have just finished that amazing trilogy. That woman is a *genius* [Henry Handel Richardson, an Australian woman] – surely the greatest woman novelist ever. I think she is an even greater novelist than Tolstoy.

It's wonderful having Lyndall over here – we snatch lots of moments together and she rings me up almost daily.

From her reading of the *Observer*, sounds almost as if the house in Sussex up for sale is Binesfield. Not at all surprised that Marshall-Dorman has decided to sell it!

5 Feb   Arnold has just rung up to say that Helen has died. This is a great shock. Only a few days ago Arnold wrote to me that her leg was mending well after the operation. He has no idea what caused her death. One thing is to me a relief – that she died before Arnold. I dread to think how awful *Arnold's* death would have been for her.

6 Feb   I think it very unlikely that Helen committed suicide. Can only wait for news.

9 Feb   I now know from Arnold that Helen died some weeks after the operation on her leg. I think it must be from an embolism.

Lyndall has been wonderfully enterprising on Sue's behalf. Getting all the information she can about 'Crisle'[?], a place which sounds a much more effective alternative to Hellingly where it is obviously doing Sue no real good. Lyndall and Cordelia are going down to Bow tomorrow to discuss the whole situation with Thomas. Thomas really needs prodding into doing something definite. Thanks to my windfall via *F. in M.* I can help Lyndall to cope with the financial problem. It will be an expensive treatment – £125 a week. But it *might* be the solution to Sue's problems.

17 Feb   Respite from treatment. During this various unguents to relieve the soreness. Not brilliantly successful. Lyndall may have to stay longer than the 26th. The difficulties at Knowsley Rd. are incredible. Every day a new disaster for Lyndall to cope with. I live in a permanent state of tiredness and lethargy. Inevitably my life for the time being centres around the cancer. Doctors are pleased with results of the radiotherapy. I wish there could be better news of Sue. She must be living in the same sort of suspended animation. The bitter weather continues. You feel spring will *never* come. I suppose my 80th birthday will be a kind of landmark. It would be nice to have some sort of celebration – but what? Nicest would be if Sue were herself again. At least she sounds a little better when Thomas saw her a week or two ago. Stood upright instead of hunched, had read a novel.

2 March   To receive after April
   Royalties   £700
   Repub[lication]   £300
   Possibly   £675 TV
   Probably   Something from BBC – Radio Portrait   Radio play
   But big Income Tax and Hartley Fowler [accountants]. Could be £400 and there will be Marler [landlord] – maybe £200.

31 March   My 80th birthday. Lovely cake.

7 April   Time I brought myself to make some kind of entry in this notebook. My 80th birthday was very nice. Sue and Thomas brought up lovely things they'd cooked. Phyllis was there too. Wonderful that Sue seems definitely better at last. She rang up yesterday to say that they were all going down to Cornwall next Saturday and staying for about 10 days. Lyndall went back to Italy on Wed, March 21st. Phyllis came to London on Sunday March 18th, spent 3 nights at Lindsay [Hotel], then moved to Harley Gardens. She was able to know on April 3rd that I've virtually got a clean bill for the cancer.

I am ludicrously tired after the course of treatment.

Have been having an orgy of Julien Green . . . the last was what I most enjoyed, being straight autobiography. Too stupid to comment on J. Green, one of the great influences on my life.

Lyndall is probably coming [back] to Harley Gdns for a few days. Renzo is too ill to come back with her, even for the dentist appointments. He seems to have suddenly gone downhill. Lyndall *must* come to London for a few days, to settle final purchase arrangements of Knowsley. Great problem for her now, how to find someone to look after Renzo at the Mill.

I think Phyllis had some good moments here. Carmen's visit with actual contract for *Shutter of Snow*. Carmen is wildly enthusiastic about [it]. Phyllis suddenly *feels* really old. She doesn't look it – getting on for 74 I think. But to me it's amazing to see someone who can walk so far and fast, doesn't need a stick, can travel on buses and trains – things now impossible for me!

Finsit remains incredibly lucky. *F. in M.* is to be translated into Spanish and I *should* get about £750!!

If my mind will begin to function again one day, I still toy with the idea of having another try at the autobi.

9 April   Had a sudden impulse to go out to a restaurant – just to vary these months of monotony. But impulse soon faded and I was too tired and lethargic to make the effort. Nurse Snee says it will be some weeks before I get over the effects of the treatment. Don't want to eat anything. Shall go to bed though it's only 7.45. All I really want to do is sleep, sleep, sleep.

10 April   Still absurdly tired. But managed to write 3 notes, walked round the Square gardens, wash 2 jumpers and do some washing-up.

Spent much time lying down and once again shall go to bed v. early. There are some flowers out in the gardens and some leaves coming out at last. Almost a touch of spring for the first time . . . milder and only light wind. But at 7 p.m. more than ready for bed.

13 April   Rose 4 p.m. Went to Tyburn with Lillis and 'John' [both unknown] – lovely day – flowers out in park. Felt well, came back to tea with Lillis.

19 April   Leg was so painful that Wilks came.

20 April   No better. He came again with colleague. V. anxious I should keep appointment at Marsden on 23rd.

22 April   Easter Sunday (April 15th) was lovely. Delightful lunch with the dear Marnaus. On Wed. last had rather a shock. Angela informed me that she was off to Athens on Fr. 20th for 3 weeks. As Joan [Harris] won't be back till Mon 30th I was in a quandary, with no one to shop for me. This became more acute as that Wednesday I became seriously lame. Something in my left groin seemed to 'go'. Impossible to get down the stairs. Dr Wilks came to see me. He said there was an inflamed muscle in the groin, another after effect of radio-therapy.

I am more and more conscious of my own sinfulness. How selfish, how cowardly, how self-indulgent, how *un*loving I have always been. I look back with shame on my selfishness – Susan, Aunt Agnes, all the people I've shamelessly neglected.

23 April   Yesterday was pretty alarming. The leg got so painful and weak that I could hardly move at all. Took me ages to get down the passage leaning on stick and clutching the wall. By a miracle Lyndall arrived and came to see me in the evening. She has been able to arrange for friends to look after Renzo – at *most* for 10 days. Poor Renzo has gone down very badly – become completely apathetic – no longer wants to come to London again or anywhere.

Am feeling pretty bad myself. A very poor night. Have now got a streaming cold – every time I sneeze my leg gives a painful spasmodic twitch.

I have never been so utterly helpless. Huge effort to get dressed even.

Lyndall contacted Cordelia before she came over here. Sue is back home. Lyndall may have rung Sue when she returned to H[arley] Gdns. Cordelia terrified of Sue's having a relapse . . . C.'s young man is in hospital having been mugged by thugs because he refused to pay the builders who'd done bad work on the Brixton flat. It all sounds very fishy. Lyndall and I like him less and less (I only of course from hearsay).

24 April   In the night I had to think seriously about what's left of my future and of my death. It cannot be more than a very few years before I die.

If leg can be patched up, can manage to go on living in the flat as long as I can manage the stairs.

But if not, what is to be *done* with me? Really one would like to be 'dealt with' as disposable rubbish!

Only thing is to leave it all in God's hands . . .

Got to Marsden in carrying chair. Lyndall came with me. Had X-ray and was put into ward that afternoon.

* * *

The cancer had not been cured and Antonia went into the Royal Marsden for a month. For the next few months she was shunted between hospitals, with spells at home under the care of agency nurses. Her confusion was understandable, and her brief, and increasingly hard to decipher, diary entries reflect it. Towards the end the lines would often run towards each other and fuse. During a spell at St Stephen's Hospital she apparently made a new will, naming Carmen Callil and Lyndall as executors in addition to Susan.

* * *

25 April   Lots of doctors examined [me] . . . P[hysio] Therapist taught me to walk with 2 sticks. Slow but possible.

29 April   Broke down on sticks.

30 April   Tried Zimmer. That worked better.

1 May   Still in Marsden. Continued with Zimmer. Improved daily.

18 May   I was 4 weeks all told in Marsden

21 May   Settled in as best I could with Angela. Dr Wilks came but [I]
was too shattered to talk.

22 May   Sue had her operation [Chelsea Hospital for Women]?

24 May   Lyn [hairdresser] came and did my hair.

25 May   Window-cleaner came. [District] Nurse washed me.

26 May   Very bad day.

27 May   Carmen came over and rang [nursing] agency.

1 June   Dr Singh came – is trying to fix St Mary Abbots Tuesday. Dr
Wilks came lunchtime – wants me to hold on for St Mary A[bbots].
Am all in favour myself.

3 June   All at 6s and 7s. Hope can be got into St Mary Abbots. Most
bewildering day. Have had nurse Leary for past few days from 9–6 at
huge cost.
    Try not to 'squirrel-cage' endlessly about religion . . .
    Find Cordelia has gone off for a week's holiday in ITALY.
    Wild rumours that Lyndall may come to London for Monday,
Tuesday or Wednesday.

5 June   L[yndall] doing her best to get things fixed. She is coming
this afternoon. I think it must be today I came into St Mary Abbots.
Yes I did into Lister Ward.

6 June   I think second day.
    Sue in Hastings Convalescent Home.

7 June   Very sick in the night after blood medicine.

9 June   Lyndall leaves . . . Worst ordeal I've ever had. See no end to it. Must remember kindness – Lyndall, Sue . . . Carmen, Angela, Joan Harris. Tom's roses.

10 June   Each day and night get more painful and unbearable. Dear Angela came in the evening. A nice and understanding Assumption Nun came on Saturday? Sister Edmund. Try to be resigned. Find it more and more difficult. Had no reason to expect this to be purely getriatric [sic] ward – all far gone and gaga.

11 June   Heart test. Physiother[apy] girl – effort to move leg at all. Dr? from ??? V. nice and human and could talk to him like human being. Last night – today very bad.

12 June   Slightly better night. Try not to be too miserable – what is the future?
   Shock   More X-rays. Hip is broken [apparently while getting out of bed unaided at St Mary Abbots]. Rushed to St Stephen's at v. short notice – operation tomorrow.

14 June   Op yesterday . . .

15 June   A terrible day. More X-rays. Painful effort to stand up and take few steps. Cordelia appeared.

17 June   Terrible day. Will Phyl really come? Yes, bless her.

18 June   Darling Phyllis came twice. Lovely flowers from Moll.

19 June   Mrs Harris [solicitor] came with codicil. Signed by Phyllis and Harriet Spicer [Director of Virago]'s mother who mysteriously appeared with roses.

22 June   Awfully painful. Trying to be 'good'.
   Frightening appliance room – Jesus hold my hand.

26 June   Sue to come.

29 June   I *think* that must be the day I was moved from St Stephen's to the Joan Bartlett [Ward] St Mary Abbots.

27 July   Came home from hospital. From then on have had day and night nurses – Sabina and Monica.

4 Aug   I am in an extraordinary situation. Absolutely crippled – can only walk with Zimmer – and have 2 nurses – 8pm – 8 am and 11 am – 5 pm. Astronomical costs. On Aug 24 have to go to St Mary Abbots for a week. What happens then?

Trying to establish some sequence since April 24th. Lyndall went with me to the Marsden. Severe pain and disability. Admitted to one of the wards. Clifton kept me in an extra week when I was packed to return home. Leg very bad. Could at first walk with stick. Now only with Zimmer. Don't know when I returned home.

13 August   Dr Wilks lunchtime.
  4   Lyn comes to do hair.

15 June[sic]   Sue and Thomas came?

19 August   Almost out of books.

21 August   'The Shepherd's Life', Hudson. 'The Chelsea Murder', Lionel Davidson. 'Caught in a web of Words', Murray.

24 Aug   Go back to St Mary Abbots today. Trying not to be too depressed. After all I have my daughters and all my wonderful friends so I'm not going into total exile. Last night sweet little Australian nurse (Williams) verified what I've always suspected – that my left leg is now an inch or two shorter than the right. This explains why I have always to drag the right one with such difficulty when I use the frame.

Completely bewildered. Dr Gill rang seemed not to know about the Joint Clinic app[ointmen]t which was supposed to be the whole point. So I only went to X-ray. That terrifying night nurse is on. I couldn't be more wretched.

25 August   Miserable. None of the doctors available at week-end –

Dr G[ill] had said she wd. prescribe a painkiller last night but she didn't.

27 August   I need day nurse and night nurse.

Ring Angela to ask if she can be in at 8 p.m. on *Fri 31st* and at 11 a.m. on *Sat 1st*.

28 August   Ask Shirley to fix *Meals on Wheels* as from Monday.

29 August   Confirm with agency Miss Fallon. Should be possible at hospital to use phone.

30 August   Sue coming.

31 August   *Go back to flat* – need a night nurse – Ring Phyllis?

1 Sept   Yesterday I came back to flat. The week at the hospital was horrible. With Sister Bradley away, all the nurses, with one exception (Norma) were really nasty to all of us, though there were only 9 of the 14 patients left. We were all very unhappy.

I have different day and night nurses. Day one v. kind but find it a bit of a strain talking to her as I can't hear half what she says.

Dr Tibble at St Mary Abbots can't understand why, after the hip operation 10 weeks ago, I should still be virtually a helpless cripple and always in pain.

Darling Emmi rang me up today. She would have so much liked to die but God decided otherwise! She says she has the gift of the giggles! I can't help feeling that God's jokes are very cruel. I'm getting dreadfully irritable and short-tempered, though I've behaved reasonably well in hospital.

I had a letter from Lyndall to say that Renzo wants to live in Florence. Poor Lyndall has had a headache for 3 days, worrying about the fate of a little stray black kitten with a broken (but mended awkwardly by nature) leg. Most of the letter was about the little cat.

I live from day to day and hand to mouth – not knowing what will eventually happen to me.

5 Sept   Phyllis here (staying in Lyndall's flat)

17 Sept   4.30. Sue

18 Sept   St Stephen's – afternoon. Only day we ever got there and had the physio. Didn't get back till 7.30.

20 Sept   St Stephen's afternoon. Ambulance never turned up.

24 Sept   4.30   Sue and Lyn. Get Joan to get something for tea.
   Frantic clearing up and throwing away until Oct 31 –

25 Sept   Lyn Isbell [over from USA to say goodbye] went down to Bow Cottage.

26 Sept   Lyn Isbell, smoked salmon, final feast.

30 Sept   Last night when Angela came home about midnight she found a rolled-gold broken watch on a long chain in her room. How it came there is a complete mystery. I have never had a watch like that.
   Other mystery is disappearance some weeks ago from my living-room of *Great Donkey Walk*. I had seen it one night when I was sitting on the loo in the book corner. Next morning it had vanished. Never reappeared in spite of extensive search for it.

2 Oct   Tonight, after long talk to Angela about her sleeplessness, Vera Maloney [nurse] changed all the bedroom furniture back to its old place. V.M. did not leave till 6.30. Hospital situation unchanged. Physio and Transport quite helpless. New routine difficult for Tricia [nurse]. She is rather cross with Angela. Don't know if A[ngela] slept better last night. Ear plugs no good.

3 Oct   Routine was much better for me. Had a really splendid night. For A[ngela]'s sake did not get up till nearly 7 and slept wonderfully even in the last period (1½ hours) after I could no longer have sleeping pills etc.

9 Oct   Miss Mann, physio came for 1st time. Terribly difficult and painful session but she's obviously extremely competent.

11 Oct Wonderful news from Carmen. They are going to republish the four novels in America . . .

Angela now insists on having furniture removed from the passage. Poor Vera had to do this! Can't help being cross with Angela and apprehensive about Angela's DIY plan of taking up carpet and nailing the floorboards [in corridor].

12 Oct Really terrifying day with the 'physio' (Miss Mann). *Very* painful and difficult. Worst is trying to walk on 2 sticks and the new performance in the bathroom. Mann says I'm making good progress. She's a real Sergeant-Major.

* * *

At the end of October a room came vacant at St Raphael's, Danehill, Sussex, a nursing-home for the elderly run by nuns and recommended by Isabel Quigly. Antonia would no longer have to be cared for in her flat by a rota of expensive private nurses. She was particularly anxious for Thomas to install a desk in her room at the nursing home, where she proposed to continue to sit as she had sat at home. She refers to a biography of Elizabeth Bowen which she was reading when she went into St Raphael's – presumably Victoria Glendinning's, published in 1977.

* * *

26 Oct Since I agreed to Sue and Lyndall's keen desire that I should go to Raphael's I have been in a mental turmoil. Yesterday I learnt that my room will be only 8 ft wide.

This last week has been a nightmare of sorting out and clearing up all my possessions – like amputating a huge part of my life. The biggest upheaval I have ever known . . .

27 Oct What a day! Last night we discovered that poor Vera was in St Stephen's with a broken leg. Much phoning to agency – now a new nurse can come today.

30 Oct Discovered FINSIT much worse than I expected. Carmen's big lump sum had gone into current a/c.

31 Oct Arrived here [St Raphael's] on Oct 31. Room very tiny but very pretty. 4 ft window with view on Walled Garden (whole width),

pale blue walls and white furniture. All spotlessly clean. Rearrangement will be very difficult owing to Zimmer frame without which
I'm helpless. Lyndall came angelically on Monday 29th and accompanied me down to St R. and unpacked for me. Sue helped too. Sue
came yesterday.

2 Nov   Margot here today.

Too tired to make comments yet but wrote notes to Phyllis, Lillis,
Tom, Carmen, Emmi. Hope later to write to Meyjes, Winifred,
[James] Cairncross [Catholic actor from Edinburgh], Senta and Fred
. . .

1979 [Date unknown]   Was it Monday breakfast?

Was it Tuesday priest and surgeon came?

It is a trifle easier to read and write [at the desk] in this position? i.e.
held firm in left hand position and leant on lap cushion to full extent,
allowing to lean forward or back. Can't truly say it's comfortable
either way. Still one can move a shade more forward or back . . .

What I remember specially about Elizabeth Bowen.

Her kneeling (in a beautiful white wool dress) in the dust as the
Corpus Christi procession went past . . .

[On a visit to Bowen's Court in 1956] We had breakfast alone in
our rooms and worked all the morning: (at translating. In the
evening lovely parties or talk – sometimes at Bowen's Court or a
drive 20 or 30 [miles] to these fascinating gatherings. Glad I'd taken
some sort of evening outfit with me.

The only word Elizabeth always stammered over. MOTH . . . Was it
in some way [connected] with her mother's death? It hd. many
distressing connections for her mother's death who died young of
cancer. But all I'm trying to do now is to unfuddle my mind a little –
days have past since Oct 31st in a dazed kind of nightmare – Today
I'm making yet another effort to get a little saner and above all sit at
desk in a more comfortable position . . . and write without reading
glasses.

I also greatly wish to get the time right. Tray removers are kind but
too busy to get time properly set.

Must persevere if I'm not to go completely gaga. Washing and
dressing are enormous and exhausting efforts . . .

Sue's Friday visits are all too brief. I wish they could be a little longer.

Friday (?th)   Sue and Thomas came to see me. Sue will be in Paris but will send Thomas some time the next Friday. They have brought *F. in May* that Sister Clement wants to read. Wonder what she'll think of it!! Two nuns came today – did something painful to my ears but had splendid result of being able to hear *much* better!! Lines still read double but are improving. Elizabeth Bowen book a severe eyestrain. Lap cushion a great help and new desk-chair a lot more comfortable.

Sue has brought me stationery and stamps. Will try to buy me a warm M[arks] and S[pencer] woolly with pockets and a set of dispensable cigarette lighters.

Today is Saturday. Sue can't come next Friday. (Gwen John research in France I think) but Thomas will come. I spilt a lot of mess over the desk. Always difficult to replace tray in a collectable position – parallel with wire trays for lady to remove. Begin by shifting tray to left?

It has been a v. difficult day. Not possible to wash myself but with huge effort managed to get dressed.

People are so kind but it is an ordeal being dragged down to the chapel.

In such a hopeless muddle that I'm trying all over again from Wed Oct 31.

The next day was Nov 1st ALL SAINTS DAY so I was taken down to Mass. That must have been a *Thursday* and the Sunday . . . the 4th. The next Sunday was the 11th. After that the 18th Nov. Then Sunday must have been 25th Nov. I must have been 4 times to Mass now. I was wrong because I believe Sue and Thomas came on a Friday . . . it must have been a Saturday. Yet they said they would regularly come on Fridays. Perhaps no definite day had then been fixed. The last time I saw them they said definitely Fridays. And this next Friday would be Thomas only; Sue having to go for a week's Gwen John's research in France – or Gruneliuses? But Thomas will come regularly on the next Friday and Sue after that.

Hope very much to procure lighter that can be thrown away. Odd how you miss the ability to light a cigarette.

Have to remember *no* aperient on Saturdays because of Sunday
Mass.

I would like *very* much to regain some of my ability to read and
write. And to be able to use throwaway lighters and be independent
of these gadgets.

Chair at desk is much better but it isn't really comfortable yet.

What a strange day. Have done literally nothing.

Glanced at *Sunday Times* and *Sunday Times*.

Filled some 9 months in abeyance.

Fiddled with odds and ends. Have almost no possessions at St. R.
Suppose I went to Mass on Saturday.

Very tired as am always on 3rd day. Nights v. disturbed. Must try
and regularize these days.

Muddle about the Elizabeth Bowen book. Rather dismal. Seems
endless repetition of names. E[lizabeth] so much more interesting
than the others.

Blue [pen] v. capricious. Sometimes work sometimes don't. Blue
ditto.

Attempt at finance

There will certainly be large sums for Private nurses.

Can we then start more or less clear?

Is 5% reasonable on capital?

If flat sells for £30,000 5% would it be £300?

No good I can't work it out.

TODAY SEEMS DEFINITELY TODAY A WEDNESDAY. IS IT WED
21ST CERTAINLY NOVEMBER.

Certainly hairwash and bath today.

26 November   I think it must have been Monday   bath and hairwash.   Muddle over Phyllis and Mary [Siepmann]. Hope we can
sort it out by post.

Sue did not come this Friday. More Gwen John research with
Mme Grunelius. Thomas *did* come though. Helped me find (and pay)
a cheque and was very sweet and helpful. Got in touch with Mrs
Harris (the trustees one) and was very good and useful. He must have
found me pretty dotty! Thinks I've been here 4 weeks. It is high time
Sue got started on the book and considered research more than done

on it. Her publishers are getting impatient for the book. She has a deadline for it.

I think the moves have badly [affected] my sight, as have all these shocks and complete subversal of my ordinary way of life. It is v. hard to try and explain to people. My brain is so muddled and I cannot say the words I mean.

December date? 1979   What has happened to the new copies of my other books? I think all the 3 other novels but I can't find them anywhere.

Darling Sue. It was very sweet of Thomas to come yesterday (Friday) though Sue had another bout of Gwen Research. I think with Mme Grunelius. I'm not 'quite myself' yet – am still 'all to pieces'. Another week or two make me feel more normal. I trust! These complications and ordeals have gone on so long that I feel like an incurable Humpty Dumpty! The nuns carry me heroically down to Mass (4 times I think). Isabel [Quigly] has twice been to see me. She was *so* sweet. Phyllis writes to me every day and I write to her. I'm sure I'll soon feel human again. I *do* long to see you . . .

Date some time late in December I think   I'm very fuddled. A doctor came I think he said I could have painkiller. No need to suffer unnecessarily. Actually cried out with pain. Never have before.

Doctors seem to say that I'm to have painkillers.

Oh, I want my family close and some sign of painkillers. None after all these hours.

I think the last 3 days have been the worst of all.

If only someone could come in and offer a crumb of consolation! But they don't.

Antonia White died on 10 April 1980.

Biographical Sketches

Arnothy, Christine The Hungarian version of Anne Frank. She was born in Budapest in 1930 of a scholarly family, and her parents were determined that she should be a concert pianist. She was equally determined to be a writer. During the Russian siege of German-occupied Budapest she and others took shelter for long periods in a mildewed cellar by the Danube. Throughout this time she kept a diary in which she based her autobiographical first book, *I am Fifteen and I Do Not Want to Die*, which won the Grand Prix Vérité in 1954 and was acclaimed by *The Times* as 'outstanding in the literature of war.' Arnothy eventually escaped to Paris, married a Frenchman, Claude, and had a child. She became a personal friend of Antonia, who stayed with her in Paris in August 1960. Antonia translated both Arnothy's autobiographical books and four of her novels between 1956 and 1964. These included *The Charlatan* (1959), and *The Serpent's Bite* (1961).

Bence-Jones, Mark Antonia met Mark through his eccentric parents whom she visited at Glenville Park, County Cork, in 1958, on her second trip to Ireland. Mark's father was a retired Indian Army colonel of the stentorian variety with a 'most uninhibited flow of language' which shook Antonia at dinner to such an extent that 'I chose the wrong piece of Irish silver and put pepper instead of sugar on my raspberries' (letter to Susan Chitty, 1958). He claimed that he was descended from eleven royal saints and heated the *prie-dieux* in the chapel electrically. Mark, his son, a novelist and historian, has written books about both India and Ireland. He and his wife Gill used to invite Antonia to stay with them on their farm at Nacton, near Ipswich.

Bertram, Anthony Catholic author of books on art history including *Life of Rubens* (1928) and *A Century of British Painting* (1951). He fought in both World Wars and was awarded the Legion of Honour.

Antonia used to stay with him and his wife Barbara at Coates Castle, Fittleworth, Sussex.

Bertram, Barbara Wife of Anthony. 'They are celebrating their 40th anniversary, the only couple of my contemporaries, except the McCleans, who got *that* far! And in the Bertrams' case, without a single glance aside by either party' (letter to Susan Chitty, 1969). Barbara was a devout, practical woman whom Antonia much admired. She moved to Petworth after Anthony's death, and remained closely in touch with Worth Abbey, where their son, Jeremy, was educated.

Birch, Lionel Known as Bobbie. Journalist, protégé of Tom Hopkinson on *Picture Post*. Himself became editor of *Picture Post* in 1950s. Lyndall became his fifth wife in 1955, but the marriage only lasted a year.

Black, Ian Scottish businessman with a liking for beautiful women, the arts and France. He was briefly Antonia's lover in the '30s and let her have a room in his house in Linden Gardens, Notting Hill, early in the War. At that time, too, he published his book *A Friend of France* (1940).

Blakelock, Denys An actor whose career was ruined by his increasing claustrophobia. Trained at RADA at the same time as Antonia. Friend of Eleanor Farjeon. A Catholic, he read *The Hound and the Falcon* and recognized Peter Thorp, to whom the letters were written. He shared a flat in St Petersburgh Place with his brother, Alban, and his brother's wife, Renée. His autobiography, *Round the Corner*, was published in 1967.

Blakelock, Renée Sister-in-law of Denys Blakelock, and wife of Alban. A woman of great gentleness and understanding. Also a beauty, even later in life.

Bloy, Léon French Catholic writer who bitterly castigated political and social institutions and had a strong devotion to the weeping Madonna at La Salette – a manifestation that appeared before a peasant boy and girl in the Alps in 1846. There had been a revival of interest in Bloy's work since 1940. His *Le Désespéré* (1886) and *La Femme Pauvre* (1897) are autobiographical.

Botting, Cecil Father of Antonia White, married to Christine. Brilliant child of Sussex shopkeeper, who taught himself Latin and Greek at the age of four. Educated at Dulwich College and Cambridge, he then taught at St Paul's School where he rose to be the senior classics master and was the co-author of the well-known Hillard and Botting text books from which Antonia received royalties until 1979. Convert to Catholicism. Retired early and died in 1929 soon after the birth of Susan, his first grandchild. Antonia was his only child. Private tutor to such famous names as Victor Gollancz and Compton Mackenzie.

Botting, Christine Wife of Cecil and mother of Antonia White. One of six children of Henry White, a city businessman living in Upper Norwood. Governess in Hamburg for four years (1889–93), then married young.

Braybrooke, June Wife of Neville. She is a novelist under name of Isobel English. Her novels, including *Every Eye* (1956) and *4 Voices* (1961), were admired by Antonia.

Braybrooke, Neville Writer, critic, and editor of *The Wind and the Rain*. Partly instrumental in arranging the publication of Antonia's letters to Peter Thorp which appeared under the title *The Hound and the Falcon*.

Broom, John A librarian living in Orkney who, like many, confided his religious doubts to Antonia after the publication of *The Hound and the Falcon*. He was steeling himself to take the leap into the Catholic fold but, like Antonia, had a constant supply of scruples. He was also attempting to complete a history of twentieth-century Scottish literature. The correspondence never developed the intimacy of *The Hound and the Falcon*. Antonia's letters started as somewhat laborious sermons (they are now greasy with handling). But it is evident that she gradually found the length of Broom's letters, and his passion for the Scottish poet George Mackay Brown, equally trying. Only at the end of Antonia's life did he send her his book about his battle against alcoholism, *Another Little Drink* – 'a most terrifying . . . account. I feel that after all these years I really begin to know you!'

Chitty, Sir Thomas, Bart Novelist (Thomas Hinde). Author of *Mr Nicholas* (1952) and many other novels and historical works. Public relations for the Shell Petroleum Co. in the 1950s, Visiting Professor, Boston University, 1969–70. Married Susan, 1951. Father of four children, Andrew, Cordelia, Miranda and Jessica.

Coleman, Emily Holmes American writer whom Antonia met in 1933. Friend of Peggy Guggenheim and Djuna Barnes, the latter describing her as 'a girl hiker in the realms of the infinite, complete with Primus stove'. Born in California, she was a tall, passionate blonde, the daughter of a wealthy businessman. She was married young, to Deke Coleman and published *The Shutter of Snow* (1930), a novel about the period of insanity that followed the birth of her son Johnny. She returned to the USA during the War, where she married a cowboy, Jake Scarborough, and was converted to Catholicism by Jacques Maritain. Back in England from 1953 to 1968, she lived first in a cottage in Rye with Phyllis Jones, and then in the retreat guest-house at Stanbrook Abbey, the famous enclosed Benedictine convent at Callow End, near Worcester.

Emily spent her last years on a Catholic Worker Farm in New York State near the Hudson River, painting pictures that Antonia described as 'pretty awful' and being waited on by a young man called Joe.

When she died of a brain tumour in 1974 Antonia wrote of her: 'For 40 years . . . she was one of the main people in my life, since she burst into a party given by Wyn Henderson (supposedly "to meet me") and spent the whole time in animated conversation with James Strachey. The next day she asked me to tea and when we'd had tea said, "By the way, I've asked that young man Tom Hopkinson to come in for a drink. I hope you don't mind, but he seemed so keen on you at the party." I had to explain he was my husband' (letter to Susan Chitty, 1974).

d'Erlanger, Charlotte A convent schoolfriend of Antonia at Roehampton, the original of Léonie de Wesseldorf in *Frost in May*. She and Antonia were reunited after many years when she was living round the corner from Antonia in South Kensington. Antonia went to stay with her and her companion Madeleine at her cliff-top house in Cornwall, looking out across the Atlantic.

Demenge, Françoise Wife of Robert Demenge, she was a close friend of Antonia, but died comparatively young. In memory of their friendship, Robert continued to see Antonia when he was in London and even helped her occasionally financially.

Demenge, Robert French businessman, related to Antonia's friends the Grunelius family. A devout Catholic, and the father of Dominique and Marie Odile. (A third child was tragically killed in the bombing of Strasbourg during the Second World War.) The family used to spend their *grandes vacances* at the château of Otrott in Alsace, where Antonia visited them. Besides being generous, Robert had a nice sense of humour. When he visited Antonia in 1965 he apologized for his loss of an eye, explaining that 'his body was leaving him, not he his body'. She in turn regretted that 'I was so deaf that I couldn't hear the nice things he was saying about *The Hound and the Falcon* which was torture!' (letter to Susan Chitty, 1965).

Freeman, Frank Freeman studied mining with Silas Glossop but spent most of his life trying to be a painter. It was he who introduced Antonia to Silas, when she was still married to Eric Earnshaw Smith. He was married first to the painter Joan Souter Robertson, then to Pamela, who, with his encouragement, became a painter of flowers. They had three children. One who knew him describes him as an unpleasant little man who wore 'the wrong kind of yellow shoes', a mixed-up kid.

Garvin, Viola Widow of James Garvin, famous editor of the *Observer* (1908–42). She lived in North Oxford and Antonia used to stay with her when visiting Susan at Somerville.

Glossop, Rudolph Known always as Silas, a mining engineer from Derbyshire, educated at Cheltenham College and the Royal School of Mines in London. Worked in Canada and on the Gold Coast. Met Antonia in Chelsea in 1928, and father of Susan. He attempted to persuade Antonia to leave Eric Earnshaw Smith and marry him, but while he was in Canada earning enough money to support her and Susan, Antonia became involved with Tom Hopkinson. During the War Silas married Sheila and joined John Mowlem, civil engineering company, rising to be a managing director. By Sheila, he had a daughter, Emma.

Graef, Hilda A German theologian based at Oxford. Wrote *The Case of Thérèse Neumann* (1950), about the nineteenth-century German girl with the marks of the stigmata on her hands and feet; and a book on Cardinal Newman which was never published. Antonia originally described her as 'a most interesting woman who is translating *The Hound and Falcon* into German' (letter to Susan Chitty, 1966). To John Broom Antonia wrote, 'She is very learned and took a degree in Anglican theology before she became a Catholic.' Miss Graef wrote for the religious review, *Search*, in one issue defending Vatican II's approach to dogma.

Green, Julien French Catholic novelist and diarist. His parents were from the deep south of America but he was born in France and has lived in Paris all his life apart from a spell as a student in the United States and another during the War. On his return to Paris in 1946, with his sister Anne, he became a friend of Antonia, who found in his guilt-tormented diaries an echo of her own difficulties. Novels include *Minuit* (1936) and *Moïra* (1950).

Green-Wilkinson, Daisy Daisy's son Reginald was married to Antonia in 1921, and separated from her the same year. He was the gentle, gangling, ne'er-do-well son of a wealthy and aristocratic family, his uncle being Tom Sopwith, the designer of the Sopwith Pup aeroplane. Antonia was sorry for Reggie, and she shared his passion for the theatre and toy soldiers. They lived in a tiny house on the corner of Glebe Place, Chelsea, described in the novel *The Sugar House*, but his drinking and irresponsibility drove her to despair. He died young, in South Africa. Daisy, widow of the impossible Fred, remained a friend and benefactor to Antonia for many years.

Haughton, Rosemary Whizz-kid theologian of the '60s, writing for confused Catholic wives and mothers. Antonia met her when she (Antonia) was giving a lecture at Ampleforth in 1966, soon after publication of *The Hound and the Falcon*, and came immediately under her spell. Mrs Haughton wrote frequently for the religious review, *Search*. She has now returned to the USA.

Henderson, Ian Older son of Wyn Henderson. Educated at Stowe and Cambridge, he was preparing for the Civil Service examination, possibly at the suggestion of Eric Earnshaw Smith, when Antonia fell in love with him. He appeared a rather solid, unimaginative person, but their physical partnership was successful for longer than most of Antonia's, although (perhaps because) they never shared a home. It ended when Ian went abroad with the armed forces at the beginning of the War.

Henderson, Wyn Wyn was the mother of Ian and Nigel. Originally a dancer, she at one time managed Peggy Guggenheim's London gallery, Guggenheim Jeune. She recommended *Frost in May* to Desmond Harmsworth, its first publisher.

Hoare, Sir Samuel Known to his friends as Peter, a distinguished civil servant who had risen to be head of the international division of the Home Office. He led a double life, being a member of the Oakley Street set of writers and poets during the mid 1930s (George Barker, David Gascoyne, Dylan Thomas). He even published an essay on Rimbaud. Emily Coleman pursued him passionately for years but he preferred the privacy of his Chelsea flat. He was a close friend of Silas Glossop.

Holms, Dorothy Estranged wife of John Holms. Amateur astrologer.

Holms, John A 'bearded and ethereal' English gentleman, supposed to be a writer and a sage. Emily Coleman had discovered him in the

South of France but Peggy Guggenheim fought for him and won (at the cost of a black eye). He was the guest of honour at her house, Hayford Hall in the summer of 1933, but was dead within the year, never regaining consciousness from an anaesthetic administered on Peggy's kitchen table after a minor riding accident.

Hope, Lieutenant-Colonel C.E.G. Known to his friends as Anthony, formerly cavalry officer in India. Writer of books on equitation and editor of magazines *Light Horse* and *Pony*. Antonia's neighbour in South Kensington.

Hope, Beryl Wife of Anthony Hope. Convent schoolfriend of Antonia and later, neighbour in South Kensington.

Hopkinson, Amanda Tom Hopkinson's youngest daughter, born just before he left Gerti. She became a Catholic in her teens, partly as a result of reading *The Hound and the Falcon*, and asked Antonia to be her 'stand-in' godmother when she was confirmed in 1966. She later married Peter Binns, her tutor at Warwick University and has four children. (Antonia found her sexual morality puzzling, since Peter was already married.) Later Amanda left Peter and went to Paris to research Simone Weil. Though Antonia confessed to being 'allergic' to Weil, she agreed with Amanda that, in matters of religious belief, it is not 'necessary to entirely suppress one's mind' (letter to John Broom, 1967). Amanda published a short biography of Julia Margaret Cameron, the Victorian photographer.

Hopkinson, Dorothy Third wife of Tom Hopkinson, whom she married in 1953. Formerly married to the writer, Hugh Kingsmill by whom she had four children, one of whom, Edmée, at first a dancer, became an Anglican nun. Dorothy set up as an amateur psychologist after the War and treated Antonia, Tom Hopkinson and Gerti Hopkinson. She was a follower of the Indian holy man Meher Baba, and with Tom wrote a book about him, *Much Silence*. After Tom's death in 1990 she moved to a retirement home near Edmée's convent in Oxford.

Hopkinson, Gerti Viennese photographer who came to London before the war and met Tom Hopkinson when he worked on *Weekly Illustrated*. Married Tom in 1939 and had two daughters by him, Nicolette and Amanda.

Hopkinson, Lyndall see Passerini, Lyndall.

Hopkinson, Sir Tom Author and journalist, editor of *Picture Post* during the War. He was the second son of Henry, an archdeacon living at Cockermouth. His brothers were Jack, Paul and Stephan; Esther was his only sister. Antonia met Tom, a fellow copywriter, at W.S. Crawford's advertising agency in the late '20s when she was already involved with Silas Glossop. Hopkinson was some years younger than Antonia. They were married in 1930 and divorced in 1938, during which period Tom worked on *Weekly Illustrated*. Lyndall was Tom's daughter by Antonia. Nicolette and Amanda were the children of his second wife Gerti Deutsch. His third wife was Dorothy Kingsmill, widow of Hugh Kingsmill. Tom later edited *Drum* in Johannesburg and returned to become professor of journalism at Cardiff. He and Antonia remained virtually estranged from the time of his marriage to Dorothy though they met briefly in 1966 and in 1977. His early novels included *The Wise Man Foolish* and *The Man Below*. His short stories were his most imaginative work. He died in 1990.

Horley, Georgina see Smith, Georgina Earnshaw.

Jackson, Lady (Barbara Ward) Originally writer on foreign affairs on *The Economist*. Became a close friend of Antonia in 1943 after giving a speech to members of the Catholic Society, Sword of the Spirit. Antonia wrote an article about Barbara for *Picture Post*, and asked her to be Susan's godmother when she entered the Catholic Church in 1945. She married the international economist, Robert Jackson (1950) and had a son by him. She became Professor of International Economic Development at Columbia University (1968). Latterly she was one of the first to champion the cause of the environment. Her many books include *Only One World; the care and maintenance of a small planet* (1972).

Johnes, Virginia Wife of an antique-dealer, Raymond Johnes. A hysterical Kensington Catholic, she became infatuated with Antonia in 1953, writing to her and telephoning daily. She made anonymous donations of money in subsequent years, which caused Antonia much embarrassment when she discovered from whom they came. Virginia Johnes continued to trouble her with letters for many years.

Jones, Phyllis One of Emily Coleman's closest English friends. A lean, handsome redhead whose dry comments concealed a great deal of kindness. 'Send for Phyllis' was the constant cry of those with domestic problems. Though much pursued, she never married. She farmed in Sussex during the War and devoted many years to looking after her mother, eventually moving down to a tiny terrace house at 19 Chapel Street, Buckfastleigh, in Devon, where she kept Emily's 'dratted' papers stored in the cellar. Antonia often stayed with her and Phyllis typed all her later manuscripts at absurdly low rates. A neighbour in Devon was Mary Siepmann (Wesley).

King, Cecil Harmsworth Director of the *Daily Mirror* from 1929 and subsequently chairman of the *Daily Mirror* and *Sunday Pictorial* Group and then of the International Publishing Corporation (1963–8). Married to Margaret Cooke, who remained a close friend of Antonia after the Kings' divorce. They had four children: Michael, Francis, Colin and Priscilla.

Legg, Robert Officer in the King's Own Scottish Borderers. When he was on leave from Ireland Antonia fell ecstatically in love with him for three weeks in 1923, between the collapse of her marriage to Reggie Green-Wilkinson and her own collapse into insanity. Robert had a sister, Dorothy, who was an artist in Chelsea. In *Beyond the Glass* they became Richard and Nell Crayshaw.

Lingham, Elaine Elaine Lingham was the daughter of Agga Lingham, a Catholic friend of Antonia. She had abandoned her Carmelite vocation shortly before taking her final vows as a nun and worked as an unpaid secretary to Antonia for a time. Later she left to go to Germany.

MacAlister, Dorothy Dorothy Seaton was an attractive pupil of Cecil Botting, who became a personal friend of his. They corresponded about Catholicism before his conversion. She later became Lady MacAlister.

Sister M. Madeleva CSC President of St Mary's College, South Bend, Indiana, where Antonia was writer-in-residence for a term in 1959. She was a self-styled 'poet, saint and scholar', and winner of a National Poetry Centre Award. She collected English Catholic celebrities like Barbara Ward and Robert Speaight. Also walking sticks. Her *Collected Poems* (1947) were described by Antonia as '*awful* sexy religious stuff'. Her prose works included *My First Seventy Years* (1959). Antonia first met her on her Jubilee trip to Europe. The College President thought the splendid Green Park Hotel 'a homey little place', and amazed Antonia by sipping champagne (letter to Susan Chitty, 1959).

Marcella, Dame A nun at Stanbrook Abbey, the famous Benedictine house at Callow End, near Worcester. Emily Coleman lived for some time at St Mary's Guest House, attached to the Abbey. Dame Marcella was a deeply spiritual woman who later became a hermit. (The title 'dame' is now more often replaced by 'sister' in the Benedictine Order.)

Maritain, Jacques French Thomist philosopher who became a Catholic in 1906 and held professorial chairs at Paris, Toronto, and (during the War) Princeton. In many books, including *On the Philosophy of History* (1957), he sought to apply the classical doctrines of Thomism to philosophy, history and art. In 1970, after the death of his wife Raïssa, he joined the unenclosed order of the Little Brothers of Jesus at Toulon, spending his summers with the Grunelius family at Kolbsheim. He shared with them and the prophet Léon Bloy a deep veneration of the apparition of Our Lady at La Salette. There is now a study centre dedicated to his memory at Kolbsheim.

Maritain, Raïssa Wife of Jacques Maritain. Raïssa Oumançoff and her sister Vera were Jewish émigrés from Rostov on Don. Raïssa met Maritain when she was a student at the Sorbonne, and with him became a convert to Catholicism. The couple agreed not to consummate their marriage, and, with Vera, they eventually set up house at Meudon, near Paris. Raïssa spent many hours of each day in meditation while Vera preferred cooking. Raïssa wrote several devotional books and also *Les Grandes Amitiés*, about the not very devout who frequented her salon. She predeceased Jacques by several years. Antonia translated her journal at Jacques' request.

Marnau, Fred Catholic German poet whom Antonia met after reviewing his novel, *Free Among the Dead*, in 1950. Chairman of the Latin Mass Society and organizer of a pilgrimage agency. 'Dear Fred', his wife Senta, and their daughter, Corinna, became close friends of Antonia. Fred read the lesson at her funeral.

McClean, Douglas Medical research scientist with strong left wing sympathies. Keenly interested in wine and for many years on the committee of the Wine Society.

McClean, Kathleen (Hale) Artist and author (as Kathleen Hale) of children's books, especially the 'Orlando the Marmalade Cat' series, first of which published in 1938. She was married to Douglas McClean. They had two sons, Peregrine and Nicholas, and lived at Radley Willows.

Moody, Ronald Sculptor born in Kingston, Jamaica, who came to London in 1923 to study dentistry. Produced fine works in wood of male figures with Buddha-like faces (*John the Baptist*, 1936). Married Hélène Cowan in Paris before the War and then crossed the Pyrenees on foot to escape the Nazis. The couple then shared flats with Antonia both at 29 Thurloe Street and 13 Ashburn Gardens. A statuette of the Virgin for Antonia's Christmas crib was Moody's first work on his return to England and, in spite of its size, remains one of his finest works. Hélène died some years before him. His niece, Cynthia Moody, is writing his biography. Some of his work was exhibited at *The Other Story* exhibition of Afro-Asian artists at the Hayward Gallery in 1989.

Muir, Richard Temple Known to friends as Dicky. Businessman. Graduate of King's College, Cambridge. Engaged to Lyndall in 1948. Publisher of magazine *Autocourse*. Proprietor of London restaurant, La Popotte. Married Patricia, ex-wife of Humphrey Lyttelton.

Nicholson, Basil Journalist working on the *Daily Mirror* for Cecil King, who said of him, 'He was among the half dozen most brilliant men I ever met. He threw off ideas like a catherine wheel.' Also a copywriter, said to have invented the strip cartoon with his Horlicks series. He wrote a novel, *Business is Business*, and was an amateur ornithologist.

Passerini, Count Lorenzo Civil engineer who worked for many years in Africa. Inherited Il Palazzone, Cortona, Tuscany, but gave it to the University of Pisa. Met Lyndall while she was working in Rome and married her when the Italian law allowed him to divorce the former wife from whom he had been long separated. He was some twenty-five years older than Lyndall.

Passerini, Lyndall Antonia's daughter by Tom Hopkinson, two years younger than her half-sister. Educated at Headington School, Oxford, followed by a secretarial course in Cambridge and a production course at the Old Vic Theatre School. She fled from her fiancé, Dicky Muir, to Rome on 16th September, 1952 to join Willy Mostyn-Owen, the art historian. For years fitted a brilliant social life round a job with the Food and Agriculture Organization of the United Nations. Briefly married Lionel Birch, her father's successor on *Picture Post*; now the widow of Count Lorenzo Passerini. She lives in Tuscany and is the author of *Nothing to Forgive; a Daughter's Life of Antonia White*, 1988.

Raine, Kathleen Author of several volumes of verse, including *Stone and Flower*, 1943 and *Collected Poems*, 1956. Also of two-volume *Blake and Tradition*, 1968. Kathleen was the daughter of a school-teacher and spent part of her childhood in the wilds of Scotland. She has something of the beauty but also the severity of the northern hills. Her years at Girton College added to this severity. Antonia met her in

1943 when they were both working for SOE (Special Operations Executive). Kathleen, almost ten years her junior, later declared 'in a dark year [she] was to me a light-bearer'. Through Antonia, Kathleen became a Catholic. The two women quarrelled violently (Antonia always insisting that it was Kathleen who turned on her) but ended 'fellow traveller[s] for so many years' as Kathleen put it. She lives in Chelsea at 47 Paulton's Square, divorced from Charles Madge (founder of Mass-Observation) and has two children, James and Anna. She is also a translator from the French.

Sawyer, Denyse Belgian author of an autobiographical novel, *L'Aube* about a young girl who survived the German occupation of Brussels. Antonia chose *Till the Shadow Passes* as the English title of the book, and it appeared in 1960 under a pseudonym, Julie Storm. Antonia described her meeting with Denyse in a letter to Susan Chitty (9 Nov 1958): 'I was sent a MS by a Belgian woman asking if I could spare time to see a foreigner of 40ish who was at a crisis in her life. Expected a sad lady just left by her husband! Instead there appeared a pretty, smart, *radiantly* happy wife with an adored and adoring husband! Crisis was only about writing . . . She's just written her first book – in French . . . could she or couldn't she? I think she definitely *can*. I went down and spent the day with them at Tunbridge Wells, was fussed, flattered and fed like a VIP. Imagine my being curtseyed to by daughters of 9 and 12!'

Collins also published Julie Storm's second book, *Madeleine* (1964), this one about the violation of Belgium in the First World War, but by then Antonia's honeymoon period with her and her businessman husband Geoffrey was over, and someone else translated it. 'She's been in England so long she's forgotten how to write French,' Antonia commented in a letter to Susan Chitty (3 August 1959).

Senhouse, Roger Literary critic, adored young friend of Lytton Strachey. He abandoned his ancestral northern home at Maryport (it fell down shortly afterwards) to join dubious friends in the south. His translation of Colette's *Gigi* appeared in the same volume as Antonia's of *The Cat*. He was a director of Secker and Warburg, who published it.

Siepmann, Eric Diplomat of German origin, subsequently author and journalist. Antonia became involved with him in the '30s and went to stay at a villa he was renting in Spain, but did not have an affair with him. It seems probable that she was more in love with him than he was with her. After the War he married the novelist, Mary Wesley and in 1956 he set fire (unintentionally) to Antonia's sitting-room-cum-study by throwing a lighted cigarette end into the waste-paper basket before going down to dinner. All her work on the Dougal book was destroyed (somewhat to her relief).

Siepmann, Mary see Wesley, Mary.

Smith, Eric Earnshaw Antonia met Earnshaw Smith, her second husband, in 1919 while she was still at the Academy of Dramatic Art, and married him in 1925. He was a homosexual and considerably older than herself, having been wounded in the First World War. He was a senior civil servant for the rest of his working life, keeping his interest in the arts and philosophy for outside office hours. His older brother Harold was Vicar of All Souls, Langham Place. Eric talked Antonia out of the Catholic Church but shared her interest in cats. After the Second World War he married Georgina Horley, but remained a close friend and adviser to Antonia. When he was in financial difficulty after his retirement, she handed on two books for him to translate from the French, one of them Pierre Jean Jouve's *Mozart's Don Juan* (1957) and the other Henry Muller's *Clem* (1962). Both caused him exquisite agony, as he was not in the habit of putting pen to paper.

Smith, Georgina Earnshaw After leaving home as a teenager she took the name Georgina Horley, under which she also wrote. Known to her friends as Georgie. Author of the novel *Bus Stop* (1955), of which Eric was the hero, and of the Penguin Handbook, *Good Food on a Budget* (1969). A close friend of Tom Hopkinson in his *Picture Post* days. She married Eric Earnshaw Smith, Antonia's second husband, in 1947. After the War she held many good jobs in journalism and publishing, including at Penguin, but usually let them go again, being, in Antonia's words, 'too good' for them (letter to

Susan Chitty, 1959). She moved from Worthing to Twickenham after Eric's death.

Smith, Leslie Earnshaw Eric's younger brother, always referred to as 'dear little Lel', appears to have suffered most in the unhappy home at Cambridge where his father died of alcoholism. Never achieved much in life; became Antonia's lodger briefly before retiring to 'a very nice home for old gentlemen on the River'.

Speaight, Bridget Wife of Robert. Oxford graduate, painter and pianist. They met at Aldeburgh in 1949, where she lived; he was lecturing at the Festival and observed a young woman 'several decades further from the grave than the rest of the audience'. They were married with the consent of the Vatican (both had been married before) and Bridget bought Campion House, a fine but cold six-teenth-century residence in Kent, without consulting Robert. There she kept things (including Robert) in a high degree of 'shipshapeli-ness' for the rest of Robert's life. She has grown-up children from her previous marriage.

Speaight, Robert Distinguished Catholic actor who made his name preaching Becket's sermon in *Murder in the Cathedral* and was condemned thereafter to clerical roles ('sealed in the tomb of St Eliot'). He became a friend of Antonia during the War after his first marriage had collapsed but confined his sensual enjoyments to good wine and cigars. He consented to be Susan's godfather. Published biographies of modern Catholics on both sides of the channel, and his own autobiography, *The Property Basket* (1968). Introduced Antonia to many Catholics, religious and lay, in France and the USA. Antonia used to refer to him as 'the ubiquitous Bobbie. He's as mobile as Mr Kissinger' (letter to Susan Chitty, 1974). He died suddenly, some years before her.

Thorp, Peter Peter Thorp (real name Joseph) was the recipient of the letters published under the title *The Hound and the Falcon*. These letters concerned Antonia's return to the Catholic Church. Peter had trained as a Jesuit, had worked in advertising and had originally written to Antonia as a stranger about *Frost in May*. The couple

exchanged increasingly warm letters during the War but the correspondence ceased when Antonia visited him (and his wife) in Wales.
She declared, as was her wont, that his wife was much nicer than he
was.

Turnell, Martin Somewhat academic writer on French literature,
and contributor to *Horizon* and *The Life of the Spirit* (Domican).
Published *The Novel in France* (1950). Two of the seven great
novelists he selected for this book, Laclos and Benjamin Constant,
wrote only one novel apiece, yet, he declared, these were not just
'superb flukes', which was satisfactory for Antonia. His life of
Baudelaire came out in 1953. He was married to Helen.

Tyrrell, George A Catholic Modernist theologian, friend of Baron
von Hügel, the Continental Modernist. He was expelled from their
society by the Jesuits and finally, in 1907, from the Catholic Church,
for championing the cause of living faith against dead theology. In
his posthumously published book, *Christianity at the Cross-Roads*
(1909) he suggested a universal religion of which Christianity was
only the germ. Antonia had originally been given an earlier book of
his, *Nova et Vetera*, 1897 by Peter Thorp, but this was not questioned
by Church authorities. It was strongly influenced by Newman, as
were most of Tyrrell's books. His tragic life story was written first
kindly by his friend, Maud Petre (1912), and now unkindly by
Nicholas Sagovsky (1991).

Walker, Alan Alan Walker had been a friend of Eric Earnshaw
Smith at Cambridge. He was briefly engaged to Antonia in 1924. On
a pre-marital tour of France in his open car that year, his glasses flew
off shortly after leaving Calais and were never seen again. He made
such a fuss that Antonia decided there and then that she would rather
marry Eric, who was of the party. Alan entered the Diplomatic
Service and later married into the Bute family. For some years he was
Daily Telegraph correspondent in Madrid.

Wall, Barbara Wife of Bernard Wall: their names were seldom
mentioned separately, though there is no reference to her in his

autobiography. She co-operated with him in his work. She also wrote a couple of novels (*The Trembling of the Sea*, 1937) before the War: after the War her books tended to be more autobiographical (*Growing Up*, 1956). She is a niece of Alice Meynell. Antonia confided her religious doubts to Barbara occasionally.

Wall, Bernard Catholic author of *Report on the Vatican* (1956). During the '30s he edited *Colosseum* (1934) from Friburg in Switzerland, which provided a forum for European Catholics (contributors included Maritain and Berdyaev). Wall lived in Paris for two years during the '30s. In the '50s he returned to England and joined *The Twentieth Century*, where, among other things, he was introduced to a new breed, the teenager, by Colin MacInnes. (Bernard was painfully aware of his 'Oxford way of talking'.) He translated books from the Italian and the French, including Julien Green's *L'Autre* (1973). His autobiography was titled *Headlong into Change* (1969).

Ward, Barbara *see* Jackson, Lady.

Wesley, Mary Wife of Eric Siepmann. She had children by a former husband. The Siepmanns lived in a cottage in Devonshire, near Phyllis Jones. After Eric's death Mary achieved great success as a novelist.

White, Father Victor OP Dominican friar from Blackfriars at Oxford. Victor White lectured on St Thomas Aquinas, and was an expert on Jung whom he visited regularly in Switzerland. A small man in a shabby black suit with false teeth that clicked when he was enthusiastic (which he usually was), he soon became a family friend. His books included *Soul and Psyche* (1960).

Woodruff, Douglas Lionized Catholic journalist, editor of *The Tablet* 1936–1967, and author of famous 'roving, panoramic leaders,' some of which were reprinted in his *Talking at Random* books. It was said of him that he thought like Belloc and behaved like Dr Johnson.

Woodruff, Mia Married Douglas Woodruff in 1933. Her full name was the Hon. Marie Immaculée, and she was a daughter of Lord

Acton. Mia was a kind-hearted woman who could be relied upon for
'unfailing practical charity'. Robert Speaight recalls that she sent her
husband to Hilaire Belloc's eightieth birthday with a cooked chicken
under his arm.